Shanghai Faithful

Praise for *Shanghai Faithful*

"In revealing the truth of how her family helped spread Christianity in China, Jennifer Lin weaves a captivating, poignant story about the nature and power of belief. This epic study shows the high price that can be paid by those who insist on holding fast to faith and family at a time when everything is at risk."

—**Jeff Gammage, author of *China Ghosts: My Daughter's Journey to America, My Passage to Fatherhood***

"Jennifer Lin's *Shanghai Faithful* is an extraordinary story about a family in a rapidly changing world. Its wide-ranging narrative links family members on two continents and covers more than a century of tumultuous change. Lin's research is meticulous and combines archival precision, sophisticated historiographical framing, and memorable storytelling. I will surely be assigning *Shanghai Faithful* in my own teaching, because its story brings to life a remarkable era in Chinese, American, and global history."

—**Robert André LaFleur, Beloit College**

"This engrossing book offers rich insights on faith and loyalty in a Christian family in Shanghai. Jennifer Lin's compelling narrative, often immensely emotional, will be of great interest for anyone who wishes to know about the everyday struggles of Chinese Christians as they endured persecution and suffering during the most hostile years of Mao's rule."

—**Joseph Tse-Hei Lee, Pace University**

"Capturing the epic sweep of a turbulent Chinese century through a personal lens, Jennifer Lin tells a poignant, riveting, and deeply researched tale of her family's journey of faith, from the nineteenth-century Chinese villager who first encountered Western missionaries to the twentieth-century Christian leaders—one working within the system and one pushing for something new. Persecuted under Communist rule, each left a mark still felt in China today, where ever more people seek something to believe in."

—**Mary Kay Magistad, creator and host of "Whose Century Is It?" podcast, former NPR and PRI China correspondent**

Shanghai Faithful

Betrayal and Forgiveness
in a Chinese Christian Family

Jennifer Lin

ROWMAN & LITTLEFIELD
Lanham • Boulder • New York • London

Published by Rowman & Littlefield
A wholly owned subsidary of The Rowman & Littlefield Publishing Group, Inc.
4501 Forbes Boulevard, Suite 200, Lanham, Maryland 20706
www.rowman.com

Unit A, Whitacre Mews, 26-34 Stannary Street, London SE11 4AB, United Kingdom

British Library Cataloguing in Publication Information Available

Library of Congress Cataloging-in-Publication Data Available

ISBN 978-1-4422-5693-4 (cloth : alk. paper)
ISBN 978-1-4422-5694-1 (electronic : alk. paper)

♾™ The paper used in this publication meets the minimum requirements of
American National Standard for Information Sciences—Permanence of Paper
for Printed Library Materials, ANSI/NISO Z39.48-1992.

Printed in the United States of America

To my father,
Paul M. Lin

Contents

Part V. Bad Elements

Part IV. Revival

List of Characters

LIN FAMILY (SHANGHAI)

Lin Pu-chi	My grandfather	Lin Buji 林步基
Ni Guizhen	My grandmother	Ni Guizhen 倪规箴
Martha	Aunt	Lin Maozhi 林茂芝
Jim	First uncle	Lin Junmin 林俊民
Tim	Second uncle	Lin Tingmin 林挺民
Paul	Father	Lin Baomin 林保民
Sylvia	Mother	
John Sun	Martha's husband	Sun Yuguang 孙毓光
Emma	Tim's wife	Hu Yimei 胡苡梅
Julia	Martha's eldest daughter	Sun Zhongling 孙钟玲
Terri	Martha's second daughter	Sun Tianlin 孙天霖
Kaikai	Tim's son	Lin Kai 林恺
Lin Yu	Tim's daughter	Lin Yu 林愉

LIN FAMILY (FUJIAN)

Old Lin	First convert; great-great-grandfather	Lin Yongbiao 林永标
Lin Dao'an	Great-grandfather	Lin Dao'an 林叨安
Zhan Aimei	Great-grandmother	Zhan Aimei 詹爱美

NI FAMILY

Watchman Nee	Brother of Ni Guizhen	Ni Tuosheng 倪柝声
Charity Chang	Wife of Watchman Nee	Zhang Pinhui 张品惠
Lin Heping	Mother of Watchman Nee	Lin Heping 林和平
Uncle George	Brother of Ni Guizhen	Ni Huaizu 倪怀祖

Note on Spellings and Reporting

*T*he spelling of Chinese names and places can be a knotty dilemma. In most cases, I use the modern pinyin spelling. But since this is a family memoir, I have made some exceptions. With my father, aunts, uncles, and cousins, I use their Christian names. This is how I knew them. And for people who had public identities before 1949, I default to the old Wade-Giles spelling or the most recognizable version of their names. For instance, I use Watchman Nee instead of Ni Tuosheng and Lin Pu-chi instead of Lin Buji. Also with some cities, where the modern version is vastly different from the one used in missionary times, I use the older version or the more familiar spelling in the local dialect, so, for example, I use Funing instead of Xiapu in Fujian Province.

This is a work of nonfiction. All quotes were gleaned from primary sources or through the recollections of relatives. In order to tell this history as a story, I have re-created scenes based on my understanding of events, which I explain in more detail in the notes at the end of this book.

Introduction

$\mathcal{I}$ had never seen my father like this, and it frightened me.

His face was ashen and blank, his eyes puffy and bloodshot from a night without sleep. He stood beside me on the second-floor balcony of his childhood home in old Shanghai in what used to be his parents' bedroom. It was the first morning of my first full day in China—June 18, 1979—and I listened as he recounted for me what he had learned only hours before from an elderly uncle. His words came out mechanically, as if he were running the information through his brain again, still struggling to grasp the meaning. In that moment on the porch, I began to feel that everything I knew about his family had been a façade carefully constructed to obscure the truth by the relatives I had met for the first time only the night before.

One of those people was no longer there; my grandfather—my dad's father—had died six years earlier. He had been our window into the house on Jiaozhou Road. Every month, without fail, he wrote to us in Philadelphia with an update on family life. He reported on everyone's health. He recounted a trip to the mountains, a visit to the zoo, a morning stroll in the park. He quoted a Tang dynasty poet or a verse from St. Paul. He described the bowl of noodles he had for his birthday and the blooming rosebush outside the front door. Sometimes he tucked black-and-white photographs of family members into the folds of the blue airmail letters. With impeccable English, he often ended his notes with reassuring words: "We are all well as usual. Do not worry about us."

And we didn't. A world away, I lived in a large, loud household in the suburbs of Philadelphia with four sisters, a brother, our parents, and our Nana from my mother's Italian side of the family. We had a sprawling house with a pool and a lush lawn that was big enough for pickup softball games. My mother, a nurse, put her career aside to raise her brood and shuttle us in our

1

red Ford station wagon from swim practice to ballet and piano lessons. She was from a rowhouse neighborhood in Camden, New Jersey, that was bedrock Italian. In 1952, when Dr. Lin, who worked on the same floor at Temple Hospital as Nurse Spina, pulled up to her stoop for their first date, neighbors craned their necks from windows for a glimpse of "the Chinaman." Their wedding a year later was the talk of Fourth Street.

With the Vietnam War playing in the background of my childhood, I was indifferent to my Chinese heritage. I wanted nothing more than to look like my best friend, an auburn-haired Irish girl whose four sisters presented a stark contrast to the mongrel look of my four sisters and me. My mother was the face of the family at our Catholic school and church. She provided some links to her husband's homeland at the dinner table, cooking daily servings of rice in a tin pot he bought when he first arrived from Shanghai. After Mass on Christmas Eve, she served Peking duck along with her traditional beef stroganoff. But my busy father, a neurosurgeon, had neither the time nor interest to properly introduce us to Chinese ways. Every now and then, he would make a comment about his family's religious life. His father, he told us, had been an Anglican priest who had studied as a young man at a seminary right here in Philadelphia. And he mentioned that another relative—an uncle with the curious name of Watchman Nee—was a Christian leader as popular in his time as the Reverend Billy Graham. That's all I knew and all I cared to know. My mother had a firm hand on our Catholic upbringing. My Protestant roots in China would remain an exotic curiosity.

But when I was twenty and a college student, President Carter normalized diplomatic relations with "Red China." The era of the Cultural Revolution had ended in 1976, and China was beginning to recover from decades of isolation. Beneath all the formal State Department language was this: families like ours would be permitted to visit. Up until then, we could communicate only through letters. Now my father would be able to return home to see the brother and sister who stayed behind. His parents by then were deceased, as was Watchman Nee. Only two of my sisters and I could make the trip; the others were tied up with school or jobs. It would have been awkward for my mother to join us. We planned to stay in my father's childhood home in the old International Settlement, and the Chinese government permitted that privilege only to "overseas Chinese" and their children, not "foreigners" such as my mother. The bamboo curtain had been pulled back, but not all the way.

We arrived on the tarmac of the Hongqiao Airport in Shanghai on a blazing hot June afternoon. For the relatives who welcomed us, it had been a mere three years since the end of the Cultural Revolution, the dark decade when Red Guards attacked anyone with educational status, religious background, and Western ties.

The first moments of the reunion were all sweetness and smiles. In the airport reception area, under the gaze of an avuncular Chairman Mao smiling down on us from a giant mural, my father melted into the embrace of his older sister. A tinier version of him, she had an easy smile and a girlish demeanor for a woman in her fifties. Best for us, she spoke English. Like my father, she had graduated from the medical school of St. John's University, run by American missionaries, and had recently retired as an obstetrician.

At the airport, our entourage split up into two borrowed vans that picked their way down a bike-choked road. Cousins who had been only faces in photographs came to life with names and personalities. To make it easier for us, they let us refer to them by their Western names. Maozhi was Aunt Martha. Her daughters Tianlin and Zhongling were Terri and Julia. Rice paddies and squat brick buildings gave way to tree-shaded avenues with storefronts that looked like they belonged in Paris of the 1930s. What few cars were on the road were antiques from decades ago. The streetscape, too, flashed by in black and white, with everyone wearing white short-sleeved shirts and dark pants.

The family lived in House 19 on Lane 170 on Jiaozhou Road. It was a narrow, three-story brick house sandwiched among identical dwellings along a common walkway. In another era, British neighbors would have called it a

On June 17, 1979, at the Hongqiao Airport in Shanghai, Martha Sun welcomed her younger brother Paul to Shanghai. They had not seen each other for thirty years. Courtesy of Jennifer Lin.

"terraced house." Entering through a rear door off a damp alley, we climbed a winding staircase to my uncle's third-story bedroom, which doubled as the family's catchall living space. It had a musty smell. I felt like I had entered a time capsule. In the stairwell was an old-style wall phone with a separate mouthpiece and receiver. Next to an armchair with a lace antimacassar was a mirrored, wooden armoire from the 1940s. I noticed that the tiny tiled bathroom with a proper Western, sit-down toilet was also the kitchen, equipped with a single gas burner that straddled the width of a claw-footed, cast iron tub. There was no refrigerator. Food was stored in a cabinet in the tight stairwell.

Everyone jammed inside the main room. Neighbors who heard what was going on stood in the doorway, straining to glimpse the foreigners. My father held court for hours, filling the gap of thirty years and answering a battery of questions. His Shanghai dialect was rusty. We relied on Julia's husband, an English teacher named Victor, to translate for us. *Who looks most like your Italian wife? How big is your house? Do you have a car? How many?* Scanning the room, I tried to match names with faces. The eldest cousin, Julia, was polite and demure and, we were told, worked as a pianist for a theatrical troupe. Her younger sister, Terri, cradled a newborn and said little.

My father was still talking when I retreated to my aunt's room a floor below and climbed into her bed, exhausted from our trip but happy to see my father home.

That first morning, blaring patriotic music from a loudspeaker mounted on a pole in the alley woke me. The energetic voice of a young woman roused the neighborhood. I didn't understand a word, but it was obvious this was our wake-up call, and I got dressed. Outside, bike bells thrummed like cicadas. A stream of cyclists already choked Jiaozhou Road. In the distance, the baritone moan of ships on the Huangpu River joined the morning chorus. Standing on the balcony off the bedroom, I could peer into the lives of families on the other side of the alleyway, or *longtang*. A woman plopped dumplings into a wok of sizzling oil. An older man in a white undershirt stood on his balcony, swinging his arms like a windmill for exercise.

That was when I heard my father coming down the steps and turned to see him approaching me on the balcony. His words that morning would stay with me forever: "My god, this is so depressing."

He explained. After my sisters and I had turned in for the night, he stayed up talking to his Uncle George, the younger brother of Watchman Nee. George asked him in a hushed voice, "Do you have any idea what happened to us?"

The uncle proceeded to tell him about the madness of the Cultural Revolution, when good people committed sadistic acts to curry favor with rebels and to protect themselves. My grandmother, his older sister, had it the worst. She was brutalized again and again for not disowning her brother, Watchman Nee, who had been branded an enemy of the people. Many times, her tormentors dragged her from her home, forced her to kneel on the pavement, and pressured her to denounce him.

The constant humiliation and physical torture, this uncle told my father, had hastened her death. But the family's hardships began long before the Cultural Revolution started in 1966. Did my father know that his father, Lin Pu-chi, had been pushed out of his church work in the 1950s? Did he know that Watchman Nee had been sentenced to prison in 1956 after a trial, public shaming in the press, and the arrest of his "counterrevolutionary clique"?

The answer, sadly, was that my father had been clueless. Of course, we had read about the destructive Cultural Revolution, a decade of anarchy and struggle, when friends betrayed friends and children turned on their parents. And we knew that Watchman Nee had been sentenced in 1956 as a counter-revolutionary. But what we didn't understand—what I didn't sense until that trip—was how the political drama of the era had played out within the walls of this very house. We had been assured time and again by my grandfather that everything was fine. "Do not worry," he wrote to us. "All's well." Now as I thought back to the faces that surrounded us the previous night, I wondered: Who were the victims? Who the collaborators?

During our two-week stay, my father tried to draw more details from his siblings but failed at every turn. No one wanted to talk; George alone revealed the truth, but even then only fragments. Fear kept their voices in a tight vise. They had been targeted once before; no one could assure them it wouldn't happen again. My father didn't press it. Instead, he vacillated between enjoying the here and now and brooding over disturbing scenes from the past that played out in his mind. It was as if an uninvited guest kept showing up as we went sightseeing from the Bund in Shanghai to the Forbidden City in Beijing. One moment, we would be sitting around a big table, laughing, enjoying a banquet, and listening to stories from long ago. The next moment, my father would drift off, anguished over thoughts of his mother in pain and his inability to help her.

When we returned to Philadelphia, my father seemed to take what he had learned, place it in a box, and put it somewhere far away. Maybe it was his temperament and training as a brain surgeon: *assess, intervene, cure. Next patient.* There was no way he could undo the past, so he would not dwell on it. He moved on. My reaction was different. Maybe it had something to do with the way I was wired. I was emerging as the reporter I wanted to be, and I couldn't let go. I had read the last page of a mystery and needed to read all the preceding chapters. I wanted to know: What happened to them and why?

For the next three decades, I worked for a newspaper in Philadelphia. As a reporter, I learned how to talk to people and to peel back layers on complex issues. I parachuted into breaking news events all over the world—from Lower

Manhattan after 9/11 to protests in the streets of Jakarta. Investigative work taught me how to drill into a topic like a miner until I reached the core of truth. But of all the subjects I took on, of all the events I covered, there was the story I could not shake, the one right in front me, the story of my family in China.

My grandfather and Watchman Nee both devoted their lives to nurturing the growth of Christianity in China. My grandmother was so devout that she clung to her Christian beliefs even in the face of unspeakable torment. All of them paid dearly for their choices. But the story of the family didn't begin there. My grandparents and Watchman Nee were third-generation Christians. Who came before them? What were their experiences? And why, in a culture steeped in the teachings of Confucianism and Daoism, did they embrace the ideas of "foreign ghosts" from a world away?

The questions that disturbed me after that first morning in Shanghai in 1979 only led to more, pushing me deeper into the past. Over the passage of many years, I returned to my relatives, coaxing them gently to tell me what they knew. I pored through the records, letters, and memoirs of missionaries and learned that Lin Pu-chi's troubles did not start in 1966 with the closing of churches or even in 1950, when the new Communist regime began to exert its control over all religions. My grandfather felt the harsh sting of China's innate distrust of foreign influences from his earliest days as a young minister in Fuzhou.

Lin Pu-chi had been born into his faith, but what about those who came before him? In missionary archives in England, I unearthed records about his father—my great-grandfather—who had been trained as a doctor by a British missionary and worked with him in a small hospital, treating opium addicts. But he was not the first convert—that man came a generation earlier and was a simple fisherman from a bayside village on the coast of Fujian. At the Lin Ancestral Hall in the town of Erdu, my branch of the Lin clan kept genealogical records in a thick book called a *jiapu*. There, I found fragments of information about the fisherman's life.

As I mined the past, I returned again and again to a thick folder with every airmail letter from my grandfather, composed in flawless English, starting on May 12, 1953, a month before my parents' wedding. My Italian mother had saved each letter, written in neat handwriting on pale blue airmail stationery. I have deconstructed every sentence, trying to discern what he was trying to tell us—or not.

After three decades, I can finally fill in what he had left out.

I came to understand that the journey of our family over five generations was the very story of the rise of Christianity in China, a saga of hardship and hope, of pain and perseverance that started when a fisherman from Fujian heard the ideas of strangers and did not turn away.

Prologue

Shanghai, 1956

*T*he Tian Chan Theater was the most glamorous in all of China when it opened in 1926, its double doors a gateway to the dramatic, stylized world of Peking opera, an art form that had bloomed in the emperor's court more than a century earlier and become a national treasure. An opera star, it was said, had not arrived until he set foot on the stage of the Tian Chan Theater before the vast house of three thousand. The brilliant costumes, the evening dress of patrons, the art deco ornamentation of the lobby—all of this coalesced under the bright lights of Jazz Age Shanghai into a spectacle that dazzled even Western visitors.

On the cold afternoon of January 30, 1956, armed guards stood at each entrance. A sullen line of people, clad in padded gray and blue cotton coats, filed through the doors. They were Christians, summoned by the Communist government to the theater just off the new People's Square in the city's center. They had been identified as followers of the teachings of Watchman Nee, and they were about to learn what it meant to be an enemy of the people in the People's Republic of China.

On this Monday afternoon there would indeed be a performance—a carefully scripted "political struggle meeting." The target was not present. Watchman Nee sat in isolation in a concrete cell in the Number One Detention Center of the Shanghai police. He had been in custody for four years, following his arrest on a train en route to the northeastern city of Shenyang.

It was chilly inside the theater. Watchman Nee's followers, called the "Little Flock" by outsiders, filled every seat. Most of them went to the same Christian assembly hall on nearby Nanyang Road, including the preacher's frail, sickly older sister, Ni Guizhen. Seated in the first row were sober-faced representatives from other religious groups—Protestant clerics, seminary students, an Anglican bishop, a Catholic priest, and a Buddhist monk. Onstage were a dozen party officials and prosecutors, who sat under a banner with Chinese characters that read: "Down with the counterrevolutionary clique of Watchman Nee."

The head of the Shanghai Bureau of Religious Affairs stood and approached a microphone. For the first time since the arrest of Watchman Nee, the government would reveal its case against him. The bureau chief told the audience that prosecutors had accumulated an overwhelming file of evidence—2,296 pages of confessions, documents, testimonies, and photographs—to prove that Watchman Nee tried "to supersede revolution with evangelism."

In the seven years since the dawn of Communist China, the new regime had asserted control over nearly all churches, mosques, temples, and religious groups. Some, however, resisted joining the new party-approved "patriotic" Protestant movement. Among them were Watchman Nee and many who followed his religious teachings.

Next up onstage was the head of the Shanghai Public Security Bureau, the omnipotent agency that kept tabs on all of the city's residents. He had an announcement. Late the night before, several elders with the Nanyang Road assembly had been arrested at their homes and sent to the bureau for further interrogation. They were, he declared, members of Watchman Nee's "counterrevolutionary gang."

The thousands in the audience listened, stunned and mute. Bodies froze and minds raced. The official was talking about respected associates and confidants of Watchman Nee. No one dared react: There were no cries, no gasps, no movement. Had there been, officials of the Religious Affairs Bureau seated at either end of each row were there to take note.

Prosecutors next laid out their case for imprisoning Watchman Nee. They did not scrutinize his religious teachings or Christian beliefs. They went after his character.

Act I: he was a spy.

Watchman Nee, an official recited, fed information to enemies in the United States Air Force and the Chinese Nationalist Party about Liberation Army troop movements during the civil war. He concocted an insidious plot to infect the troops in Jiangsu with a parasitic worm by dropping snails into their water supply from Lake Tai—and then withholding the materials for a curative drug. He encouraged the Nationalists to target attacks on water and electric plants, a strategy that had succeeded in Shanghai.

Act II: he was an economic criminal.

The pharmaceutical factory that he ran with his brother—the China Biological and Chemical Laboratories—evaded taxes, bribed officials, and dodged foreign-exchange rules.

Act III: he was "a dissolute vagabond of corrupt and indulgent living."

Watchman Nee was accused of forcing himself on young women; taking nude photos and movies as licentious mementoes; and frequenting prostitutes, including one particular "White Russian" refugee.

The meeting went on for hours. A handful of his followers took to the stage to vent emotions of anger and betrayal about their spiritual leader. Some shouted, "We will smash the reactionary clique of Watchman Nee!"

Finally, it was the vice mayor's turn. Religion, the Communist leader told the audience, should not be used as a cover to spread poison against the country and people. He urged the men and women in the Little Flock not to be afraid to wash their dirty linen in public.

"This struggle has just begun," Xu Jiangguo encouraged. "We will not draw back until we have completed it victoriously and rooted out every counterrevolutionary hidden within the Little Flock."

On cue, the audience was prompted to repeat, "We will smash the reactionary clique of Watchman Nee!"

Weeks later, Lin Pu-chi sat at his desk in the attic of his home on Jiaozhou Road in the International Settlement. The quiet house was drafty. It had been a mild winter, but just a week before, the first snow of the year dusted the city.

Lin Pu-chi and his wife outside their Shanghai home in the early 1950s. Courtesy of Lin Family Collection.

The sixty-one-year-old wrapped a wool scarf around his neck. Lin Pu-chi was an ordained Anglican priest, a Western-trained educator, and a respected editor. But in this new China, he had no church duties and preached only intermittently, filling in for others when they were busy or went out of town. He passed his days looking after his granddaughters.

Lin Pu-chi reached inside his desk for a sheet of airmail stationery, dipped his pen into a well of blue ink, and dated the letter March 24, 1956. It had been an uncharacteristic lapse of two months since he last wrote to his youngest son and daughter-in-law in the United States.

So much had happened. He paused, thinking how to begin. He wanted to tell his son that his mother, Watchman Nee's older sister Ni Guizhen, lay motionless in her bed with the curtains drawn. He wished he could explain how after the rally at the theater, she endured further "accusation sessions" with other members of the Little Flock. And how the *Liberation Daily*, the most influential Communist newspaper in Shanghai, had attacked his uncle Watchman Nee for three days with front-page articles, editorials, testimonials, and a scathing political cartoon showing him siphoning gold and money from obedient followers. The caption read: "Abandon the family. Give it all out. Give up your job."

Lin Pu-chi knew that once he placed his letter in the mailbox, it would be reopened and reviewed by agents with the Public Security Bureau. His youngest son had become an American citizen, and since the Korean War, the United States was China's number one enemy. Anything he had to say to his son would be scrutinized.

Telling the truth, confiding his fear and anger, was not an option. Instead, Lin Pu-chi did what was expected. He pulled the curtain down on their lives. In effortless English, he asked about Paul's two young daughters and marveled at how the eldest was already starting to talk. He mentioned that Paul's sister had used money he had sent the family to buy fabric for sewing dresses for her daughters. He thanked his son and daughter-in-law for the card they sent for his wedding anniversary on March 4 but remarked how the day passed quietly as his wife was not feeling well. Not quite knowing the words to describe her traumatized state of mind, he obliquely referred to her condition as "brain storm."

In closing, he wrote:

I wish I had a long telescope and could look across the ocean and see how you all are faring! But I can see with my mind's eyes just as well.

Love from,
Mom & Dad

I

FOREIGN GHOSTS

• 1 •

Cook

Fujian Province, Mid-1800s

*O*n New Year's Day in 1847, the schooner *Petrel* arrived at the mouth of the Min River and sailed upstream toward the port of Fuzhou, carrying opium from India and a missionary from Connecticut.

The *Petrel* was well suited for the voyage, fast across the open sea, quick and nimble along the coast and in the shallow rivers. Seamen who required speed and agility as well as a large cargo hold—slavers, privateers, fishermen— favored the double-mast schooner with its trapezoidal sails. The *Petrel* was laden with wooden chests packed tightly with heavy balls of dried, hardened opium from India. She had set sail from Hong Kong, four hundred miles to the southwest, racing up the coast through the Taiwan Strait to the mouth of the Min, where she slowed her pace as she headed west into the interior.

The river soon narrowed into a gorge named Five Tiger Gate, less than a half-mile across, with towering cliffs on either side and riven with spectacular cascades. The ship handled this passage well and then negotiated the growing cluster of Chinese junks that gathered alongside in hopeful expectation of business. As the river widened again, the landscape took on spectacular dimensions that reminded Europeans of the Rhine, Americans of the Hudson. Presently a pagoda came into view, a white tower of some 120 feet atop a hill on an island. This was Pagoda Anchorage, the schooner's destination. The captain dropped anchor in the deep water.

The next day, Stephen Johnson of Griswold, Connecticut, climbed into a smaller sampan and traveled another ten miles upstream to the port of Fuzhou. Johnson stayed for a few weeks at the house of the opium skipper before setting up his own residence and establishing the first Protestant mission in Fuzhou. He viewed this city of seven hundred thousand with the fervor of a revivalist, determined to convert China's millions one soul at a time on behalf of the equally optimistic New England churches that had sent him.

His arrival as a passenger on an opium schooner was an inauspicious way for a man of the cloth to make his entrance. Johnson, however, had no other way to get to Fuzhou. It was either sail on the *Petrel* or not at all. The port had been officially opened to foreigners and trade only three years before, in 1844, and profiteers selling opium and buying tea provided the only transport from the new British colony of Hong Kong. Johnson was keenly aware of the destructive and demoralizing influence of the opium trade. As he wrote to his supporters back home, "Not less than one half of the male population in this city are more or less enslaved to the use of opium, an appalling and melancholy fact!"

Three years after Johnson's arrival, a pair of British missionaries from the Church Missionary Society (CMS)—the Reverends Robert David Jackson and William Welton, also a physician—established the first Anglican mission in Fuzhou. They didn't have to rely on an opium captain; in Hong Kong, they chartered a lorcha, a smaller vessel with the bat-wing sails of a Chinese junk and a Portuguese-style hull. The Americans may have gotten to Fuzhou first, but the British missionaries did them one better. Through diplomatic channels, they were able to find rooms to rent in a Daoist temple on Black Stone Hill inside the walled city, the beating heart of Fuzhou. The other missionaries had to live outside the gates of the oldest neighborhood.

But in another way, the British were just like the Americans before them. Both were met with open hostility as interlopers who had forced their way into China in the wake of gunboats and a battle over opium. It didn't help that in the early years, the only way missionaries could exchange money without making a trip all the way back to Hong Kong was by calling on an opium skipper to cash a bank check for Mexican-minted silver dollars that were used in China at the time. Chinese cynics noticed: a missionary visits an opium schooner and returns with bags of cash. How could he not be complicit? But the missionaries in Fuzhou accepted the taint of their connection to the opium traders as the price of a toehold in China.

Opium had been officially banned in China in 1729. But the United Kingdom saw profit in the addictive drug derived from poppies that grew in Indian provinces controlled, conveniently, by the United Kingdom. For a century, usage spread as the British East India Company built a thriving business. This helped balance a trade deficit. Middle-class Britons craved all things Chinese: fine silk for their wardrobes, porcelain dishes for their dinner tables, and tea for their teacups. The Chinese had little interest in British cotton or pottery. But opium—now there was a product in demand, with an ever-growing customer base (fed, too, by American traders).

By 1839, Emperor Daoguang had had enough. He dispatched a scholar-statesman from Fuzhou, Lin Zexu, to the port of Canton to suppress the opium trade. British traders flouted the ban, and when Commissioner Lin discovered twenty-two ships carrying one thousand cases of opium each, he had his men seize the cargo and destroy it by digging trenches and using water, salt, and lime to dissolve the raw opium. Britain struck back, setting off a series of military clashes along the coast in the name of capitalism, open markets, and free trade. After three years of fighting, the humiliated emperor signed the Treaty of Nanjing, the first of several unequal treaties with other nations, and agreed to open four more ports to unfettered trade and foreign residents. Along with Canton, the emperor had to allow foreign ships to dock in Shanghai, Xiamen, Ningbo, and Fuzhou while ceding control of the island of Hong Kong to Britain.

Missionaries seized the moment. They looked upon these cities with great expectation requiring great effort. The evangelical movements in the British Isles and the United States were reaching outward, insinuating themselves into distant countries to plant their message. In Fuzhou, Protestant missionaries began preaching in the streets, handing out pamphlets in Chinese with Bible stories and Christian teachings, and opening small "chapels" in storefronts.

But Fuzhou, a center of learning, was hard ground. Every year, tens of thousands of scholars came to the city to sit for grueling imperial examinations that tested their knowledge in the Confucian classics. A successful scholar might join the emperor's government as a bureaucrat while gaining great status in society. To this class of scholar-bureaucrats, foreign missionaries were the ones who needed enlightenment. The barbarians had much to learn from the Middle Kingdom, not the other way around.

Above it all loomed opium. In the eyes of many Chinese, there was no distinction between missionary and merchant; both were foreigners, and foreigners brought opium. How many addicts did they supply? No one kept precise figures, but since a pipe could hold one mace—a Chinese measurement equal to about four grams—the number was thought to be in the tens of millions. At the peak of the drug trade in 1879, foreign captains delivered more than thirteen million pounds of opium. An Anglican missionary, John R. Wolfe (who would become known as the "Moses of Fujian"), lamented that he often faced the scornful remark: "You destroy us with your opium, and now you insult us with your offer of peace and salvation."

Inside the ancient walls of Fuzhou, the Christian message failed to take root. "I preach and preach and preach, but no one seems to regard my words," wrote one exasperated Anglican missionary to his London home office. After a decade in Fuzhou, the CMS missionaries had converted not one person to Christianity. The bishop in Hong Kong, who oversaw the Fuzhou mission, wanted to abandon the effort. But finally, in 1861, he had reason to celebrate: he traveled to Fuzhou to baptize the first convert.

When Wolfe arrived in Fuzhou the following year, he proposed a new tack. Fuzhou, he declared, was an "obdurate city," and it made little sense to waste time on the educated elite and worldly city dwellers. He wanted to look beyond the walled city and focus his energy on the multitude in the countryside. Wolfe knew what it was like to be poor. The son of tenant farmers from hardscrabble County Cork in Ireland, he felt he understood farmers and fishermen struggling from one day to the next. Obdurate himself, he set off for the far corners of the province, traveling for months on end into the mountainous interior or following the tortuous coastline.

In 1866, Wolfe headed north to the city of Ningde, a four-day walk from Fuzhou. Traveling on foot or carried by porters in a sedan chair, Wolfe was awestruck the first time he crossed Snow Mountain into Ningde. The sea seemed to run right up to the walls of the city, Wolfe wrote, bringing trading boats to its very gates. "The city in the valley, the mountains rising high on every side, the sea stretching off in the distance, and the boats spreading their sails before the breeze . . . it was grand beyond description."

In Ningde, he set up a CMS station and recruited a pair of Chinese helpers to assist him. They soon headed out to neighboring fishing villages, including the hamlet of Erdu on Sansha Bay.

The sight of a foreigner coming over the mountains by sedan chair was enough to bring life to a halt in a place like Erdu.

Wolfe was tall and pale with a bushy, dark beard. He wore leather boots, slim-fitting pants, and a wool coat. Farmers with shaven foreheads, long queues, and hairless faces dropped their rakes in the field to get a closer look at the stranger. Wives put down their water buckets. Startled children took off, squealing. Word spread of the "foreign ghost"—*yang guizi*—with his craggy, white skin. They wanted to touch his sharp nose, peer into his pale eyes, feel the metal buttons on his coat, hear the ticking of his watch.

Wolfe didn't mind; he knew he could cast a spell over villagers. In a letter home, he described how he would "quietly submit to the unpleasant results of their excited curiosity" and "the torture of being the most popular creature in these regions."

Wolfe talked to them about his "Lord on high," his *shangdi*. He told villagers to put away their idols and kitchen gods. His God could help them and save them from their sins. But what was sin, villagers were left to wonder. Confucius, whose moral teachings guided the country, never spoke of sin-stained souls. The great sage described neither heaven, nor hell, nor any path toward immortality.

The missionary laid out the essentials: Know right from wrong, follow these ten commandments, honor our God, and you will find eternal bliss. He told stories that came from his holy book and spent days patiently explaining the meaning to villagers. His Chinese assistant, in contrast, tailored the Christian lessons for the villagers. Once, speaking to a group about giving up their worship of idols, the catechist asked, "You say there is a spirit inside the idol. Well, are there not very often rats living inside the idol?"

"Yes, yes," the people responded. "Of course."

"Now, if I die, the spirit leaves my body and living things soon swarm inside. That is proof there is no spirit in me?"

Everyone nodded.

"Well, then, the rats in the idol show there is no spirit within it either!"

His point was that wooden idols were just that: wood. Some villagers looked at Wolfe and his helpers with suspicion and anger; their ideas were blasphemy. Renounce idols? Refuse to bow before ancestors? A man could lose his right to ancestral land for that.

Many turned away from the strangers. But others stayed to hear more.

One of the men to come back again and again whenever a Christian preacher came to town was a fisherman named Lin Yongbiao.

OLD LIN

By this time, Lin Yongbiao was an old man. His first wife died and he married another, but still he had no son. It weighed heavily on him. Without a son, a man had only a past and no future.

Old Lin was not educated. He knew little of Confucius. He fished in the morning and farmed in the afternoon. The landscape that Wolfe found so breathtaking also made it brutally hard for peasants like Old Lin to survive. Mud flats in Sansha Bay yielded rich harvests of oysters, shrimp, and eels, but the mountains were stingy and left little room for farmers and their crops. Hunger was constant, death always near.

The message brought by missionaries that their God had something better in store for everyone would have soothed someone like Old Lin. It was not something he heard from the Buddhist monks or Daoist priests. He was intrigued by the story of this Christ, who could free him from the drudgery of his earthly life. But he could not let go of everything. Straddling two worlds—one traditional, one Christian—he clung to some old ways. How could he not pay homage to his ancestors?

In the year that Old Lin turned fifty, his second wife delivered the son he had been waiting for. In the Lin Ancestral Hall, a two-story courtyard building guarded by a pair of stone lions in the center of Erdu, the time and date of the birth of the boy were later logged in a genealogical record of the clan's family

Records for the author's branch of the Lin family are stored in this ancestral hall in the bayside village of Erdu in Fujian Province. A genealogical book called a *jiapu* holds information on the first convert in the family, Lin Yongbiao, and his son and grandsons. Courtesy of Jennifer Lin.

tree, a *jiapu*, which was stored in a big wooden box and opened only once a year. According to the lunar calendar, the child was born just after 5:00 a.m. on the twenty-first day of the twelfth month in the ninth year of the Tongzhi reign—or, in the Western calendar, on February 10, 1871.

Old Lin finally had an heir who would walk the same stone paths, plant the same fields, and fish the same waters as all who had come before him for more than three centuries. His life was complete. But only months after his son was born, Old Lin watched his world go mad.

Up and down the coast of South China, villages and towns were seized with a fast-moving rumor that foreigners were out to poison everyone. Posters went up by the thousands, accusing God-talking missionaries of peddling "magical powder" that would kill unsuspecting victims. Placards warned of these "barbarians" with their "hideous faces" masterminding the plot. One read: *Whenever any of these persons, whether male or female, enters any village, reject their poisonous medicine. They should be treated like vagabonds. Don't by any means spare them!*

It was all a hoax, probably concocted by critics among the educated elite in the city trying to undermine the work of the missionaries. But it worked, and the panic was real. Throughout Fujian, mobs destroyed chapels and attacked the homes of Christian converts. A terrified Anglican missionary in Fuzhou wrote a frantic letter to his colleagues in London warning that the entire region was "on the brink of a volcano which was ready to open and send forth death and destruction all around us."

In his village, Old Lin could feel the eyes of his neighbors on him. Everyone knew he was one of *them*. He was a Christian.

Old Lin had waited a lifetime for the arrival of this son. Now, with the frenzy brought on by the poison scare, he worried about the safety of his family. He had heard that the missionaries in Fuzhou needed helpers. Maybe he could find work with them? It might be better to leave.

One morning, Old Lin and his wife loaded a basket with provisions. In another, he placed their baby boy. He attached the baskets on the ends of a bamboo pole and swung it over his back. Together, the couple took off over the mountains and away from home.

ROAD TO FUZHOU

Wealthy men could pay porters to carry them in palanquins for the slow trip to the city so that their black felt slippers need never touch the ground. Old Lin and his wife would walk in sandals made of straw. The road to Fuzhou started as a path wide enough only to put one foot in front of the other. Ahead, rugged mountains ran into the diamond waters of the bay, resurfacing on the horizon as small islands. He labored up steep steps, keeping his eyes focused straight ahead. A false step could send him plunging into a ravine with his precious cargo.

The footpath turned into a mosaic of stones, smooth and gleaming from generations of wear. Old Lin and his wife passed through dark bamboo groves and over hills with ruffles of wild red azaleas and pink roses. On the fourth day, the land opened into a valley with rice paddies spread before them like bolts of green velvet.

They were approaching Fuzhou, the capital of Fujian Province, which was the size of England. On the busy Min River, British captains picked up cargo of bales of black tea grown in the hills—and unloaded shipments of opium from India. A long, low bridge linked the old city with a newer settlement for foreigners on Nantai Island.

In the final miles to Fuzhou, travelers jammed a road that now was as wide as a pair of fat oxen. Old Lin turned his bamboo pole sideways to maneuver past coolies with sedan chairs. Men cleared the way by calling out the cargo of porters blocking their path.

"Slop buckets, out of the way!"

"Turnips, to one side!"

"Opium chests, give us the road!"

Shops with names like Perpetual Longevity or Myriad Profits lined both sides of the road. Proprietors burned incense to the gods of their trades outside oval doors shaped that way to keep out evil spirits. In the span of a few feet, Old Lin (if he'd had the money) could have bought a bolt of red silk from a dry-goods store or mackerel and cuttlefish for dinner from the smelly fishmonger's stall next door. Aching tooth? A sidewalk dentist wearing a necklace of molars knew just what to do: cover the spot with a corroding powder until the gum became soft, and yank out the offending tooth.

For Old Lin, who had spent his life in a fishing village, the city would be an adjustment. But for missionaries who were fresh off the boat from San Francisco or London, walking through the tight, smelly, crowded streets was a shock to the senses. More than one missionary—exhausted from the ocean crossing, overwhelmed by the crush of people, sweating from the heat, ignorant of the language, repulsed by leper beggars—privately wondered, *What am I doing here?*

Many a foreign lady, teetering in rigid leather shoes, twisted her ankle in the ruts and holes of the stone paving. Housewives threw kitchen waste on the street. Sewage stagnated in puddles. The streetscape had no comparison to anything back home. A missionary from New Jersey was aghast at the Chinese-style justice he saw on display in the city. He wrote home about a scene at a teahouse. Refined men on stools sipped from porcelain cups and nibbled rice cakes, while just at their elbows, a criminal stood in a tight iron cage with only his head free and his feet barely brushing the ground. The man had been charged with kidnapping. His sentence: starvation in full view of the languor and luxury of the teahouse.

Old Lin entered the walled city of Fuzhou from the South Gate. To the left was Black Stone Hill, the highest spot in the walled city. He followed the zigzag of alleys and crossed Bird's Tongue Bridge. At a walled temple, he pounded on a wooden gate.

The volcano did not blow, as the frightened missionary had warned in his letter home in 1871. Officials in Fuzhou refuted the poison claims and threatened to punish anyone who continued to spread false rumors. But for the nascent Christian community, the poison scare became part of a larger pattern of building up and tearing down. The antagonism between missionaries and some among the educated gentry, part of the legacy of opium, only grew more virulent.

When Old Lin arrived in Fuzhou, he went to work for the Anglican missionaries as a cook. Most of them lived in a compound on Black Stone Hill, the most prominent spot inside the walls of the city and a sacred place, with many Daoist temples. There wasn't just one hall, but many temples where different groups would gather with priests to perform ceremonies and rites set forth by Laozi, the sixth-century BCE philosopher and poet. When the first British diplomats arrived in Fuzhou, they were able to secure rooms in one of the temples. Anglican missionaries who came later followed their countrymen to Black Stone Hill and leased a small temple from a Daoist priest. They began making changes to fit their needs. They built a tall wall around the compound to keep out beggars. After a fire, they replaced a traditional Chinese wooden dwelling with a taller colonial-style stucco home. They built another Western dwelling when a new family arrived. They also opened a small school for girls on the temple grounds, further irritating the educated elite. These literati, who had social clubs nearby, saw no value in the education of girls.

The kitchen staff, including Old Lin, tended a garden inside the compound. House servants planted vegetables and flowers—from seeds arriving by mail to missionary wives from sisters and mothers back home. They cared for a buffalo kept in a shed. Foreigners needed milk for their tea and butter for their bread, two culinary oddities that perplexed the house staff. Old Lin learned how to prepare bland Western meals like boiled celery and potatoes.

Black Stone Hill, with its elegant temples, rose high above the tiled roofs of the cramped city. Locals believed it had ideal feng shui, the ancient belief that the harmony flowing from nature required the proper placement of buildings. From its highest reaches, a resident like Old Lin could peer over the jumble below like a sailor scanning the sea from the mast of a ship.

In the temples on Black Stone Hill, scholars and students gathered in courtyards for discussion and contemplation. During a special festival each autumn, thousands climbed with torches to the Altar of Heaven and Earth to burn incense in an iron cauldron at the top of the hill. From evening until daybreak, a long line of worshippers snaked up and down the hillside steps. Writing to London in 1878, a recently arrived CMS missionary, the Reverend Robert W. Stewart, described the procession: "We watched it from our windows last year and it seemed as if the whole city had turned out."

It was on this hallowed mountain that British missionaries decided in 1878 to build a school to train Chinese helpers. Wolfe needed more assistants to work in the field. At the time, the mission employed eighty catechists, plus five native clerics, to tend to more than two thousand followers scattered throughout the province. On an unused slip of land on the grounds of the Daoist temple where they lived, the clerics began erecting a three-story center from which they would advance their Christian agenda.

* * *

Through the spring of 1878, Chinese workers filed in and out of the temple grounds, hoisting timbers on their shoulders for the frame of a three-story building rising against a rock face. Using wheelbarrows, they lugged gray tiles for the roof. Carpenters blocked out forty-eight little rooms, seven and one-half feet square with shuttered windows. It was a top-heavy structure, the third floor wider than the second, which was wider than the first. The locals didn't know what to make of it, but it was clear the feng shui left much to be desired.

Stewart was in charge of the project. The grandson of an earl, he and his wife came from wealthy Irish families who financially supported their endeavors in China. His pedigree was many notches above the modest background of his colleague Wolfe, the farmer's son whose education was limited to a training college for missionaries. The twenty-eight-year-old Stewart, on the other hand, had studied law at the prestigious Trinity College in Dublin before joining the ministry. He arrived in Fuzhou in 1876 with a strong sense of purpose and the money to back it up.

As the school took shape, the Chinese scholars who had social clubs in the neighborhood didn't like what they saw. They viewed the construction as another affront by the foreigners, who had no business living on the sacred mountain in the first place. The scholars argued that the Chinese priest who had rented them rooms in 1850 lacked the authority to do so.

To offend the educated elite was to court trouble. The elite had extraordinary influence in Chinese society. Some held government jobs, and some merely served as links between officials and ordinary people. They were the intellectual stewards of the Middle Kingdom, their power drawn from their knowledge of Confucian thought. And they were not about to have these hairy foreigners, yammering away about their God in an ugly, guttural language, ruin the feng shui of their temples.

In June, a Chinese official who dealt with foreign affairs relayed to the British consul the mounting complaints of the scholars. Charles Sinclair politely broached the subject with Stewart. Yes, the diplomat conceded, the college building was within the walls of the temple grounds. Yes, Stewart had sought and received permission from the consul to begin construction. And yes, the work was nearly complete. Even so, the intellectuals had raised questions about several of the new buildings and whether the missionaries had encroached on land they didn't control. The head of the mission, Deacon Wolfe, was away at the time. The consul asked Stewart whether he could hold off on further construction until Wolfe returned and the matter could be sorted out with Chinese officials.

"I greatly regret I cannot comply," Stewart responded, even at the risk of "incurring your displeasure." The roof was finished, he noted, and all that remained was the detail work of fitting windows and doors.

Stewart had the callow self-confidence of a bright law student fresh from a lecture on treaty law. "The whole thing rises from two or three members of that most idle worthless class, the literati," Stewart wrote to the CMS board. "And that they should try to throw us about like this with our Treaty—giving us equal rights with other nations—straight before their eyes seems to me, I must confess, most unfair."

In an attempt to broker a compromise, Fuzhou officials offered the CMS mission a large piece of land in the Nantai foreign settlement on the other side of the Min River. They would throw in five thousand dollars in Mexican silver, too, to cover moving and construction costs. Consul Sinclair endorsed the settlement—not mentioning to the missionaries that the mandarins were also offering another piece of land for expatriate traders in order to build a track for racing their horses.

Stewart refused. He thought it would set a dangerous precedent to capitulate to the demands of the Chinese. "If I stopped work in this treaty port to please a few of the literati, who disliked foreigners and the spread of Christianity, all over the country the same thing would be tried," the former law student reasoned. "It would be impossible to hold our ground."

The Anglican missionaries offered a small concession: they would take the mandarins and neighborhood scholars on a tour of the compound so that they could see there were no violations. Chinese students had already moved into some of the forty-eight rooms of the college.

A date was set for August 30 at 11:00 a.m.

At the appointed hour, mandarins in formal silk robes arrived at the home of Stewart with an unexpected entourage of more than fifty men.

"Attendants," mandarins insisted.

"Ruffians," missionaries later charged.

In the drawing room, a missionary wife brought a tray with five cups of tea, sweetened with sugar, to serve the Chinese guests. Wolfe demanded that the officials throw out the hangers-on, including some of the literati who were temple directors. He accused one of them of being the ringleader and hiring thugs from the countryside to foment trouble.

"The greatest vagabond I have ever known!" Wolfe exclaimed.

The Chinese magistrates explained to the agitated Irishman that there was nothing they could do. Wolfe stormed out of the room, shut a hall door, and hurriedly called on house servants to lock an outer gate to stop others from coming into the compound. Impatient, he tried to push the crowd off the veranda himself, triggering a thunderbolt of raised voices. A messenger ran back into the parlor. In Chinese, he urged an interpreter for the officials to hurry. "Mr. Wolfe is pushing people about, attempting to clear them out of the house!"

Wolfe returned to the parlor, breathless and enraged. He claimed he had been punched in the chest and head and kicked in the stomach by "desperados."

"If anything happens to the mission," Wolfe shouted, "I will demand that an admiral send a dozen man-of-war ships into the port!"

As the missionaries tried to take the officials on the inspection tour of the school building, the situation spiraled out of control. Men began smashing rattan chairs on the Stewarts' veranda. In the garden, they upended pots and pulled up shrubs. As the day passed, the mob grew. The British consul arrived, as well as several Chinese officials with forty unarmed troops.

At one point, local men and teens began picking up rocks. Someone lobbed the first stone. Others followed, launching a fusillade of debris at the structure. A man with a torch set the wooden structure ablaze.

Soldiers, sensing a license to loot, threw off their uniform jackets and joined the mayhem. All through the night, as Stewart and his students took cover inside his house, soldiers and marauders ransacked the compound. Old Lin and the house servants watched helplessly as the mob took plates and cooking utensils, hurled rocks through windows, and ripped off shutters. By dawn, the crowd had wrecked the cowshed and pulled up all the plants in the kitchen garden.

In twenty-four hours, the mission compound was ruined, the college nothing but a heap of smoldering embers.

TRIAL

The clash at Black Stone Hill was resolved in a most unexpected way. Not about to accept blame, four Chinese temple directors sought a Western-style solution to the dispute. They sued Wolfe in a British consulate court in Fuzhou, alleging that the mission had an illegal lease. To argue their case, the temple directors hired the best English lawyer in Hong Kong, a debonair barrister by the name of Thomas C. Hayllar. Arriving in Hong Kong from Bombay in 1867, Hayllar was a good friend of the colony's governor, John Pope-Hennessy—and apparently also of his pretty young wife, Kitty. On the eve of the trial in Fuzhou, the governor had walked in on Hayllar and his wife in the bedroom of the governor's summertime mountain retreat. Days later, on April 27, 1879, the men met by chance on the street, and the cuckolded governor lunged at the barrister with his umbrella, nipping his chin. Hayllar wrestled the umbrella from the governor. He later hung it over his mantel like a trophy.

Sporting a nasty cut, Hayllar arrived in the courtroom of the Fuzhou consulate on April 30 for *Chow Chang Kung and others v. The Rev. John R.*

Wolfe. The trial dominated news from Hong Kong to Shanghai. The Irish cleric did not come off well on the stand. In three days of questioning, Hayllar made Wolfe seem evasive, obfuscating, and untrustworthy. It was left to Hayllar, this cad who had a hard time abiding by the commandment "Thou shalt not covet thy neighbor's wife," to encapsulate what the Black Stone Hill case was really all about.

The Hong Kong barrister noted that neither the government of the United Kingdom nor that of China had contemplated missionaries when five treaty ports were opened in 1844. Fuzhou, as Hayllar explained, was "a city of literates."

"The Athens of China," Chief Justice George French concurred from the bench.

On the rocks of Black Stone Hill, Hayllar went on, were inscriptions in many languages, including Sanskrit, dating back more than a thousand years. "The city is a place with a very strong literary element in it," the barrister told the court, "and before 1850, so far as I can discover, the people knew nothing of that particular product of civilization, the Protestant missionary."

Residents had shown admirable forbearance toward the expanding missionary presence, the barrister said. "The Chinese mind and the Chinese temper will bear a great deal before it is forced into active hostility against any foreigner, much less a missionary." But between the new houses and relocated walls, the girls' school and the training college, it was all too much. Hayllar disdainfully recounted his questioning of Stewart, who had ignored Chinese demands to stop building. His tone drenched with sarcasm, Hayllar addressed the judge: "This gentleman of 1876, who has been here two years, from Trinity College, Dublin, knows *all about* feng shui and the views of these people! And he says, 'I am not going to stop my work, I am only doing them inside.'"

"Well," Hayllar concluded, "the storm did break."

Of the violence, he continued, "I don't stand here to justify; it is a pity, but it is what everyone must have known would have happened."

A fellow CMS medical missionary who was observing the trial, Birdwood van Someren Taylor, wrote to his colleagues in London, "There was quite enough to make us hide our faces."

Chief Justice French issued a split decision. The missionaries, he concluded, had a valid lease to occupy the temple land. But that lease also allowed the owners to evict them with three months' notice. And that is just what the temple directors did. They sent a notice to Wolfe that everyone had to vacate the premises by January 1, 1880, because the directors needed the property. When one of the missionaries protested that they had no place to go, the Chinese officials reminded him that there were 140 CMS chapels in the province.

Out of options, Wolfe was forced to relocate to the telegraph office site in Nantai, the same location that was offered to him before the mob attack. Old Lin and the house servants packed up the belongings of the British families. They loaded up baskets, carts, and wheelbarrows for the long walk to new homes in Nantai.

Old Lin was on the move again.

• 2 •

Doctor

Fujian Province, 1890

*A*nyone crossing the Bridge of Ten Thousand Ages in Fuzhou to the Nantai neighborhood could spot in an instant where foreigners lived and worked. Their homes and offices loomed tall and white on the south shore of the Min River, like flags staking a claim.

The stone bridge, an engineering marvel eight centuries old, two lanes wide, and a third of a mile long, pulsated with commerce at either end. English merchants haggled through compradors to buy timber floated downstream from forests in the far interior. Coolies hauled bales of tea that had been picked in mountain plantations and then were pressed into brick-size blocks in warehouses and readied for shipment to Russia, Australia, Japan, Europe, and America. The powerful Hong Kong trading house of Jardine, Matheson & Co. kept a ship—the *Mahamoodie*—anchored nearby for receiving and unloading the most lucrative cargo of them all: opium, grown in India and shipped to China to be packed into the pipes of millions of addicts in Fujian and beyond.

The foreign community—mostly American, British, and Japanese traders with some French and Russian residents—was small, but its members felt compelled to re-create the worlds they left behind. They had tennis courts, a cricket pitch, and even a racecourse for play. The English had one cemetery; Americans another. Missionaries had opened schools, hospitals, and churches. A vicar from Sussex would feel quite at home in Nantai's chapel for expatriates, tucked behind a wrought-iron fence and fashioned from granite, not brick.

To get to the walled compound of the Anglican mission, house servants like Old Lin had to climb steps from the waterfront to a ridge a half-hour away. Old Lin knew some of his countrymen looked down on him, deriding him as nothing more than an opportunist who accepted the religion of foreigners only to fill his bowl with food. *Rice Christian*, they sneered. But like any father, Old Lin wanted a better life for his son—status, wealth, good fortune. *Fu*, the Chinese called it. More than anything, he hoped to see his son wear the long silk tunic of a scholar rather than the baggy hemp-cloth shorts of a peasant. Old Lin knew the missionaries with their schools and books could help his son. They could mold him into a thinking man.

The cook enrolled his son, Lin Dao'an, in a mission school in Nantai. His classmates were the sons of local church workers as well as boys from remote villages in the interior of Fujian. Missionaries taught the Chinese classics and Christian scripture in the local dialect—as well as composition, mathematics, and science. Most graduates went on to jobs as teachers in mission schools in villages throughout the province. But Lin Dao'an was handpicked for a different assignment; he would become a doctor's assistant. The CMS station in Fujian did not have a medical school, but it did have a new hospital in the walled city of Funing on the northern coast. It was started and run by a respected, energetic physician with the impossibly long name of Birdwood van Someren Taylor. He selected the cook's son as a trainee, giving the cook's family a hand up the social ladder.

DR. TAYLOR

To reach Funing, a town of only ten thousand, Lin Dao'an sailed to the farthest end of Sansha Bay, passing waterfront villages like the one his father had left two decades earlier. Travelers getting their first glimpse of Funing were often disappointed. Set on a plain surrounded by mountains, the city appeared trapped in the claustrophobic embrace of a twenty-six-foot-high wall, built four hundred years earlier to keep out marauding Japanese pirates. Anglican missionaries described it as "the backwater of the backwater."

But every three years, the sleepy city stirred to life. Funing was one of the host cities for imperial examinations. Thousands of scholars from surrounding counties passed through the city gates to endure long days of tests for official jobs and government appointments. It was the backwater's saving grace; other than that, Funing was in a sorry state of slow decay. Even the cannons mounted on the fern-cloaked city wall were rusted and useless.

The town presented an enticing challenge for Dr. Taylor, one of the most effective Anglican missionaries in Fujian province. Born in India to missionary parents, he trained at the esteemed Edinburgh Medical School and arrived in China in 1879, shortly after the destruction of the mission compound on Black Stone Hill by anti-Christian agitators. In the wake of the hostilities, Deacon Wolfe thought it would help to repair relations in the neighborhood to have a doctor offering medical help. Locals may not have accepted the religion of the foreigners, but they could not deny the results of their medical methods. Taylor began seeing patients for a few hours a day in a makeshift dispensary in between language training with a tutor. The young doctor was soon overwhelmed. He had only one Chinese helper, who knew nothing of either English or medicine. Taylor suggested to Wolfe that he start training a few local young men as medical students.

The deacon immediately dismissed the idea.

"You have been sent out to do mission work, not to train medical students," he said.

"Surely, this is mission work," Taylor replied. "Do you not have boys' schools, girls' schools and colleges? Do you not regard education as a very important part of mission work?"

"Oh, yes," the senior cleric said. "But it is not quite the same. We teach the Bible and train men to be catechists."

"Do you not teach them a great deal more than the Bible?" the doctor asked. "You teach them geography, the knowledge of the earth made by God. I teach them anatomy, the knowledge of the body made by God."

The doctor added: "You teach them two and two makes four. I teach them that the result of a good dose of quinine in ague relives them of fever and a good deal of misery."

Taylor suggested that he recruit trainees from the CMS boys' high school in Fuzhou.

Wolfe relented, begrudgingly. "Well, we might let you have a few boys," he said, "but only the ones who are not fit to be catechists."

In his first years in China, Taylor traveled by foot across the entire province, visiting towns and villages for weeks at a time to see patients and to scout for a place for a hospital. American missionaries had hospitals in Fuzhou and other towns across the province. The CMS decided to place Taylor in coastal Fu-ning, a small town with a handful of Christian followers and a Chinese cat-echist who worked for Wolfe but no hospital or dispensary.

Taylor brought the pragmatism of a scientist to his work as a missionary. He shared the same ardor for his faith as his fellow missionaries, but reason and respect guided his approach to the challenges of life in China. He knew, for instance, that the Chinese would not give up their belief in ancient remedies and herbal treatments. But he could clearly see the need for Western surgical techniques and standards of hygiene. In his travels, Taylor was aghast to see infected wounds that had been treated with putrid poultices or folk therapies such as raw chicken skin. Worst were the cases where people had taken medical matters into their own hands. He once had to repair the damage done by an old man who had trouble seeing and decided to cut away part of his eyelid with his knife.

When Taylor settled in Funing in 1882, his first challenge was finding a building to rent for a hospital. The very concept of a hospital was met with deep-set resistance. The Chinese believed that a person's spirit stayed behind after death. Nobody wanted to lease a property to this foreigner and his army of spirits. If a property owner rented to him, who would ever want to live again in a house overrun with the ghosts of dead patients? Taylor was forced to use a small spare room in the chapel for his dispensary. On Easter Monday in 1883, he opened his door to villagers.

He quickly felt deep suspicion among residents of the walled city.

"We were thought to be spies, to be agents of some political organization that was to overthrow the present dynasty! To be buyers of tea! To be sellers of opium!" the doctor recounted.

His medicine, rumormongers warned, was enhanced with human eyeballs and kneecaps and had the power to cause people to become followers of Christianity. When the doctor offered a cup of tea to a guest, it was often declined for fear of instant conversion. Taylor saw the hesitation and concluded that only through medical success— and patients in high places—could he overcome his doubters.

Taylor sensed an opportunity when a military officer asked him for help. The man was gaunt and pallid, and the doctor quickly recognized the symptoms. The "angel of death," as missionaries called opium, was pulling him away. The officer told Taylor that he'd heard foreign physicians had ways to break opium addiction that traditional Chinese doctors lacked. Taylor was forthright in his warning: There was no easy cure. Withdrawal from the grip of opium would be a violent process, the doctor cautioned. He must prepare for an extended stay to break the habit all at once, not gradually.

First the military man had to put aside his pipe. If he was caught sneaking a stash of opium—in the folds of his sleeves, between his toes, or woven into his braided queue—he was out. No exceptions. The officer agreed, and treatment began. The first two days were the toughest: explosive diarrhea, uncontrolled vomiting, even spontaneous ejaculations. His stomach and bowels felt like they had turned to ice. Worse, he was awake through it all. Taylor administered doses of chloral hydrate to put him to sleep; it would allow the officer to escape inevitable thoughts of suicide. For the aches that racked his body, the doctor offered a tonic of quinine.

The man ate very little during the first days, only a little rice porridge. He took eggs and juice a day or so later. By the tenth day, the pain was gone. His craving for opium eased. He was eating and sleeping on his own and restless to go home.

The cured officer was not one for a quiet thank-you. He expressed his gratitude in a distinctly public, military way. A brass band played as a flag bearer carried through the streets of Funing a silk banner declaring the wondrous works of the foreign physician. The procession ended at the hospital, where the banner was hung—an eye-catching endorsement from an influential man. Perhaps this, Taylor thought, would end the rumors and reassure the local citizens.

"Do not you Englishmen bring us this opium?"

The question was asked time and again. Taylor could not escape the truth in it or the embarrassment it caused. At his hospital, two out of three patients were addicts. Missionaries, disgusted by the opium trade, wrote home to friends and family that the hospital only mirrored the rest of the city. Every village in the area had at least two or three opium dens, where addicts could easily smoke away half their wages. A wealthy person could indulge his habit in the privacy of home. Even if he was in a stupor, he could depend on his trusty servants to feed and bathe him, even change his clothes. A military officer, too, could hide his addiction by having an assistant cover for him. But pity the coolie who carried a sedan chair for a living or loaded boats at the docks. He retreated to the darkness of a filthy opium den. And there, with dozens of other addicts who rotated all day long on bug-infested daybeds, he could escape the hardship of life in an opium haze.

Smoke opium long enough, and your body stops absorbing food. You waste away. You stop caring. You stop living. In this desperate state, some patients listened a little more closely to the message of missionaries. And if Jesus could not save them, there was always suicide. Women who were tethered to the pipe, in particular, felt so trapped that they viewed death as the only alternative. They swallowed large doses of opium extract at night, knowing that by the time they were discovered in the morning, it would be too late. Taylor could try to pump a patient's stomach or induce vomiting with sulfate of zinc. But if a woman was unconscious or couldn't be forced to vomit, it was useless. The angel of death would take her away.

Some were better than others at hiding their addictions. Another British cleric in Funing, the Reverend Hugh M. Eyton-Jones, received a rare invitation to dine with the highest-ranking government official in the district. To be a guest of the mandarin in charge of the entire prefecture of Funing indicated great progress for the mission. As servants placed dishes on the table, Eyton-Jones took the opportunity to ask the official directly about the opium epidemic.

"It is bad," the man replied soberly. "It's a waste of life, of time, and of money." It was clear the official had given the topic much thought, and he went on to speculate on how it might be fought. "If the foreign import were stopped, we could control the use inland," he noted, "as the native-grown opium is so much milder than the foreign."

After dinner, the men adjourned to an anteroom in the official's quarters, known as his yamen. Eyton-Jones assumed they were settling in for more conversation, but the missionary's Chinese servant appeared restless and anxious. He paced the room. Soon he brought in their traveling lamp, signaling that it was time to go.

"Why were you rushing to get me out of there?" an irritated Eyton-Jones asked his servant when they arrived home.

"Could you not see?" the servant replied. It was so obvious to him: the official could not sit still; he was fidgeting constantly. The man explained to his British employer: "The hour for his opium smoking had come and he was most uncomfortable."

The missionary stared in disbelief. His servant leaned in closer and said in a low, disgusted voice, "All of them were opium eaters."

The opium pipe, Eyton-Jones would later lament to his colleagues in London, "becomes a rod of iron, and the smoker a slave."

MEDICAL MEN

When Lin Dao'an arrived in Funing, the hospital was established, respected, and growing. From a spare room in the chapel, Taylor and his staff of trainees and nurses could treat sixty men and women at any given time in a compound of buildings. With his new students, Taylor was not about to have anything—or anyone—ruin the reputation of the medical mission. At the start of training, the doctor issued a stern warning. If any student was found stealing bottles of medicine from the dispensary, he was finished.

"For the first year," he told them, "you are simply on trial. At the end of six months, I will let you know if you can stay or not until the end of the year."

Word of the hospital had spread throughout the coastal area, and people traveled great distances for treatment. Each year, the staff treated as many as five hundred inpatients and more than four thousand outpatients. Village patients, accustomed to pigs eating slop in the courtyards of their homes, found the hospital startlingly sterile. It had a private section for paying patients; separate rooms for examinations, operations, and recovery; and a classroom and quarters for medical students. For the foreign staff, however, this was primitive medicine. Patients slept on beds that were boards resting on wooden sawhorses and covered themselves from the night chill with thick quilts. Their families followed them to the hospital to provide meals. And if the efforts of

A map of coastal China with a close-up of Fujian Province marking the location of Erdu, home of the Lin ancestral home; the port of Fuzhou, and the town of Funing, a center for Irish missionaries. Courtesy of Sterling Chen.

the medical staff were failing, they hurriedly carried their relatives back home. The Chinese dreaded the thought of taking a last breath away from home. The hospital even had a "dying room" that could be completely shut off from the rest of the facility. That way, any patient who took a sudden turn for the worse could be quickly sequestered so as not to alarm other patients.

Taylor treated his trainees as if he were mentoring men at his alma mater in Edinburgh. Lin Dao'an and the others studied physiology, anatomy, and surgical techniques, mostly using textbooks that Taylor had translated into a Romanized version of the local dialect. Like British students, they consulted Heath's *Student's Guide to Surgical Diagnosis* as well as Fenwick's *Medical Diagnosis and Treatment*. They learned how to suture a cut, something that never

A portrait of Lin Dao'an, who was trained by missionaries as a doctor. Courtesy of Lin Family Collection.

failed to awe local patients. They dressed wounds using rolls of bandages made from the old calico dresses that mission ladies cut into strips. They lanced boils, removed cataracts, and set broken bones.

When a new patient arrived at the hospital, Taylor would let one of his students present a diagnosis, and then he would critique his assessment. Every day it was something different: pinkeye that could cause blindness; fevers from malaria and typhoid; the chronic bronchitis and asthma of opium smokers. The most pathetic patients were those afflicted by the bacteria causing leprosy. And unlike students in Edinburgh who might hear about elephantiasis in a class on tropical diseases, Lin Dao'an saw it firsthand—patients with legs swollen to grotesque proportions because of a parasitic worm.

The molding of young doctors went beyond the clinic. Taylor mixed passages from the Gospels of John or Matthew into his class time. And during off hours, he introduced his students to his other passion: tennis. The Irishman was not about to give up his game, even in China. Within the hospital compound, where his house also was located, he had a house servant build a court, using a fishing net strung between two wooden poles. One day, the doctor invited his students over to try their hand at the game with some of the newly arrived unmarried British ladies who were studying Chinese in Funing before being posted to remote mission stations.

Lin Dao'an, wearing his loose, ankle-length tunic, was paired with the daughter of a vicar from Birmingham, Elsie Marshall. Flailing about, he tried to imitate his skillful mentor but kept tripping on his long robe as he ran to swat the ball in felt slippers. Lin Dao'an had no clue how to play the game or how to run, for that matter.

Elsie tried not to laugh. "It was a curious experience playing tennis with a Chinaman," she wrote home to her family in England. "I believe the literary men think it degrading to run."

While Taylor tended to the sick, his wife, Christiana, circulated with recovering patients and their families in the hospital courtyard. One or two Chinese Christian men assisted her. She handled the women; they handled the men. Christiana was the first foreign woman ever to pass through the city gates of Funing. As she made her rounds, she told patients Gospel stories. Over cups of tea and bowls of peanuts, she might pass on a little prayer, jotted on the back of a Christmas card she'd received from home. The Chinese catechists might share with patients a book of rhymes explaining Christianity or teach them a favorite hymn, such as "Rock of Ages."

All around the hospital, the tenets of Christian faith were on display. Military officer or beggar boy, all patients were treated the same by the hospital staff. Lepers, who had no hope of recovery, received equal compassion from doctors and nurses. So when the Chinese catechist quoted from the Bible—"Come unto me, all ye that labour and are heavy laden, and I will give you rest"—the patients and their families could see that these were not mere words.

The missionaries raised nonreligious matters with the locals. The foreigners found the crippling practice of binding women's feet barbaric and cruel. Nurses winced as they changed bandages on young feet being molded into three-inch human hooves. Christiana tried to persuade Chinese wives to free their feet and those of their daughters. With converts, she would reason: would Jesus want you to distort your body and cause such pain, all for the sexual titillation of men?

One woman who was led into the hospital on tiny feet could barely see. The doctors performed successful cataract surgery. During her recovery, the woman listened to Christiana's reasoning. When the woman returned home, her neighbors were so shocked and excited that the nearly blind woman could see that they didn't notice her feet. They were unbound.

A GOOD WIFE

The interior of the small Anglican chapel in Funing felt like a barn. Made of rough-hewn wood, the open space had small windows with no glass. The baptismal font was a big bowl. Women sat in the rear of the chapel behind a screen. Chinese custom forbade them from having direct contact with men other than their relatives. In the city of ten thousand, the little congregation attracted one hundred or so people on Sundays—some simply curious and inquiring, others baptized or about to be. With so few members, there were no strangers among the small band of foreign and Chinese Christians. Lin Dao'an could not help but notice the petite Chinese teacher who played "Jesus Loves Me" on the little pump organ during services.

You could read the lineage of Zhan Aimei in her face. Her full lips and dark skin suggested generations of farmers who never knew the luxury of a rich man's home. Zhan Aimei was the youngest of four, born in 1874 in a tiny village deep in the mountains west of Ningde. She was given a name that meant love and beauty. Zhan Aimei lived a simple life, learning how to tend to household chores as well as how to plant crops and care for barnyard animals. Her life would have begun and ended in the tiny hamlet of Meiyu. But when she became a teenager, her path took a remarkable turn: her parents decided to send her to a missionary school in Funing.

A girl born into a poor peasant family faced a precarious future. Just feeding her would have been a struggle. A few years after the birth of Zhan Aimei, China faced one of the worst famines in its long history. Between 1876 and 1878, an estimated thirteen million Chinese starved to death. Missionary women wrote home to sisters and mothers about tragic examples of desperate parents abandoning their daughters, or worse. One British woman in Fujian theorized that in some parts of the province, three out of every four female newborns were victims of "infanticide."

Many poor fathers agreed to send their daughters off to missionary schools less out of a zeal for education than mere indifference. If these foreigners wanted to support their daughters, feed them, care for them, maybe even find them husbands, so be it. One desperate father sent his daughter to the mission school in Funing only to withdraw her when a better opportunity came around: he sold her for sixty dollars to work as an indentured servant for an official.

Missionary women traveled from town to town trying to recruit students for the mission schools. Chinese women led cloistered lives, unable by custom to leave their homes. Dr. Taylor's wife, Christiana, would call on former patients under the pretense of checking on their health. While her husband believed that the way to a man's soul was through his health, she knew that the way into a woman's home was through her children. On visits, she tried to persuade mothers to send their daughters to the boarding school in Funing. "If we can get the children," Christiana wrote in a dispatch to supporters back home, "we have every hope of getting the mothers. If we can reach the mothers and children, we shall reach the fathers. There are exceptions, but women can rule here in their own way."

When Zhan Aimei arrived as an adolescent at the boarding school in Funing, it had about two dozen girls. Mornings were for scriptures, afternoons for practicing Chinese characters and studying a map of the world, and the time after that for mending clothes, knitting and needlework, cooking and cleaning. The students would, after all, become wives one day. In another break from Chinese tradition, British teachers put girls through daily exercises with calisthenics and drills to keep them fit.

For a farm girl like Zhan Aimei, the world opened up inside the classroom.

"Can blood really run up and down your leg?" an incredulous student asked during a session on the human body.

Teachers told the girls about cities beyond the borders of the Middle Kingdom. They passed around a magazine, *The Church Missionary Gleaner*, with articles about converts in Bombay and West Africa and drawings of chapels in the American West and Madagascar. Sometimes, the missionaries would hang a sheet on the wall and light a candle behind a "magic lantern" slide projector. The walls of the simple classroom were suddenly filled with astonishing scenes from England—a cityscape of impossibly large buildings; a mechanical trolley on a city street; a massive steam locomotive. In this part of China, where trains were unknown, the idea of traveling faster than a donkey was too fantastic for the girls to imagine.

The education of the girls wasn't limited to books. For the students, as young as seven and as old as twenty, the women from England and Ireland were odd birds to study. A Chinese girl wore a loose-fitting, embroidered tunic made from indigo cotton that breathed in damp, hot weather. Her raven hair was slicked back with tea oil, braided into a long queue, and tied with red thread. Her earlobes were pierced for hoops or dangling earrings made of tin.

Her teacher, in contrast, wore a heavy long woolen skirt cinched so tight at the waist that the girls wondered how she could breathe. Her only jewelry was a cameo brooch, pinned at the high neck of her cotton blouse. Her hair was so wavy that tendrils fell around her face. And the green Wellington rubber boots she sometimes wore on her big feet to hike in the hills seemed more fit for a farmer than an educated woman.

Zhan Aimei had been a bright student. Since she had shown promise, the missionaries sent her to a bigger and better boarding school for high school girls in Fuzhou. After graduation, she followed a path laid out for her by returning to Funing to teach at the school she had attended as a child. Training more Chinese teachers was a vital part of the mission system of schools. The other was molding girls into proper brides for boys who would become Chinese catechists. The mission teachers considered it a failure if a Christian convert married a nonbeliever. But most of the country girls already were betrothed by the time they arrived at the school. The fate of some was sealed in infancy; in the business of marriage, the younger the bride, the less a groom's family had to pay.

Zhan Aimei, coming from humble roots, had no engagement plans. The missionaries played matchmaker and thought the young teacher would make a fine wife for one of Dr. Taylor's assistants, Lin Dao'an. With much joy and re-lief for the Funing Christians, they wed in 1893 and celebrated with a banquet at a dining hall. In keeping with custom, Chinese women sat in one room, men in another, and the foreigners in a third. The bridegroom himself waited on the missionary ladies, scurrying in and out of the kitchen with steaming bowls of food that he placed in the center of the table. After seven courses, the young teachers told him they'd had plenty.

Lin Dao'an looked perplexed. "We're not even halfway finished," he protested. "We have thirty dishes!"

The ladies looked at one another, smiled gamely, and picked up their chopsticks.

On Christmas Day a year later, all the Christians of Funing filled the chapel, which smelled of fresh pine. The day before, schoolgirls had climbed into the hills to cut branches to decorate the church. A young English lady showed them how to bend the branches into wreaths, which were placed inside the church. Girls hung lanterns from the ceiling and made strings of paper roses in red and pink to drape across the pulpit. They traced big Chinese characters on red paper, cut them out, and pasted them on white cloth. The banner was hung above the altar: "Glory to God in the highest and on Earth, peace and goodwill toward men."

At 11:00 a.m., schoolgirls sang in Chinese, "Hark! The herald angels sing." The benches of the chapel were filled. But behind the curtain, in the seats saved for women, Zhan Aimei was absent. A murmur rippled among the Chinese wives.

Did you hear? Lin Dao'an and his wife who married just the year before? They have a child, a son, born just now.

It was Christmas morning, 1894.

The couple named their firstborn Lin Pu-chi.

• 3 •

Firstborn

Fuzhou, 1907

$\mathscr{O}$n a Monday morning during the Spring Festival heralding the Year of the Goat in 1907, Lin Dao'an left his home with his eldest son in tow. Dr. Lin was a man on a mission, weaving in and out of the crowds in Nantai, his long queue swinging back and forth like a metronome. His son Lin Pu-chi, tall and lanky at twelve, followed behind, his gaze fixed on his father's back.

Occasionally the doctor would nod to a passerby he recognized, if not by name then by medical history. He had settled in Fuzhou a few years earlier, after more than five years working with his mentor, Dr. Taylor. He had helped the missionary to open and run a new hospital in the southern coastal city of Xinghua. But his health was poor, and with a growing family, Dr. Lin decided to return to the city of his youth. He took a position as the head Chinese assistant of another well-known Scotsman, Thomas Rennie, who ran the main port hospital in Fuzhou. Dr. Rennie was renowned in the province for his medical skills and cut a striking figure on the streets of Nantai, riding his dappled gray mare to call on patients. Once, on a visit to a CMS school, the Scotsman noticed from across the room a girl with a tiny white speck on her cheek. He whispered to the teacher. The child was brought to him. His suspicion was confirmed; the child had leprosy. Sadly, she had to be removed from the classroom and sent to a settlement for lepers outside the West Gate of the walled city, where she died soon after.

Dr. Lin and his son, arriving at the gate of a foreign home, bounded up the front stairs to a second-floor veranda. A tall, mustached Irishman stood among a group of Chinese boys and men.

"Oh, Dr. Lin," the middle-aged cleric enthused, with surprise and relief in his voice. "Thank you for bringing your son."

With his thick Irish brogue coloring his Chinese, the cleric was sometimes difficult for the doctor to understand. But his command of the local

39

dialect was beside the point. What brought Dr. Lin racing to his house this morning was the man's offer to teach his son the Queen's English.

Just the day before, Dr. Rennie had told Dr. Lin about the Irishman, the Reverend William S. Pakenham-Walsh, who was looking for students for a new school. Pakenham-Walsh had been in China for ten years, teaching in a variety of capacities: at a school for Chinese boys; theology classes for church assistants; even religious training at a home for lepers. While the Anglican mission already had a boys' high school, this new venture would be unique. English would not be merely the subject of a class; it would be the language of instruction for all courses.

That was all Dr. Lin needed to hear. Then and there he determined that the eldest of his five boys, Lin Pu-chi, would enroll. Many Chinese had little patience for foreign evangelists. But Dr. Lin, who had grown up among them, saw their system of education as superior. He believed the missionaries, with their schools and hospitals and ideas, were agents of change at a time when China desperately needed help.

The century had started violently, with the antiforeign Boxer Uprising in North China. In 1900, a sect of self-described warriors, abetted by the xenophobic empress dowager, slaughtered hundreds of foreigners and tens of thousands of Chinese Christians before falling to an eight-nation military force in Beijing. China's defeat only amplified the cry for reform. Men like Dr. Lin believed that the Western world was not to be feared or disregarded; China had much to learn from others. The doctor wanted his son in the vanguard of that transformation.

On his veranda, Pakenham-Walsh was explaining his plans to the assembled fathers and boys, some as young as Lin Pu-chi, others in their late teens.

"We wouldn't be here today if I hadn't said hello to this lad last Saturday," Pakenham-Walsh said, gesturing to one of the older teens.

Pakenham-Walsh had been walking by the English cemetery when he bumped into a former student named Li.

"Where are you going?" Pakenham-Walsh had inquired.

"I'm on my way to the American school to sign up as a student."

Pakenham-Walsh was stunned. The teen had already graduated from the Anglican school for boys and was now qualified to return to his village as a teacher.

"What happened?" Pakenham-Walsh needed to know.

"Teacher," the former student answered, "you do not understand. I'm young. I want to get on and I can't if I don't know English. If your mission won't teach me, I'm forced to go to an American school."

The student was right.

For years now, the most senior cleric in the Anglican mission—the seventy-five-year-old Wolfe, who had spent more than half his life in Fuzhou and was now an archdeacon—resisted introducing English into the curriculum. He thought it was a waste of time. What the mission needed, Wolfe argued, was to train Chinese boys to help with evangelizing. For that, all they needed was their mother tongue. Leave the English to others.

The Americans had no such reservations.

"Do you know of any others who are leaving our schools?" Pakenham-Walsh asked.

The teen sheepishly nodded.

Pakenham-Walsh recognized that this was serious. If the English missionaries lost graduates to their American counterparts, all the time and effort that they were putting into their own schools would be for naught. Mission schools were feeders for the church, shaping not only teachers and catechists but also future members.

"When do you start at the American school?"

"Thursday."

Pakenham-Walsh made him an offer: "Hold off on enrolling, and bring the others to my house on Monday. I will start a school to teach you English," he said. The student agreed.

Now all Pakenham-Walsh had to do was persuade the CMS leaders that this was a good idea. He was blunt. He told his peers that in the eyes of the Chinese—and himself—the Anglican mission "was half asleep." Enrollment in its schools was declining, and the quality of its students, quite frankly, "diminishing." Wolfe, naturally, voiced his doubts. But the other missionaries sided with the younger man, albeit with certain conditions: Pakenham-Walsh had to recruit at least ten students; they had to pay tuition; and the venture had to pose no extra burden to the financially strained mission.

"Walsh," the cantankerous Wolfe needled, "you will never get ten boys in our mission to enter your school."

At Pakenham-Walsh's home that Monday, the doctor's son made nine.

But time was running out, and Pakenham-Walsh had no tenth student or even the prospect of one. He had promised the boys that if he couldn't fill a class, they would be free to go to the American school, which started in three days. The Irishman despaired. Wolfe's words kept him awake at night.

Thursday morning arrived, his enrollment stuck at nine, when his house servant announced a visitor at the gate. A Chinese pastor whom Pakenham-Walsh knew well had arrived with his very young son, no more than eight and too young for the school.

"Here is my son," Pastor Ding Ing-ong told him. "I will lend him to you. But when you get a real tenth boy, please return him to me."

The local pastor wanted Pakenham-Walsh to succeed. "The time is soon coming," Ding told his friend, "when a Chinese man will not be looked upon as an educated man unless he knows English."

And so it began: St. Mark's Anglo-Chinese School.

ANALECTS AND ENGLISH

Throughout China, a rush was on to build schools. The catalyst was an edict from the empress dowager on September 2, 1905, ending more than one thousand years of the imperial examination system. It was an act of apparent enlightenment spurred by fear: the Qing Empire was lagging behind other nations economically and militarily. Even the small island kingdom of Japan was modernizing and adopting Western science and technology. If China was going to catch up, some in the imperial court argued, it needed to change, starting with its educational system.

In Chinese society, there was no greater rank than scholar. It opened doors to official jobs, status, and respect. The road to scholarship for a young man began—and just as often ended—at a literary examination hall. Only elite cities had halls, where would-be scholars endured grueling tests. The one in Fuzhou sprawled over more than fifty acres just outside the North Gate. There, candidates for imperial degrees passed under a gateway with characters that read: *For the empire, pray for good men.*

Teenagers sitting for the first time and old men trying again and again took the examination and subjected themselves to nothing less than a kind of voluntary incarceration. Each candidate brought bedding, food, a pitcher of water, and a chamber pot to his "cell," a tiny chamber only three feet deep, four feet wide, and eight feet high, roofed but open at the front. Rows and rows of cells—enough to accommodate twelve thousand scholars—were lined one next to another. If typhoon winds brought downpours, or if the sun beat down, it didn't matter. The scholars had to write on. It wasn't unusual for candidates to die from exposure—or stress.

Rigid though it was, the examination system allowed anyone to advance in society based on intellect alone. Even a farmer's son, tutored in the books of Confucius, could sit for the imperial exam, and if he passed, possibly rule a city. But the exams were narrowly focused on knowledge of the nine books of Confucianism, called the Four Books and Five Classics. There was no testing on science or mathematics. Instead, candidates were given many questions and had three days to write a total of three eight-part essays and one poem. They also had to provide recommendations on an actual issue, addressing the eternal question, *What would Confucius do?* When the empress issued her edict in 1905, scholars at some examination centers were in the midst of their tests. They had to put down their pens and go home.

For Lin Pu-chi, his first taste of modern learning was reciting English words in a ramshackle house by the edge of a rice paddy. The makeshift school was the best Pakenham–Walsh could do on such short notice. The boys met for class on the first floor and slept on the second. When floods came, putting the classroom under a foot of water, everyone headed upstairs to the dormitory for lessons.

The first class of ten was a comical hodgepodge of ability and ages. Several students were little boys who hadn't stopped growing; the oldest student had whiskers, a wife, and a baby but desperately wanted to learn English and convinced Pakenham–Walsh to give him a spot. The "faculty" consisted of a Chinese assistant, Pakenham–Walsh, and his wife, Gertrude, who had sailed to China a year before her future husband. She and her sister, a physician, were part of a wave of adventuresome single women who traveled to China for the challenge and intrigue of missionary work. At St. Mark's, Gertrude treated all the boys with the gentleness, patience, and intuition of a mother. In Chinese schools, it was unusual for boys to even encounter women, let alone be taught by them. With no teachers to spare in the Anglican mission, her presence was a lesson in modernity for the students.

It was left to the minister's wife to introduce the students to English. Like toddlers, they started by learning their ABCs. With this new language, Lin Pu-chi had to wrap his tongue around different sounds. The soft "th" of a simple word like "the" was not familiar to him. And what was the meaning of "the" anyway? An *article* of speech? Useless, he privately groused. Lin Pu-chi kept putting tones where there were none. A word in the Fuzhou dialect had a different meaning, depending on which of eight tones were applied. Rising? Falling? Low? High? Quick? Long? Heavy? Light? Different tone, different word entirely. Pronouns, meanwhile, confounded Lin Pu-chi. Chinese had no gender-specific words. He kept using "she" for the reverend and "he" for his wife. But Lin Pu-chi delighted in hearing English words pronounced with proper form and inflection. He realized he liked the sound of his English voice.

Word of the school spread. More boys began showing up, and Pastor Ding got his young son back. Some of the new students traveled great distances from villages to attend the school. It pained Pakenham–Walsh to have to turn anyone away, but space was tight.

At the end of the first term, Pakenham–Walsh attended a tennis party at a foreigner's home. At courtside, Archdeacon Wolfe took a seat next to him. The elder Irishman, with his long white beard and brusque manner, knew he intimidated everyone around him. But Pakenham-Walsh had been secretly hoping for this moment.

"Walsh, how many boys have you got?" Wolfe gruffly asked.

"Thirty," the schoolmaster succinctly replied with obvious pride.

Standing to get up, the older man put his hand on his shoulder. "Walsh," he said, "you'll get hundreds."

Thirty soon became seventy. Pakenham-Walsh found a bigger building to rent only a hundred yards from the existing CMS high school, which taught boys in Chinese. Those students were being trained for meager-paying jobs as village teachers or religious assistants. For them, a command of scripture was more important than fluency in English. But the St. Mark's students were subtly taught from the start that they were special, even a cut above. Pakenham-Walsh encouraged them to think about advancing to one of the many universities in China started by American missionaries. Their prospects were brighter. British managers at the postal service and customs office needed English-speaking clerks, who could earn two hundred dollars a month, compared to the sixteen-dollars-a-month salary of a village teacher. The boys at the CMS high school knew that this pay discrepancy put them at the lower end of a caste system. It rankled them. But at least in sports, they had a level playing field. Team athletics were not part of the Chinese experience. It would be inconceivable for a traditional Chinese tutor, drilling his charges in the ideas and sayings from the *Analects* of Confucius, to worry about whether they did their morning calisthenics. But the two CMS boys' schools lived by the British credo of "strong body, strong mind" and could play out their rivalry in matches of soccer or basketball, even field hockey. Far from the nearest sports equipment vendor, a Chinese carpenter fashioned hockey sticks for the boys by bending the soft roots of bamboo trees.

Lin Pu-chi, who was somewhat on the frail side, was no one's first choice when picking teams. Although hopelessly nearsighted, he liked to play billiards and had a modicum of success with tennis. But this didn't mean he wasn't competitive; his drive to win played out in the classroom. Words became his sport. For training, he read the *Encyclopaedia Britannica* and memorized pages of the *Oxford English Dictionary*.

When Pakenham-Walsh suggested a debate contest, Lin Pu-chi prepared with intensity. The topic: Would railways benefit China? This was an issue preoccupying the entire country. In the early twentieth century, China was woefully behind other nations in developing a national rail system; Fujian Province did not have one mile of railroad. The conservative Qing rulers placed no value in railways and did not recognize how a modern transportation system could help the kingdom. Instead, the court fretted that trains could make the interior vulnerable to attacks, or worse: the thundering locomotives could disrupt the delicate feng shui of the countryside. In 1888, a reformer in the Qing court presented the empress dowager with a gift of a miniature train from Germany for her to ride in her garden. Instead of a steam engine, eunuchs pulled the six cars over tracks in the Forbidden City. It worked. She came around.

At the century's turn, foreign companies were eager to use their capital to develop railways in China. In time, British, German, French, American, Russian, and Japanese enterprises extracted from the Qing government the right to build, operate, and control railways. For the most part, Chinese people supported railway construction. Indeed, in November 1907, thousands jammed into a meeting hall in Fuzhou to support connecting Fujian Province to a rail line. The Chinese in attendance pledged to back the project by buying eighteen thousand shares in the venture.

"China must have railways," Lin Pu-chi told an audience of students and teachers in the inaugural competition of St. Mark's debate society.

"But," he blurted with emphasis, "we must build it ourselves."

Heads nodded. "China is not strong," he continued. "China should make a Chinese railroad for Chinese people."

Students applauded at the conclusion of the debate. Pakenham-Walsh walked to the front of the room and announced in Chinese, "First prize in our first debate goes to . . ."

But everyone already knew it would be Lin Pu-chi.

ANOTHER SUNNY SUNDAY

Autumn winds brought rumors sweeping into Fujian Province in 1911. In markets and teahouses, from farmer to peddler to merchant, whispers of revolution rustled among the people.

On October 10, 1911, the accidental explosion of a bomb being made by underground rebels in the Yangtze River town of Wuchang triggered a national uprising against inept Qing rulers. Fighting spread into full-fledged revolt. After rebel forces took Wuchang, they took the revolution to other cities, defeating imperial troops in Hankou, Changsha, Jiujiang, and Shanghai. The foundation of the Qing dynasty, started by Manchu invaders from the north more than 250 years earlier, was collapsing. Clearly, Fuzhou would be next to fall.

In the walled city, Manchu leaders fortified their compounds. The officer in charge, known as the Tartar general, threatened loudly and repeatedly that he would detonate the city's entire stockpile of weapons and gunpowder if revolutionaries made one move on his garrison.

"We will all die," he promised.

Residents panicked. They threw possessions, food, babies, and grannies with bound feet into carts and wheelbarrows, jamming all roads out of the city. Every sedan chair and boat was put into service. In days, half the population fled, many going to the Nantai neighborhood that was thought to be safer. Streets in the walled city fell silent.

On November 6, a gloriously sunny Monday, the boys at St. Mark's did not flee; they went about their classes but could not stop talking about the impending showdown. They handicapped the fighting. If Beijing or Tianjin fell, they reasoned, there was no way the Tartar general in Fuzhou could resist. By that afternoon, a clerk at the Eastern Telegraph office in Nantai raced to the British consulate with a telegram: Qing troops had been defeated in Hangzhou and Suzhou.

A delegation of reform-minded Fuzhou citizens appealed to the imperial viceroy to resign and hand over the city without bloodshed. The viceroy was willing, but the Tartar general held on to his scorched-earth strategy.

Peddlers and beggars who used to stake out every inch of the long bridge over the Min River cleared out. Men hurriedly erected wooden barricades across the span. Gunboats from Britain, the United States, Germany, and Japan dropped anchor near Fuzhou to protect their citizens if the fighting endangered them or their property. English sailors took positions guarding British buildings in Nantai, setting up tents on flat rooftops.

In the walled old city, news of the impending danger arrived in the form of messages wrapped about copper coins and thrown into shops and homes by phantom rebels. They warned: *Run! The viceroy and general will lose their heads. Blood will flow. Chinese will rule under a flag of righteousness.*

On Wednesday night—November 8—a full harvest moon illuminated the sky. Along the main roads leading to the city, Manchu troops doused bales of cotton with kerosene and set them ablaze to cut off access. But revolutionaries in white armbands stealthily infiltrated the city. Part of the city's ancient wall had crumbled after a typhoon a month earlier, allowing the rebels to creep into position.

After midnight, shooting erupted. The whiz and ping of metal on stone echoed through narrow corridors. Revolutionaries, staked out on a hill, lobbed three-pound shells that rattled the ground.

In Nantai, Pakenham-Walsh sat bolt upright in bed. He reached for his pocket watch and made a mental note: the revolt began at 1:30 a.m. From the street below, he heard the crash of gongs and blare of horns. Citizen brigades patrolled the streets to scare off river pirates who might be tempted to take advantage of the outbreak of fighting in the old city to loot stores in the foreign enclave.

All eyes in Nantai were riveted on the action across the river. Residents emerged from their homes to watch the fighting as if they were finding seats for a soccer match. At daybreak, Pakenham-Walsh and some of his students climbed a hill near school for a better look. A few boys armed themselves with the best weapons they could find: hockey sticks. Fires raged from the area where the viceroy and general had their quarters. In just a half hour, four blazes swelled into a curtain of flames.

As plumes of smoke blackened the sky, soldiers didn't notice that the Manchu viceroy had slipped out of his compound, using his hands to feel his way in the darkness along the city wall. At the West Gate, he saw an empty paper shop and slipped inside. He removed a coil of rope from under his long tunic. He climbed atop a stool, swung the rope over a beam, and placed a knotted loop around his neck. He stepped off. His legs flailed in the air and then stopped.

The Tartar general fought into the next day. He played possum with his adversaries. Twice, he commanded his troops to wave a flag of surrender—and then twice ordered them to resume the charge on rebels. The third time, his soldiers no longer followed his bluff. Five hundred Manchu troops put down their rifles and bayonets. Their general had been wounded and tried to escape but was easily captured before nightfall.

The next day, he was executed.

"Another sunny Sunday," Pakenham-Walsh wrote in his diary on November 12, "but what a lot has happened within one week."

St. Mark's reopened the next morning. But many of the students were late getting to class. School would have to wait. Pakenham-Walsh understood why. The boys were anxious to get rid of their braided ponytails. From the dawn of the Qing dynasty, the queue had been a symbol of submission for the majority Han people of China. Manchu victors from the north wore queues, and so must they.

But in the aftermath of the battle, men and boys all over Fuzhou stood in line at sidewalk barbers, patiently waiting for them to lop off the braids with shears. Others asked rebel soldiers to do the honors with their swords. Lin Pu-chi and the older students viewed the queue as if it were the bit of a horse, forced on them as a symbol of subjugation. But even with the exuberance of the regime change, some men hedged their bets. To be on the safe side, they retrieved their queues and brought them home. If the Manchu people returned to power, they could revert to long braids in a hurry by stitching their queues into seams of hats.

This portrait of the Lin family was taken in 1913. Note the lack of queues on the males, a sign that this was taken after the end of the Qing dynasty. Courtesy of Lin Family Collection.

TRINITY COLLEGE

The collapse of the tea trade in Fujian presented an unexpected opportunity for Pakenham-Walsh and his school. The Irishman had been searching Nantai for land on which to expand St. Mark's, but the only space he could find was in the outlying hills, which were dotted with gravesites. That presented myriad problems. Landowners were loath to remove graves—the equivalent of evicting ancestral spirits—especially if it was to make room for foreigners. Luckily for Pakenham-Walsh, tea drinkers in Europe were proving to be fickle customers. Tastes shifted and they began preferring stronger tea from the highlands of India to varieties grown in South China. Business was so bad that three Russian trading firms pulled up stakes. And with no subjects to protect, Russian diplomats decided they would have to follow suit.

Before word got out, a British tea inspector who was a friend of Pakenham-Walsh tipped him off that Russian diplomats would want to sell their consulate before leaving town. The schoolmaster seized the moment. With the backing of the bishop in Fuzhou, he made an immediate offer to the Russian secretary. That very day, they sealed a deal, and Pakenham-Walsh signed a purchase agreement under the gaze of a full-length portrait of Czar Nicholas II.

Pakenham-Walsh went home and excitedly mapped out a layout for a new campus, using his children's blocks and books on the floor of his parlor. The Anglican mission had decided to group all of the boys' schools in Fuzhou under the direction of Irish clerics who were working in China as part of the Dublin University foreign mission. So that meant Pakenham-Walsh had to have a new school not only for St. Mark's but also for the other CMS high school and a middle school.

In the fall of 1912, four hundred students passed through the gates of the new Trinity College, named after the Dublin alma mater of Pakenham-Walsh and most of the faculty. With five acres of land, athletic fields, and a majestic banyan tree at the heart of the campus, Trinity College rivaled any school in Dublin or London.

Lin Pu-chi was seventeen when St. Mark's moved into a new, two-story building on the Trinity campus. With a full head of post-Qing hair tamed into a center part with gobs of pomade, he looked every bit the modern man. He and his classmates took to wearing Western hats. Felt fedoras, straw boaters, and rakish caps were all the rage in Fuzhou. His generation was caught up in the spirit of revolution and change, of possibility and invention. The five-striped flag of the new republic fluttered from government buildings. China had its first president, and everything Western—schools, railways, factories, telegraph wires, electricity, even fashion—was sought with urgency. Many students, including Lin Pu-chi, dreamed of studying abroad in England or the United States.

Compared to his peers, Lin Pu-chi left little room for frivolity. This made him seem, even to his teachers, intense and a bit high-strung. He delighted in spinning a new phrase, correcting someone's spelling, or lobbing a multisyllabic word as if he were playing a match point—habits that classmates found tiresome. He used a word like "verdure" in a sentence simply because he could, knowing that it would send any academic rival scurrying to the pages of his dictionary.

Clearly, he was a student with a plan, and it was this: he hoped to leave home after graduation and enroll in the American-run St. John's University in Shanghai, the best school in China for studying English. Lin Pu-chi ranked first in his class. By now, he spoke and wrote English flawlessly but still enjoyed studying the Chinese classics. In the dense text of philosophers such as Confucius and Mencius, Lin Pu-chi felt as if he were peering into the past life of the country, seeing all of the thought, sentiment, imagination, and will of the Chinese people.

Pakenham-Walsh encouraged this pursuit. He had Lin Pu-chi and other senior students read the *Analects* of Confucius next to an open Bible. They compared sayings of the great sage with passages from the New Testament, seeing how the message of one was flowing into the meaning of the other.

The thought of joining the ministry was something Lin Pu-chi carried all through his years at St. Mark's. It was something his father wanted for him, too. Dr. Lin and other lay leaders in the Anglican Church fretted about the future. If the mission could not recruit more local men and women to carry on their work, Christianity would wither like an alien weed with shallow roots.

One night during the first fall term at Trinity, Lin Pu-chi rapped on the door of Pakenham-Walsh's study. He told his mentor he had come to talk to him about an important decision.

On the third Sunday in February, just after Chinese New Year and the heralding in of the Year of the Cow in 1913, the Anglican community braved a downpour for the consecration of the chapel on the Trinity campus. Clerics from all over the province, Chinese as well as foreign, arrived by rickshaw and high-stepped through puddles and mud to make their way up a hill to the chapel. Their own doubting Thomas—Archdeacon Wolfe, who only five years earlier had predicted Pakenham-Walsh's failure—proudly joined the bishop to bless the building.

The chapel was the centerpiece of the college as well as the entire Anglican diocese in Fujian. A foreign architect in Shanghai designed the building, which was striking for its lack of any attempt to blend in with the surrounding Chinese architecture. Instead, it looked like the Episcopal chapel at the American-run St. John's University in Shanghai. With the new Trinity chapel, everything about it—the pointed steeple, ivy-covered brick walls, tall windows—exalted the Anglican roots of the missionary society.

Just as they would back home, missionaries donned their university robes for the consecration, which was religious pageantry of the highest order. Many wore blue hoods marking them as graduates of Trinity College in Dublin; others sported the white silk of Cambridge. And humbly dressed in their Sunday vestments were Chinese clerics, including Pastor Ding, father of the now legendary tenth student of St. Mark's who made the whole venture possible.

Senior students, including Lin Pu-chi, ushered guests to their seats while Pakenham-Walsh himself manned the organ and the choirmaster led boys in *Jesu, Joy of Man's Desiring*. As the procession began, heads craned over high oak pews. One missionary woman leaned over to whisper in the ear of another. "That's Dr. Lin's son," Eleanor Harrison remarked, nodding in the direction of Lin Pu-chi. "I understand he's decided to join the ministry."

"This means so much," she commented. "These days, a boy from a mission school can earn so much in official or commercial work. Everyone is glad about it."

II

PATRIOTS

· 4 ·

Light and Truth

Shanghai, 1913

$\mathcal{I}$nside Alumni Hall at St. John's University in Shanghai on a stage festooned with chrysanthemums and ferns, the father of modern China waited to speak.

Earlier in the day, he had watched four companies of cadets in navy blue jackets and caps march behind a fife and drum corps on the campus parade ground. Now indoors, he prepared to address the entire student body, ambitious young men from all over China drawn to the American university with the Confucian saying in characters on its crest: *Learning without thought is useless; thought without learning is dangerous.*

It was the last day of the winter term in 1913. With a fanfare of cornets and organ, the assembly stood to sing the school song in English.

> Sons of the Orient,
> Children of the morning,
> Seekers of Light,
> We come!

The university president introduced the speaker as a leader who had stirred the hearts of the Chinese people as no one before.

Dr. Sun Yat-sen strode to a podium flanked by two flags: the stars and stripes of the United States of America and the black, white, blue, yellow, and red bars of the new Republic of China.

The man who inspired a revolt against imperial rule congratulated students at St. John's for their good fortune at being at such an esteemed seat of learning. Two hundred hopefuls had applied that year for admission, but only fifty were selected.

Even though he was fluent in English, the language of the university, Sun Yat-sen chose to address the students in Chinese. He had a critical message for

53

them—their duty to the country. China needed educated leaders now more than ever, he told them. Only a year earlier, the last emperor, six-year-old Puyi, abdicated the throne, but his departure left a perilous void as China struggled to create a unified republican government. The current president, Yuan Shikai, was a military strongman from the north who plotted against rivals, including Sun Yat-sen and his allies, as he tried to consolidate power.

For centuries, China had depended on the teachings of Confucius for answers to its problems, Sun Yat-sen told the students. It was sufficient for young men to immerse themselves in the words of the great sage. But Confucius alone was not enough to pull China through its current problems. Foreigners brought new ideas, science, medicine, and technology. Chinese students needed practical and useful knowledge to complement what was lacking in their country's ancient civilization.

The Chinese people, he continued, had a respect for learning and willingness to follow educated leaders. This was their moment.

"As you learn from the Bible, when you have the light, show others the way," Sun Yat-sen stressed. "When you receive knowledge, teach it to others. The basis of a democratic country is education. With people who are always ready to learn, it is your duty to teach. Give unto others what you have received. Let your light shine."

This students rose to their feet with thunderous cheers and applause.

CITY ON THE SEA

In September 1915, two graduates from Trinity College sailed north to Shanghai to enroll at St. John's University. They were the first students from the school to matriculate at the famous university. One was the son of a clerk for the British post office in Fuzhou and an accomplished athlete. He was captain of the soccer team but never could claim the top spot in academics. That honor went every year to his traveling companion, Lin Pu-chi.

The ideals of St. John's appealed to Lin Pu-chi. It was the notion of new learning for a new country, and no other college in China did it better than St. John's. It was the perfect place for a twenty-year-old with the intellect, drive, and confidence to think he was destined for much more from life. The two Trinity graduates skipped two grades and entered as juniors, a nod to the quality of their education. Both had full scholarships for the annual tuition of $120, plus $100 for room and board—sums paid in silver coins minted in Mexico, the preferred currency in the foreign enclaves in China.

When the pair stepped off a coastal steamer from the south, they entered the disorienting, grasping, gritty maw of Shanghai. Their hometown of Fuzhou was a treaty port like Shanghai, but there the similarity ended. Nearly half of all the trade in China passed through Shanghai, the capital not only for manufacturing but also for finance and shipping.

Long before the arrival of foreigners, Shanghai was a trading hub on the banks of the Huangpu River near where the Yangtze River enters the East China Sea. Junks carrying tea, silk, and cotton docked at the old city, fortified behind a wall to keep out Japanese pirates. In 1844, after the ratification of the Treaty of Nanjing, a mere fifty foreigners lived in Shanghai. But the race was on to carve up the area. The British were first, staking out a sparsely populated stretch of the Huangpu for a settlement that would be independent of Chinese law. Next came the French, who created a separate concession, as well as Americans, who later combined their holdings with the British to form an "International Settlement." By 1915, the foreign population included people from more than thirty nations, with Japanese residents representing the largest group (7,397), followed by British (5,521), Portuguese (1,352), American (1,448), German (1,425), and French (608) nationals. But for all its Western veneer, manners, and architecture, Shanghai remained a Chinese city: it had a foreign population in 1915 of close to twenty-one thousand people and about a million and a half Chinese residents, some of whom lived in foreign concessions.

The Bund, just a footpath by the river's edge a century earlier, now stood like a crowded trophy case, with each European-style building representing profits from global trade. All that China craved, as well as all that it offered, passed through the hands of Shanghai traders: silk and cotton, tobacco, chemicals, oil, coal, and, always, opium. Number 27 on the Bund was the Ewo Building, home to the foreign *taipans* of Jardine, Matheson & Co., Ltd., the trading house from the British colony of Hong Kong that reaped its fortune packing the pipes of addicts with "foreign mud." It stored chests of opium grown and processed in India in floating wharves moored on the Huangpu.

Along the Bund were hotels with rooftop terraces for tea and social clubs such as the Shanghai Club, with its legendary 111-foot Long Bar. At the north end, on the other side of Suzhou Creek, the Astor House Hotel reigned as a hub of expatriate social life, with a banquet hall for five hundred and hot water in every room. Trumpeted as the best hotel in Asia, it welcomed dignitaries and celebrities the likes of former Olympian Jim Thorpe, who, as an outfielder for the New York Giants, came to town in 1913 for exhibition games against the Chicago White Stockings.

St. John's University was in the Huxi neighborhood, located west of the International Settlement about five miles from the Bund. Wealth and poverty lived cheek by jowl in the area, with the villas of tycoons on some blocks and shantytown hovels for mill workers on others. One of the mansions belonged to a British property developer, who decided to give his fifty-acre garden to the Shanghai Municipal Council, the settlement's governing body of British and American men. The council created an urban oasis with expansive beds of roses and peonies, hothouses, undulating paths, stately trees, manicured lawns, and a bandshell. Jessfield Park opened to the public in 1914—but only the public that was not Chinese. A sign with nine rules, posted at each entrance, gave notice that Jessfield Park was "reserved exclusively for the foreign community." Also barred were horses, dogs, and vehicles of any kind, including bicycles. Another "foreigners only" park on the Bund had a tenth rule: Chinese nannies watching foreign children were not permitted to occupy chairs during band performances. They had to stand.

The entrance to St. John's was just across the street from the northern entrance to Jessfield Park. To get to the university from the waterfront, travelers like Lin Pu-chi would have ventured by electric tram along Nanjing Road, the city's busiest shopping corridor jammed with rickshaws, bicycles, horse-drawn carriages, and motorcars. Signs in windows urged shoppers to buy "patriotic" consumer goods—locally made clothing to replace hard-to-find imports. With the European continent embroiled in the First World War, shipments to Shanghai had dropped off sharply, leaving local mills and factories to fill the vacuum.

On the eve of classes at St. John's starting in September 1915, hundreds of young men passed through the wrought-iron gates of the forty-five-acre campus, which jutted like a bent elbow into Suzhou Creek. Students arriving by rickshaw alighted on Jessfield Road in a neighborhood with a candy store, pawnshop, and cluster of tenements that housed laborers who worked in mills making silk, cotton, flour, and oil. Those from nearby farm villages pushed their belongings in wheelbarrows, while more cosmopolitan classmates pedaled onto campus, flaunting their wealth and privilege from the seats of expensive bicycles.

Only eight years earlier, Lin Pu-chi was attending a one-room school run by an Irishman and his wife in a wooden house on the edge of a Fuzhou rice paddy. Now he was matriculating in a university with two hundred students and forty professors with doctorates from Harvard, Cornell, Yale, Princeton, Penn, and Columbia. St. John's was started by missionaries with the Episcopal Church in the United States. An architect from Newark, New Jersey, designed the quadrangle of buildings, brick structures that blended Western design with Chinese flourishes such as tile roofs with swooping eaves. One of the newest additions was the $22,000 Anniversary Hall with the Low Library and its collection of 8,600 English and 5,000 Chinese books.

St. John's was not simply run like an American university; it *was* an American university. In 1905, the American Episcopal Church registered the school in the District of Columbia, allowing graduates to easily pursue advanced degrees in the United States. Students celebrated Thanksgiving Day as well as the birthday of Confucius. They studied constitutional law, American history—from the American Revolution through the Civil War—and the industrial and political rise of the United States as a world power. China's history, too, was examined through a Western lens, with a class on foreign relations focusing on the years from 1834 to 1860—the beginning and end of the Opium Wars.

The history of St. John's dated back to 1879, when a missionary sent by the Episcopal Church in America started a school for boys that later would expand into the university. The founder was a linguistic genius with the Old Testament name of Samuel Isaac Joseph Schereschewsky, a Lithuanian Jew who studied to be a rabbi before immigrating to the United States, converting to Christianity, and entering a seminary in New York. A polyglot fluent in Yiddish, Polish, Russian, and German, the Reverend Schereschewsky singlehandedly translated the Bible into Chinese. At the urging of Western merchants in China, St. John's added English to its curriculum and, in 1905, switched to teaching all classes in the language of commerce. Most students were scions from China's burgeoning merchant class, coming from families as far away as Hong Kong and even the US territory of Hawaii. Their parents expected them to build business careers or, short of that, run the government.

The bar for admission was set high. Students had to pass an English grammar test as well as demonstrate their understanding of English literature. They were expected to be able to analyze great works such as *Silas Marner* by George Eliot or *Pilgrim's Progress* by John Bunyan. Proficiency in Chinese language and literature was also required, but the study of the Confucian classics was not why someone enrolled at St. John's. A student could flunk Chinese year after year and still graduate with a St. John's diploma. Eventually, it became so difficult to attract students to study classical Chinese literature and philosophy that the courses became optional. Undergraduates still had to spend two hours a week practicing translation of Chinese to English and vice versa. But the required six hours of Chinese studies could be substituted with only three hours of French or German.

In 1915, Lin Pu-chi plunged into his course work, studying the poetry of Wordsworth, Pope, and Milton, and taking classes in German, political science, European history, metaphysics, and religious instruction. Outside the classroom, his peers tutored him in fashion and trends. Lin Pu-chi promptly added to his wardrobe a Western-cut suit, purchased from one of the tailors who catered to St. John's students, such as "Mr. Goodcut" on Burkill Road in the International Settlement. Lin Pu-chi started wearing leather shoes instead of black felt slippers and followed the seasonal rotation of hats, going with a gray felt fedora in cool months and a straw boater for warm weather.

A new acquaintance who lived in his dormitory was a young, single alumnus who taught sociology and was an assistant chaplain. The thirty-year-old Y. Y. Tsu had recently returned from graduate school in the United States. Lin Pu-chi and other students enjoyed hearing his tales of New York City—taking the Ninth Avenue Elevated Railway from the downtown Episcopal seminary to classes uptown at Columbia University; frequenting the ghetto known as "Chinatown"; combing bookstores and buying for a half dollar a rare Chinese-language copy of the New Testament dating back a half century. Y. Y. Tsu also told them about meeting the pastor of the First Chinese Presbyterian Church in midtown and his American wife of Dutch descent. Sun Yat-sen often stayed with the couple during his trips to New York. But of more interest to Y. Y. Tsu was their charming third daughter, Caroline, who would later become his bride.

In the culture-blending world of St. John's, the university president, the Reverend Dr. Francis Lister Hawks Pott, was the inverse of Y. Y. Tsu. Raised in Manhattan, Dr. Pott shocked the missionary community by flouting convention and marrying a Chinese woman, the daughter of the first Chinese priest ordained by the Episcopal mission. Dr. Pott, who became president in 1888, often could be seen strolling around campus in a floor-length Chinese gown instead of his clerical collar.

Pott, also a Columbia man, brought to St. John's the American tradition of sports to foster camaraderie and community in college. He was the antithesis of the aloof headmaster and treated his students as if he were a coach, ascribing as he did to the principle of a strong mind in a strong body. At 7:15 a.m. every morning, students had to do fifteen minutes of exercises with dumbbells, and on Mondays, Wednesdays, and Fridays, all but the seniors and juniors ran through a battery of military drills.

Students took a ferry dubbed "the Ark" to athletic fields on the other side of Suzhou Creek from the main campus. At their disposal were a soccer field, nine clay and grass tennis courts, and a quarter-mile cinder track. St. John's athletes taunted their crosstown rivals at Nanyang University by calling themselves "the Ever Victorious." Matches between the two schools drew thousands of spectators who waved school pennants and sang school fight songs. Male cheerleaders belted out a favorite chant:

> Bon chicka bon! Bon chicka bon!
> Bon, chicka-ricka-recka.
> Bon, bon, bon!
> Wa-hu-wa! Wa-hu-wa! St. John's, St. John's!
> Rah! Rah rah!

Pott also wanted St. John's students to embrace "America's pastime" and promoted baseball as a major sport, even displaying his own prowess on the

diamond by playing first base during the annual faculty-student game to celebrate the Chinese Mid-Autumn Festival. While baseball never matched soccer or tennis in popularity, the St. John's squad had standouts from Hawaii,
who grew up playing the game and gave the university an edge over the three
other American schools in Shanghai with teams.

The bookish Lin Pu-chi lacked prowess on the playing field. He enjoyed
tennis, but his game was unexceptional. Instead, he focused his competitive energy on the Literary and Debating Society. No one at his alma mater
back in Fuzhou could match his wits in oration. He brandished words like a
fencer's saber, a skill he displayed proudly when he arrived at St. John's. But
after the first few meetings of the debate club, Lin Pu-chi came to an unsettling realization.

For the first time, he was no longer the smartest one in the room.

THE TWO LINS

This other man could write.

He published long essays for the *St. John's Echo* newspaper, which he
edited, often with a barbed pen. In one piece, he took aim at classmates who
put on airs by sprinkling English words into their Chinese conversations just
because they could. "What other earthly reason, I ask, than the poor childish love for show can cause a student to put an 'although,' a 'so far,' and an
'all right' in the midst of a Shanghai talk with Shanghai friends?" He thought
they sounded as ridiculous as an Englishman attempting to pronounce with his
Oxbridge accent the name of China's president, Yuan Shikai.

This other man could talk.

He spoke clearly with graceful gestures, never stiffly. His arguments
flowed logically, escorting his audience to a conclusion that could only be accepted as the undeniable truth. Extemporaneously, he was even better, nimbly
moving among quick thoughts and finding the weak spot in his opponent's
position.

Most of all, this other man could think.

He was a senior theology student and won every award for writing and
debate that the university had to offer. Nonetheless, he was ridden with doubt
and later would describe St. John's as part of the "protective shell of Christianity," which, while educating him, was also cutting him off from Chinese
philosophy, folklore, and the stream of thought of his country. It embarrassed
him that his calligraphy was poor, the telltale mark of an uncultivated man. "I
had been cheated of my national heritage," he would later observe. "That was
what a good Puritan education could do to a Chinese boy."

This man also was named Lin. He also came from Fujian Province. The son of a Christian pastor, he also was considering joining the ministry.

Lin Pu-chi studied him for months. He deconstructed his essays in the *Echo*. He watched him debate. He analyzed his delivery.

He would finally get his chance to test his mettle and intellect against the "other Lin"—twenty-year-old Lin Yutang—during Christmas recess and the annual oration contest, a highlight of the university calendar.

At dusk on Christmas Eve, the campus twinkled with strings of electric lights and hundreds of colorful lanterns dangling from wires on either side of the long entrance driveway. Bursting firecrackers ushered in the night, which began with a ten-course feast for students in the dining halls.

Outside the gates of St. John's, it was an ordinary Friday night in the village of Caojiadu. Workers made their way home for bowls of rice after long days in the silk and cotton mills along Suzhou Creek. But inside Alumni Hall, more than six hundred people—university men, teens in the St. John's preparatory school, and guests—were transported to a holiday celebration like any found in America.

On one side of the stage stood a freshly cut pine tree with burning tapers and dangling glass ornaments. On the other were banks of flowers in yellow and red. Across the top of the black curtain were the words *A Merry Christmas* cut from white cotton cloth. No Christmas would be complete without an appearance of Santa Claus, and a student dressed with a white cotton beard and padded belly made his grand entry, pulling gifts out of his bag for young boys from the surrounding neighborhood.

The drama club staged two plays about love and marriage, followed by the glee club serenading students with carols and songs like "Hail! Smiling Morn." Between acts, musicians on harmonica and violin performed Christmas selections. No one seemed to mind that the program went on for more than three hours, concluding just before midnight.

Christmas Day broke warm and bright. After chapel service, Lin Pu-chi retreated to his room to polish his speech and wait four days until the oratorical competition.

At 8:00 p.m. on December 29, the seats in the Alumni Hall auditorium again filled with students. In the front row sat three judges, invited from outside the university community to ensure impartiality. A professor introduced them: Mahlon Fay Perkins, the young deputy US consul and a Harvard man; J. W. Crofoot, with the Seventh-Day Baptist Mission in nearby Wuxi; and S. K. Tsao, the first Chinese secretary of the local YMCA.

Only three students competed for the top honor, one from each class. All spoke in English on the theme of China's future. Four years after the downfall of the Qing dynasty, the entire country was on edge. Any hope of an independent, progressive China was dashed by the stunning power grab of President Yuan, who proposed creating a new constitutional monarchy. Ever the shrewd political manipulator, the military veteran offered himself up as the next emperor.

A sophomore spoke first on "Nation and Nobility." Next up was the junior class representative. Lin Pu-chi's topic was "The True Greatness of a Nation." In his wire-framed glasses and center-parted hair, he was the picture of the modern scholar. When he spoke, his sentences were complex and layered, requiring the concentration of his listeners. His voice was loud and strong, but his delivery somewhat stilted. He addressed the situation in Beijing. Compared to the violent revolutions in America and France, China had made a quick break from imperial rule. Now was the time, he said, to give the new government a chance to solidify before the country backpedaled into a monarchy.

"We are living in a century and in a civilization under which absolutism is no longer tolerable," Lin Pu-chi intoned. "Although the mass of the Chinese people cannot be entitled to the full rights of democracy, they have awakened to a consciousness that autocracy is a thing of the past."

His countrymen would not be led around like "the cattle and horses of an almighty monarch." The republican government must be given a chance. "It is childish to be too optimistic," he told the audience, "but it is impious to be pessimistic."

He took his seat. The last competitor, senior Lin Yutang, rose to speak on "China's Call for Men."

"Every day we hear our elders say to us, 'You are the hope of China.' And our foreign friends and the whole world say to us, 'You are the hope of China.'"

Don't be flattered, he told his classmates. That phrase was actually a plea for help—"a howl from the Valley of Death."

"Fellow young men, realize when you hear this line again that the situation is a dangerous situation, and the call a desperate call, and be serious about it."

China's biggest problem lies with its citizens, he asserted. "It matters not whether you have a monarchy or a republic in a country of robbers, assassins, selfish intriguers and political swindlers. Before the Revolution of 1911 people thought that a republic would save China, and now that a Republic has been established and set on running, they say that a monarchy would better serve her. Well, will a monarchy then save China? The fact is, republic or monarchy, both have more or less failed and both must fail, when the officials are corrupt and debased. It is all a question of men. Men, men, able men, strong men, honest men, are alone China's hope."

His words made the audience squirm.

"Examine yourselves and find there the answer to the question. For as I said before, you are the last hope of China, you, and you alone, hold the fate of China in your hands, and it is all up to you to save and uplift China, or to send her along her line of destruction."

The judges huddled and conferred in whispers. But the decision was obvious.

Perkins from the US consulate rose to announce the winner. He said the speeches were free from the common fault of Chinese speakers of misusing difficult words of the English vocabulary. "The winning speech," the diplomat said, "excelled in all around character, having the best combination of material, an exquisite choice of words and phrases and the best way of presentation."

"And the winner is Lin . . ." Perkins announced, pausing a few seconds for extra suspense.

"Yutang!"

The audience cheered as the victor stood to shake the hands of judges and accept the oratory medal for the second time in his university career. With a pinched smile, Lin Pu-chi offered congratulations.

DOUBLE TEN

The wheel of China's leadership turned again by the time Lin Pu-chi entered his senior year in September 1916. Yuan Shikai, who had crowned himself the Hongxian Emperor, had died from kidney failure the previous June and was replaced by his vice president, another military man, named Li Yuanhong. Expectations were low for this political survivor who had been marginalized and isolated by President Yuan, but he was the best alternative at the moment. Away from Beijing, provincial governors filled the power void at the center by exerting their own authority politically and militarily. Some warlords declared their outright independence.

The precarious Republic of China marked the fifth anniversary of the Wuchang Uprising on October 10, 1916. On "Double Ten Day," the entire student body of St. John's gathered at dusk in front of Moore Memorial Church in the heart of the city to join a procession of students from all over Shanghai. In a nod to their status in the city's social order, the senior men of St. John's stood at the front, leading a parade of 2,500 young men and women behind two brass bands. Lin Pu-chi and his classmates held paper lanterns as they proudly passed local and foreign onlookers cheering them from sidewalks.

Everywhere people looked, they saw the five-color republican flag— hanging from lampposts, decorating shop windows, draping trams, even covering the hoods of motorcars. All the ships in the Huangpu, including US Navy vessels, fluttered with banners from bow to stern in honor of the day.

Students marched south on Honan Road under a canopy of giant flags. Behind them in a second procession were one thousand workers from the largest printing house in Asia, the Commercial Press, who trailed a brass band and fife and drum corps playing the Scottish classic "Auld Lang Syne."

Lin Pu-chi honored President Li with a National Day editorial in the *Echo*, penned as a plaintive poem:

> Since that momentous day five years have passed,
> Again the nation's eyes are turned to thee,
> The state to reconstruct, the plan to cast
> For true reforms; this now we yearn to see.

With the start of a new academic year, Lin Pu-chi stepped out of the shadow of Lin Yutang and into many of his predecessor's campus roles. He became president of the campus debate society and was voted by his classmates onto the staff of the *Echo*. The other editors elected him as their chief. Lin Pu-chi freely experimented with his English writing. He covered news, dabbled in

The Board of Editors and Business Managers of St. John's Echo for 1916-1917.

At St. John's University, Lin Pu-chi was elected editor in chief of the St. John's *Echo* for the 1916–1917 academic year. This staff photograph appeared in the student publication. Lin Pu-chi sits in front, arms crossed, second from the right. Courtesy of St. John's *Echo*, Yale Divinity School Library.

satire, editorialized about politics, tried literary criticism, and explained folk-tales. The results were varied but the effort constant.

His first news story took him to the jetty in front of the Maritime Custom House on the Bund. On the second Saturday in September, he watched as almost a hundred of China's best and brightest, including fifteen women, climbed the gangplank of the SS *China*. Graduates of colleges across China, they were all bound for San Francisco by way of Yokohama and Honolulu and heading to elite US universities on government scholarships, a legacy of the Boxer Uprising. The United States, instead of taking taels of silver from the defeated Qing Empire after the conflict in 1900, agreed to have the Chinese government cover its indemnity by underwriting the cost of sending students to the United States for graduate study. Chinese students competed for scholarships covered by the indemnity fund.

Watching the students waving from the deck, Lin Pu-chi imagined being in their place. In his article, he asked his readers to imagine what it would be like to leave your homeland for five years or more. What emotion, what reflection would be going through your mind? There was no doubt that in the United States they could get a broader liberal education, better than anything available in China. But he compared China to a parent who bids farewell to a child with a blessing yet expects loyalty and faithful service in return.

He wished that on foreign shores "their memory and fealty for their beloved Republic might still remain with ever-accumulating intensity. The nation cherishes no small hope in this group of young men and women."

COMMENCEMENT

With thirty-six graduates, the class of 1917 was the largest in the history of St. John's. They joined an elite fraternity. Alumni were serving as ambassadors to Germany, the United States, and England. They managed steel mills and railways. They were university presidents and college deans; judges and surgeons; church rectors and directors of the YMCA in China.

Class Day exercises on the eve of graduation showcased the melting pot that was St. John's. Students performed scenes from *A Midsummer Night's Dream*, sketches adapted from *Les Miserables*, and an original play in Chinese. A Hawaiian student sang a Polynesian tune while playing the ukelele. Others followed with a selection of songs on Chinese instruments and a banjo number.

Delivering the day's keynote address was a senior known as the class's own Cicero, the great Roman orator. For the last time in his college career, Lin Pu-chi held the attention of his peers who were about to go forth with a Western education that would open doors all over the country. With everyone's focus on the future, Lin Pu-chi used the occasion to look into the past, deep into the past, and made a plea for a renaissance in the study of classical Chinese literature. Among the Shanghai literati in 1917, it was more fashionable to quote the women talking of Michelangelo in T. S. Eliot's "The Love Song of J. Alfred Prufrock" than the quiet night imagery of the great Tang dynasty poet Li Po.

That was the problem with progress, Lin Pu-chi said; it made people forget what came before, making them lose touch with their culture and traditions. "Literature reveals the thought, sentiment, imagination, and will of the people from whom it springs," he said. "It is the outcome of the entire past life of a nation and it molds the thoughts of succeeding generations." When the old system of learning in China was replaced, interest in the classics waned as a fascination with all things Western gained. "It is impossible to push back these influences as it is to stop the stars in their courses," he told his peers. But "we owe it to posterity to preserve our literature. . . . It is part of our patriotism, a part of our spirit of nationality. We should guard against the scientific current . . . being strong enough to sweep away the zest for literature and homage paid to it."

The rain held back on the Saturday of commencement, but the heat of the June afternoon hung heavy as guests assembled in seats on the south lawn. Men donned straw hats, while women opened black umbrellas for shade.

At 5:00 p.m., the ceremony began with a procession of the student body, the graduating class, alumni, faculty, and the guests of honor: the American consul-general and Shanghai's Chinese commissioner of foreign affairs. Professors sat on a platform against a backdrop of giant replicas of the US and Chinese flags, plus the university crest and the numbers "1917" made out of flowers.

After an opening prayer, Pott handed out academic and athletic prizes. Twice, Lin Pu-chi climbed the red-carpeted steps to receive individual awards—the gold medal for fiction for his short story "The Tragedy of the Jade Ring," and the gold medal for best English essay for "An Estimate of Yuan Shikai." A third time, he joined two other seniors in accepting a sterling silver cup, engraved with their names, for winning the interclass English debate.

The sky was beginning to darken by the time Dr. Pott got to the presentation of diplomas. "A degree of the bachelor of arts is awarded to the following," the headmaster read. "Lin Pu-chi, with honors."

In his black robe and mortarboard, the twenty-two-year-old shook the president's hand and returned to his seat to watch the others. Two classmates were going to work for the Episcopal mission in other cities. Three had jobs with businesses, including Nanyang Iron Works, while another found employment with a hospital. His classmate from Fuzhou who started with him had accepted a faculty post teaching English at their alma mater, Trinity College.

But Lin Pu-chi was not returning to Fuzhou. He had plans that would take him far from China. He was anxious to take the next step and to act on the ideals of national service and duty that he had written about so frequently during his years at St. John's.

It was his moment, his time, and if everything went as he imagined, he would not see his family for many years to come.

· 5 ·

A Modern Man

Aboard the SS *Nanking*, 1918

*H*eavy smoke poured from the twin stacks of SS *Nanking*, leaving smudges in a cloudless Pacific sky. From the rear deck, passengers watched porpoises leaping in and out of the ship's wake, a welcome diversion from the tedium of onboard life. Even more entertaining for the bored and weary were the schools of flying fish skimming over the water, wings outspread, tails wriggling in a frantic escape from underwater danger.

The *Nanking* left Shanghai on August 14, 1918, headed east to Yokohama, Japan, and now was steaming toward Honolulu, the halfway point of a three-week voyage.

Lin Pu-chi had never been out of China or on a ship this grand. Foreigners were nothing new to him. He came from Shanghai, after all, and knew their customs and manners. But this was the first time he was in such close quarters with so many Americans. They were merchants and missionaries, diplomats and teachers, all returning home after adventures in the Far East.

The owners of the *Nanking*—Chinese entrepreneurs from San Francisco—promised "Passenger Service of Unusual Excellence." Days passed slowly after morning calisthenics taught by some of the "Y" men onboard—athletic missionaries with the YMCA. Travelers played shuffleboard or practiced putting on an artificial golf green. For fun, mothers and children competed in tug-of-war matches or wheelbarrow races.

After dinner, waiters pushed back the tables to make room for the ship's band. Ladies dragged their husbands to the dance floor for a fox-trot or waltz. On other evenings, Chinese acrobats entertained guests with contortions and stunts, or a magician dazzled them with sleight-of-hand tricks.

The *Nanking* was a veritable ship of scholars. The manifest listed 594 passengers, of whom 149 were Chinese men and women, most in their twenties, heading to graduate schools in the United States for the fall semester. They were China's best and brightest, graduates of top colleges, bound for elite universities in the United States to study engineering, finance, medicine, law, political science, mining, agriculture, sociology, philosophy, and literature. A majority had scholarships from the Chinese government's indemnity fund, which underwrote graduate study in the United States as part of a financial deal to cover US losses after the Boxer Uprising in 1900.

When the ship pulled into Honolulu Harbor, passengers had less than a day to explore. For the Americans, surfers riding waves on Waikiki Beach were a source of fascination. But for the students, the city was hallowed ground: this was where the heroic revolutionary Sun Yat-sen was educated as a teenager. The missionary-run Iolani School, his alma mater, held more interest to them.

The final destination of twenty-three-year-old Lin Pu-chi would be Philadelphia. After graduating from St. John's in 1917, he had spent a year teaching English at the university's high school before leaving for the States with a full scholarship from the Episcopal Church to attend its seminary. If all went according to plan, he would spend six years, maybe more, studying abroad.

In their well-cut suits and straw boaters, the students from cosmopolitan centers like Shanghai or Tianjin carried themselves with confidence. But for many others, the voyage was their first awkward encounter with Western ways. Suppertime, in particular, was cause for anxiety. Some Chinese passengers had never eaten with a knife and fork. The taste of butter and milk was nauseating, steaks were too big and bloody, and cakes and pies were cloyingly sweet. And if the cutlery was confounding, the folded napkin on a dinner plate was an utter mystery. Where did it go? Placed over their forearms like the waiters serving them their meals? And why did foreigners insist on ruining tea? They added lemon to make it sour and then sugar to make it sweet.

The dinner conversation was more satisfying. Eager to flaunt their knowledge, students dissected the pitiful state of Chinese politics over plates of striped bass with lemon butter sauce. They deconstructed the fiction of Lu Xun or the journalism of Liang Qichao over slices of blackberry pie. Lu Xun taught this generation how to write in the everyday spoken language of people, while Liang Qichao showed them how newspapers and periodicals could spread political ideas and foster patriotism.

In the ship's dining room, Lin Pu-chi noticed a familiar face, the younger sister of his St. John's friend, Y. Y. Tsu. Her name was Tsu Lan-tsung, and she was heading to Ann Arbor to enroll at the University of Michigan. She had attended high school at St. Mary's Hall on the campus of St. John's. In snatches of conversation, Lin Pu-chi found out that she would be studying literature *and* medicine. He was interested in her—*such a voracious learner!*—but he held back. He bowed to propriety. It would not be correct to spend so much time in the private company of a pretty single woman. Social custom in China still left the matter of selecting partners to parents, and rumor had it that she was already spoken for.

The inevitability of arranged marriages weighed on the minds of many of the scholars on the *Nanking*. One of the students, Xu Zhimo, was twenty-one and already a father, married off by his parents at eighteen to a seventeen-year-old girl. Each of the students could recite the examples of filial piety that were the bedrock of Confucian thought. Social order dictated that children defer to the judgment of parents. Yet the graduates were leaving their homeland to travel to the other side of the world in the name of modernity. They wanted knowledge to make China stronger and to save the country from disintegrating. But as their minds changed and evolved through education, what would become of their hearts? Would they ever be free to decide for themselves whom they married?

The narrative of his life would not be for Lin Pu-chi alone to write. So he did what came naturally: he began to write a story that he could control. It would be a love story. It opened in the Jiangsu mansion of a scholar-official with a headstrong nineteen-year-old daughter, Ah-Tsu, who pined to study in the United States. Her parents had arranged her marriage to a student whom she had never met but who was already studying engineering at an American college. Her conservative father, Mr. Faung, objected to the idea of her studying abroad, but her mother pressed the matter for her.

As Lin Pu-chi wrote, using the precise English he had studied for years:

"I can't see any sense," said Mr. Faung in a peremptory tone of voice, "for a girl of nineteen to go to a foreign country. It's entirely a different country, her people, her manners and customs are all different from our own."

"Yes, it's all true," replied Mrs. Faung, "but you know Ah-Tsu is such a persistent girl. She won't give up an idea when she has determined to bring it to completion. Moreover, she goes for education."

"Education? You women can't fool me. I know what education is. The teachings of our saints are good enough for me, and for anybody. What do I care for a smattering of astronomy or geography or arithmetic? That's all for fashion."

"No, Mr. Faung, you are certainly biased here. Our saints certainly have very good teachings. But we live in the twentieth century, and in an age of science; modern education is of more material importance."

"What has that to do with girls?"

"Girls ought to be educated too; if for no one else, she ought to be educated for her husband and children. If you love your daughter, won't you care for her future happiness?"

The father relented. In his short story, Lin Pu-chi had Ah-Tsu sail to America on a steamer like the *Nanking* among men and women like the author and his shipmates.

BEAUTIFUL COUNTRY

From the deck of the *Nanking*, America seemed a vision, and here it was, coming into view. Burnt yellow hills flanked the gateway to San Francisco Bay.

On September 4, 1918, Lin Pu-chi and the other sea-weary scholars stepped onto American soil. At the wharf in San Francisco, a band of Chinese students from the University of California in Berkeley greeted them with signs and Chinese flags. At the time, there were about 1,500 students from China studying in the United States, mostly at Ivy League institutions or midwestern universities such as Michigan but also at a smattering of private colleges such as Beloit in Wisconsin and Lehigh in Pennsylvania.

The students had no problem entering the country. They were spared the brutal interrogations that awaited Chinese passengers who intended to live in the United States. The Chinese Exclusion Act of 1882 had put tight controls on Chinese immigration and effectively legalized racial discrimination on the grounds that the influx of people from China was disruptive.

The Berkeley students ushered the newcomers across the bay to the train station in Oakland. Lin Pu-chi caught the Pacific Limited to Chicago that left every afternoon at 1:30 p.m. He marveled at the constantly changing landscape—the unbroken farmland in California; the mighty Wasatch Mountains near Ogden, Utah; the heaving cattle stockyards of Omaha, Nebraska; the manmade peaks of the Chicago skyline.

Railroads had fascinated Lin Pu-chi from the time he was a schoolboy in Fuzhou. The strength of nations was undergirded by rails of steel, which was precisely China's problem. It lacked a cohesive national rail network. Too many of its railways were controlled by foreign investors, reducing China to the status of an economic protectorate. Lin Pu-chi could not imagine traveling by train from one end of China to the other. But in the United States, he had done just that in a mere five days, changing trains once in Chicago and again in Pittsburgh.

Less than a month after leaving Shanghai, Lin Pu-chi arrived at the Broad Street Station across the street from Philadelphia's elegant city hall tower, the tallest building in the country at 548 feet, topped with a bronze statue of city founder William Penn.

He stepped off the Pennsylvania Railroad car and into the night, just as an invisible assassin was infiltrating the city.

SPANISH LADY

Home for Lin Pu-chi in Philadelphia was a three-story brick townhouse in a genteel section of the old city. The Episcopal Church had rented the entire property at 901 Clinton Street as temporary quarters for seminarians. It had recently sold its seminary on the west side of the Schuylkill River and planned to build a new one. But construction was put on hold because of the lack of laborers due to the First World War.

The war effort consumed Philadelphia. Even before Congress voted to declare war against Germany on April 10, 1917, factories and shipyards in the city were supplying American allies with ammunition, helmets, locomotive engines, and trucks. The work in Philadelphia became a magnet for immigrants fleeing conflict in Europe and African Americans fleeing Jim Crow laws in the South. The Frankford Arsenal made one hundred thousand artillery shells a month; the Ford Motor Company's factory on North Broad Street pressed forty thousand steel helmets a day. Tens of thousands of men worked in the dozen shipyards along the Delaware River, building submarines, destroyers, cargo ships, and gunboats.

Buoyed by patriotic fervor, the city erected a twenty-nine-foot-tall plaster replica of the Statue of Liberty and placed it on a two-story wooden pedestal in front of city hall. At its unveiling in the spring of 1918, more than a thousand schoolgirls dressed as Lady Liberty paraded down Broad Street.

In the weeks before Lin Pu-chi arrived, hopes were rising that World War I would soon come to a victorious end as Allied troops began their final advance on German positions. A corps of female volunteers in the city had planned a colossal parade to drum up interest in a fourth round of war bond sales. John Philip Sousa and his band did their part by performing "Liberty Loan" concerts amid the roller coaster and carousel of Willow Grove Park. War, however, was not the only news making headlines. The Shubert family of Broadway fame opened a new theater on South Broad Street on August 26. The premiere show was the British hit musical *Chu Chin Chow*, featuring actor Tyrone Power Sr. as a Baghdad chieftain up to no good disguised—in yellowface—as a Chinese merchant.

In late August a deadly influenza virus, most likely originating in China, began to sicken people in Europe and Africa. No one paid much notice when a sailor who arrived at the Philadelphia Navy Yard after a stop in Boston showed signs of influenza. No one panicked on September 18, when eight hundred sailors fell ill the next day. Health officials in Philadelphia assured the public that the sickness was confined to military personnel.

On September 28, the Liberty Loan parade on Broad Street went off as planned. More than two hundred thousand people crammed both sides of

South Broad Street, cheering as thousands of marchers—many wearing gauze masks—passed them. Crowds watched soldiers with bayonet rifles and tanks pulling cannons, oblivious to any coughing and sneezing among onlookers.

A week after the parade, the city had 636 cases of Spanish influenza and 139 deaths. In four days, the death toll almost doubled. The city shut churches, schools, and theaters to prevent the spreading of germs in crowded spaces.

By the third week in October, the death toll in Philadelphia, a city of 1.7 million, hit 4,500. Hospitals and morgues could not keep pace. Bodies were piled on sidewalks. A streetcar factory shifted to assembling coffins. Police stations became makeshift emergency rooms. At a Catholic cemetery on the outskirts of Philadelphia, seminarians worked into the night digging mass graves. By November, the "Spanish Lady" had killed more than twelve thousand Philadelphians, the worst death toll in the country.

From his window on Clinton Street, Lin Pu-chi could see the sick waiting to enter Pennsylvania Hospital, which took up the entire block just on the other side of Ninth Street. Scientists at the hospital had taken cultures from sick sailors and determined that the virus was the same Spanish flu ravaging Europe and other American cities. Lin Pu-chi had to don an "influenza mask" from the Philadelphia Red Cross every time he ventured outside to explore his new neighborhood.

The great influx of workers to Philadelphia factories and shipyards left most sections of the city overcrowded and unsanitary. But tree-lined Clinton Street maintained an air of understated Quaker gentility. Even animals had it good. On the sidewalk at Ninth and Clinton Streets was a stone water trough for horses with the inscription, "A merciful man is merciful to his beast."

Lin Pu-chi could walk six blocks to the east and find himself at the front door of Independence Hall. If he traveled ten blocks to the west, he arrived at city hall. North on Ninth Street took him to the retail emporiums of Market Street, great palaces of spending named after merchant princes like John Wanamaker and his archrivals, the Strawbridge and Clothier families. Farther north at Race Street was the block-long Chinatown, home mostly to single men from Canton who worked in restaurants and spoke a different dialect, unintelligible to most of the Chinese students.

On November 1—All Saints' Day—Lin Pu-chi officially became a student of the Divinity School of the Protestant Episcopal Church in Philadelphia. The dean of the seminary, the Reverend George Bartlett, led an evening service in the living room of the Clinton Street residence for the matriculating students, all three of them. Enrollment was down sharply due to men shipping off to the western front of the war. In a leather registration book, Lin Pu-chi signed his name in English script and Chinese characters. His two classmates were a man from nearby Bethlehem, Pennsylvania, and a Japanese graduate of Waseda University in Tokyo.

Lin Pu-chi split his time between Clinton Street and the University of Pennsylvania in West Philadelphia. Penn automatically accepted divinity students into its graduate program, and Lin Pu-chi seized the opportunity to enroll.

At the seminary, which held classes in a parish house at nearby St. Andrew's Church, Lin Pu-chi took classes in canon law, Hebrew prophets, and the history of world religions. Miss Blaylock, the elocution instructor, taught him how to be more effective from the pulpit—how to modulate the tone of his voice, how to control his breathing, how to sound out English vowels and consonants. At Penn's ivy-covered College Hall, he delved into ethics, economic theory, and modern philosophers. His adviser was Dr. Edgar Arthur Singer Jr., who was trained as a civil engineer before becoming a philosopher with a special interest in the emerging field of psychology.

If his course load was heavy, Lin Pu-chi wanted it that way. Partly it was raw ambition. But partly it was from a sense of duty and guilt. Every Chinese child was brought up studying the *Analects* of Confucius and taught, "While your parents are alive, do not journey afar." Every minute that he violated that rule had to be a minute of purpose.

On November 8, Lin Pu-chi caught the number thirteen streetcar on Walnut Street, crossed the Schuylkill, and got off at Thirty-Ninth Street to walk two blocks south to the International Students' House.

The local branch of the Chinese Students' Alliance was holding its first meeting of the school year in a new clubhouse for foreign students, located in a former mansion on Spruce Street. One of the founders of the International House at Penn was the Reverend A. Waldo Stevenson, who came up with the idea for a center after a chance encounter with a group of Chinese students in 1908. Stevenson was dismayed to learn that he was the first American to befriend them. The minister and his wife began inviting foreign students into their home and eventually partnered with the university's Christian Association to buy the mansion and start the International House.

At the Friday night gathering, the influenza scourge was all that anyone could discuss. There were only thirty-two Chinese students studying at Philadelphia schools, and three of them—all Penn medical students—had been called into the trenches of the flu pandemic. Because of the war, more than a quarter of the city's physicians were serving in the military.

At the meeting, the students learned that one of the medical students, K. H. Li, a St. John's alumnus from Suzhou, had been dispatched to help at an emergency hospital. He contracted the virus and had to be hospitalized for three weeks. Another friend of many of the Chinese students, Dr. C. W. Low, was returning from the home of a stricken family when the ambulance transporting him crashed. He was thrown from the vehicle and suffered a deep cut on his face.

As one of the newest members of the club with the freshest news from home, Lin Pu-chi was invited to share his thoughts at the meeting. The others were particularly keen to hear his take on political developments back in China.

It was a precarious time, a transition period, he told the students, some of whom had not been home in many years. The world stood on the threshold of peace, but China remained divided by hostility between the warlord-backed government in the North and allies of Sun Yat-sen and the Kuomintang in the South. It was less a geographic divide than an ideological one, pitting a conservative wing of the government against a more progressive one, between old ideas and new ones. But the stakes were nothing less than China's ability to remain an independent nation. The most baneful policy of the country was conservatism, he believed. The so-called official party was miserably under the fetters of the past and failing to keep pace with the march of progress of the rest of the world.

Three days after the club's meeting—at the eleventh hour of the eleventh day of the eleventh month of 1918—the war ended with the signing of the armistice between the Allies and Germany in the northern French town of Compiegne. Newspaper headlines screamed *End of the War!* In Philadelphia, cheering throngs jammed the blocks around city hall and Independence Hall. Lin Pu-chi witnessed peace in the making. But like other Chinese students, his attention shifted to his homeland. China had entered the war hoping to regain concessions controlled by Germany in the province of Shandong. Would that finally happen?

THE SHANDONG QUESTION

The afternoon sun was just beginning to soften as the New York Central left Grand Central Terminal en route to Albany.

The train steamed north, and the Hudson River widened to more than a mile across at Tappan Zee—the Dutch word for "sea." The mighty Hudson, or the North River as locals called it, was an estuary, with salt water pushing at high tide as far upriver as Troy.

Lin Pu-chi set his book down to stare out the window. Forested shoulders of land heaved into view, reminding him of the mountains along the Min River back home but on a scale that was breathtaking. He was again struck by the immensity of the countryside and the striking absence of people. The train passed through villages with intriguing names that evoked Dutch settlements and Mohican history—Ossining, Peekskill—and over small rivers like Wappinger Creek and the Casperkill. He recalled reading a story by an American author who had lived here, Washington Irving, about a hermit with the funny name of Rip Van Winkle, who fell asleep for twenty years. He awoke to find his gun rusted and his country entirely changed—gone was King George, and in his place, President George Washington. When Lin Pu-chi had read the story in English, he had recognized the Chinese legend of "Lankeshan Ji," or "The Rotten Axe Handle"—the same story, but about a woodchopper. Lin Pu-chi wondered how different China would be after his time spent abroad.

It was almost a year to the day since he had arrived in Philadelphia. Everything was going as planned. His academic record at the seminary was so strong that the school awarded him a hundred-dollar prize. He knew where the money had to go: he sent it to his mentor in Fuzhou, the Reverend William Pakenham-Walsh. He asked his teacher to use the funds for St. Mark's School of Trinity College. He would later write to him, "The teaching of English was a minor thing in that little school, but the purpose manifested of leading young Chinese to better and higher things was the all important thing."

With the start of a new semester only weeks away, Lin Pu-chi was making his first trip outside of Philadelphia. His destination was Troy, New York, where Chinese students on the East Coast were gathering for the annual meeting of the Chinese Students' Alliance. The host college this year was the Rensselaer Polytechnic Institute, a respected engineering school with many Chinese alumni.

Lin Pu-chi half expected some notice from his peers once he got to the conference. In the previous issue of the alliance's magazine, editors awarded him second prize in a fiction contest for "The Comedy of Ignorance." This was the short story he had started while en route to Philadelphia, the love story about a headstrong young woman, Faung Ah-tsu, who convinced her father to send her to America to study. For all of his cerebral coursework and pondering of the great moral questions of the day, he could not resist writing a Cinderella ending to the saga of Ah-Tsu.

In the story he crafted, Ah-Tsu ended up at the same university as her fiancé, Dyau. In America, she followed the fashion and adopted an English name, introducing herself as "Sophia" Faung. Dyau noticed that she bore a slight resemblance to the photograph of his betrothed in China, but he did not connect one to the other. Sophia, for her part, did not share her true identity. They met at gatherings of Chinese students, went sightseeing and shopping, and studied together. Dyau professed his love for Sophia, ignoring the ties that bound him to someone else back home.

Two years passed. Dyau was working for a US railway company when he received a telegram from home: his father was seriously ill and he must return immediately. Dyau was his only son, and the dying man longed to see him married and settled before he passed away. The news sent Dyau into a panic. Should he return and marry someone he'd never met? How could he discard his true love, Sophia?

"And yet," Lin Pu-chi wrote, "it was necessary that he should return; his sense of filial obligation compelled him to his father's death-bed."

The doorbell rang. Dyau was face to face with Sophia. She had news, too. Her father had also sent a telegram, instructing her to return home—for she was the Faung Ah-Tsu who was arranged to become his wife. They embraced, their hearts intertwined for eternity.

The story left readers with an ending that many of them thought unimaginable—that the hand of fate could lead them to a marriage based on love.

Troy was a small enough city—population 70,000—that the arrival of 150 Chinese students was big news. If Troy residents had any contact with someone Chinese, it was the launderer ironing their shirts or the waiter serving them American-style chop suey.

As the *Troy Times* prepared its readers on the eve of the conference, "Many of the students have a far better grasp of the English language than the average American student, and they are keen tennis and golf players." The paper even noted that Rensselaer's football team had a second-string quarterback who was Chinese.

Merchants hung Chinese flags in their store windows. Churches and the YMCA opened their doors, and prominent families held dinners and lawn parties for the visitors. City fathers were eager to show off Troy's manufacturing might to the Chinese students, who were just as eager for a close-up look at legendary American industrial ingenuity. A hundred Chinese students hopped on trolleys to travel across the Hudson to tour the US Army's Watervliet Arsenal. A colonel showed them workshops making heavy field equipment and guns. Another afternoon, after students saw workers making precision instruments at W. & L. E. Gurley Co., the widow of a former company president had them over to her mansion for tea.

All of the attendees at the conference knew what it felt like to be the only Chinese person in a classroom or on a streetcar or in a dining hall. The meeting gave them ten days to escape those feelings of isolation and to imagine, if only for a short while, that they were back home.

Like true Americans, they bonded over sports. Students came to the conference armed with college pennants from their alma maters in China as well as from their US schools. Old rivalries between universities like St. John's and

Nanyang transformed into new ones. Harvard men challenged Yale rivals in tennis. But it was the Cornell athletes at the conference who hammered challengers not only on the courts but also in track and field.

One night, a student from Columbia donned his varsity wrestling uniform to demonstrate the sport with a freshman teammate, who was also Chinese. It was an odd sight compared to the martial arts of China. Afterward, the gymnasium was cleared and turned into a dance floor. That's when the intercollegiate competition really heated up: there was only 1 woman for every 10 men among the 150 attendees.

But there was more to the gathering than bonhomie on the athletic field and flirtation on the dance floor. There was work to be done, a call for this privileged generation of overseas students to return home and continue the fight for a free, independent China.

The first speaker at the conference set the tone. Quo Tai-chi—Penn class of 1911, Phi Beta Kappa in political science—was just back from the debacle of the peace conference in Paris, where he had served as a technical adviser to the Chinese delegation. China, he told the students, was locked in a battle for survival.

Japan had pulled a fast one on China, he said. With the defeat of Germany, China expected to reclaim German concessions in Shandong. But Japan wanted to replace Germany and had finagled the secret support of Great Britain, France, and Italy. In a quid pro quo, Japan had traded its naval support during the war for the right to take over German concessions in Shandong afterward, particularly the port of Qingdao.

Quo Tai-chi and the other delegates learned of the secret deal only when they arrived in Paris. President Wilson, who had promised to stand with China, capitulated on April 30 and, in order to move the peace process along, did not block Japan. Beijing students by the thousands took to the streets, marching in protest to the foreign legation on May 4, 1919. But the backlash in China had little effect. The Treaty of Versailles was signed on June 28—without the signatures of Chinese negotiators.

"The Shandong settlement by the peace conference in Japan's favor amounts to a moral and legal sanction by the civilized world of Japan's policy of aggression and despoliation in China," Quo said. "It is not only a glaring injustice to China, but an outrage against the present worldwide awakening spirit of democracy for which Young China is fighting."

Students cheered him with thunderous applause.

On the last day of the conference, the members needed to elect new officers. It was a small exercise in the democratic process of voting as well as a bit of a popularity contest. Getting the most votes for chairman was a Harvard-Penn-Indiana man from St. John's. In a nod to modernity, his vice chairman was a Radcliffe woman from Fujian. And rounding out the slate as secretary was another St. John's alumnus, Lin Pu-chi.

With the election, Lin Pu-chi joined the inner circle of leaders of the eight-hundred-member eastern branch of the alliance. In the closing hours of the conference, they had one final act of business. They drafted a protest letter to the Foreign Relations Committee of the United States Senate, declaring that the Shandong deal "violates the principles of justice and equity for which the Great War has been fought and won, and upon which the future stability of world peace rests."

Lin Pu-chi and the others appealed to the moral leadership of the United States. Americans, they wrote, "will not tolerate such an outrageous act of international brigandage" and will push to alter the Shandong decision to restore "all political and economic rights and privilege once enjoyed by Germany absolutely and unconditionally to their rightful sovereign owner, the Republic of China."

The patriots had spoken.

PIETY

The Western Union messenger rang the doorbell at 901 Clinton Street.

"Telegram for Mr. P. C. Lin," he told the housekeeper.

Later that day, when Lin Pu-chi returned home from the library, he saw the telegram addressed to him on a table in the foyer.

In an instant, he knew it could be from only one place.

His heart pounded. He ripped open the letter and frantically read the message:

Your brother will marry later this year.
Return home.
Made arrangements for your marriage.
Father

His hands shook. He read the words again and again.

His brother was the third son, Lin Buying. The second son had died at a young age. Lin Buying also graduated from Trinity College but went to work for the postal service in Fuzhou instead of going to St. John's. Chinese custom dictated that if Lin Buying wanted to marry, he could not do so until the eldest son—Lin Pu-chi—was married.

In the back of his mind, Lin Pu-chi always knew that the day would come when his parents arranged his marriage. But this wasn't *his plan*. This wasn't supposed to happen now. His graduate studies were going well, but it would take many more years to earn his doctorates from Penn and the seminary. He had scarcely started. How could he return now?

And besides, there was no reason, no logic to this insistence that the oldest son had to marry first. Why did it matter? This was just an old-fashioned way of thinking. He was a modern man.

His mind raced. He thought of ways to explain this to his father. Should he send a letter right away? Should he spell out for him why this was not a good idea? If he wanted to serve the church in China, he needed to get the most out of his study at the seminary. And if he wanted to serve China, he needed to drink up as much as he could from his professors at Penn.

That was rational. That was logical. A summons home was not.

But was his father asking him to return or telling him? And if it was an order, could he defy him? Was he prepared to break from Confucian convention and let his individual desires guide him?

There could be only one way.

The weather was warm with a light breeze on the first of Lin Pu-chi's two graduation days. On May 27, 1920, Dean Bartlett handed him and four others their seminary diplomas at a service at St. Andrew's Church.

In 1920, Lin Pu-chi graduated from the Divinity School of the Protestant Episcopal Church in Philadelphia. He stands in the back row, second from the right. *Source:* Class Photos, RG-7, Student Records, Box 5, The Archives of The Divinity School of the Protestant Episcopal Church in Philadelphia, at Episcopal Divinity School, Cambridge, MA. Used with permission.

Some received doctorates. With his studies cut short, Lin Pu-chi had earned enough credits for only a bachelor's degree of sacred theology. For the second year in a row, the dean awarded Lin Pu-chi a prize of one hundred dollars for academic excellence.

Twenty days later, Lin Pu-chi walked down the aisle of the Metropolitan Opera House on North Broad Street for the 164th commencement of the University of Pennsylvania. He received a master of philosophy.

Back at 901 Clinton, he packed up his books in boxes to ship to China via the American Express Company. Lugging his leather suitcase, he walked to the Broad Street Station to catch the Pennsylvania Railroad's Day Express to Pittsburgh, the first leg of his long journey home.

· 6 ·

Second Daughter

Fuzhou, 1920

*E*ven with her door shut, Ni Guizhen could hear her father's voice raised at her mother.

"It's your daughter's wedding," he implored from another room. "How can you not be here?"

"Your sister can handle everything," her mother answered. "I'm needed in Fuqing."

Inside her room, Ni Guizhen did not try to hold back her tears. She did not want to get married. And now, as the days counted down to December 20, 1920, she faced the prospect of standing at the altar to marry a virtual stranger without her mother in the front pew. Making the situation even harder to accept, it was Ni Guizhen's mother who had pushed for this union in the first place. Her husband and the father of Lin Pu-chi had served together on the board of directors of the YMCA, and she had her eye on his eldest son, the student in the United States. When a go-between suggested a marriage, she accepted wholeheartedly.

The bride's mother, whose name was Lin Heping (but not related to the groom), had never bowed to the opinion of others and was not about to start. Her decision to miss her daughter's wedding had been abrupt. Only in the past few months had she embraced a new desire to spread her Christian beliefs. To her delight, she found that she was much in demand among missionaries. A few weeks before the wedding, an American woman had invited her to give a series of talks about her faith at a school in Fuqing, a coastal city to the south. Foreigners depended on local women like Lin Heping, who understood the Bible and could act as cultural conduits to other wives and girls who were inquiring about Christian beliefs. Women did not mix freely with men in proper Chinese society, making a female approach necessary. On top of that, though missionaries had been around for seventy years, it was more effective to have Chinese believers rather than foreigners conveying the religious message.

Lin Heping viewed the invitation as a test, coinciding as it did with her daughter's wedding. It pitted her spiritual devotion against her maternal responsibility, a choice of one love over another.

Short and stout with her weight approaching two hundred pounds, Lin Heping ruled her household and marriage by intimidation. She craved social status and nurtured her reputation as the wife of a senior official in the maritime customs office. Her meek husband gave her wide berth.

For all her imperious manners, Lin Heping was not born into a high station in life. She was the daughter of peasants who could not afford to feed another mouth—another female mouth. Out of desperation, her father sold her to a merchant in the city. The man gave the girl to his concubine, who could not have children and wanted a child to coddle. Only girls were sold, never precious boys, and so the concubine gained a daughter.

Following Chinese tradition, the woman began to bind Lin Heping's feet when she was six. The child resisted and wailed each time the cloth wrappings were tightened. That same year, the merchant became stricken with an illness that defied traditional Chinese treatments. A colleague from his business asked members of his Methodist Episcopal church to pray for the man's recovery. The merchant rebounded and, convinced that the faith of the Christians had saved his life, decided to convert. To prove his commitment, he threw out the Kitchen God in his home and other traditional wooden idols.

The conversion of the family had a profound impact on Lin Heping's upbringing. Her parents sent her to a mission school run by a Methodist missionary from West Virginia. Julia Bonafield, the principal, had a strict rule: no girls with bound feet allowed. "Bound feet should be looked upon as a mark of heathenism and should not be tolerated in a Christian school," Miss Bonafield wrote in a letter to the *Chinese Recorder*, a missionary magazine. Lin Heping's mother heeded her admonition and unbound her daughter's feet.

When Lin Heping was sixteen, she asked Miss Bonafield to write a letter to her contacts in America. She told the school principal of her deep desire to travel to the States and follow in the footsteps of the famous Dr. Xu of Fuzhou. Every Christian girl in Fuzhou had read about the remarkable achievement of Dr. Xu. The physician Xu Jinhong was a missionary success story, touted from church to church. In 1884, her parents, who were converts, broke with tradition and not only educated their daughter but also accepted the suggestion of a missionary to let her continue her education overseas. It was such a novelty at the time for Chinese students to study in America, let alone young women, that the *New York Times* reported on her arrival in Delaware, Ohio, to enroll at Ohio Wesleyan University. After four years at the school, she moved to

Philadelphia to attend the Women's Medical College of Pennsylvania. Dr. Xu returned home and managed a missionary hospital in Fuzhou, treating women and children and training other Chinese women as nurses.

Miss Bonafield did reach out to her colleagues in the United States about the prospects for Lin Heping, and she received an encouraging reply. If her student could handle the language and maintain good grades, it might be possible for her to enter medical school. With that, Lin Heping urged her father to send her to Shanghai, where the Methodist missionaries ran the more academically rigorous McTyeire Home and School for Girls. She reasoned that she could better hone her language proficiency at a better school.

Even as a seventeen-year-old, Lin Heping could be persuasive. Her father yielded to her wishes, and Lin Heping left for Shanghai with another girl from her school, the daughter of a local pastor, who also wanted to become a doctor. In 1897, McTyeire was in its infancy with only two dozen students, mostly girls from affluent families. One of her classmates was Song Qingling, who would later become the wife of the revolutionary Dr. Sun Yat-sen. Lin Heping's mother, however, worried about losing her daughter to the modern world and leaving China. So when a matchmaker came to her home to inquire about a marriage between her daughter and the son of a local pastor, the concubine eagerly endorsed the idea. Lin Heping's father acquiesced, preferring harmony under his roof over honoring his daughter's wishes.

The news of their decision, delivered in a letter to McTyeire, shattered Lin Heping. "I knew that useless girls planned to get married, but others could be independent and become teachers, doctors and important people," she wrote many years later. "Me? Finished—go and get married!"

When she returned home, her parents gave her a photo of her betrothed. "My ambition had come to nothing. I had no alternative," she said. "Within me was born a hatred of my mother. I regarded her as the one who ruined my future."

But for all her bitterness, for all her thwarted ambition, she felt no compunction about doing the same thing many years later to her second daughter, Ni Guizhen.

NEW PATH

At the start of her eighteenth year, Ni Guizhen was going to school in Shanghai and was happy, blissfully happy.

She was thriving as a student at the McTyeire School, the same mission school attended by her mother. When she left home, she felt liberated. She was dispensable as a second daughter—or as she was viewed by her tradition-bound mother, a second disappointment. Though China had entered the modern era, ancient customs still cemented families. Boys were coveted; girls endured. When Lin Heping gave birth to her second daughter in 1902, she feared that she was cursed like her husband's sister, who had produced nothing but girls—*six* of them! When she delivered her third child, her husband was the first to see the newborn. He whispered in his wife's ear, "It's true! It is a son, thank God." They named him Ni Shuzu. As their family grew, he remained the sun with everyone else mere planets.

Ni Guizhen grew up knowing she was not the answer to her mother's prayers but rather the reason for them. She had a plain, round face, and absent the attention of her vain mother, she found contentment at school.

She loved everything about McTyeire. She loved her teachers, adventuresome Methodist Episcopal women from states like Georgia and Tennessee, who had been teaching Chinese girls since 1892. There was Miss Smith, who taught her how to play the piano, and Miss Clairborne, who showed her how to use a microscope in biology class.

She loved the idyllic campus, sequestered in the western part of Shanghai behind a tall wall that looked like the undulating spine of a dragon. She loved the magnolia tree by the front gate, transplanted from the American South to China, and the constant parade of flowers on campus—white peach blossoms, lavender wisteria, pink cosmos, and cardinal-red geraniums. She loved playing croquet on the manicured lawn, singing in the school choir, and tending a botany class garden with beans, strawberries, asparagus, blackberries, lettuce, and mustard greens.

She loved that she could dream at McTyeire. Even girls could have aspirations, and hers was to leave China for the United States and become a physician. Like her mother before her, Ni Guizhen wanted to be like Dr. Xu, a virtuous woman with purpose. At McTyeire, she focused on science as she polished her English language skills.

The school song was her anthem.

> Near the yellow Yangtze River
> In the heart of old Shanghai,
> There's a school for China's daughters
> Bringing truth and freedom nigh.
> May she live and grow forever,
> Scatter knowledge far and near,
> Till all China learns the lessons
> That we learn at old McTyeire.

Everything was going as planned until the day the principal called her to the office and handed her a letter from her mother. The note said her marriage had been arranged and she must cut short her studies to return home.

Just like that, Ni Guizhen's dream ended. She would not graduate from high school, not travel to America, not study medicine. What she wanted from life did not matter; her parents had made the decision for her.

Ni Guizhen silently raged against her fate but mostly against her mother. She could not understand how her mother could do this to her.

How could she allow history to repeat itself in such a cruel way?

FORCE OF NATURE

The religious transformation of Lin Heping in the year before her daughter's wedding had been nothing short of startling. If someone had to describe Lin Heping—the *old* Lin Heping, the one before 1920—you would hear words such as "forceful," "imperious," "striving," "stubborn," "overbearing," "headstrong," and "opinionated." The phrase "exemplary Christian" would not have been among the descriptions.

She spent her days at the mahjong table, gossiping and gambling with her friends. She draped herself in fine silk and velvet and flaunted her valuable jade rings and pendants. Given a choice between a service at church and the latest Hollywood movie at the cinema, she had no trouble choosing Charlie Chaplin or Rudolph Valentino ahead of the apostles. She could be downright rude if a local pastor made the mistake of coming to her home and interrupting her gambling to ask for a church contribution from the family. "Sit down here," she would say mockingly. "Let's see what my winnings amount to. If I win plenty, I'll give God some!"

With her four daughters and five sons, Lin Heping had a short fuse. Once, she came home and found a valuable vase shattered in pieces on the floor. She immediately accused her eldest son, Ni Shuzu, then sixteen, of breaking it. Despite his denial, she gave him a thrashing.

But at forty, Lin Heping experienced a spiritual awakening that started when an old acquaintance came to Fuzhou in February 1920. The visitor's name was Yu Cidu, a popular female evangelist who went by the English name of Dora Yu. A second-generation Christian, she was seven years older than Lin Heping and a well-known preacher in coastal China. Lin Heping had met her as a student at the McTyeire School and attended one of her talks. So inspired was Lin Heping by the preaching that she gave the evangelist a valuable ring that had been a gift from her own mother. She wanted Yu Cidu to use it, if need be, to cover her expenses. The older woman at first refused, but Lin Heping insisted.

Yu Cidu was part of a generation of Chinese women and men who, at the dawn of the twentieth century, began to preach independently across the country. The early part of the century, a time of great political upheaval and change, was a golden age for missionary work. The ranks of Chinese Protestants numbered about one hundred thousand in 1900, increasing to almost three hundred thousand by 1915. It was during this period that Yu Cidu began conducting revival meetings in Methodist Episcopal churches in Shanghai and other major cities.

In February 1920, when Lin Heping heard that Yu Cidu was coming to Fuzhou for two weeks, she was both pleased at the prospect of seeing her old acquaintance and somewhat uncomfortable. In the twenty-two years since they had last seen each other, she was a Christian in name only.

The day of Yu Cidu's arrival, Lin Heping invited her to her spacious home for dinner. The family lived in a two-story brick house behind a wall in the foreign settlement of Nantai. The other guests included a few church members and some of the gambling friends of the hostess. At the dinner table, Lin Heping kept the conversation between the disparate guests moving along and mentioned the good work of Yu Cidu, who would be holding a two-week revival meeting.

At the close of the meal, she said, "Tomorrow morning at eight o'clock, Yu Cidu will preach at the Church of Heavenly Peace. Please all go."

"And what about you?" a mahjong friend playfully taunted.

Put on the spot, Lin Heping stammered, "Of course, I will go."

On February 15, the Methodist church, built by American missionaries and located on a hillside overlooking the Min River, was filled to capacity and included Lin Heping and her friends. For the day's lesson, Yu Cidu told the story of Adam and Eve, tempted by the serpent in the Garden of Eden.

The second day, Lin Heping felt obligated to return to hear her friend talk. Again, the topic was man's descent into sin from the book of Genesis.

By the third day, Lin Heping needed a break. She resumed her spot at the mahjong table with her friends. "We've wasted two days without playing mahjong," a friend protested. "Her preaching was unintelligible."

Lin Heping kept quiet. While the others laughed and chatted, she felt torn. She surprised herself by deciding after two days of gambling that she needed to return to church for the sake of Yu Cidu. "She came here from a great distance to preach," Lin Heping explained to her friends. "How can I decline to go?"

She rose at four the next morning, unable to sleep. When she arrived at church, Yu Cidu immediately asked about her whereabouts for the past two days.

"I wasn't feeling well," Lin Heping lied sheepishly.

The day's talk was on lapsed Christians. Lin Heping felt as if her friend were looking right at her. She felt uncomfortable in her gaze and resolved that tomorrow she would not return to church.

But at the end of the talk, Yu Cidu made a point of asking her whether she would come back for the next day's session. Lin Heping nodded yes.

Again the topic was nominal Christians. "It was as if she had seen my way of life with her own eyes," Lin Heping later wrote. "I sat there as though yesterday she had not scolded me enough."

On the following Sunday, the seventh day of her revival meetings, Yu Cidu delivered her main message—that Jesus was the Son of God who endured pain and shame and willingly died on the cross to save man from sin. The preacher's zeal was so intense and effective that when Lin Heping returned home, she wept uncontrollably. "When people go to worship, they come home happy," her husband lamented. "You went for several nights and you can't sleep or eat. After this, don't go anymore."

But she felt compelled to confess all of her shortcomings in an outpouring of remorse and contrition. It was as if she was seeing herself for the first time and disapproving of what she saw. Lin Heping told her husband she regularly skimmed money from household funds to gamble with her friends. And when she finished with him, she turned to her eldest son. She apologized for accusing him of breaking her favorite vase.

"I confess to you that the time when I beat you unjustly was a sin against you," she told him. "Please forgive me."

"I truly hated you for beating me without cause that day," her son replied.

"Please forgive me," she repeated.

He did not answer. But the next morning, after seeing how his mother's demeanor had changed and how her contrition seemed real, he was curious about what this preacher had said and decided to go with her to the revival meeting.

Her eldest son was a student at St. Mark's, the high school that was part of the Irish-run Trinity College, the alma mater of Lin Pu-chi. Ni Shuzu was the type of student whose intellect allowed him to coast through school with little effort. The older this son got, the more he developed an aversion to the organized church. He found it pathetic the way Chinese pastors came around, knocking on the door of his family's home, begging for donations for their foreign-run churches.

At the revival meeting, he listened to his mother, who stood next to Yu Cidu and interpreted her words into the local dialect spoken in Fuzhou. He returned the next day to hear the preacher again, and then another day, eventually attending every meeting for a week.

The experience left the seventeen-year-old tormented and changed. He felt repentance, joy, and confusion: was he being called to follow a new path, a religious one? Two months later, as he would later recall for friends, "I was alone in my room, struggling to decide whether or not to believe in the Lord.

I pictured his hands stretched out on the cross, and all at once they seemed to be welcoming me."

His mother also felt compelled to make decisive changes in her life. She no longer would be a Christian in name only. Every Tuesday at 2:00 p.m., she began to hold Bible study meetings in her spacious home. She played the piano at big revival meetings across the province. She accepted invitations to share her story, testifying to Methodist and Anglican groups as well as members of the Young Women's Christian Association. Word of her speaking ability spread, and soon Lin Heping received invitations to talk to groups in other towns, including a girls' school in neighboring Fuqing. In the autumn of 1920, she stayed for a month at the school. No sooner had she returned to Fuzhou than she received another invitation to return. She agreed, even though she knew it overlapped with an important family event: her second daughter's wedding.

Facing the prospect of missing the ceremony, Lin Heping asked her husband's younger sister to fill in for her.

"Guizhen has a mother," her sister-in-law clucked. "Why is it necessary for an aunt to help? Don't be crazy."

Even in the face of intense disapproval from the family, Lin Heping intended to follow through with her plans. Her daughter was despondent. Her husband tried to talk sense into his wife, but she would hear none of it.

Relief came in the form of a letter sent by messenger to the Ni family. Lin Pu-chi had returned to Fuzhou in the summer of 1920 and was not oblivious to the drama unfolding within the Ni household. He wrote a letter to the patriarch informing him that he was "ill" and it would be better if the families postponed the wedding for a month or more. Lin Heping packed her suitcase and hired a sedan chair for the daylong journey to Fuqing.

DOUBLE HAPPINESS

In her room, the bride took her wedding dress into her hands, unbuttoned the back, and slipped the column of blush-white satin over her arms. The gown came to just above her ankles, showing off her dainty feet in white silk stockings and white kid pumps. She broke from Chinese tradition, eschewing a red embroidered wedding outfit in favor of this Western bridal gown with a high neck, long sleeves, and a scalloped hem with fringe. It was modern yet modest, just like her. Her hair was pulled into a loose bun that covered her ears and softly framed her face. Her only jewelry was a gold necklace with a locket. On her head she wore a crown of flowers that held a long veil of white tulle. In her hands she clutched a bouquet of daisies with soft tendrils of ferns.

Lin Pu-chi and Ni Guizhen pose for their wedding-day portrait. Courtesy of Lin Family Collection.

At his house, the groom put his long arms into the sleeves of a formal morning jacket with a black waistcoat and starched, high-collar white shirt. He used pomade to slick down his thick, black hair in a straight center part. He pinned his boutonniere on his lapel and adjusted his wire-framed eyeglasses. Last, he pulled white gloves over each hand and placed a black bowler on his head.

The ceremony on March 4, 1921, would be a double wedding. Lin Pu-chi's younger brother dressed differently for his nuptials. He opted to wear a traditional Chinese black silk coat over a long gown with black felt slippers. He had never traveled beyond Fuzhou and was not about to put on the airs of a westerner like his older brother.

Hundreds of guests filled all the pews of the stone chapel on the campus of Trinity College. Heads turned as the brides made their way down the aisle—Ni Guizhen to marry Lin Pu-chi, now a deacon in the Anglican Church; and Yu Yujie to marry Lin Buying, a clerk with the postal service.

After the Christian ceremony, friends and family crossed the campus for an outdoor reception. Coming from such prominent families, the couples drew guests from many different quarters—Chinese and Western, missionary and medical. Directors of the YMCA mingled with doctors from the Tating Hospital; deacons and pastors dined alongside clerks from government offices.

For the double wedding on March 4, 1921, both grooms—Lin Pu-chi (right) and Lin Buying—pose with their brides, parents, and siblings. Courtesy of Lin Family Collection.

For the wedding banquet, round tables were set up around the soccer field by the middle school. The North of China may have been reeling from a famine, but the double wedding of Dr. Lin's sons was cause for a feast. Each table was set with plates of fruit and a sampling of cold dishes, including duck and preserved plums. Kitchen staff brought out a procession of steaming dishes, featuring the bounty of the sea, Fuzhou's specialty. There were fish balls in broth, shrimp baked in custard, sea urchins, curried fish, and the grand finale, generous bowls of shark's fin soup.

Each set of couples posed for photographs with their parents and siblings. Lin Heping, back from her preaching, smiled for the camera; the bride stood over her right shoulder with an impassive expression. Her young brothers and sisters surrounded them.

Neither the bride nor groom wanted this marriage, but the power of Confucian obedience was stronger than individual will. Lin Pu-chi was twenty-six. He had lived abroad and was building a career in the Anglican Church. He taught at the Union Theological Seminary and ran the small Ming Do Chapel near the family's home in the foreign enclave of Nantai. Ni Guizhen was nineteen and had only one path in front of her. Her clothes may have been modern, but tradition dictated that her next step was raising a family.

She accepted her fate. But on her wedding night, Ni Guizhen vowed that if she ever had a daughter, she would not let history repeat itself.

· 7 ·

Running Dog

Fuzhou, 1924

*T*he procession was about to begin. Boys from a home for orphans launched into "Thy Kingdom Come, O Lord" on trumpets and drums. It was All Saints' Day—November 1, 1924—and the high-noon sun beat down on hundreds of Chinese and foreign guests standing around trenches in a neighborhood a few blocks from the Min River. Western men shielded their heads under pith helmets. Women tiptoed around puddles and piles of rubble. They pressed close to a wooden platform that marked the exact spot of the front door of the future Jidu Tianzhu Tang, or Christ Church Cathedral.

In a house near the construction site, Lin Pu-chi and other clergy donned their robes before stepping into the sunlight for the laying of the cornerstone. For the twenty-nine-year-old priest, the ceremony marked a personal achievement. The trenches outlined the foundation of a new mother church for the Fujian diocese. The stone and wood structure, which would be shaped like a cross, would have twin square towers and stand as an architectural expression of the aspirations of the Anglican Church. It would have classrooms for a school, a meeting hall, and a sanctuary vast enough to seat a thousand people. And the cleric selected to run it was Lin Pu-chi.

Addressing the assembled, an elderly Chinese pastor recalled the trials of Archdeacon John Wolfe, the "Moses of Fujian" who died in 1915 after a half century of work in the province. The cathedral was being dedicated in the memory of the archdeacon, who evangelized beyond the walled city of Fuzhou to villages like the ancestral home of Lin Pu-chi's family.

Workers pulling on ropes and rigs positioned the massive cornerstone, chiseled with the English words "Glory be to God." Before it was lowered into place, they placed in a time capsule mementoes of the era: a Chinese Bible, the charter for the Fujian parish, a list of cathedral donors, a bank note worth one thousand yuan in silver, and a copy of a local newspaper.

If everything went according to plan, the cathedral would be finished in time for a dedication ceremony on May 1, 1927. The national synod for the Chung Hua Sheng Kung Hui, as the Anglican and Episcopal Church in China was called, would congregate in Fuzhou on that day, and church members from all over China could bear witness to how far they had come in Fujian.

Anglican missionaries needed men like Lin Pu-chi to carry on their work in the province. It had been nearly seventy-five years since they arrived in Fuzhou, and control of chapels, schools, and hospitals was still very much in their hands. Until the church could shake its foreign profile, Christianity would be seen as an alien religion. Bishop John Hind, the head of the Fujian diocese, was not resistant to transferring more responsibility to Chinese Christians, but there were practical matters to consider, such as finances—paying salaries, covering debts, subsidizing budgets for hospitals and schools—and a shortage of capable local clerics. Mission help was still necessary in a diocese with 15,000 baptized members in 316 churches.

But the slow pace of change made Lin Pu-chi impatient. He recognized the undeniable tide of anti-Christian sentiment rising throughout China, linked to equally strengthening feelings of national pride. The Chinese people, especially those who were younger, urban, and educated, resented how other nations treated their homeland. They wanted to do away with "extraterritoriality," the right given to foreigners after the Opium Wars to be beholden to the laws of their home countries and not China's. Increasingly, Christianity and its institutions were viewed as part of the problem—and their Chinese followers as unpatriotic instruments of imperialism. The attacks against them were well organized, with rallies, articles, and slogans. There were even printed instructions on how to organize an anti-Christian campaign: conduct parades to arouse public attention; make speeches to discredit Christianity; distribute attack literature; and recruit sympathizers. Mission schools were singled out for criticism, accused of robbing students of their Chinese identities by perfecting their English at the expense of their Chinese—a form of cultural imperialism that conquered minds and fostered feelings of deference and inferiority.

Even among Chinese Christians, some believers distanced themselves from the Protestant churches run by missionaries. The brother-in-law of Lin Pu-chi—the oldest brother of Ni Guizhen—was one of these outliers. A self-taught preacher with no denominational ties, he felt no need for these foreign institutions. He openly disparaged Chinese pastors who came to his home to ask for donations from his wealthy parents. Instead, he sought out mentors, Chinese and foreign, to teach him the scriptures, and he voraciously read English works by well-known European mystics and evangelists. He was baptized by immersion in the Min River and took to the streets with a band of friends to spread their beliefs. They dressed in white tunics emblazoned with red cloth characters that translated to "Jesus is coming." They handed out pamphlets about the Gospels, banged gongs for attention, and played hymns on accordion. So consumed was he with his newfound mission that he changed his name to reflect his spiritual quest. He picked a moniker that was a nod to a popular Welsh evangelist he admired and studied who had penned a prayer for "all the faithful watchmen on the watchtowers." In a decade, he would be known throughout China by this new name, Ni Tuosheng, or to English speakers, Watchman Nee.

Watchman Nee rejected denominational churches, but Lin Pu-chi was trying to change the Anglican mission from the inside out. His new appointment as dean of the cathedral would elevate his standing not only within his church but also with the larger foreign community in Fuzhou.

Erudite and ambitious, Lin Pu-chi eagerly shared his thoughts, sometimes bluntly, on the pages of the *Chinese Recorder*, a Protestant magazine published in Shanghai and circulated to missionaries throughout the country.

His barbed opinions could rankle foreign readers. When editors sent a survey to Chinese theologians, asking them among other questions whether

Lin Pu-chi's first job in Fuzhou was on the faculty of the Union Theological Seminary, pictured here around 1920. The Reverend Lin Pu-chi represented the Anglican Church and sits in the front, second from the left. Courtesy of Yale Divinity School Library.

they wanted missionaries in their country, he replied yes but added with emphasis, "the *right kind* of missionary." China didn't need missionaries who were ensconced in spacious compounds with maids and cooks, protected by treaty law and isolated from the very people they were trying to help. The people, he wrote, needed missionaries who choose a life of self-denial and sacrifice to "entirely work for the advancement of God's Kingdom and not for the prestige of their nations; those who can sympathize with the people among whom they work, who are humble enough to see their viewpoints, to share their aspirations."

What Chinese Christians sought were advisers, not rulers who overstayed their welcome. "The missionaries are a valuable asset to the Chinese Church but we need not attach undue importance to them," Lin Pu-chi wrote in the magazine.

Another time, he challenged missionaries who objected to demonstrations every year on May 9 to mark the "Day of Humiliation." It was the anniversary of China's acceptance in 1915 of an ultimatum from Japan to cede to it control of Manchuria and German concessions in Shandong Province. Many mission schools banned students from protesting, saying it fed hatred and animosity. Lin Pu-chi openly disagreed. He argued that the actions of Japan constituted a crime of international proportions. "And no Christian, if his religion is worth anything, should or can tolerate . . . a crime," he wrote in the *Chinese Recorder*.

The Beatitudes, he acknowledged, may teach Christians that "Blessed are the peacemakers." His rebuttal: "It is a very different thing to refuse to assert one's national rights, or to be so shamefully servile as to accept any treatment, however vile, accorded another nation. The Christian Church should take an active part in the keeping of the Ninth of May, 'Lest we forget!'"

Missionaries would get a blunt warning about the depths of the antipathy toward foreigners in the spring of 1925.

On May 15, 1925, the foreman of a Japanese cotton mill in Shanghai shot and killed a Chinese worker during a labor strike. Protesters marched into the heart of the International Settlement in Shanghai on May 30. They rushed a police station run by the Shanghai Municipal Council near busy Nanjing Road. A British inspector ordered them to halt. He counted to ten before commanding Sikh and Chinese officers to fire into the surging crowd. Forty-four shots from automatic pistols killed eleven and wounded twenty demonstrators.

In Fuzhou, as many as ten thousand people—some with signs saying "Exterminate Foreigners"—protested in sympathy for the victims of the "May Thirtieth Incident." Residents launched a boycott and stopped buying everything from British American Tobacco cigarettes to coal imported from the

Japanese colony of Formosa. The newly formed Fujian Student Union, whose ranks included Chinese Communist Party activists, terrorized local employees of foreign firms. A mob attacked a deliveryman with the British-run Asiatic Petroleum Company and cut off his left ear with a pair of scissors.

The protests in Fuzhou shifted in the summer toward mission schools. The Student Union pledged to prevent them from opening in the fall and, in particular, vowed to destroy the most prominent British school in the city, Trinity College. Provocateurs sent anonymous letters to parents of students and teachers, warning them of an attack if they dared to return.

On August 30, 1925, as a violent typhoon buffeted the coast of Fujian, nine leaders of the Anglican Church—all Chinese—huddled for an emergency meeting on the fate of Trinity College. They were taking matters into their own hands. The highest-ranking Chinese cleric in Fujian, Archdeacon Ding Ing-ong, had called the meeting. The older man spoke no English, so Lin Pu-chi took notes. He later drafted a letter to the missionary in charge of Trinity College, relaying the group's concerns and trying to impress on him how this political storm was different.

"The fact that there is an element of patriotism gives weight to the attacks," Lin Pu-chi cautioned in English. "And no doubt the recent attempt to overthrow British schools is different in nature from former attacks."

In spelling out options, the group recommended that the three foreign principals who ran the primary and two middle schools step aside and allow Chinese men to take their places. The foreign staff complied and then went a step further by naming a new executive committee to run Trinity, made up of a Chinese majority of directors. The president of the college, the Reverend W. P. W. Williams, also offered to resign. But in the end, he remained because he felt there was no qualified Chinese candidate to replace him.

On October 2, Williams sent a coded telegram to London: TRINITY REOPENS UNDER CHINESE MANAGEMENT.

ORPHANS AND RADICALS

Lin Pu-chi could mark the passage of time by his rise through the ranks of the Anglican community: ordination as deacon in 1921 and priest in 1922; selection as cathedral dean in 1924.

For his wife, time was measured through the lives of her children. After the disappointment of their arranged marriage, both assumed the roles expected of them in a Confucian society. Their relationship was amicable and respectful, with children coming at a regular interval. Lin Pu-chi was preoccupied with his career and professional duties, leaving the household and family to his wife.

Ni Guizhen bore their first child—a daughter—almost nine months to the day after their wedding. Another daughter arrived the next year, but the baby did not survive, a victim of dysentery, which took the lives of many children in the teeming, unsanitary city. Two healthy sons followed in quick succession in 1924 and 1925.

The couple lived on Nantai Island, a place that in some neighborhoods felt more foreign than Chinese. The Western community was tiny compared with Shanghai's, numbering in the hundreds rather than the thousands. But the foreign presence—all the consulates, banks, trading firms, shipping lines, and social clubs—was concentrated in one place. A British man could spend the morning at the office, play an afternoon game of field hockey on the grounds of the racecourse, and then relax in a leather chair at the Fuzhou Club with the latest London edition of the *Times* and a whiskey and soda. At night, he might bump into a visitor such as the British author W. Somerset Maugham, staying at the Brand Hotel on the waterfront.

Lin Pu-chi knew every corner and alley of the neighborhood, as did his wife. Both had grown up there: the young priest near his father's hospital and Ni Guizhen near her father's waterfront office for the customs service.

The couple now shared a brick house with Lin Pu-chi's widowed mother and his younger brother, the postal clerk. It was a stately building, three stories tall, designed by an American architect out of gratitude for the good medical care he had received from the late Dr. Lin, who died in 1922 of tuberculosis.

In the fall of 1926, Ni Guizhen was pregnant for a fifth time when the mood in the city turned dark. Newspapers told of the movement of troops from the south toward Fuzhou. It was part of the unfinished revolution of Sun Yat-sen. Since the debacle a decade earlier, when the first president tried unsuccessfully to reinstate a monarchy, the country lacked an effective central government. China, a republic in name only, was carved into districts controlled by warlords with private armies.

Loyalists of Sun Yat-sen and his Nationalist or Kuomintang Party were backed into a corner, operating from a base in the southern city of Canton. The revolutionary statesman had died in 1925, but in one of his last acts, he negotiated a tenuous military coalition between Nationalists and the Chinese Communist Party. Chiang Kai-shek, the Nationalists' military man, vowed to carry on the fight to unify China once and for all. In the summer of 1926, he headed north with a combined army.

The Northern Expedition, as it was known, faced little resistance. When coalition forces reached Fuzhou in December 1926, most of the fifty thousand soldiers under the nominal control of a local warlord scattered without a fight.

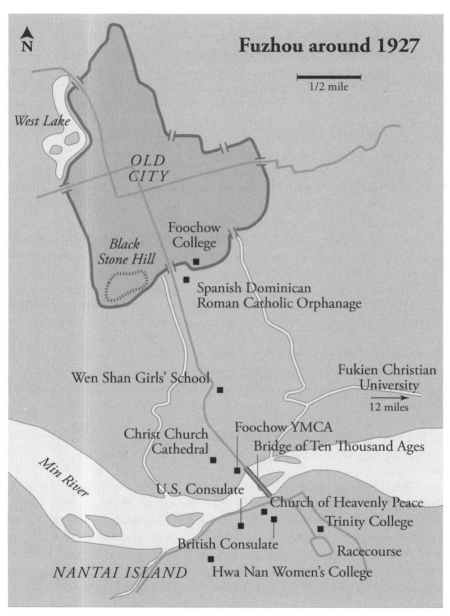

This map depicts Fuzhou in 1927 and shows Christian landmarks and locations that were relevant to the life of Lin Pu-chi. Courtesy of Sterling Chen.

Many were former bandits and mercenaries with little loyalty and much hatred for the warlord. When a Nationalist commander marched into Fuzhou, these soldiers simply did an about-face and traded in one uniform for another.

By the time the Lin family gathered to celebrate the thirty-second birthday of Lin Pu-chi on Christmas Day in 1926, Nationalist forces controlled Fuzhou. Overnight, the city was ablaze with flags for the victors—a blue background with a white sun. Some students set up soapboxes to extol like preachers the late Sun Yat-sen's three principles of the people: nationalism, democracy, and socialism. Local newspapers carried editorials on the topic; one explained that this was Abraham Lincoln's theory in Chinese terms.

The Northern Expedition pushed into the next province but left behind in Fuzhou some of the Soviet advisers who had been helping behind the scenes. The young Soviet Union was the only country willing to help the Nationalists with funding and military and political assistance. Masters of propaganda, they were intent on advancing a socialist agenda in China and began organizing workers into unions. The Fujian Students Union, with its anti-Christian members, gladly worked with the Soviets against foreigners and Christians. Young provocateurs plastered posters against Christians and brazenly sauntered through the streets, swinging crude homemade bombs from ropes. They staked out mission schools and other properties, skulking in the shadows and setting up surveillance.

One group of students planted themselves outside the compound of an orphanage run by Dominican nuns from Spain. When a Chinese worker left the compound carrying two baskets balanced over his shoulder, they demanded to know what was inside.

The man nervously answered, "Fish."

Someone lifted a cloth to inspect the baskets, detonating an explosion of rage among onlookers.

What they saw was the sad evidence of the Chinese preference for boys. Newborn girls who perished from malnutrition or illness or who simply weren't wanted by their parents often ended up in the "baby tower," found among the gravesites outside the city walls. It was a conical stone structure, slightly taller than a man, with an opening at the top where someone could drop a baby—dead or alive. Towers like this were built to help poor people who could not afford the expense of funerals. They were not supposed to be used for living children, but it happened. At the tower's base were baskets with strings, left behind by bearers after they lowered newborns into the putrid pile. Another way to dispose of girls was in the river. City dwellers tried to discourage the practice. On the waterfront in Nantai stood a stone with the chiseled message: "Little girls are not to be drowned here."

Peasants came to know, however, that the Dominican nuns at the Holy Childhood Orphanage in Fuzhou would pay for their girls—twenty cents per baby. The government discouraged such transactions, but the sisters viewed it as an act of mercy. The mother superior felt payment would encourage parents to make the effort to turn over their daughters to them. The Spanish sisters supported hundreds of orphans by making lace embroidery, a skill they, in turn, passed on to their wards. In a little chapel with a statue of the Blessed Virgin Mary, they also taught the girls how to recite the rosary.

The Spanish nuns accepted five to twelve babies a day. They arrived in deplorable condition and after being washed and clothed were quickly baptized. All too often the children were moments from death. For practical reasons, the sisters waited a few days until there were several corpses before giving the deceased a proper blessing and burial outside the orphanage.

The worker who was accosted by students was on his way to bury babies. As soon as the crowd discovered his cargo, they stormed the compound, where they found even more corpses, some stored outdoors and crawling with rats.

Rioters tore apart the dormitories, playrooms, and classrooms. When they were finished, they moved across the street and ransacked the church and the rectory for Dominican priests. The violence started at 4:00 p.m. and ended six hours later. The Spanish nuns fled with as many girls as possible, escaping the city aboard a British steamer.

Protesters had what they needed. They put some of the tiny corpses on display in front of a local court and hung posters with images of babies being boiled. They passed out leaflets with the message: "Do you realize the dark purposes of the Christian religion? Are your hearts not moved by their cruel acts?"

The destruction of the orphanage was on a Friday—January 14, 1927. The following Sunday, Lin Pu-chi traveled by rickshaw across the Bridge of Ten Thousand Ages to a small Chinese chapel near the old city. With him were his wife and their daughter, five-year-old Martha; the younger toddler boys stayed at home with a nanny. The pastor of the church, founded by American missionaries, had invited him to be a guest speaker at that day's service.

The day was bright and clear, and the pews were filled mostly with girls from the Wen Shan Girls' School across the street, one of the oldest mission schools in the city. The students sang joyfully, their sweet voices filling the chapel.

After the service, a pair of sisters from Rhode Island invited the Lin family over for dinner. Betty and Mary Cushman had been sent to China by a mission organization for the Congregational churches. The pastor and his wife were easy guests. Lin Pu-chi spoke English effortlessly, and Ni Guizhen, from her years at the McTyeire School, could follow along. It was well known among American missionaries that Lin Pu-chi had studied in Philadelphia. The sisters' elder brother, a sailor, had died in that city in September 1918, a victim of the Spanish flu pandemic.

As they finished their meal, the nephew of a Chinese teacher burst into their house, shouting. The big Methodist Episcopal church in the city was being looted by a mob. Betty tried to calm him. Then three girls charged into the compound with another breathless warning. Their school, the Anglo-Chinese Girls' School a few blocks away near the South Gate of the old city, was under attack. Rioters were ripping apart their campus and had seized two British teachers. The attackers used knives to tear the dresses off the women's bodies, took off their shoes and stockings, and sent them barefoot into the streets in only their undergarments.

Betty received more reports of destruction. Looters were targeting mission buildings all over the city: schools, hospitals, a YMCA, and homes. Student demonstrators egged them on, riding up and down the streets in cars and shouting through megaphones, "This is the day to overthrow Christianity!"

"What should we do?" Betty anxiously asked her sister. Their students were on the edge of panic. Without a telephone at the school, Mary agreed to run for help from the American consulate across the river in Nantai. Someone else from the school slipped out the back to reach Nationalist soldiers, billeted at a nearby temple.

Protesters kept pounding on the front gate, but the gateman refused to let anyone inside. At 4:00 p.m, he opened the door just a crack, thinking an officer from the temple had arrived to help them. More than thirty men—not the troops—forced their way inside.

Betty stood outside her house, arms folded, a forced smile on her face. The trespassers circled her, quizzically studying her and three other American teachers. Lin Pu-chi, his wife, and their daughter stayed out of sight. The men spoke Mandarin—evidently northerners. Betty felt there was nothing she could do but stand there, praying that the nearby soldiers would come to their rescue. She kept the mob at bay with sheer friendliness and calm.

"Are you French?" someone asked in Mandarin.

"No, no, American," answered another teacher who spoke the northern dialect.

"Meiguo," Betty repeated, mimicking her friend, for she spoke only the Fuzhou dialect.

After ten minutes, more rioters from the streets began pushing their way inside and racing up the walkway toward the campus. Now there were more than a hundred men eyeing the tall brick school building and missionary homes. Someone clapped his hands and yelled, "Let's go!"

Ni Guizhen raced down the steps of the Cushmans' home and held out her arms, trying to halt the advancing men. She pleaded with them to do no harm. Just then, twenty uniformed guards with bayoneted rifles marched into the compound. They pushed the mob back through the gate and onto the street.

The officer in charge posted guards at every gate and plastered a sign on the front door: "No foreigners here, just Chinese students and teachers."

Lin Pu-chi hurried with his wife and daughter back to their home in Nantai. The officers ordered Betty and Mary to stay indoors. The American women went to bed with their clothes on that night. Outside their window, a hundred troops encamped in the schoolyard.

The next day, the US consul in Fuzhou, Ernest B. Price, surveyed the damage. He no longer trusted Chinese officials to keep Americans safe. Even though the Wen Shan School had been spared, authorities had not stopped the systematic looting elsewhere. Indeed, some of the culprits were renegade soldiers wearing the KMT military insignia. At 3:00 a.m. on January 18, Price sent a telegram to the legation in Beijing and circulated a letter to all Americans in Fuzhou, urging women and children to evacuate. "We are now in a lull before the storm which may break at any time upon us," Price warned American residents.

Later that week, Betty and Mary Cushman boarded the destroyer USS *Pillsbury* bound for Manila. Fewer than a hundred Americans remained in Fuzhou.

MARKED MAN

Local authorities immediately captured and executed a dozen men for robbery and spreading rumors. Justice was swift, but the undercurrent of discontent, especially within mission schools, was surging.

Any foreigner who thought the January outbreak was only momentary lawlessness didn't see what was happening at a deeper level in China. Apathy was turning into action as Chinese people began seeing themselves as citizens responsible for the direction of their country. It was nothing less than a political awakening, and mission schools became a point of attack.

The Nationalists, now in control of vast swaths of China, launched a drive to "Recover Educational Rights." Mission schools would be tolerated but had to register with the government and install Chinese principals and directors. Religious services would become voluntary and the Bible excluded from the curriculum. Instead, students would attend a weekly ceremony to honor Sun Yat-sen.

Some schools, like Trinity, struggled with the question of registration, arguing that it would undermine their religious purpose. But others, such as Fukien Christian University (FCU), were swift to change. The ten-year-old university, supported by four American and British missions, had been built at the base of a mountain on the Min River, six miles downstream from Fuzhou.

Its American president, John Gowdy, understood what was happening and in December 1926 tendered his resignation. The university trustees in New York City balked, but Gowdy insisted, saying the political situation demanded it. He told them bluntly that he was standing in the way of the legitimate aspirations of the Chinese. "Nothing that I have seen in China has gone so deeply into the lives of the students as has this movement," Gowdy wrote.

At the start of 1927, the debate over the future of FCU turned into open confrontation. A pair of Chinese teachers had come under the influence of one of the originators of the anti-Christian movement in China, Tsai Yuen-pei, fifty-nine, a former chancellor of the elite Peking University. He advanced the ideas that science and religion were incompatible and that Christianity was a tool of imperialism and capitalism and a means of oppressing weaker nations.

In February, Tsai traveled to Fuzhou to work with a nucleus of young men and women who had studied in Beijing and now taught at mission schools, including FCU and Wen Shan Girls' School. He took the group to Amoy, another treaty port in Fujian, and as Gowdy described to his trustees, "thoroughly indoctrinated them so they came back here with the declared purpose of breaking up all the mission schools."

One of them was H. H. Chen, an alumnus of the university and one of the few Chinese professors on the faculty. Chen had been such a promising student that after he graduated from FCU, he went to Peking University for two years of further study. It was there that he met Tsai and other activists behind the anti-Christian movement. Chen thought it was not enough for the American president to resign or for the university to register. He demanded that the entire institution—buildings and all—be turned over to the government.

"Our university is too Christian, too ideal," Chen complained as he pressured students to see his way.

Late at night on March 21, 1927, his supporters called a meeting of the student body to put the matter to a vote. The students had no power to effect change, but it would send a potent message. Chen had invited two speakers from Fuzhou. Each delivered virulent anti-Christian harangues.

The student body was split. Opponents of the resolution tried to stop a vote with a two-hour filibuster. A vote was about to be taken when the lights in the hall went out—and forty-four opponents walked out, leaving the student union without a quorum. Not about to give up, Chen and his allies moved their fight to the city and a bigger audience. They boarded river launches for the trip downstream to Nantai. Armed with pots of glue, they plastered thousands of anti-Christian posters in red, yellow, and blue on walls. Chen rustled up more than a hundred supporters for a demonstration, including many younger students from mission high schools.

On Thursday, March 24, they took to the streets of the foreign settlement.

At 8:25 a.m. every morning, the chapel bells at Trinity College summoned students to morning prayers. The pealing chimes mixed with noisy magpies and warblers in the banyan trees on campus.

Lin Pu-chi still enjoyed attending the chapel at his alma mater. As he left campus after the short service, he thought of all the things he had to do that day. He needed to check on the cathedral, now nearly finished, with only a few furnishings to add. The consecration on May 1 was only five weeks away. Lin Pu-chi was proud that his extended family had donated a wooden lectern

The Reverend Lin Pu-chi (far right) traveled to Shanghai for the consecration on November 1, 1927, of the Reverend Ding Ing-ong (far left), who became an assistant bishop in Fujian. With them was the Right Reverend John Hind, the bishop of Fujian. Courtesy of Church Mission Society Archives, Cadbury Research Library, University of Birmingham.

for the altar. It was carved from hardwood and fashioned like an eagle, an Anglican symbol of unflinching faith: a bird capable of staring into the sun.

Lin Pu-chi, wearing his clerical collar and a Western-cut suit, headed toward the Bridge of Ten Thousand Ages.

Approaching from the opposite direction was a crowd spread across the width of the street. The protesters were young and loud, mostly teens and young men, all chanting. Lin Pu-chi was unconcerned; protests nowadays were common.

As they neared, he could start to make out their chants: *Down with Christian schools! Down with religion! Down with the church!* The closer they came, the more menacing they seemed, their faces contorted with anger, fists pumping, voices strained.

Lin Pu-chi kept to the sidewalk. He looked ahead, averting his eyes. Someone shouted his name. Others turned in his direction. Lin Pu-chi was easy to pick out—tall with an elongated face and so nearsighted that he was never seen without his eyeglasses. The mob flew toward him like wasps on the attack.

A hand reached out and grabbed him at the scruff of his neck. He fell back.

Others seized his hands and pinned them behind his back. He strained to break loose but there were too many arms, too many hands reaching at him, grabbing. He felt them wrapping twine around his wrists and then a thicker rope around his neck. An attacker tightened it with a quick tug.

Someone jammed a straw wastebasket upside down on his head and hung a big poster from his neck. *Waiguoren de zougou*, it screamed in crude black brush strokes. Running dog of foreigners!

The anti-Christian agitators needed a Christian to parade through the streets, and they'd just caught the dean of the Anglican cathedral. Everyone knew Rev. Lin Pu-chi. If they could scare him enough to recant his faith, even just for a terrified moment, they would be able to declare a victory that would resound through the city and beyond.

The man holding the rope yanked Lin Pu-chi forward like a dog on a leash. He tripped and fought to keep his balance.

He heard laughter. His glasses were cockeyed. He had trouble seeing.

Terror gripped Lin Pu-chi. Everything was happening so fast. There was one of him and a hundred, maybe more, of them. He caught the glint of a pistol in someone's hand. Out of the corner of his eye he could see police officers in the distance, but they did not come to his aid.

The mob was leading him somewhere but moving too fast. If he fell, he feared he would be trampled. His attackers could say it was an accident, not murder. *Was this how he would die?*

They took him to a platform built for the protest near the gates of Trinity. As he stood there, people slapped him in the face and cackled, *Running dog!*

Amid the screaming, he closed his eyes. He prayed for bravery and for his tormentors. He instinctively thought of St. Stephen, one of the first deacons of the apostles, who died from a stoning, becoming the first Christian martyr. He summoned the saint's last words: *Lord, lay not this sin to their charge.*

"Are you a Christian?" a ringleader shouted.

"Yes," Lin Pu-chi replied resolutely.

"Renounce your faith and we'll let you go," his tormentor bargained.

"Never," he said, unperturbed. "Kill me if you want."

"We will drag you through the streets if you don't renounce!"

He calmly refused. The students pulled him off the platform.

The parade had begun. They led him past the seminary where he taught; past the big church on a bluff overlooking the Min; past a Methodist mission school for boys. When the American principal saw the commotion, he dispatched a student to get a message to Lin Pu-chi. The teen was able to get close enough to offer to send for help from the US consulate.

"Tell him no," Lin Pu-chi replied. "This is a Chinese affair. I'll handle it."

The mob now headed in the direction of Hwa Nan College, a missionary school for women that was registered in the United States. The crowd was a mile away. A teacher from the college who saw the protesters ran ahead to warn its president. Ida Belle Lewis, a missionary from Iowa, raced from class to class, telling students to take cover in the home economics room in the basement. She ordered a guard to lock the front gate. But when the protesters arrived, they jumped over the wall, opened the gate, and dragged Lin Pu-chi inside. From the basement, Lewis could hear them outside. She took a deep breath and stepped outside to face the protesters.

Lewis started talking to demonstrators, not all of them local students. They badgered her on the evils of Christianity. She switched from the local dialect to Mandarin, even English, depending on whom she was talking to, and held her ground.

An exhausted Lin Pu-chi stood under a palm tree, bedraggled, his hands still bound with rope. While most of the protesters were engaged with Lewis, he maintained a calm demeanor with the captors nearest him and tried to reason with them.

They responded with bitter slogans.

"Christianity is a foreign religion that devours us!"

"No it's not," the priest quietly replied.

Taken aback by his mild response, they allowed him to continue.

"Do you know Confucius? Do you know Mencius?" asked Lin Pu-chi, ever the teacher. "Christianity is not a foreign faith. It's what the great sages told us to look forward to. And that is why I will never deny my Lord and Master."

The others had had enough of Lewis and turned to leave after nearly an hour of back-and-forth questioning. They pulled Lin Pu-chi on his leash out the gate.

"We'll go now," a leader shouted over his shoulder. "But we'll be back."

For all their bluster, the protesters had failed to garner support from onlookers in their attack on Lin Pu-chi. After three hours, Chinese marines finally intervened and freed the young priest from his captors. The next day, he went about his work as usual.

Twelve days after his trauma, Lin Pu-chi took his wife to the hospital. She delivered a son, Lin Baomin. They baptized him with the Christian name Paul, the name taken by the biblical Saul after his miraculous conversion on the road to Damascus—not long after he had encouraged a mob to stone to death St. Stephen.

· 8 ·

Alma Mater

Fuzhou, 1928

*T*he clock on the dormitory wall read half past midnight when a teenage student at Trinity College shuffled down the empty corridor on his way to the lavatory. He stopped. He sniffed and followed the scent of smoke to a stairwell leading to the attic.

His shouts woke the other boarders on the floor. The Chinese housemaster and older students grabbed heavy blankets and flailed at the fire in the stairwell. They snuffed out those flames, but above them, in the attic packed with surplus furniture, paper lanterns, and decorations for Christmas, an inferno roared.

A fire brigade raced through the streets of Nantai, bells clanging. Volunteers with buckets hurried past students and teachers standing in their nightclothes by Trinity's front gate. Other men on ladders with hoses worked through the night to prevent the fire from spreading to other buildings on campus.

At dawn on January 2, 1928, all that remained of the Anglo-Chinese School, one of three schools at Trinity, were its brick walls and foundation. The dormitory was in the same building as classrooms. Everything was lost. Desks, blackboards, chemistry beakers, microscopes, textbooks, notepaper, inkwells, fountain pens—gone. Only the absence of wind that night and a downpour kept the fire from destroying the entire five-acre campus. And no one that night could shake the thought that perhaps that was exactly what the blaze had been intended to do.

Maybe it had all been an accident. Certainly, it would have been hard for an arsonist to run up to the attic, start a fire, and fly down the stairs and out of the building without being detected. Yet eyewitnesses swore they smelled oil that night, raising the specter that an accelerant had been used to start the blaze. Rumors circulated, too, that all the pulleys on campus wells were broken. Had someone tried to sabotage the rescue effort?

But the most unsettling theory, the one that no one could entirely rule out, not even Bishop John Hind, was that someone from within the Trinity family had set the fire. For months, critics of mission schools, including extreme Nationalist and Communist supporters, had been contacting Trinity students and faculty in order to agitate from the inside. They viewed an elite school like Trinity, with its foreign pedigree, as hostile to the patriotic spirit of the times. The college was three schools in one, with 370 students split between a primary school, the Anglo-Chinese School (formerly called St. Mark's), and another middle school. The latter two were the equivalent of high schools in the American educational system.

The agitators could be patient: Bishop Hind suspected that a handful of students had enrolled that fall just to cause trouble. The Chinese principals of the three schools as well as some students had received anonymous letters warning them to leave or face danger. In one incident, an older boy in the Anglo-Chinese school, the son of a Chinese pastor, was returning to campus with friends after attending a political rally. Just outside the school gates, the group was jumped and the pastor's son was stabbed five times and injured. His attackers escaped.

Two days after the fire, Bishop Hind wrote "a wail" for help to the London office of the Church Missionary Society (CMS). The destruction of the Anglo-Chinese School was a severe blow to morale. He cautioned that if the school did not reopen, it would be a major defeat for all concerned. "We cannot desert our Chinese brothers at a time like this," Bishop Hind wrote. "It seems well, if possible, to keep the schools going, and yet the strain is very great, not only at TCF [Trinity College Fuzhou] but indeed all through the mission."

Trinity College set up temporary quarters and classrooms for the sixty students from the Anglo-Chinese School in private houses around Nantai. Still the violence continued. The following month, the American-run Foochow College in the old city was damaged by fire—its second arson attack in five months. And on May 28, a dormitory at Fukien Christian University (FCU) went up in flames while students and faculty were attending evening chapel. American and British diplomats urged missionaries to shut down their schools in protest. If provincial leaders could not guarantee their safety, they contended, the city should lose access to its finest educational institutions.

At FCU, the board of managers opted to remain open and replace the two-hundred-thousand-dollar dormitory. To close the university, they reasoned, would play into the hands of critics. Trinity College also moved to rebuild its damaged Anglo-Chinese building. But internally, the school struggled with the question of its future. The Nationalist government was insisting that all private schools register and abide by new regulations and limitations. Some senior missionaries on the faculty had threatened to resign, arguing that some of the rules would strip Trinity of its Christian identity and mission. Religious classes and chapel services had to be voluntary. English would be reduced to a subject taught in class but not the principal language for instruction. And foreigners could teach at schools but not run them.

Before the fall term started for the 1927–1928 academic year, the Anglican community had sent two emissaries—Lin Pu-chi and the first Chinese bishop in Fuzhou, the Right Reverend Ding Ing-ong—to meet with a recently appointed education commissioner for the province. The official was Christian and had studied at Columbia; his wife and mother attended Christ Church Cathedral. Sympathetic, he assured the men that Trinity could maintain its religious aim while complying with new rules. After the meeting, the school submitted an application, which was accepted by the government and confirmed in a letter delivered to the school on January 2, 1928—the very day of the fire.

The missionary in charge of Trinity, the Reverend W. P. W. Williams, placed the letter in a safe in his office. But the process of registration had one more step: finding his replacement. Williams had worked in Fuzhou for more than a quarter century and at one time had been principal of the Anglo-Chinese School, where he taught physiology and scripture. Given the new rules, Williams could not remain as president; it would have to go to a Chinese educator.

The board of managers for Trinity began searching for a Chinese candidate. The most obvious choice was an alumnus who wanted the job the least—Lin Pu-chi.

FILIAL DUTY

With the opening of Christ Church Cathedral in 1927, Lin Pu-chi's workaday world shifted to the main part of the city on the north side of the Min River, opposite his home in the foreign settlement in Nantai. Fuzhou was rapidly changing. Gone was the five-hundred-year-old city wall with its stone gates, replaced by a boulevard broad enough to accommodate automobiles. The city now boasted auto showrooms for Ford and Chevrolet and got its first paved road in 1928. Lined with trees and electric lights, the avenue stretched from the old city to the waterfront and was twice as wide as before.

Lin Pu-chi fell easily into his new role as the dean of the cathedral. It suited his intellectual temperament with its balance of church and educational

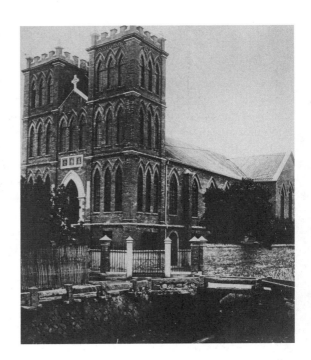

Lin Pu-chi was named dean of Christ Church Cathedral in Fuzhou, pictured here in 1927. Courtesy of Church Mission Society Archives, Cadbury Research Library, University of Birmingham.

responsibilities. On Sundays, he oversaw religious services in the cross-shaped nave, and on weekdays, he supervised a primary school in classrooms on the ground floor. Two mornings a week, he left the cathedral and sailed downstream to the FCU campus. The new Chinese president of the university, Lin Ching-jun, a youthful returned student who had studied at Oberlin, Harvard, Columbia, and Drew Theological Seminary, had asked Lin Pu-chi to teach theology. Lin Pu-chi readily agreed. He already was a member of the university's board of managers, representing the Anglican community, one of four missions jointly running the Protestant university. The invitation to teach was another attempt by local Christians to raise the Chinese profile of their schools.

Every day at 11:30 a.m., youngsters at the cathedral school attended morning chapel and listened to Bible stories told by their teachers. Sometimes, Lin Pu-chi invited guests to speak. On the first anniversary of the cathedral, an Australian physics professor from FCU gave a demonstration of one of the man-made wonders of the world: electricity. All the children from the cathedral school, plus students from three other Anglican schools in the neighborhood, filled a hall in the cathedral to see how electricity could light a room or power a motor. Afterward, everyone posed for photographs to mark the big day.

Lin Pu-chi was immersed in the day-to-day life of the cathedral. But in the fall of 1928, the board of managers of Trinity asked him to relinquish his

This photo of Lin Pu-chi, surrounded by students in Fuzhou, was published in a 1935 memoir by his mentor, the Reverend W. S. Pakenham-Walsh. Courtesy of W. S. Pakenham-Walsh, *Twenty Years in China.*

post as dean to take over as president of the college. Both the cathedral and Trinity were controlled by the diocesan synod for Fujian Province. Another time, such an assignment would have been an honor. But Lin Pu-chi had been at the cathedral for little more than a year, enjoyed the work, and did not want to leave. He respectfully declined. Bishop Hind asked a second time. Lin Pu-chi was caught in the enduring Confucian dilemma of duty versus ambition. If he declined again, it would be nothing less than canonical disobedience—as severe an offense as a son refusing the request of his father. Again, he had no real choice.

Lin Pu-chi cut short his tenure at Christ Church Cathedral and returned to Nantai as the first Chinese president of Trinity College.

BANYAN TREES AND LYCHEE NUTS

The Lin boys could not believe their good fortune. Their father's new job came with a new house, and not just any house. This was the former Russian consulate, a stately residence befitting a top diplomat in a major port city. The Russians sold it to missionaries from Dublin University in 1912, and the Irishmen used the property to create the Trinity campus.

After years of sharing a house with siblings and in-laws, Lin Pu-chi and his wife, Ni Guizhen, had more room than they could use. The two-story square residence was situated at the top of a tree-lined walkway. Its stucco walls were a pale shade of ochre, and it featured tall Palladian windows, a front portico, and a small balcony above the entrance. The first floor had a commodious parlor on one side, a formal dining room on the other, and a grand staircase leading to separate bedrooms for the couple and their children.

What Ni Guizhen liked most about her new home was the piano in the parlor. She played every night, often hymns that her children knew and could sing with her. She taught her eight-year-old daughter how to play; Martha showed true promise. She was a quiet, studious type, content to stay indoors and practice her scales. But her rambunctious brothers had the run of the campus. The two eldest, ages five and four, loved clambering up the branches of a giant banyan tree next to the house or gorging themselves on lychee fruit that they picked by the armful from trees on campus. The youngest son, only two, was too small to keep up with them and clung to his mother's skirt.

Lin Pu-chi could not pass through the gates of Trinity College without feeling waves of nostalgia. His mentor—the Irishman who had taught him English as a twelve-year-old—was the founder of Trinity. In the heart of campus stood a four-story brick tower with a brass bell from Dublin, erected in memory of the Reverend William S. Pakenham-Walsh after he retired in 1919 and sailed home. Lin Pu-chi was still in Philadelphia at the time. Teacher and student never met again. But every time Lin Pu-chi looked up at the bell tower, he was reminded of the legacy that had been entrusted to him.

Not everyone in the Trinity community was happy about his appointment. A faction of teachers and students bristled under his leadership. Their objections stemmed from old rivalries that divided the campus along lines of class and social standing. Trinity could be split into two castes. The upper one included the boys in the Anglo-Chinese School. They mainly came from Fuzhou and paid considerable tuition to be taught in English. Their education gave them ample options in life. They could continue to university, enter business, or become a clerk for the postal service or international telegraph company, which needed bilingual staff. The lower caste included students in the Middle School. They came mostly from villages, were too poor to pay for tuition, and were taught in Chinese. They were destined for low-paying jobs as teachers in mission schools or religious instructors in the field. It rankled them that they were made to feel beneath the boys in the Anglo-Chinese School, who mocked their peasant roots by calling them *digua*, or sweet potatoes. And it wasn't just the Middle School students who felt inferior; many of the Chinese teachers on the faculty, who were graduates of the school, shared their resentment.

While missionary supporters saw Lin Pu-chi as someone who was strong enough to pull all the schools together, the Middle School saw him as a polarizing figure. He was one of *them*, and some students felt that their principal, the Reverend Huang Yangying, had been passed over for the top job. Huang was older than Lin Pu-chi and came from a more humble background. He grew up in a village, graduated from the Middle School, and studied at the local seminary before joining the faculty to teach mathematics and scriptures. Students took their dissatisfaction with Lin Pu-chi straight to Bishop Hind, but he stood by the appointment.

One by one, teachers in the Middle School resigned, including Huang, who left Fuzhou for the British colony of Malaya. The Reverend E. M. Norton, a faculty member and onetime principal at Trinity, tried to bridge the rift. He explained with exasperation the dilemma to the CMS office in London: "I did all I could to get the teachers to stay on, but failed—not one of them would serve under Mr. Lin. I need not remind you that he is an old Anglo-Chinese school boy."

Lin Pu-chi scrambled to replace the teachers, but the new hires were universally seen as inferior to their predecessors in scholarship, teaching ability, and class management. Norton wrote: "This, plus the critical attitude of the boys, provided material for an explosion."

Explode it did. One night in May, Williams was making his evening rounds in the dormitory of the Middle School. As was his custom, he patrolled the hallway, telling students to turn out the lights. When he peered inside one room, he was aghast at what he saw: three teenagers sitting on a bed, naked from the waist down. The flustered priest accused them of indecency. The students claimed they were merely darning their underpants, which was why they had taken them off in the first place.

The next morning, Williams told Lin Pu-chi to expel the boys. He complied. The students were accused of "immorality" and thrown out of school. The other roommates protested, calling the punishment too harsh. Neither Williams nor Lin Pu-chi backed down. News of the expulsions rocked the Middle School. In a gesture of solidarity, all of the classmates of the accused held a sit-down in their classroom, refusing to study or even move from their desks. Williams called for their expulsion, too.

Three days later, ten students from the Middle School appealed to the administration for leniency. Sympathetic teachers lent their support to the students to no avail. Not to be cowed, students circulated a protest petition and began organizing a demonstration. They would exploit the expulsion of the students as yet another example of the imperious ways of foreigners and their Chinese minions.

On May 17, the Lin children and their mother left the big house on the hill for the safety of a relative's home. A brother-in-law on the Ni side of the family, meanwhile, lurked in the street by Trinity. He had a switchblade and pistol in his pocket if anyone tried to harm Lin Pu-chi.

Outside the locked front gates of Trinity, as many as three hundred protesters shouted slogans and held banners. The mob included students and teachers from the Middle School plus anti-Christian agitators from town. Their jeers echoed through the campus.

Down with the imperialist running dog Lin Pu-chi!
Down with British imperialist Williams!
Williams get out of China!

Police were summoned to guard the gates. Demonstrators took their protest to the city, marching in two lines to deliver petitions to the provincial offices of the education commissioner and the ruling Nationalist Party. Along the way, they passed out pamphlets denouncing Trinity and its leaders.

The following day, the city's main Chinese newspaper ran a front-page article under the headline "Great Tempest: Trinity's Anti-imperialist Student Movement." Editors published the full text of the protesters' leaflet.

It was happening all over again for Lin Pu-chi—"running dog" taunts, threats, angry mobs, verbal assaults. His mentor in Ireland, the Reverend Pakenham-Walsh, would later describe him as a "marked man" for the anti-Christian movement stirring up students. The hostility toward him, which first flared in 1927, showed no signs of abating. Lin Pu-chi did not help the situation. Just as he was resolute in his faith, he stubbornly resisted any challenge by those he viewed as misguided. His critics saw this as arrogance; he would have called it certitude.

The board of managers of Trinity, chaired by Lin Pu-chi and including Chinese and Western staff, held an emergency meeting. They acted decisively. On May 29, they voted to shut down the Middle School and send students home. The provincial government was not happy with the decision, and an official with the education commission criticized Lin Pu-chi for his handling of the situation.

But the damage from the incident was irrevocable. Families received letters over the summer announcing that the Middle School would not re-open for the fall semester. Instead of maintaining warring schools, the board of managers decided that Trinity would be better off with only one—the Anglo-Chinese School. If the diocesan synod needed teachers and religious instructors to fill their mission schools and chapels, the supply would have to come from those students.

In his report to the CMS headquarters in England, Lin Pu-chi explained: "The board of managers had several long and very careful discussions . . . and on July 11 they decided that the department should be closed in the autumn. . . . The students, some seventy of them, were given letters of transfer to other institutions in the province and elsewhere. How things would develop eventually remains to be seen, but we are confident that the managers would have the best interests of this college and the Church in view of whatever action they may adopt, and that nothing but good would come out of the sad turmoil."

A CHINESE CHURCH

When classes resumed in the fall of 1929, the reorganized Anglo-Chinese School had 192 students and the primary school an additional 191. "Things went on without a hitch," Lin Pu-chi assured the CMS office. "Our anticipated fears and troubles vanished like mist."

On the surface, life did go on. Interest in the school remained strong, with more boys applying than could be admitted. Trinity had twenty-six teachers and no trouble recruiting new ones from mission universities such as St. John's. There was much to commend on the part of students, too. Lin Pu-chi reported to England that senior boys were teaching laborers who worked on campus how to read and write. Other students joined a citywide health campaign, sweeping roads with brooms and clearing fetid ditches around campus.

But the troubles at Trinity did not "vanish like the mist." Instead, Lin Pu-chi was racked with doubt. He had returned from Philadelphia a decade earlier with high aspirations, both spiritual and professional. He saw himself as being in the vanguard of a great transformation of China. The quest for truth, he wrote in 1924, was central to man's search for meaning. In an English-language article in the *Chinese Recorder*, he explained:

> Says Christ, who is the Truth, "The truth shall make you free." China as the oldest existing nation in the world has contributed her quota of truth, which her ancient sages and heroes discovered. But in no era of her prolonged history did she need, nay, hunger for more truth than she does at present. She craves for new, practical truths in relation to every phase of her national existence. In arts, in science, in government, and in all civic problems, she craves for the right principles.

He said his generation was eagerly searching for spiritual guidance as well, and it fell to the church to show them the way. But how? On this, he echoed the sentiments of the times, the feeling that China as a nation needed to stand on its own and control its destiny. Over the millennium, he wrote, China had been very capable of absorbing alien cultures. Lin Pu-chi cited as an example Buddhism, which was introduced from India two thousand years earlier and transformed into a virtually indigenous religion. "The Chinese have given

Buddhist literature a Chinese vocabulary, a Chinese style, and a Chinese presentation," he wrote. "Chinese accretions of thought have become part and parcel of the original Indian religion, and have been made her own. The whole system has been 'Sinified.'"

In his article for the missionary magazine, he asked why Christianity couldn't be "Sinified":

> This has in recent years become a household phrase. It means that the Chinese Church will ultimately take over all evangelistic, medical, educational, financial and administrative responsibilities. In the matter of architecture, liturgy, polity, theology, literature and various other things, there may be modifications and alterations to suit the Chinese psychology and usage. And not until then will Christianity in China become "Chinese." But he greatly errs who thinks that a "Sinified Church" will be so much transformed as to be totally different from the rest of Christianity in this world. There will still be traces of former connections. Continental Christianity, English Christianity, American Christianity will all leave indelible marks upon Chinese Christianity.

He had been thirty when he wrote those words. Now he was thirty-five and feeling ineffective, toiling in a job that was not of his own choosing. More than half the students at Trinity did not come from Christian families. The hope, indeed the mission of the school, was to lead them to the church through the teaching of scripture and exposure to Christian ideals. But in his first three terms, only one student had elected to be baptized. "It may be that the recent anti-Christian movement in China has a deterring effect upon the progress of the Church in general," Lin Pu-chi explained with great understatement to the CMS office in London.

Lin Pu-chi felt thwarted in his work. Even though Fuzhou had close to a million people, the foreign settlement in Nantai where he lived and worked was small and confining. Try as he might, he could not shake the stigma of being a lackey for foreigners, even though he was the one pushing and prodding missionaries from the inside to make the church more Chinese. He felt trapped and exposed in Nantai. In this current environment, he was like a carp swimming in a barrel. Whenever anti-Christian critics needed a target, he was an easy shot.

He tendered his resignation but was turned down.

SHANGHAI BROTHER

In the spring of 1930, Lin Pu-chi had to make an emergency trip to Shanghai with his wife, Ni Guizhen, whose health needed immediate attention.

She suffered from endometritis, an inflammation of the lining of the uterus. Doctors in Fuzhou advised her to have a hysterectomy and suggested she have it done in Shanghai. The medical school of St. John's ran a top hospital for women and children, St. Elizabeth's. Ni Guizhen had given birth to five children in the span of seven years, one of whom did not survive past infancy. Her mother had nine children, her mother-in-law ten. But Ni Guizhen's childbearing days were over.

On May 9, 1930, the couple boarded a coastal steamer and headed north to Shanghai, a city both of them loved from their school days, Lin Pu-chi at St. John's and Ni Guizhen at the McTyeire School. Back in Shanghai, the couple was able to reconnect with Ni Guizhen's younger brother, Watchman Nee. From the hospital, Lin Pu-chi had to walk only a few blocks to visit his brother-in-law, who lived on a lane off Hardoon Road in the center of the International Settlement.

The fitful political unrest across the nation made headlines. But a quieter, spiritual hunger was evident among many young Chinese—a yearning that was fed by popular Christians like Watchman Nee, who operated outside the zone of mission churches. Watchman Nee had a personality that drew people in. Tall and handsome with a sonorous voice that was not loud but soothing, he felt established churches, with their foreign ancestry and traditions, were too removed from the experience of most Chinese converts. He sought a simpler form of worship, separate from denominational groups, and his appeal was strong.

This troubled clerics such as Bishop Hind, who warned that such independent evangelists were starting what amounted to new Christian communions. They were fostering disunity, the bishop cautioned. Lin Pu-chi had to agree that there was much about his brother-in-law that was unorthodox. But he privately held an abiding respect for the younger man. Watchman Nee was only twenty-seven and already had written his magnum opus, *The Spiritual Man*. It was not a textbook but a chronicle of his religious pilgrimage and an attempt to lead Christians to the innermost core of their spiritual being. Like Lin Pu-chi, Watchman Nee was trying to quench man's eternal thirst for truth. But unlike his Anglican brother-in-law, Watchman Nee was drawing followers by the thousands in Shanghai and beyond. Lin Pu-chi, on the other hand, struggled to find even one student at Trinity to baptize into the Anglican church.

Ni Guizhen's surgery went well, and a month later the couple returned to Fuzhou. Lin Pu-chi went back to work, but a change had come over him. He knew he was at a crossroad in his life. He could stay at Trinity and try to battle the unrelenting anti-Christian forces aligned against him. Or he could leave Fuzhou and maybe return to Shanghai in search of more meaningful work.

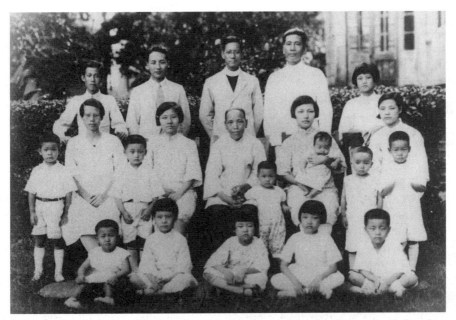

Before Lin Pu-chi departed Fuzhou, the entire family posed for this 1931 portrait. Rev. Lin, wearing his clerical collar, stands behind his mother, who is seated in the second row. The author's father, Paul Lin, stands in the second row, the second child from the right. Courtesy of Lin Family Collection.

At the end of the fall term in 1930, he submitted his resignation. This time, Bishop Hind accepted.

Lin Pu-chi told the bishop that he would seek new work outside of Fujian. Temporarily, his friends at FCU had found him an assignment as an interpreter. A fact-finding team of Christian laymen from America was visiting China to appraise the work and efficacy of missionaries at the request of philanthropist John D. Rockefeller Jr. The anti-Christian hostility was raising deep questions among American churches about the value and direction of missionaries not only in China but also around the world. The group would visit FCU, and Lin Pu-chi would serve as a translator during their stay. After that, he was unsure of his family's next move. He told Bishop Hind that he eventually hoped to find a position on the faculty of St. John's.

"In many ways I am sorry that we were not able to keep him in the diocese," Bishop Hind wrote to the CMS office. "But I am not sure that he was wrong in thinking that it would be better for him to leave us for awhile. He has had to encounter many difficulties and opposition in his work and is consequently rather unpopular with certain people. He may not always have acted in the wisest possible way, but he has been in some very tight corners."

III

A HOUSE DIVIDED

· 9 ·

Watchman Nee

Shanghai, 1932

The rector rushed from room to room. At any hour, St. Peter's Church in the International Settlement of Shanghai could start to receive an onslaught of people fleeing for their lives. The clergyman directed volunteers as they carried bedding into classrooms and cleaned out a janitor's closet for use as a makeshift washroom. Men rearranged pews in the sanctuary and made room for more people in the parish house. They carried crates of vegetables and burlap sacks of rice into the kitchen. Women sorted through a pile of donated coats, sweaters, pants, hats, scarves, and other winter clothing.

It was January 28, 1932. Pastor Yu Ensi, who had been at St. Peter's for only four months, knew he had to act quickly and decisively. The clock was ticking: at 6:00 p.m., Japan would "take necessary steps" if the Chinese mayor of Shanghai did not apologize for anti-Japanese provocations. St. Peter's was a safe haven, neutral territory inside the International Settlement. But the rest of the sprawling city was vulnerable to attack by Japanese marines. To the north of St. Peter's, in Hongkou Park on the opposite side of Suzhou Creek, more than two thousand Japanese soldiers waited for orders. Their presence already had sown panic. Chinese men, pulling wheelbarrows and rickshaws piled with belongings and topped with children, pleaded to get through checkpoints into the International Settlement before the deadline.

The city had been bracing itself for four months. It was back on September 18 that relations between China and Japan ruptured with an explosion in northeastern China, known as Manchuria to outsiders. A bomb damaged a Japanese-owned railway, prompting Japan to invade the territory and establish the puppet state of Manchukuo. Since the so-called Mukden Incident, anti-Japanese sentiment had spread throughout China, whose citizens boycotted Japanese products. On January 18, a Chinese mob in Shanghai attacked five

121

Japanese monks, killing one. A Japanese gang retaliated by burning down a Chinese factory and stabbing a constable to death.

Japan then issued its ultimatum. It demanded an official apology for the attack on the monks; punishment for the assailants; compensation for the victims; and the suppression of anti-Japanese organizations and activities. In case anyone thought this was a bluff, the Japanese navy positioned a dozen gunboats and an aircraft carrier on the Huangpu River. The flagship *Ataka* tied up at the dock next to the Japanese consulate. British and American troops assumed positions to defend the International Settlement.

With preparations at St. Peter's complete, Pastor Yu put his daughter on a train for Hangzhou, where she could wait out the situation with family there. His wife stayed at the church while Yu returned to their home in the Chinese Zhabei District. He bolted the door and waited.

That afternoon at 1:50 p.m., radios crackled with a news flash: the mayor of Shanghai had accepted the demands. That night, Pastor Yu and most of the city went to bed thinking a crisis had been averted.

At 11:10 p.m., under a moonless sky, an elite unit of Japanese marines bowed to the east, toward their emperor in Tokyo, and yelled "Banzai!" A Japanese admiral had been tipped off that Chinese troops still were massed in the Zhabei area. Columns of Japanese soldiers, on foot and in trucks, advanced through deserted streets, firing flares to light the way. Searchlights mounted on armored cars picked out Chinese snipers on rooftops or in alleys. Residents behind closed doors would hear the crack of a sniper's rifle followed by the drumming of machine-gun fire. On the Huangpu, Japanese seaplanes on the deck of the aircraft carrier roared to life and rose into the night sky. The planes wheeled toward carefully selected targets: factories, cotton mills, certain houses, shops, cinemas, a railway station—even the sprawling Commercial Press with its inventory of six hundred thousand books. The bombing began.

Pastor Yu's house rocked from the explosions. He crept out his front door but ducked back inside as gunshots ricocheted off the walls.

Urban warfare dragged on in Zhabei, street by street, for weeks. From the eerie safety of the International Settlement, expatriates sipped martinis at rooftop restaurants and lifted binoculars to get a closer look at the fires destroying Chinese neighborhoods after bombardments from Japanese planes. By mid-February, Japanese forces had essentially taken over the city. Down at street level, Japanese soldiers at checkpoints pointed bayonets at the chests of Chinese refugees, who were searched for weapons before being allowed to pass into the city's foreign zones.

Five weeks after the fighting began, Pastor Yu was able to make his way back to St. Peter's. When he arrived on March 5, he found 226 refugees—45 men, 119 women, and 62 children—crammed inside the church compound.

At night, the sanctuary became a dormitory, end to end with bedrolls. Most of the refugees were from sister churches around Shanghai, mostly Anglican as well as some Presbyterian and Baptist congregations. They came from the other side of Suzhou Creek and from nearby cities that had been drawn into the conflict—such as Wusong, fifteen miles downstream, where Japanese gunships had fired at close range into a Chinese fort.

Pastor Yu organized volunteers. One committee handled sanitation; another helped with the children. A medical team inoculated everyone against the spread of diseases such as cholera. Pregnant refugees overwhelmed St. Elizabeth's Hospital next door. Triple the usual number of newborns filled the nursery; when cribs ran out, nurses placed bookcases flat on the floor and placed babies inside the shelf space.

China's appeals to the League of Nations led to a ceasefire on May 5. The members of St. Peter's raised $1,369.69 to help families return to their homes or find new places to live.

Pastor Yu returned to the spiritual needs of his congregation, organizing Sunday services, weekday classes and meetings, and prayer services in five locations. The church's strong social mission also demanded his time and attention. An assistant priest was clearly needed.

Pastor Yu had someone in mind: a cleric from Fuzhou who shared their belief that the future of the church depended on shifting responsibility from foreign missionaries to Chinese Christians. The rector knew him from Kaifeng, where he had replaced Yu as headmaster of a small Anglican school. The pastor sent a message: Would this priest be interested in joining them in Shanghai?

The Lin boys fidgeted and fussed in their seats on the train to the city. Their parents passed out hard-boiled eggs to keep them quiet. The boys were eight, seven, and five. Their eleven-year-old sister did everything in her power to ignore them, keeping her eyes fixed on the expanse of flat farmland flashing past her window.

Kaifeng had not been a good fit for Lin Pu-chi, and he had welcomed the invitation to join St. Peter's. When he left Fuzhou in 1931, he had expected to join the faculty of his alma mater, St. John's University in Shanghai. But with the world economy collapsing, the position never materialized. The post at St. Andrew's was the best he could do. Remote, flat, and dusty, the ancient city of Kaifeng—the country's capital a thousand years earlier—was strafed by Gobi Desert winds in the winter. Once, when the youngest of the boys stepped outside to urinate, a frigid gust was so strong that it blew him off the back porch.

Lin Pu-chi's ambitions were too large for Kaifeng. In Fuzhou, he held important positions with the largest Anglican diocese; in Kaifeng, he ran a school for one of the smallest. Confident and exacting, he was critical of the work of those around him, which made him unpopular with coworkers.

But St. Peter's in Shanghai—now that was exceptional, like few other churches in China. The American Episcopal Church built the church in 1898, but the parish became independent of the foreign mission in 1914. This absence of missionary ties appealed to Lin Pu-chi. Since his days as a young priest in Fuzhou, he had advocated for a thoroughly Chinese or *Sinified* church. Here was one of the few parishes actually doing it. It was self-governing and self-supporting and engaged in its own evangelizing. Less well known was that some of its members had communist leanings, which they kept private. The previous rector, the Reverend Dong Jianwu, had secretly joined the Chinese Communist Party, and during the war with Japan, he hid confidential party documents under the altar of St. Peter's as well as under floorboards in the choir's changing room and parish house.

Lin Pu-chi would draw no salary from St. Peter's. Instead, like Pastor Yu, he found work as an assistant headmaster for a public school for Chinese boys operated by the Shanghai Municipal Council (SMC), the governing body of the International Settlement. Pastor Yu had a similar job at another SMC secondary school. The secular position paid Lin Pu-chi more than twice what he could earn at a mission school.

In September, the Lin family moved into a new home in Wing On Terrace, a development of identical brick houses packed tightly on a curving *longtang*, or lane, only as wide as a car. The Hong Kong millionaires who owned the giant Wing On Department Store on Nanjing Road in the International Settlement built the homes and rented out many of the units to their employees. The neighborhood was drab and utilitarian, consisting of four parallel lanes of about two hundred houses with electricity and running water but no flush toilets. Because Lin Pu-chi earned enough money through his school job, the family could afford to hire a cook and an *ayi*, or "housekeeper."

Only four months after the ceasefire with the Japanese, Lin Pu-chi had moved his family into the heart of Little Tokyo. Around the corner from their home loomed the Japanese garrison, a modern, concrete building with a courtyard where from dawn to dusk passersby heard menacing shouts and grunts coming from soldiers running drills. Japan, like Britain and the United States, kept troops stationed in Shanghai for the defense of the settlement. The Lin boys tittered to see Japanese officers walking naked from their barracks to a bathhouse across the street. But it made their father uneasy to live next door to the masterminds of Yi Erba, or One-Two-Eight, as the January 28 attack had become known.

A few blocks west of the family's home, the Zhabei District lay in ruins. Pastor Yu had lost everything—his house, furniture, and clothing. Lin Pu-

The Lin brothers in Shanghai around 1937. Left to right, Paul, Jim, and Tim. Courtesy of Lin Family Collection.

chi's indignation was further piqued every day when he went to work at the Public School for Chinese Boys on Haskell Road in Hongkou. A wall topped with barbed wire and bolstered with sandbags stretched across the far end of the street, a glaring line of demarcation between the unscathed Japanese enclave and the destroyed Chinese side.

Lin Pu-chi had been at St. Peter's for only a month when he decided to use the Sunday pulpit to rouse the congregation. It was October 9, the eve of National Day in 1932. With his wife and children sitting in a pew before him, he delivered a sermon on "National Day in a Time of National Crisis." This was not a sermon about turning the other cheek. It was more a call to action, backed by a belief that God was on their side.

This crisis, he said, was cause for heartache. "We, all without exception citizens of the Republic of China, take Japan's invasion of three provinces in the Northeast as an occasion of great shame," Lin Pu-chi told the crowd of three hundred. "We must inure ourselves for future trials, and we swear that one day we will wipe out this humiliation."

Stay optimistic and positive, Lin Pu-chi encouraged in a strong, firm voice. "Many believe that Manchuria has already been completely forfeited to Japan. I believe this is a major misconception. If we four hundred million Chinese do not allow Manchuria to be lost, then who can take it? If we maintain a spirit that we will 'stage a comeback,' how can we say that Manchuria will not be again part of China? We Christians, on this National Day with nothing to celebrate, still have one thing worthy of celebration. We believe God is just and is the advocate of justice."

It was his gift to them, a reminder of the righteousness of God.

HEADMASTER LIN

The Lin children felt they had arrived in another country the first time the family strolled along Shanghai's Bund, the fabled promenade on the western bank of the Huangpu River. They tilted their heads back to see the tops of the grand granite buildings. They paused at the Hongkong and Shanghai Bank, where a pair of giant brass lions stood guard. For good luck, the boys rubbed the paws of the lions, which gleamed like gold from so many visitors doing the same. In later years, their parents sometimes rewarded them for good behavior with lunch on Nanjing Road. It could be a bowl of borscht at a white-tablecloth Russian restaurant or a hot dog and frosty bottle of Coca-Cola at an American café.

The Lin family had joined three million people in Shanghai, the sixth-largest city in the world, behind London, New York, Tokyo, Berlin, and Chicago. Despite the city's international profile, Shanghailanders, as foreigners were called, accounted for a mere seventy thousand residents. The Bund gave first-time visitors the impression that they had arrived at a cohesive, Western-style city. In fact, Shanghai was a patchwork of many disparate districts, with the fetid, black waters of Suzhou Creek serving as a key dividing line. Lin Pu-chi conducted services at St. Peter's on the south side of the tributary but lived and worked on the north side.

It was not easy to be a son of Lin Pu-chi. Martha, the eldest child and only daughter, had it better than her siblings. Her father didn't dote on her, but from the perspective of the boys, he treated her more gently. She was quiet to begin with and preferred to stay indoors practicing the used piano her parents bought for the Wing On house. Studious and obedient, she caused her parents no worry. Of the sons, the youngest, Paul, was sickly and unable to keep up with Jim and Tim, who were only a year apart. The two elder sons spent their days racing scooters in the lane or chasing each other on wooden stilts. For Christmas one year, each received the same gift: one roller skate. Jim got the left one, Tim the right one. They were going to have to learn to share, their father told them.

If Lin Pu-chi was stern at home, he gave his sons a double dose of discipline at school. The Public School for Chinese Boys was the largest of five secondary schools operated by the SMC for the benefit of local boys. With seven hundred students, it was far bigger than any of the schools Lin Pu-chi ran in Fuzhou or Kaifeng. Students studied Chinese classics as well as spoken English, with most heading to jobs in commerce at foreign banks or trading firms. Classes took field trips to the theater and had special assemblies, such as a film screening about the snow-capped American territory of Alaska, presented by the Eastman Kodak Company. Lin Pu-chi helped to start a student magazine and, ever the orator, coached students for the annual Speech Day competition at the end of the academic year. One year, the event drew six hundred VIP guests to the Ritz Theatre in Hongkou and ended with his wife's handing out prizes onstage to the winners.

At school, Lin Pu-chi shared a spacious office with his English counterpart, Mr. J. Moffat. At lunchtime, when most students went home to eat, the Lin boys had to dine with their father in his office. A school cook prepared them a light meal of soup, noodles, or dumplings. Afterward, everyone took a fifteen-minute nap. On a table next to his desk, Lin Pu-chi kept a stack of papers and tests from his classes. Once, Jim could not help himself and took a peek at his own exam for biology class, which his father taught. He had studied more for that test than any other and sailed through the questions. He was crestfallen to see in his father's handwriting a disappointing "B."

"B?" Jim asked incredulously. "I got everything right. Why did I get a B?"

"You're my son," Lin Pu-chi replied. "I couldn't give you an A because everyone would think it was favoritism."

Lin Pu-chi set a high bar, expecting from his children what he demanded of himself. Martha and Paul consistently delivered. But for Jim and Tim, earning top grades did not come easily. One semester, Jim proudly presented his father with his report card that had a smattering of hard-earned As. His father reacted with a tepid, "Oh." In one syllable, he conveyed his disappointment, a sting that never went away.

Family provided pleasure. The children looked forward to seeing their uncles on their mother's side; Watchman Nee and his younger brother George often came over for supper. Dinnertime came alive with conversation. Watchman Nee loved to drive and had access to a Fiat sedan. "Why don't we call your uncles?" Ni Guizhen might tell her children on a sunny Saturday. When they arrived, the boys would squeal, "Take us for a ride!" Two people would sit up front with Watchman Nee, and everyone else would cram into the back. The boys hung out the windows as Watchman Nee motored up and down North Sichuan Road. As a treat for Martha, Watchman Nee once took her and her mother—minus the boys—on a special sightseeing trip to Hangzhou, the capital of neighboring Zhejiang Province, set on the idyllic West Lake.

A quiet moment for Ni Guizhen at a park in Shanghai in the 1930s. Courtesy of Lin Family Collection.

Despite the differences in their church lives, Lin Pu-chi enjoyed seeing his younger brother-in-law. Watchman Nee, almost six feet tall with an open face and toothy smile, had a magnetic personality—the opposite of the older, intimidating Lin Pu-chi. Over steaming plates of food, the men talked of everything but religion, at least in front of the children. But when Watchman Nee openly groused about the paternalistic way missionaries treated local Christians, he privately had the sympathetic ear of his brother-in-law. Missionaries, Watchman Nee once complained, treat Chinese Christians like they were "just a kind of little toy terrier to be taken up and set down without their opinion being consulted." Lin Pu-chi did not take such an extreme view but understood full well the younger man's impatience and frustration.

Lin Pu-chi, who had spent two formative years in the United States, enjoyed listening to his brother-in-law talk about his world travels and adventures. In 1933, Watchman Nee had circled the globe, traveling to London by way of Singapore before sailing to New York and crossing Canada by rail to Vancouver. An evangelical Christian group known as the Plymouth Brethren had extended the invitation to him to visit them in various cities. They wanted to meet the man whose vast biblical knowledge and flair for speaking were generating attention and excitement in China.

Watchman Nee once regaled the family with stories about a motor trek through the snowy mountains of southwestern China. Watchman Nee had a friend, a fellow Christian and wealthy businessman who went by the name Shepherd Ma, who owned a Ford. In the spring of 1934, the pair loaded the backseat of the car with cans of gasoline and boxes of gospel pamphlets. With Shepherd Ma doing most of the driving, they took off from a port city on the Yangtze River in Hunan and headed south to the capital of Changsha before crossing Guizhou Province and reaching elevations as high as six thousand feet in Yunnan. Whenever they stopped, Watchman Nee stood up in the car and spoke to crowds. They were twentieth-century versions of the early missionaries, motivated by an intense need to evangelize, but instead of being carried in sedan chairs by porters, they traversed rough roads from behind the wheel of a black sedan. (A few months later, Mao Zedong and thousands of Red Army troops embarked on their legendary Long March through the western and northern parts of China to evade Nationalist troops.)

After he came back from that trip, Watchman Nee's life took a major turn. He was going to marry his childhood friend, Charity Chang. The news thrilled Ni Guizhen. The women also had been friends in Fuzhou, but Charity moved to Shanghai when she was still young. She went on to study biology in Beijing at Yanjing University, an elite missionary school, and returned to Shanghai, where she taught at an SMC school. The marriage announcement was as much about love as the willpower of a headstrong mother, in this case Watchman Nee's. Lin Heping was anxious to see her thirty-one-year-old son betrothed and, after some initial hesitation about the attractive and educated Charity, agreed to the match. Not everyone reacted well to the idea. Charity's aunt thought the poor preacher beneath her accomplished niece and publicly said so. Some of Watchman Nee's followers, conversely, thought Charity too worldly for such a pious man. Lin Pu-chi tried to mediate, assuring all sides that the young couple should have a chance at happiness. But his mother-in-law forced the issue. In October 1934, as Watchman Nee concluded a series of religious talks in Hangzhou, Lin Heping surprised him: he was getting married right then and there.

On October 19, Watchman Nee and Charity exchanged vows before hundreds of guests, including a beaming Ni Guizhen. Her friend was now family.

In 1934, the population of Shanghai was swelling, and the congregation of St. Peter's grew with it. Members wanted to open a new branch on the western edge of the city and took advantage of an offer from a Chinese Christian headmistress to use her school's assembly hall on weekends for free. Lin Pu-chi was asked to lead the worship while his wife, Ni Guizhen, was recruited to play the piano for services.

Lin Heping surrounded by two of her daughters and two daughters-in-law. Ni Guizhen stands top left, and her childhood friend and the wife of Watchman Nee, Charity, stands next to her. Courtesy of Lin Family Collection.

The family's Sunday commute thus changed from a tolerable two-mile ride to St. Peter's to a grueling hour-long journey to the far western suburbs of the International Settlement. It prompted Lin Pu-chi to act on an idea that had been brewing for some time. The atmosphere in Hongkou was becoming worse as tension between Japan and China intensified. All-out war seemed inevitable. Japan was making more demands for territory in the northeast, in effect hacking off one province after another. Lin Pu-chi felt it was time to move. He found a terraced house on a quiet lane off Jiaozhou Road that was closer to St. Peter's as well as the western chapel. The building was erected before 1900 and was not as modern as the Wing On home, but its location was more convenient. And it was far from the Japanese garrison.

In 1935, the family packed its belongings and headed across Suzhou Creek. Ni Guizhen was enthusiastic: she'd live across the street from her brother and his new wife, her friend Charity.

HARDOON ROAD

Watchman Nee and Charity had a soft spot for the youngest Lin son, who was cute and precocious, having skipped several grades in primary school.

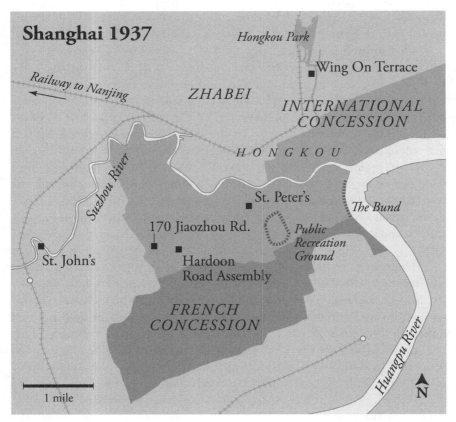

The layout of Shanghai in 1937, including points of interest for the Lin family. Courtesy of Sterling Chen.

The couple had an open-door policy for their nephew, who was allowed to visit whenever he desired. Their house was down a lane on the other side of Jiaozhou Road. Young Paul enjoyed his uncle's vast collection of books and American magazines. He would curl up in his uncle's library, flipping through issues of *Life* and *Reader's Digest* as well as the occasional rare find like a Ford Motor Company magazine with an article about his uncle's car trip across southwestern China.

Ni Guizhen saw Charity often, and it was only natural for her occasionally to accompany her sister-in-law and brother to religious gatherings at the Christian assembly they attended on Hardoon Road. Outsiders called their group the Little Flock, a moniker they detested. It came from the name of a hymnal Watchman Nee had published, *Xiaoqun Shige*, or *Little Flock Hymns*, which included a collection of songs he had written or translated from English.

They disliked the Little Flock label because it made them sound like they were part of a denomination, similar to calling someone an Anglican or Methodist.

That was the last thing they wanted. The popularity of Watchman Nee had as much to do with how he worshipped as what he taught from the scriptures. The Shanghai Christian Assembly had no ties to missions, no affiliation with Protestant groups. They did not attend a church in the traditional sense but shared fellowship in a "local church." Their meeting place had no pews, no stained-glass windows, no cross on the roof. There was no formal liturgy; the only customs they adopted were traditions directly from the Bible, such as baptism by immersion and the breaking of bread. Most significantly, they were not led by clerics. Members called each other "brother" and "sister" and rejected the stepladder hierarchy of deacons, priests, and bishops that characterized other churches. This, they felt, was a more pure form of worship, as close as modern Christians could come to the ways of the early followers of Christ, as exemplified by the original missionary, Saint Paul.

Theirs was a truly homegrown movement, free of the history and foreign baggage of establishment missions. This appealed to many Chinese whose swelling sense of national pride and purpose fostered a desire to distance themselves from institutions with a foreign taint. They yearned for guidance and hope amid the chaos in China, marked by not only warfare between China and Japan but also civil war between the Nationalists and Communists and economic hardship from the Great Depression. Splendor and squalor lived side by side in Shanghai. Thousands existed hand to mouth in overcrowded shantytowns, unable to find work and too frightened to venture beyond the stability of Shanghai.

Watchman Nee offered the assurance of salvation at a time when people needed an escape from the misery all around them. He made people think about how they related to God at the core of their being, their spirit—not just in their rational mind. He took this message beyond Shanghai to neighboring cities such as Hangzhou and Nanjing; north to Beijing and Shandong Province; south throughout Fujian; and west to the ports of Wuhan and Chongqing. Worshippers wrote down his talks and sermons and gathered them into books that were not only distributed among Christians in China but also translated for believers around the world.

The focal point of his activity was the assembly hall off Hardoon Road in the heart of the International Settlement. In 1927, Watchman Nee took over three adjacent houses and combined the ground-floor space to create one open room. The buildings were old frame structures with pillars inside and squeaky floors. On Sunday morning at 9:30 a.m., a crowd would gather in the main meeting room, sitting on little stools packed one next to the other. When space ran out, people stood at open double doors or windows or put their stools in the lane, listening to the service via a loudspeaker. In the main room, women sat on one side of the room, men on the other. They were a mixed crowd, doctors and teachers mingling with laborers and rickshaw drivers.

What they heard was not bombast. Watchman Nee's speaking style was gentle. There was no pulpit, and he made those around him feel that he was listening and not judging. Standing before a crowd, dressed in the dark blue cotton gown of a traditional Chinese man, he prayed slowly, letting the words out deliberately, and he distilled his thoughts in language that anyone could understand. Never referring to notes, he relied on stories or anecdotes to convey his message, prefacing his remarks with "I remember a true story" or "One day I was walking down the streets of Nanjing when . . ."

The Bible, he told them, was God's way of directly communicating to them. He explained that it was sixty-six books, divided into the Old and New Testaments and written by no fewer than thirty people in a span of more than sixteen hundred years. The writers were lawyers and fishermen, princes and shepherds, men of different backgrounds, languages, nationalities, and periods. He preached that there was a time in history when simply holding the Bible could mean death. "Everyone who possessed it would be inhumanly persecuted and later killed or burned," Watchman Nee said. The book, he assured

Watchman Nee photographed in Shanghai with an unidentified foreigner in the 1930s. The photograph is part of a private collection of Angus Kinnear, the biographer of Watchman Nee. Courtesy of Angus Kinnear family collection.

the gathering, was simple and easy. "It tells the origin of the universe, the earth, the plants, human beings, how they established their kingdoms, and how they will eventually end."

"This," he would say, holding up a Bible, "is *all*."

From her first visit to Hardoon Road with her sister-in-law, Ni Guizhen felt a strong connection. For years she had listened to her husband speaking from the pulpit and following word for word the Book of Common Prayer for private and public devotions. But in this simple hall, with its low ceiling and humble stools, people seemed more spontaneous, more engaged.

She went back another Sunday instead of joining her husband and children at St. Peter's. It wasn't long afterward that one Sunday became two, then three, four, five . . . until she realized that she preferred the fellowship at Hardoon Road over the services at St. Peter's. And so she told her husband.

"What do you mean?" he exploded. "You can't be serious!" He didn't try to keep his voice down for the sake of the children.

"It's what I want," she replied.

"I'm a pastor at St. Peter's. You are my wife. What will people think?"

Ni Guizhen held her ground. Here was someone whose life dream as a young woman was thwarted by an imperious mother. She was not about to relent to an equally forceful husband who framed her choice as a matter of spousal obedience.

"You have a duty," Lin Pu-chi insisted.

Her response cut him to the quick. "Your sermons have no life to them," she said. "You have knowledge, but no passion, no spirit. I want to stay at Hardoon Road."

Lin Pu-chi moved out of their bedroom on the second floor and slept with Jim in his room on the third floor.

More than his pride was wounded. He could not let the matter rest. He had his position with the church to consider. Not only was he an assistant pastor at a prominent parish in Shanghai, but the Anglican community also had made him editor of the *Chinese Churchman*, a vital Chinese-language magazine that circulated among clerics and church members throughout the country.

If his wife stopped playing piano on Sundays, people would notice. If she disappeared entirely, their whispers would gather force.

This was more than a family squabble. The popularity of independent preachers was a matter of concern for all Protestant churches. Watchman Nee? He was a "sheep stealer," clergymen decried, who was poaching their flocks. And he was just one of many. Others, such as Wang Mingdao in Beijing and John Sung with his "preaching bands" in almost ninety cities, were gaining followers at the expense of establishment churches. The Anglican and Episcopal Churches in China—or known jointly as the Chung Hua Sheng Kung Hui—was so worried about the trend that when its general synod convened in Fuzhou in April 1937, members cited the trend as an obstacle to church unity. The Little Flock and Watchman Nee, the general synod later reported, "induce people to leave their own churches and be immersed by some of their people as a sure way of salvation. They preach against organized churches and an official ministry."

Lin Pu-chi felt conspicuous when the topic came up. They were talking about his relatives; they were talking about his wife. And she was now sometimes taking their daughter, Martha, with her to Hardoon Road, though the three boys dutifully followed their father to St. Peter's.

One Sunday, the eldest son, Jim, humored his mother by going with her to Hardoon Road. When he arrived, he was shocked. People were praying, but spontaneously. They were not reciting devotions from memory or reading from the Book of Common Prayer. His mother leaned toward him and whispered, "Let the Holy Spirit descend on you."

At the end of the meeting, some of the congregation began clapping with excitement, jumping, laughing, and then, to Jim's astonishment, began spouting indecipherable words. Jim looked around and joined in, babbling gibberish. He wasn't sure what was happening, so he made a game of it. He found the service more entertaining than inspiring.

The following Sunday, Jim returned to St. Peter's, sitting in the last pew with Tim and Paul, listening to the familiar cadence of his father's voice from the pulpit.

MARCO POLO BRIDGE

In July 1937, Watchman Nee left for Manila at the invitation of an old school friend from Fuzhou who had moved there. His former classmate wanted him to address Little Flock members in the Philippines. With her husband traveling, Charity accepted an invitation from the Lin family to join them on a holiday to Yantai, a popular resort on the Bohai Sea, north of Qingdao in Shandong Province. They had made arrangements to rent rooms through a friend of Watchman Nee.

Much of Shanghai cleared out in August, when temperatures climbed so high that St. Peter's cut back hours and canceled choir practice. Missionary friends, as was their custom, took off for Lushan, a cool mountain retreat a day's travel from Shanghai.

The US Navy used the port of Yantai as a base of operation. Shortly before the family arrived, part of the US Asiatic Fleet—four American destroyers and a flagship—left for the Soviet naval base in Vladivostok. The two nations wanted to make a show of naval power to discourage Japan from further incursions in China. Tensions had recently escalated: on July 7, Japanese and Chinese forces exchanged gunfire at the Marco Polo Bridge on the outskirts of Beijing.

The vacation house was a block from the beach. The Lin boys enjoyed swimming in the calm water and climbing atop a rock jetty to spy on American sailors splashing in a cove—sometimes without bathing suits and in the company of giggling women. Their mother, meanwhile, stayed indoors with Charity. Neither dared to put on a bathing suit. Women in the Little Flock dressed modestly in long, black skirts and would never wear anything remotely revealing. Instead, Ni Guizhen had a houseboy carry buckets of seawater into the bathtub in order to soak privately and gain what she thought were its therapeutic benefits.

On August 13, news from home shattered their idyll: that morning, more than ten thousand Japanese troops fanned out across Shanghai. By 4:00 p.m., Japanese warships on the Huangpu River began shelling the city from all directions. Inside Lin Pu-chi's school on Haskell Road, terrified staff escaped from the building as bombs rained down on the neighborhood.

This was war.

Frantic, Lin Pu-chi bought tickets for the family on a cargo ship bound for Hong Kong. They did not have a berth but would instead have to sleep on the deck with hundreds of other evacuees. Lin Pu-chi gave his wife instructions that once they arrived in Hong Kong, they could wait out the fighting— a few weeks, maybe months—with his sister and her husband, a close friend of Watchman Nee.

After they were safe at sea, he purchased a one-way rail ticket for home.

· 10 ·

Island of Shanghai

Shanghai, 1937

*T*he family had just sat down to dinner when there was a tap at the door. Ni Guizhen rose to answer it. Standing before her on the front step was a tall man with a weathered face, Caucasian, not Chinese, and a scraggly gray beard that reached down to his chest. His jacket was filthy, and he gave off a pungent odor. Was he Russian? A German Jew? He said nothing but cupped his hands and raised them to Ni Guizhen in the universal wordless plea: "Feed me."

As her teenage sons looked on in shock, she led him inside their home. She gestured to her own stool at the round table, set with steaming bowls of noodles. The stranger's face showed relief, gratitude, and ravenous hunger as he sat down and began shoveling hot food into his mouth in one long slurp. The stranger held the bowl to his lips and tipped every drop of broth into his mouth. When he finished, he stood up, kissed the hand of Ni Guizhen— such a strange gesture!—and politely left. Ni Guizhen grabbed a rag from the kitchen and wiped the table.

The boys understood the message: Do not look the other way. They'd learned it from Bible parables like the Good Samaritan, they saw it in their mother's daily actions, and of course they heard it from their father. This was wartime, and Lin Pu-chi preached from St. Peter's pulpit about helping the refugees who had flooded Shanghai, and he wrote about their needs on the pages of the *Chinese Churchman*. As editor, he used his Christmas column to acknowledge the despair piercing the lives of all families in Shanghai. The fighting that had started in August dragged on for three months and displaced thousands from obliterated neighborhoods outside the International Settlement. "People usually sing in elation at this time of year," Lin Pu-chi wrote. "But my country, the most vast territory in East Asia, overflowing with resources, has been invaded and encroached upon. . . . We have fallen into the hands of our intruders. Millions of us struggle as we fight bloody battles.

Countless refugees fall prey to death and are left unburied. Our cities are crumbling, as are our houses and farms."

Christians, he reminded his readers, had a responsibility to help others. "At every glance our gaze captures the grief that has swept our land," he observed. At this time of year, thoughts usually turned to "Peace on Earth." But this Christmas was different. "We are up in arms, swords drawn and ready to ignite explosions that have made the Second World War so devastating. Armies have fallen in East Asia and Western Europe. But true peace can only come from inside the heart, and through the spirit."

To the rest of China, Shanghai was *gudao*. The lonely island. Terrified refugees from all over the country, indeed all over the world, struggled to reach its shores. Russians fleeing Bolsheviks and Jews fleeing fascists knew that if they could get to Shanghai, where they did not need a passport or entry visa, they would be safe.

The ten square miles of the International Settlement and adjacent French Concession, normally home to 1.5 million people, saw its population more than double with the outbreak of war in 1937. People from surrounding areas escaped the hellfire of war for this zone of neutrality. Soldiers of Emperor Hirohito controlled the area outside the boundaries of the international enclave and never let locals forget who was in power. Any Chinese resident crossing the Garden Bridge from the occupied area to the Bund, for instance, had to pass through a barbed-wire checkpoint and bow deeply to Japanese sentries.

When fighting flared in Shanghai in August, the Nationalist government tried to make a stand, throwing all of its military weight against the Japanese occupiers. The Nationalists had established a new capital in the western city of Chongqing in what became known as "Free China." But the advancing Japanese troops overwhelmed the forces of Generalissimo Chiang Kai-shek. During the three-month Battle of Shanghai, which spread to riverfront towns along the Huangpu and then west toward Nanjing, the Chinese side lost three hundred thousand troops. The enemy plundered Nanjing, raping women and slaughtering civilians.

The Sino-Japanese War would not be contained. Bombs fell on Fuzhou in the spring of 1938, triggering more streams of refugees. Among this tide of evacuees were thirty men, women, and children from one extended family who secured passage on an overcrowded coastal steamer bound for Shanghai. When they stepped ashore at the Bund, they piled into rickshaws and shouted the address of the one place they knew they would be safe and welcome: 170 Jiaozhou Road.

The Lin boys thought it an adventure to suddenly see so many relatives show up at their doorstep. There were uncles and aunts, faces they vaguely remembered from their childhood in Fuzhou, plus assorted cousins from toddlers to teens and their tiny sixty-four-year-old grandmother. The old woman brought her small-city ways with her. She had a revulsion to Shanghai's chlorinated tap water, preferring to drink rainwater collected in a barrel. Lin Pu-chi, his wife, and his four children moved into one bedroom on the third floor while his relatives spread out on the other floors. Family loyalty was the bedrock of Chinese society; you looked after your own in times of crisis. Like now.

These were the lucky ones, the refugees who had family to double up with in Shanghai. They had somewhere to go, someone to help them. The unlucky ones survived on the streets, living like barnyard animals, crammed into alleyways or huddled under straw and bamboo huts on vacant lots. Waifs in rags begged for coins and swiped steamed buns or fruit from peddlers. Mothers with nursing infants and grannies cradling tots slept in doorways and gutters. Tens of thousands of refugees survived in camps throughout the city that were plagued by epidemics of diseases such as measles. No safety net could stop the misery. Before dawn, trucks made the rounds, picking up bodies at a rate of sixty a day—beggars, indigents, babies, their bodies discovered in alleys, along roads, in vacant plots or stuffed into makeshift coffins.

By the fall of 1938, Fuzhou was calm enough for the relatives to return home, and life on Jiaozhou Road returned to an altered state of normal. Lin Pu-chi's job as an assistant headmaster remained the same, but the location of the Public School for Chinese Boys was moved to the heart of the International Settlement. During fighting in 1937, the neighborhood around Haskell Road had become the focus of gun battles and shelling. The school was destroyed, including the six-thousand-volume library, forcing it to move to a safer location inside the settlement on Gordon Road, not far from Lin Pu-chi's house.

Lin Pu-chi's three sons had transferred to the middle school affiliated with St. John's University, while his daughter, Martha, enrolled in its medical school. As an Anglican cleric, Lin Pu-chi could send his children on scholarship to the American-run St. John's.

The sprawling university campus became a wartime refuge for Anglican missionaries and their families from outlying cities. Japanese soldiers, too, were billeted in classrooms in the Science Building on the north side of Suzhou Creek, territory under their control. It galled students to stand on the banks of the creek and watch enemy troops commandeering barges to load with looted furniture, valuables, and artwork from Chinese families who lived upstream in defeated areas. They seethed at the thought of purloined property finding its way to Japanese homes in Shanghai or Tokyo. Powerless, the students would express their outrage in English compositions—which instructors immediately destroyed. If such hostile essays fell into Japanese hands, it would mean certain punishment, perhaps imprisonment, for the authors.

On campus, foreign teachers and Chinese students shared the same fear: Japan had a noose around Shanghai's neck, ready to yank it at any moment.

That moment arrived on December 7, 1941.

In the South Pacific, Japanese fighter planes screamed across the sky over the island of Oahu at 7:53 a.m., dropping bombs on American battleships in Pearl Harbor, pulling the United States into the war.

Two hours later in Shanghai, in the predawn of December 8, special Japanese forces startled the sleeping crew of the USS *Wake* and captured the river gunboat before the Americans could put up a fight. Nearby, a Japanese officer climbed up the ladder of the HMS *Peterel* and informed its captain that Japan and the United Kingdom were now at war. When the officer demanded his surrender, the British captain bellowed, "Get off my bloody ship!" Japanese gunboats shelled the *Peterel*, setting it ablaze before the ship sank into the muddy depths of the Huangpu, taking six sailors with it.

Students entering the campus of St. John's for Monday morning classes were startled by the buzz of low-flying planes that dropped a snowstorm of leaflets. As the papers fluttered to the ground, professors and students read in Chinese and English that American and British residents were now considered enemy subjects. They could go about their business but could use only certain roads to enter or leave the settlement. The leaflet said the Japanese Army would protect law-abiding citizens and respect property rights but would not tolerate anyone who disrupted public order.

By 10:00 a.m., Japanese soldiers with bayonets fixed to their rifles marched into the International Settlement to take up positions behind sandbag bunkers at major intersections. Tanks and armored cars rumbled across the Garden Bridge, past hotels on the Bund and department stores on Nanjing Road. Atop major buildings—city offices, police barracks, banks, railway stations—soldiers hoisted the Rising Sun flag. They took over the US and British consulates, the American Club, YMCA buildings, and even a hospital run by St. John's for refugees. Doctors and patients had until January 15 to clear out and make way for Japanese secretaries and military officers, who wanted the building for headquarters. The American physician in charge, Josiah Mc-Cracken, told a hospital worker not to raise the US flag; he didn't want to give the enemy the satisfaction of pulling down the Stars and Stripes and replacing it with the Rising Sun.

Japanese troops toppled symbols of British power. At the grandiose headquarters of the Hongkong and Shanghai Bank, a sign on the front door read: OCCUPIED BY THE MARINES OF THE GREAT JAPANESE EMPIRE. Soldiers removed the iconic brass lions with their polished paws that stood guard at the entrance. Across the street and down a bit, another group pulled down the statue of Sir Robert Hart, one of the most influential westerners in the Qing dynasty.

All of Shanghai had fallen.

CAMPS

The roundup of foreigners did not happen immediately. As a first step, citizens of enemy nations had to register with Japanese authorities and wear armbands, designating their country of origin: *A* for America, *B* for Britain, *H* for Holland, or *X* for other. Allied enemies also had to turn over cameras, binoculars, telescopes—anything with a lens that could be a tool for would-be spies. They also had to relinquish cars. From now on, only Japanese officials were allowed to drive.

As the weeks passed under Japanese occupation, the economy of Shanghai was crippled, and tens of thousands of Chinese and foreigners faced starvation and sickness. Runaway inflation stripped money of value. Food supplies grew scarce, and "rice riots" broke out over dwindling supplies. Ni Guizhen sent her children in pairs from Jiaozhou Road to her mother's house in a far western suburb to buy rice. The older woman, who had relocated from Fuzhou to Shanghai, lived closer to farmers where supplies were easier to find than inside the International Settlement. But the trip sent the children through Japanese checkpoints. Once, after making the long journey and loading bags onto their bicycles, Martha and Paul had to watch silently as a soldier, checking for weapons or contraband, pierced a burlap sack with his bayonet, sending a cascade of rice to the ground. The siblings quickly swept up the precious kernels with their hands, not uttering a word as they bowed and sped off.

The people of Shanghai had to accept that the city was no longer theirs. At St. Peter's Church, the parish gave free classes in Japanese. At St. John's, Japanese regiments took over two buildings on campus to use as warehouses. Mandatory Japanese classes became part of the curriculum at the middle school. In an act of passive protest, Paul, the youngest son of Lin Pu-chi and an outstanding student in every way, refused to put any effort into his language study, learning little more than the obligatory *arigato* and *konnichiwa*, "thank you" and "hello."

The summons that foreigners had been dreading for more than a year arrived on January 31, 1943. American and British residents were notified that the following day they had to report to internment camps. Each prisoner needed to bring an enamel cup and bowl for meals, plus clothing and necessities. Lin Pu-chi's colleague, the bishop of Shanghai, the Right Reverend William Roberts, was sent to a camp in the Zhabei section of Shanghai; the bishop's brother Donald, a St. John's professor, crossed the Huangpu for internment at an empty warehouse of the British-American Tobacco Company. Chinese friends gave their foreign colleagues canned food, newly knitted sweaters, and warm slippers. Ni Guizhen put her children to work making peanut butter—an excellent protein source—for missionary friends to take with them to the camps. Martha shelled and roasted the peanuts in a wok, and her brothers ground them into paste.

The Roberts brothers, along with all American and British residents, were marched through the city to waiting trucks and river launches to take them away. Chinese crowds lined streets in a show of support; some people even grabbed suitcases out of the hands of internees to lighten their loads. In the first half of 1943, Japanese authorities sent 7,600 men, women, and children to internment camps. This presented a crisis for Lin Pu-chi. Among the prisoners was the British headmaster of his school. The city's Education Department informed Lin Pu-chi that he would be expected to take over running the school. With the onset of war, the Shanghai Municipal Council, mostly made up of Americans and Britons, ceased to exist, which meant Lin Pu-chi would have to report to education officials in the new city government installed by Japanese occupying forces.

The thought of working for the puppet government repulsed him. After all he had seen in the past decade—the misery, hunger, and desperation of refugees, the wanton cruelty of Japanese warriors, the loss and suffering inflicted by years of fighting—it was unfathomable to consider working for enemy occupiers. But he needed the job. He had his family to worry about. How could he find work that paid anything in this chaotic environment?

Lin Pu-chi pushed fear aside and refused to collaborate. His conscience would not allow it. And so at the end of the year in 1943, he resigned as assistant headmaster. Now he was jobless like countless others and equally as desperate to find work. His mother-in-law pestered him to ask his brothers-in-law for help.

Without a better alternative, Lin Pu-chi relented and approached the Ni family business.

Ni Guizhen had a younger brother, George, who was a brilliant chemist with a degree from St. John's but little aptitude for business. In contrast, her other brother, Watchman Nee, was a congenial sort with innate skills for organizing but no experience in the world of commerce.

Her father brought the brothers together. He leaned on Watchman Nee to help George run the business, which the patriarch had started as Zion Laboratory in 1936. George was the brains behind the venture, mixing formulas in a home lab to create antiseptic salves and antibiotics such as sulfathiazole. When Watchman Nee became involved, around 1940, he began expanding the operation and changed the name to the China Biological and Chemical Laboratories (CBC). The factory on Jiaozhou Road, a quarter mile from the Lin home, was the first in China to manufacture sulfa drugs, in addition to vitamin B concentrates; antibacterial products such as Mercurochrome and, later, the insecticide DDT. Located in a walled compound, it occupied the former residence of a wealthy merchant and two utilitarian buildings with rooms for synthesizing chemicals, preparing liquids, packaging and sealing products, and storage. At its peak, CBC employed as many as two hundred people, including a half-dozen chemists. Before the war, some of its scientific staff included Americans. With the outbreak of the Second World War, the business shifted much of its production to a second manufacturing site in Nationalist-controlled Chongqing, playing an important role in supplying the government during the war.

Lin Pu-chi was assigned to the personnel department, but it was a job in name only. He had no real responsibilities and spent most mornings reading the newspaper or pacing the CBC compound. It was pointless yet necessary. He had close friends whose families were starving. His colleague from St. Peter's, Pastor Yu Ensi, who became a bishop, died in 1944 of complications from exhaustion and malnutrition. Instead of a salary, Lin Pu-chi received one hundred liters of rice a month, enough to feed his wife, four children, and mother, who had not returned to Fuzhou with the rest of the family in 1938. To earn cash, he picked up work on the side teaching English at St. Mary's Hall, the girls' school affiliated with St. John's, where a friend was principal. At CBC, even the sons of Lin Pu-chi were put to work. During summer breaks from school, they helped at the factory, doing manual jobs like hauling five-gallon drums of hydrochloric acid from storage to laboratories. They were paid in rice or canned vegetables.

All of the Ni brothers were part of CBC: Watchman Nee was chairman of the board; George was the chemist in chief; a third brother handled distribution with about a dozen salesmen; and a fourth oversaw purchasing. George was a constant presence at the factory, but Watchman Nee spent more time with customers, shuttling between Shanghai and Chongqing with his wife, Charity.

If it seemed odd for an Anglican priest to be working for a drug company, it was even more unlikely for Watchman Nee to be immersed in a life of commerce. He saw it as a means to an end: in addition to relatives, CBC employed many Christians from the Hardoon Road church, providing them with critical support during tough economic times. But the more the company took him away from his religious work, the more his close associates from the Little Flock disapproved of this unexpected detour into capitalism.

At the beginning in 1940, the CBC work was only part-time, taking up an hour or so a day and leaving Watchman Nee with time to continue his biblical teaching and expansion of the Little Flock. But the demands of the company soon consumed his attention and time. Some elders from the Hardoon Road assembly objected to the duality of his life, viewing his new role as a waste of time and effort. They couldn't understand how he could spend his days hosting business lunches or negotiating deals when he could be doing religious work. In their eyes, his reputation was tarnished; ultimately, they told him to stop coming to Hardoon Road to preach. He had been ostracized from the very group he started. So severe was their reproach that gossip began: the church's inner circle must have known something the rest of the worshippers did not. Rumors spread of everything from marital infidelity to the misuse of funds and collaborating with the Japanese.

Dejected, the forty-year-old preacher was nevertheless unwilling to walk away from the workers who depended on him. One day, sitting with the factory manager, a fellow Christian from Fuzhou, Watchman Nee commented, "I envy you. You are free to do what you like in the factory, and if then you go and say a few words at the meeting, they will acclaim you a very zealous brother. No one will question you. But me? Twenty-four hours a day, they need to know exactly how I spend my time. I am a marked man."

Church activity at Hardoon Road stopped, partly in response to the confusion and controversy surrounding Watchman Nee and partly in reaction to pressure from the Japanese military police, which tried to regulate and control the activities of all churches, not just the Little Flock. Rather than comply, the Hardoon Road group fragmented, with members meeting on their own in small groups, usually in someone's home. At the Lin house, Ni Guizhen often gathered with her sister-in-law Charity and three or four other women.

RECOVERY

After seven years of war came the reassuring sight high above Shanghai of a squadron of big, loud American B-29s en route to take out Japanese military targets. The high-altitude plane with its remote-control machine guns was the most advanced bomber of its time, dubbed the "Superfortress" by the US Army Air Corps. Air attacks of Japanese installations around Shanghai began in late 1944 and ended by August 1945 after two B-29s dropped atomic bombs on the Japanese cities of Hiroshima and Nagasaki within three days of each other. In Nanjing on September 9, 1945, Japanese commanders surrendered to China.

Throngs of well-wishers on the Bund cheered the arrival of the US Seventh Fleet. More than two hundred vessels, including American cargo vessels with names like *Liberty* and *Victory*, anchored stern to bow for miles along the Huangpu River. The presiding bishop for the American Episcopal Church sent a congratulatory telegram to his Chinese counterparts: AMERICAN CHURCH REJOICES WITH YOU FOR VICTORY DAY. GRATEFUL FOR YOUR STEADFASTNESS DURING WAR.

But there would be no respite for China. The end of the Sino-Japanese War had exposed battle lines between the Nationalist and Communist forces. The People's Liberation Army wasted no time filling the military vacuum of power left by retreating Japanese forces in northeastern China. No sooner had the war against Japan ended than civil war began.

Shanghai remained an island of stability under Nationalist control, allowing residents to carry on with their lives. Lin Pu-chi left the CBC factory and found work with a new national office for the Anglican and Episcopal Church in China, the Sheng Kung Hui. He became an assistant to his friend and mentor Y. Y. Tsu, now Bishop Tsu, who had been posted in Free China during the war, by the end even serving as a chaplain for the US military. The *Chinese Churchman* magazine resumed publication with Lin Pu-chi restored as editor. In one of his first articles, he told readers about the desperation of starving Chinese clerics in outlying areas. He reported receiving two letters, one from a priest and another from a village preacher. The priest barely earned enough to cover meals for his family, let alone keep socks and shoes on the feet of his children. "All my six children wear rags and look like beggars," the man wrote.

He quoted the preacher, who said families in his impoverished village were ravaged by bubonic plague, cholera, and malaria. A drought in the autumn was followed by a typhoon, destroying crops. "The hard life is unimaginable," the preacher despaired in his letter.

Lin Pu-chi spelled out what readers already painfully knew, that runaway inflation had made the Chinese currency meaningless. In the years since 1936, the cost of living for Shanghai workers had increased 5,200 times. "Suppose the pre-War salary of one church staffer was 100 yuan," he wrote. "He should be paid 500,000 yuan now. . . . No wonder they are unable to get enough food and clothing and their children unable to go to school."

The only remedy, he argued, would be more donations from those who could give as well as an inevitable plea for help from foreign missions. "Some people are against raising funds from Missions, thinking that would impede the independence of the Chinese Church. This is stupid." Rather than watch colleagues starve to death and debating whether this would hurt the drive for self-sufficiency, he said the Chinese church needed to ask for help. Foreign missions, for their part, responded to the crisis, with British and Canadian Anglicans plus American Episcopalians transferring emergency funds to help the Sheng Kung Hui.

In 1946, the Lin family had much to celebrate. The eldest daughter, Martha, continued her father's legacy by graduating from his alma mater, St. John's University. But it was her mother's dream that she fulfilled. When Ni Guizhen was a young woman, she had had to give up her studies in order to enter an arranged marriage, forever putting aside her desire to become a physician. Now her only daughter was Dr. Lin. The war years had been difficult for students of the medical school, which followed a British model of conferring a degree after five years of academic study and clinical training. The school had to relocate several times because of fighting and lost most of its foreign faculty to evacuation or internment. But it never ceased training students, who included Martha's youngest brother, Paul. Martha went on to become a resident in obstetrics and gynecology, while Paul's vaunted ambition was to go to the United States to study neurosurgery. He dreamed of returning to China as only the second brain surgeon in a country of 550 million (the first being a doctor at Peking Union Medical College Hospital). Paul even taught himself how to play the violin in order to improve his manual dexterity.

St. John's medical school had a sterling reputation in both China and the United States, thanks to Dr. Josiah McCracken, a rawboned Kansan and a graduate of the University of Pennsylvania, who joined St. John's in 1914. McCracken, a college football star who won a silver medal in the shot put and a bronze in the hammer throw at the 1900 Olympic Games in Paris, forged close ties financially and academically between St. John's and the Christian Association of his alma mater. Most of the professors were Penn men, and the

Both Paul and Martha attended the medical school of St. John's University. Paul used to wear a school blazer with a gold-threaded crest that read, "Pennsylvania Medical School St. John's University," which acknowledged the school's relationship to the University of Pennsylvania. Courtesy of Lin Family Collection.

Shanghai medical school's official title, which it bore on its crest, was changed to the Pennsylvania Medical School.

Lin Pu-chi had wanted Martha to continue her schooling in the United States as he had. Through connections at St. John's, she could have taken her residency at the Cincinnati Children's Hospital. But the thought of leaving China was too much for timid Martha, who chose a more predictable path. She decided to marry. Her betrothed, John Sun, was a gentle, quiet business-man. Even though John was a graduate of Shanghai University, he was not the scholar Lin Pu-chi would have preferred. Lin Pu-chi disregarded the Sun fam-ily's substantial wealth, which included a newly purchased Spanish-style villa with a spacious yard and driveway big enough for two sedans, a Dodge as well as a Pontiac. It mattered more to him that John did not have initials after his name signifying at least a master's degree. His future son-in-law managed his family's sizable real estate holdings as well as an embroidery store on Nanjing Road. Lace-making was a skill imported to China by missionaries, and the Sun family's shop, with its front window brimming with delicate silk slips and embroidered tablecloths, was one of the finest on Nanjing Road. American sailors on leave in Shanghai thought nothing of plopping down fifty dollars for an embroidered silk robe for a girlfriend back home.

The matchmaker in Martha's case was her mother. Ni Guizhen knew the Sun family from the Hardoon Road assembly and made the introduction. Before moving to their new house in the western suburbs, the Sun family had lived next door to the church meeting place and became active members of the Little Flock. The patriarch of the Sun family also had another connection to Watchman Nee: he was a substantial investor in his CBC pharmaceutical business and a managing partner of the company.

On the second Saturday in July 1947, twenty-six-year-old Martha was married in the Anglican tradition at the Church of Our Savior by her father's friend, Bishop Roberts. She wore a demure white gown and a veil that was longer than she was tall. Her wavy hair was loose but teased with a bouffant in front. Around her neck was a gold heart pendant and in her hands an over-flowing bouquet of white lilies and feathery ferns. After the ceremony, guests celebrated the marriage over cake and tea in the church auditorium.

PRODIGAL SON

Once married, Martha became a more regular member of the Hardoon Road assembly. By 1947, the group had begun to recover from the disruptive years of war. Witness Lee, a longtime associate of Watchman Nee from Shandong Province, helped him to heal the rift with members of the Little Flock. A change meanwhile had come over Watchman Nee. In 1948, he detached himself from the day-to-day responsibility of running the pharmaceutical business and went so far as to dedicate his profits from the business to supporting a revival of his church work. He left Shanghai for Fuzhou with the idea of using his hometown as a new base. At first, he repaired and restored his family's vacant home on Customs Lane to use as a training center but expanded from there, buying up cottages in the mountaintop getaway of Guling. His plan was to transform the former missionary hill station into a gathering place for both fellowship and religious retreats. A half century ago, missionaries had built sturdy stone houses in the mountains to escape Fuzhou's brutal summer heat. But by 1948, they were happy to sell the houses to Watchman Nee, aware that the People's Liberation Army was winning the civil war.

Witness Lee convinced Watchman Nee to return to Shanghai to face the members of the Hardoon Road assembly. He had been absent for six years. Before a room full of skeptics and critics as well as loyal followers, Watchman Nee acknowledged his failings. He compared his foray into business as being like a desperate widow who remarries in order to support many children—only to discover "unexpectedly all her children deserted her after her second marriage." He broke down, and those in the meeting who had harbored doubts and questions accepted his contrition.

In the summer of 1948, Watchman held a training conference in Guling, drawing about seventy followers. From June to the end of September, the Little Flock met in the lush, cool hill station for days of fellowship and learning. Ni Guizhen arrived with her husband in mid-July. Each morning began with Watchman Nee's delivery of a biblical message, followed in the afternoon with testimonies from participants and evening hours dedicated to discussion about how to reach newcomers. Watchman Nee, relaxed and reconnected, would walk among the others, his hands clasped behind his back as he invited and answered questions.

The revival of the Little Flock in Shanghai was so robust that the group began to make plans to build a larger meeting place to replace the cramped Hardoon Road site. More than 1,500 people regularly tried to squeeze into a meeting place big enough for only a few hundred. People sat on stairways or stood in the lane, straining to listen to the service. Soon they identified a large property at 145 Nanyang Road with a big house and vast garden, and they purchased it for 210 gold bars, equal to $105,000 in US currency. For the first of three installments, church members raised half the funds, with Watchman Nee personally contributing thirty-seven gold bars. Construction began in the garden for a one-story brick and wood hall with 2,400 seats.

But as the Little Flock was shoring up its foundation in Shanghai, Watchman Nee was well aware of the inevitability of a Communist victory against the weaker, corrupt Nationalist government. In November 1948, he delivered an urgent message to church members: some of them must leave China for Taiwan or Hong Kong to carry on their work. Communist troops, already victorious in northern China, were advancing into the Yangtze Valley with Shanghai within their grasp. One of the people he urged to leave was Witness Lee, who questioned and challenged the decision. "Brother," Watchman Nee explained, "you must realize that although in this desperate situation we trust in the Lord, it is possible that the enemy will one day wipe us out. If this happens, you will be out of China, and we will still have something left. So you must go."

• 11 •

Bund to Boardwalk

Shanghai, 1949

*T*he steady clicks of a typewriter broke the morning stillness in the Lin home. In his cramped office behind the kitchen, Lin Pu-chi dated a letter on official church stationery—May 14, 1949—and typed: *To Whom It May Concern.* He was taking no chances. He had spent months planning how he would get his sons out of China to jobs at hospitals in the United States. He put out unabashed pleas for help, accepted offers of money from friends and family, wrote to church colleagues in Hong Kong and the States, filled out paperwork for passports, and stood in line for a day and night for tickets on a coastal steamer that would leave from the Bund that afternoon. But just in case he forgot something or some link in the chain unexpectedly broke, he hoped this letter would serve as insurance for his sons. And so he wrote: *Paul M. Lin and James M. Lin come from a very good Christian family. I can sincerely recommend them to friends and fellow Christians in the United States. Any courtesy and assistance to them will be greatly appreciated.*

Lin Pu-chi folded the letter and placed it in an envelope along with a pocket-size booklet containing important names and addresses and a brief description of the family's religious lineage, as well as this parting advice for his sons, written in Chinese: *Go to church. Watch your health. Worship God. Help people.* He signed the letter with his looping signature, adding the full breadth and weight of his station as assistant secretary and editor for the Chung Hua Sheng Kung Hui—the Anglican and Episcopal Church in China.

The assuring words and steady signature hid the anxiety that was building inside him. From the time his sons were young, Lin Pu-chi had planned for Jim and Paul to study in America. They didn't talk about it much; it was understood. He had earned his graduate degrees in the United States, and so would they. But the war was rushing the timetable. Just a week earlier, Paul had finished his medical school classes at St. John's a full month ahead of

151

schedule. Administrators weren't wasting any time. Beijing had fallen without a fight in January, with the Nationalist government retreating from the capital of Nanjing in April. With each passing day, the muffled sound of explosions edged closer to campus. Students of means were making arrangements to flee, while those with Communist allegiances were eager to step out of the shadows. That spring, they had the temerity to press faculty to teach in Chinese instead of English—an affront to St. John's American roots but a foreshadowing of the inevitable.

Shanghai newspapers were filled with articles predicting how the Nationalist government would rebuff the advancing People's Liberation Army, the PLA, and hold the city. But no one believed it. There was reason for pessimism. At St. John's, the faculty families still on campus estimated that Communist troops were no more than eight miles away and advancing from all directions. Word had spread that an airfield near the Longhua Pagoda, which was lined with wing-to-wing planes ready to whisk Nationalist VIPs to safety, was under attack. Just outside the campus gate, the neighborhood of Caojiadu was on war footing. Under the eye of Nationalist soldiers, political prisoners, women as well as men, dug zigzag trenches by roadsides. Villagers, meanwhile, were hawking anything they could for food. They spread their blankets on the ground, displaying trinkets, leather shoes, pottery, towels, and pigskin dowry chests to barter for bags of rice or chickens. Even the boatmen who usually moored their flat-bottom houseboats on Suzhou Creek near campus seemed to sense that the final battle was about to begin. Days earlier, the waterway was so jammed you could get across by skipping from one deck to the next. But even the boatmen had fled. The muddy creek was empty.

To get his sons to the United States, Lin Pu-chi had to raise about $1,000 each, or the equivalent of a year's salary. He cashed in a life insurance policy and retrieved gold bars, hidden behind a sliding wooden panel in the attic. He put aside his pride to accept $100 from his boss, Bishop Y. Y. Tsu, $100 from Bishop Roberts, and $500 from Watchman Nee.

Lin Pu-chi planned to escort his sons as far as Hong Kong. It was a risky move. Assuming they arrived safely, there was no assurance he'd make it back to Shanghai anytime soon, especially if fighting intensified. His sons had no passports, no visas, and, so far, no plane tickets. The Nationalist government in Nanjing had fled to the southern city of Canton before the foreign office had time to process their applications for passports. There was no other option, Lin Pu-chi concluded. Time was against them. Rumors were rife that the Nationalist forces, fearing a Communist advance on Shanghai from the Pudong District, might shut the busy Huangpu River to all but military ships. He got three tickets on one of the last coastal steamers bound for Hong Kong.

At home, Ni Guizhen was in Paul's tiny second-floor bedroom getting her son's things ready. She moved slowly, as if trying to put off the inevitable. Reaching under his cot, she pulled out a leather suitcase she had bought just days before at a shop on Nanjing Road. On the front, in big gold letters, were the words DR. PAUL M. LIN and then, in parentheses, the three characters of his Chinese name, Lin Baomin. She ran the tips of her fingers back and forth across the embossed letters like a mother stroking the head of a sleeping child. Paul was twenty-two, barely a man; Jim, just three years older. And here she was, sending them off to work in hospitals in American cities that she could not find on a map.

Lin Pu-chi hurried up the tight circular staircase from his office two floors below and handed the envelope to his wife, who tucked it between the covers of Paul's English-Chinese dictionary, which was as big as a brick. The night before, she had used remnants from her sewing basket to stitch a cloth cover. Paul seemed to have as many books as clothes. In one pile on his bed were a small English-language Bible and two enormous medical text-books—one devoted to internal medicine, one for surgery, easily weighing more than ten pounds. In another pile was his white physician's coat with his name stitched in red; a thick gray sweater she knitted him with a giant "P" for Paul in front; and a hand-me-down tweed blazer from a missionary family. In between the pages of the dictionary, Ni Guizhen slipped a black-and-white family portrait, taken the previous autumn at a studio a few blocks away. She and Lin Pu-chi, dressed in his clerical collar, sat in the center, surrounded by Martha in a traditional floral *qipao* dress and all the men—Paul, Jim, brother Tim, and Martha's husband John—dressed in dark Western suits and ties. Ni Guizhen had gotten everyone together to sit for a portrait, sensing perhaps as only a mother can that this moment was coming. Her mind raced as she closed the suitcase and tightened a strap holding it together. Paul was going to the seaside resort of Atlantic City, Jim to a hospital in the nearby city of Paterson. Everyone reminded her that these places were not far from New York City, as if proximity to that famous city made the anonymity of their destinations somehow less unsettling. Even if they arrived safely, adjusted to life in America, did well, the thought remained: Would they ever return? When the PLA arrived in Shanghai, would there be more years of fighting? House-to-house combat—or a bloodless retreat like in Beijing? She shook the questions out of her head, but they kept returning like unwanted visitors banging on the front door.

It took hours for Lin Pu-chi and his sons to travel by rickshaw from their house to the docks on the Bund and their waiting steamer. Along the way, worlds collided at busy intersections. Displaced rural families pulling carts piled high with possessions and children were gridlocked with chauffeurs in black

In 1948, months before two of the Lin sons departed for the United States, the family posed for a final portrait. Ni Guizhen tucked a copy of the photo inside the suitcase of her son Paul. Clockwise from bottom left: Lin Pu-chi; John Sun, husband of Martha; Tim; Jim; Paul; Martha; and Ni Guizhen. Courtesy of Lin Family Collection.

sedans and shirtless rickshaw drivers trying vainly to deliver their impatient patrons to destinations. At the wharf, Paul and Jim followed the tall figure of their father as he led them up the gangplank to the steamer. They had a third-class cabin that was cramped with floor-to-ceiling bunks on each side. No one minded the utilitarian berths. They had made it. As the ship pulled away, Paul and Jim stood on deck, watching the Bund disappear.

For the Chinese of Shanghai, if you were lucky enough to have money, you could buy a seat on a steamer or plane to Hong Kong. If you weren't, you might be able to force your way onto an overstuffed train, even if it meant clinging perilously to the side of the locomotive or sitting on the roof of a car. And if you were a destitute refugee trying to stay one step ahead of the fighting, good luck. Shanghai was walled off as the city girded for a showdown with the People's Liberation Army. Outwardly, the Nationalist government flexed its muscles for the sake of residents, marching soldiers through the streets and parking howitzers side by side along sidewalks. Troops stood guard at sandbag bunkers by banks and government offices as workers boarded up the windows of commercial buildings and shops to protect against the inevitable onslaught. Newspapers, under tight government control, declared that the city could hold for months if not longer.

St. John's, on the western side of the city, was on the front lines of the action. Most students had gone, leaving only a skeleton staff on campus. Across Suzhou Creek, an encampment of Nationalist troops had taken over the athletic fields.

On May 24, as staff and teachers were nodding off in afternoon naps, a great explosion jolted everyone awake. The windows in the magnificent library and administration building shattered, sending shards of glass flying. Chunks of plaster dropped from ceilings, and a thick steel beam, hurled through the air like a red-hot spear, landed in the lawn by a giant camphor tree. *This is it*, everyone on campus thought as the dust cleared. But this was not the work of enemies; it was a desperate move by allies. Retreating Nationalist forces did not want their Communist foes chasing after them so they blew up a nearby railway bridge without bothering to warn anyone on campus.

The following morning, the PLA drew closer and occupied parts of the former French Concession, just south of St. John's. Shanghai's mayor fled by air from the Longhua Airfield after the city government flew a white flag of surrender. In the face of defeat, the Nationalist soldiers who were billeted on the other side of Suzhou Creek shifted from protecting the university to looting it. They turned their rifles toward the campus and tried to scare away the handful of Americans by shooting into their homes. Some soldiers crossed the creek by boat, tore down fences, and ran toward classrooms and residences. A history professor called the US consulate, pleading for help. The diplomats told him there was nothing they could do; they had their own buildings to secure.

Families took cover, listening to bullets whizzing by their windows and bracing for looters. Instead, as if on cue, a single file of PLA soldiers marched through the campus gate. Hundreds of young soldiers in crisp khaki uniforms and soft-soled cloth shoes streamed onto the grounds. Communist-leaning students at St. John's had tipped off the PLA about the mayhem caused by fleeing Nationalist soldiers. Coming to the rescue, Communist troops marched right up to the edge of the creek and goaded their Nationalist foes with shouts of "Fight or give up!"

All day, the two sides traded barbs and gunfire, but by nightfall, the PLA was in charge. The young soldiers set up camp around Mann Hall and dug foxholes to secure the area. Peasant fighters who had never seen anything as grand as the stately campus buildings or manicured grounds of St. John's walked around wide-eyed. Most seemed to be teenagers and, to the missionaries, surprisingly well behaved. That night, American professors looked on in puzzlement as the PLA soldiers sang and played a game that looked a lot like a Chinese version of "Farmer in the Dell."

By morning, the troops decamped, but not before asking the Chinese staff what they owed for using their electricity for one night.

On May 27, Shanghai was theirs.

HONG KONG

It took Lin Pu-chi and his sons three days to sail eight hundred nautical miles from Shanghai to Hong Kong, with stops to discharge evacuees in ports in Taiwan. After docking in the British colony, Lin Pu-chi hurried to the home of his sister, who had lived in the British port for years with her husband, a close colleague of Watchman Nee. No sooner had they dropped off their bags than they immediately returned to the docks to catch a ferry to Canton. The Nationalist government had moved its offices to the South after the capital of Nanjing fell to the PLA in April. Lin Pu-chi hoped that somewhere in the piles of paperwork of the Foreign Ministry were the passport applications of his sons.

In Canton, the makeshift offices of the Foreign Ministry were jammed with people from all over China just as frantic as the Lin sons were to escape. Just that morning, the *South China Morning Post* reported that military sources held little hope of defending Canton from the PLA, which was advancing southward from Hunan. Civil servants in the Nationalist government were making plans yet again to evacuate—this time to the safety of Taiwan. The line for passports snaked out the door and around the block, everyone pushing and jockeying to hold their positions. Lin Pu-chi felt a jolt of panic. What if all of his well-made plans for this exodus fell apart because of lost paperwork? What if the Nationalist government retreated again? He had exhausted the family's money. This was his last chance.

Hours passed before they made it through the front door and faced a harried, impatient clerk. He snapped their Chinese identification cards out of their hands and wrote down their information, noting that they were born in Fujian Province. The clerk looked at the Chinese characters for their names—Lin Baomin and Lin Junmin—and looked at their faces. Again, he looked at the characters, then at their faces.

"Do you know Lin Xinmin?" the clerk asked Lin Pu-chi.

"Yes, he's my nephew," replied the minister, recalling his younger brother's second son, who had stayed with the family in Shanghai at the start of the Sino-Japanese War.

"He works here," the clerk said, hurrying into another room and calling out, "I'll get him."

The clerk had recognized that the middle character of the Lin brothers' names was the same as his friend's—something Chinese families did to identify a generation of the same clan. He studied their faces, too, and noticed a family resemblance. Thanks to that stroke of luck, this Fuzhou cousin got Paul and Jim their blue-cloth-covered Republic of China passports in hours instead of days.

The Chinese have a phrase, *guanxi*, which describes the intricate web of relationships that help a person to survive. It's using your connections to get what you need. It's the "you-scratch-my-back, I'll-scratch-yours" strategy. And for the next week in Hong Kong, Lin Pu-chi tapped every relationship he had to see that his sons made it to America. He sought out the help of the Right Reverend Ronald O. Hall, the head of the Diocese of Victoria, whom Lin Pu-chi had met at previous meetings of the Sheng Kung Hui. The arrival of Lin Pu-chi and his sons coincided with a special service to celebrate the one hundredth anniversary of the diocese. At St. John's Cathedral, which had the letters "VR" chiseled into the bell tower in honor of Queen Victoria, Lin Pu-chi delivered greetings at the service on behalf of the Sheng Kung Hui. Afterward, the influential bishop pulled strings with the American consulate next door on Garden Road to expedite a meeting with a visa officer. The bishop's *guanxi* paid off. On June 3, three weeks after leaving home, Paul and Jim paid $2.50 apiece to an American consulate clerk for US visas.

Days later, Lin Pu-chi watched as his sons climbed up the steps of a charter flight en route to Everett, Washington.

The gunmetal-gray plane transported troops during World War II. Now all of its passengers were Chinese. Many were wealthy overseas Chinese who had been living in Shanghai and wanted to return to the United States before the inevitable Communist takeover. In the air, as American stewards walked down the aisle serving food and drinks, the brothers privately made note of this unusual role reversal. In Shanghai, they rarely if ever saw Americans waiting on Chinese customers. Now a brawny young man leaned over, asking, "Whaddya like?"

After refueling first in Tokyo and then at the Shemya Air Force Base in the Aleutian Islands off Alaska, the brothers arrived in Everett, Washington, thirty hours after taking off from Hong Kong.

In the light of morning on their first day in the United States, Paul and Jim faced a world bearing little resemblance to the one they left. The air was clear and crisp, scented with pine and saltwater—a wonderful change from the thick, fetid odors of Shanghai. Great granite peaks loomed behind a calm harbor with tall sailboats, ferries, and fishing boats. It was all so new—not only what they saw, but what they didn't see. For starters, where were the people? They knew Everett was a small town by American standards. But still, even in China, a harborside village would be brimming with humanity. Here, everything seemed empty and uncluttered. Pedicab drivers didn't swarm around cars. Vendors didn't jam sidewalks hawking steamed buns or fried *youtiao* crullers. Mothers didn't hang laundry from bamboo poles in alleys as toddlers crawled in doorways.

Even though they had spent most of their lives in the most sophisticated metropolis in China, they were still surprised in ways big and small at how things were done in America. It started from the moment they got to the Everett train station. Jim had to go to the bathroom and followed the sign for "Men." Inside the restroom, he tried opening the door of the stall, but it wouldn't budge. He tried the next door, and it, too, was locked. Jim left the men's room and asked Paul to take a look. He, too, couldn't open the doors. "Why are they all locked?" he asked Jim in Chinese.

"You need to put in a nickel," came a voice from a stall.

A nickel? A toilet flushed as a husky white man, tucking in his shirt, emerged from the stall.

"You need to put money into the slot to open the door," the man explained. "Do you have any nickels?"

Jim shook his head with embarrassment.

"Here," the stranger said, slipping a coin into the slot, turning the knob, and opening the door. The brothers left the restroom feeling like the peasant bumpkins they used to mock in Shanghai.

When they got to San Francisco, a woman from a local Episcopal church—one of the many contacts Lin Pu-chi had notified in advance via telegram—met their train and ushered them to a local YMCA. They stayed only a night and departed by ferry at 11:00 a.m. the next day for Oakland, where they caught the *San Francisco Overland* to make the same eastbound journey as their father had thirty years before.

In Chicago, the brothers parted ways. Jim boarded another train, to New York City via Buffalo, while Paul continued on to Philadelphia. They split the money they had between them, leaving each with about fifty dollars.

"*Zai jian, Xiguatou,*" Jim said in parting, using his younger brother's childhood nickname. "See ya, Watermelon Head."

AMERICA'S PLAYGROUND

As the commuter train from Philadelphia approached Atlantic City, saltwater marshes spread for miles like a welcome mat to the resort town, renowned for its Boardwalk, beaches, and hotels. No other shore town on the East Coast served up the glamour or allure of Atlantic City. Paul had ended up here because of Josiah McCracken from St. John's medical school. Now living in Philadelphia, McCracken had helped medical students fleeing Shanghai to secure work in the States. He reached out to his son, a physician in Atlantic City, who got a spot for Paul as an intern.

Forty-five days after sailing from Shanghai, Paul walked up the front steps of Atlantic City Memorial Hospital and, in his most polished English, announced to a receptionist, "My name is Paul Lin and I'm here to work as an intern."

He was taken to a dormitory for interns next door to the hospital and two blocks from the beach on Ohio Avenue. His tiny room had a bed, a dresser, a chair, and a bedside table. Setting down his leather suitcase, he tossed his wallet with $36.50 on the bed and headed to the cafeteria for dinner.

Returning to his room, exhausted from days of train travel, he flopped on his bed and reached for his wallet. Picking it up, he immediately noticed that it felt lighter. He opened it. His heart skipped. All the money was gone—every bill, every coin, gone. He looked under the bed and in the drawer of the bedside table. He opened his billfold again, just in case he was mistaken. Empty. The first day of his new job and he was literally penniless.

Welcome to America.

With those early days to himself, Paul explored Atlantic City. He walked the entire seven-mile length of the Boardwalk. Often he simply sat on a bench looking at the sea of beachgoers sunning on towels or resting on chaise longues. In an odd way, this city of sixty thousand reminded him a little of Shanghai. With its constant stream of promenading crowds, the Boardwalk was like the Bund with a beach. And certainly some of Atlantic City's grandiose hotels—the Traymore, Claridge, or Blenheim—would feel right at home

Dr. Paul M. Lin, an intern at Atlantic City Memorial Hospital, on the beach in Atlantic City in the summer of 1949. Courtesy of Lin Family Collection.

next to Astor House or Cathay Hotel in Shanghai. This, too, was the first place in the United States where he saw anything close to a rickshaw, but the Boardwalk version was made of wicker and had passengers sitting in front with someone pushing on foot from behind. Even the billboards—like the giant ad for Camel cigarettes with the smiling face of a blond model in front of the sixteen-story Traymore Hotel—made him think of Shanghai.

In late August, two months after his arrival in Atlantic City, another intern asked Paul a puzzling question.

"You ready for the big pageant?" his colleague wanted to know.

"The what?" Paul asked.

"The *pageant*. You know, *Miss America*," the intern told him.

"Miss Who?"

It seemed the whole city was ramping up for the Miss America pageant. Interns from the hospital had to work at the pageant as emergency medics in case a contestant in heels twisted her ankle or fell off the runway. The local newspaper ran stories every day about the arrival of contestants and cheesecake photos of them chasing the waves or posing on the Boardwalk.

On September 10, spectators filled the cavernous Boardwalk Hall, including one new arrival from Shanghai, whose friends gave him the best seat in the house. In his white tunic, Paul was posted at the foot of the long runway and told to help any damsel who might slip and fall face-first into the potted ferns. A giant "Miss America" banner hung over the stage. As the curtains were pulled back, a stream of contestants in evening gowns began parading down the runway. They weren't wearing the body-hugging silk dresses preferred by Shanghai beauties. Instead they looked like big bells, swishing back and forth with each stride. Paul was agog. There were brunettes, blonds, even a redhead. They came from states he never heard of: North Dakota, Arkansas. Next came the swimsuit competition. Just how this was a competition, he wasn't sure. He averted his eyes as the long-legged ladies pivoted past him in tight suits and heels. Fifteen women went on to the talent portion of the pageant. Miss Arizona recited Shakespeare, acting out the potion scene from *Romeo and Juliet*. Stagehands rolled out a giant glass tank of water for Miss Indiana, who dove in and performed a water ballet routine.

One of the last ones up was Miss Montana. The curtain parted, and she came trotting out dressed as a cowgirl, astride a golden palomino horse. Halfway across the stage, the animal stumbled, reared up over the judge's table, and nearly fell into the orchestra pit.

The audience gasped.

Paul lurched forward.

But Miss Montana steadied her horse and trotted off with a plastered smile and a tip of her cowgirl hat. That would be the last year animals were allowed to perform at the Miss America pageant. In the end, Miss Arizona,

Jacque Mercer, was crowned the winner. As she made her victory walk down the runway, Paul gazed up as Miss America in her rhinestone tiara and fake-fur-lined vermilion cape waved at the audience—and him.

DRAGON SEED

The year passed quickly. After Atlantic City, Paul transferred to Hartford Hospital for a residency in surgery, moving a step closer to his goal of becoming the second neurosurgeon in China. Hartford was a far cry from Atlantic City. With more than twice the people, the Connecticut capital was more intense and the hospital environment more competitive. This was a larger teaching hospital, drawing medical students and physicians with Ivy League credentials. A young urologist and Harvard man took a liking to the awkward resident from Shanghai and invited him home to his family's bayside vacation house in Old Saybrook, Connecticut, for the weekend.

More than a decade older than Paul, Dr. Robert Hepburn was a Yankee blueblood and a legacy at Hartford Hospital: his father also was a urologist. Robert explained to Paul that he had more than a passing interest in Shanghai. After the Second World War, he had served on the naval hospital ship *Repose*, which had anchored in the Huangpu River for six months. The eight-hundred-bed ship served as the base hospital for the Seventh Fleet and the British Far Eastern Fleet.

"I think my older sister would enjoy meeting you," Robert explained on the hour-long drive to the family home. "She just made a movie about China."

As they turned down a long driveway leading to the waterfront house, Paul soon realized that this was no family cottage. The seventeen-room, three-story, white brick house faced a lawn that led to a private beach, where the arms of two rock jetties formed a secluded bathing area. When they arrived, Robert's sister was already out golfing at the nine-hole Fenwick Golf Course, which ran past the house. Robert grabbed his clubs for a quick nine, with Paul tagging along to watch. Back at the house after the round, they were sitting in the kitchen when Robert's sister came through the door. Wrapped in a thick terry robe after a swim in the frigid sound, she gave her brother a kiss on the cheek and immediately joined them at the kitchen table.

"Paul, this is my sister Katharine," Robert said.

The introduction hit him like a thunderbolt. *Dr. Hepburn. Katharine Hepburn. My sister the actress.* Why hadn't he noticed the family resemblance? Bob had the same long, thin nose as his forty-three-year-old sister. Even in Shanghai, with its many movie houses, Katharine Hepburn was a big name.

At the moment, she was between movies, having just finished *Adam's Rib* and before the release of *The African Queen*.

"Ah, my brother told me all about you," the actress began, tilting her sharp chin upward. "You're from Shanghai, aren't you? I made a movie about China. One of Pearl Buck's novels. *Dragon Seed*. Do you know Pearl Buck?"

"Of course," Paul replied. "Even in China, Pearl Buck is very famous. Her parents were missionaries. Where did you film in China?"

"Oh, not in China. Good god," Katharine chuckled. "We filmed on a back lot in Hollywood. Built a set to look like a village."

"Did you play a missionary?"

"Missionary? No, no, I played the lead, a peasant named Jade," she said. "The movie was set in 1937. The story goes that none of the village men want to fight the Japanese. But Jade isn't afraid. She's headstrong and . . ."

As Katharine went on about the movie, Paul had a hard time processing what she was saying. *She plays a Chinese peasant?* He looked at her square face, her high cheekbones and pointed chin, her wavy brown hair. *Why would anyone think that she looks Chinese?* He tried to picture her as a farmer with indigo trousers rolled up, planting rice seedlings with an infant strapped to her back. A comical thought crossed his mind: What if a Chinese studio was making a movie about, say, the Civil War, and cast only Chinese actors and actresses? What would Americans make of that?

"Was it very horrible?" Katharine asked Paul, who hadn't heard a word she said.

"I'm sorry, was what horrible?"

"The Japanese. Shanghai. During the war?"

Both Katharine and Robert looked intently at Paul, waiting for his answer. One had played an avenging Chinese peasant against Japanese occupiers; the other had patched up wounded American soldiers during the Pacific conflict.

"It was bad, but not as bad as you might think," Paul tried to explain. "Shanghai was isolated in a way."

Sensing their confusion, he went on, "It was hard for us, don't get me wrong. But the Japanese didn't destroy Shanghai. They lived there, too. Other places had it a lot worse. But my family, we were okay. I still went to school. My father worked."

Paul went on to tell his hosts about his flight from Shanghai just days before the PLA took the city.

"And how are things now?" the movie star wanted to know.

The question seemed to stump Paul. He paused, thinking of his father's regular letters and the paucity of any details.

"I really don't know," Paul replied somewhat sheepishly. "I've been here more than a year and I can't tell you what's happening to my family. I'm not sure they know either."

IV

NEW ORDER

· 12 ·

American Wolves

Shanghai, 1950

*W*hen he said good-bye to his sons in Hong Kong, Lin Pu-chi insisted on one thing: "You must write to us every month." He expected the letters to be written in English, the language of their adopted country, and free of misspellings or grammatical errors. In a typical exchange, he once admonished Paul: "You wrote, 'My saliva was *drowling*.' There's no such word as *drowling*." Lin Pu-chi wanted to know about their new lives, about their professors and colleagues, about girlfriends if there were any, about their progress in medicine. But in his own replies to them, he established a pattern of keeping things superficial. With Paul working as a surgical resident in Hartford and Jim now with a hospital in Washington, DC, he told them only what they needed to know, never burdening them with the many matters that were racking him.

A year after the founding of the People's Republic of China, no one could predict what would happen to Christians under the new regime of Chairman Mao Zedong and Premier Zhou Enlai. The country's new leaders promised freedom of religious belief for Christians, Muslims, and Buddhists. But would that work in a political system controlled by avowed atheists? How much would the arm of government intrude into churches? And more important, would freedom of faith extend to freedom of conscience?

On the eve of the Communist victory in 1949, Lin Pu-chi had calmed the readers of the *Chinese Churchman* by quoting from Isaiah, "In repentance and rest is your salvation, in quietness and trust is your strength." China had endured a century of unrelenting warfare, he wrote in an editorial. The bloodshed stretched from the Opium Wars to the Taiping Rebellion; invasions by British, French, and Japanese forces; the Boxer Uprising; the Northern Expedition; eight years of Sino-Japanese fighting; and finally, the civil war between Nationalists and Communists.

"In times like these, heart-gripping terror is inevitable as the future looks ever so bleak," he told readers. His advice: be still, be quiet, reflect on the words of Isaiah, and put your trust in God.

Lin Pu-chi remained guardedly hopeful about the future. To cower would be useless. To flee to Hong Kong or Taiwan was no guarantee of true comfort and stability. He said as much in a letter to his friend, Bishop Y. Y. Tsu. In the summer of 1950, the older man was in Hong Kong, debating whether he should take the next steamer to Shanghai. It was a dilemma facing many Chinese, particularly those with Western ties, money, education, status, and options beyond China. Bishop Tsu had been traveling in North America, attending a conference of the World Council of Churches in Toronto and visiting his university-age children in New Hampshire, Connecticut, and California. While transiting in Hong Kong, some foreign friends, concerned about shifting political winds, advised him not to return to Shanghai.

But the bishop felt bound by duty. When he received the letter from Lin Pu-chi, encouraging him to come back, it sealed his decision.

The fact that Lin Pu-chi had been favorably disposed to the new situation did not mean that he was a supporter of the Chinese Communist Party. But like many people who had weathered decades of turmoil and humiliation at the hands of Japan, he held a deep, abiding sense of pride for his country. As a Chinese Christian, too, he saw this moment in history as a unique opportunity for the church to finally stand on its own without the help of foreign missionaries and their faraway boards. It was a growing sentiment, this notion of a love of the motherland—*aiguo*—coexisting with a love of church—*aijiao*.

Lin Pu-chi made his thoughts known to an audience beyond his immediate circle of Anglican colleagues in the Sheng Kung Hui. He added his name with eighteen other prominent Chinese Christians to an open letter to foreign mission boards, published soon after the founding of the People's Republic of China in October 1949. The widely circulated document was a public declaration that the missionary era was over and its legacy, entangled as it was with the history of imperialism in China, would be contested. Lin Pu-chi was the only Anglican priest to sign the statement. He and the others stated that this new era was a "milestone," signaling the end of a century of struggle against exploitation and feudalistic oppression. They added:

> Much of Western culture that has been introduced in recent years will be re-examined and shorn of its undesirable elements. Out of this will be born a new China, radically different from the China of old.

There was no need, they declared, for Christians to reexamine their faith. Their beliefs would endure. But the role of missionaries would be greatly limited. Lin Pu-chi and other coauthors acknowledged that they could not remain aloof from the political environment. Neither could the Chinese church expect to emerge from this historical moment unaffected. "It will suffer a purge and many of the withered branches will be amputated," the group wrote. "But we believe it will emerge stronger and purer in quality, a more fitting witness to the gospel of Christ."

Lin Pu-chi shared an office with Bishop Tsu in the Hongkou section of Shanghai. His main task was handling the minutiae of the regime change, the endless forms to fill and inventory of church property and personnel to complete. Under socialism, schools and hospitals run by the church were now national assets and had to be turned over to the state.

The bishop's return to Shanghai in the fall of 1950 came at a time of worsening relations between China and the United States over the conflict in the Korean peninsula. The communist regime in North Korea had dispatched troops across the thirty-eighth parallel on June 25, 1950, to attack the pro-Western South Korean government in Seoul. Chinese "volunteers" supported northern troops, while General Douglas A. MacArthur of the United States led United Nations forces in pushing the northern troops back to the Yalu River and the border with China. The United States would refer to the

At home in Shanghai, Lin Pu-chi wrote in a small office off the kitchen. This photograph was taken in the early 1950s. Courtesy of Lin Family Collection.

conflict as the Korean War, but in China, it was dubbed the "War to Resist America and Aid Korea."

At the Sheng Kung Hui national office, police often made unannounced visits, questioning Lin Pu-chi and others about the comings and goings of visitors, particularly foreigners. The anti-American rhetoric became so bombastic that the last of the missionaries packed up and left before they were kicked out.

For Bishop Tsu, it quickly became clear that he had made the wrong decision. Even if he wanted to stay, there was no way his wife could ever return. She was a US citizen, the daughter of a Chinese-American pastor from New York City's Chinatown. The couple had met four decades earlier when Bishop Tsu was a graduate student in the United States. In the summer of 1950, after traveling with her husband, she had stayed behind in the States. Now, with guns drawn over Korea, the bishop felt as if the political situation had forced his hand. He would turn sixty-five years old on December 18, 1950, and realized that it would be best for him to retire and leave China.

Since they were young men, Bishop Tsu had been Lin Pu-chi's adviser and confidant. He was close to the Lin family, too, and had given his younger friend some money to cover his sons' passage out of China before the fall of Shanghai in the spring of 1949. The bishop had even scouted out hospitals in America where the Lin sons might continue their medical training, approaching physicians he met in his travels across the United States about internships for them.

Fittingly for the friends, their last occasion together was at St. John's University, where they had first met as professor and student thirty-five years earlier. On November 30, 1950, members of the Anglican and Episcopal community gathered in the university chapel to mark two occasions: the retirement of Bishop Tsu as well as the consecration of a new bishop who would work in Sichuan Province. At a luncheon afterward, Lin Pu-chi and the others presented Bishop Tsu with a silk-bound book of essays, eulogizing his four decades in the church. Everyone had signed it, including all the bishops. In leaving, Bishop Tsu relinquished his title as general secretary of the national office to Lin Pu-chi.

On December 13, 1950, the older man boarded a cargo ship in Hong Kong, the SS *President Pierce*, bound for Los Angeles.

CHRISTIAN MANIFESTO

Premier Zhou had warned the Christian community—in 1949, numbering one million Protestants and three million Roman Catholics—to clean house on their own and rid churches of "imperialistic and feudalistic influences."

Some leaders in the Protestant community, disposed to working with the new government, heeded those words and advocated for a new paradigm for the church in China. They drew up a "Christian Manifesto" and urged others to publicly sign on, pledging to terminate ties with overseas missions and support the new regime. This emerging movement, dubbed by its leaders as the "Three-Self Reform Movement," envisioned a Christian community that would be "self-governing, self-supporting and self-propagating"—in real terms, free of foreign involvement of any kind in the fate, finances, or future growth of Christianity in China.

In April 1951, Zhou summoned more than 150 Protestant leaders from around China to Beijing for a high-level meeting with officials in charge of religious matters. Among them was the brother-in-law of Lin Pu-chi, Watchman Nee, who was invited as an observer. Even though he was not affiliated with any denominational church, the Little Flock, with more than seventy thousand people spread across the country, represented a significant portion of China's Protestant population.

The meeting was ostensibly to examine how Christian groups would sever their ties with foreign mission boards. For the first two days—April 17 and 18—the gathering followed that agenda. But the next two days devolved into a mass denunciation of seven men: three missionaries and four Chinese Christians.

This was a deliberate attempt to remold ideas and create a united front of Protestants, free of denominational divisions and with a clear demarcation between "patriotic" Chinese Christians and recalcitrant allies of America. Eighteen delegates took turns making "vehement denunciations" against the seven men, none of whom were present. In each case, someone close to the target—a friend or colleague—led the charge. The westerners were decried as "imperialist agents under the cloak of religion."

Frank Price was a China-born Presbyterian with the YMCA who had the misfortune of now being a former close adviser to the Nationalist pariah Chiang Kai-shek.

Edward Lockwood was another YMCA man, accused of being a "missionary spy" for thirty years in the southern city of Canton.

Timothy Richard was an unexpected target. He had been dead for thirty-six years. The Baptist educator from Wales founded the Christian Literature Society, which translated religious books into Chinese, now criticized as intellectual poison.

The four Chinese Christians fared no better. With Premier Zhou in attendance at the meeting, they were dismissed as "agents of imperialism" and "renegades and enemies of the people."

One was an American-educated bishop with the Methodist Episcopal Church.

Another was a leader of the YMCA, who was accused of taking orders from America.

A third was a Pentecostal preacher, formerly an actor, already under arrest and labeled as "Christian scum," who was accused of raping his own daughter. "Does he deserve death?" asked his accuser. "Deserves death! Deserves death!" roared the crowd.

And the final target was Bishop Y. Y. Tsu.

It fell upon his colleague Bishop Robin Chen from Anhui Province to lead the attack on him. Bishop Chen, an active and early supporter of the Three-Self Movement, was the head of the House of Bishops and the face of the Sheng Kung Hui.

"It is not an easy matter to accuse another bishop of the same church," Bishop Chen told the audience in Beijing. "Yet standing alongside of the people and for the love of the fatherland and the love of the church, today I must accuse him."

He charged that his colleague "fell into a trap and became a tool of the American imperial aggressors."

Bishop Chen went on to itemize the departed bishop's transgressions, starting with his work as a chaplain for the US Army. It was true that in the last eight months of the Second World War, Bishop Tsu accepted an offer to serve as a civilian chaplain in the Burma Road area, where troops transported supplies from the British colony of Burma into southwest China. He traveled with his church vestments as well as a GI uniform with a silver cross, which he donned when addressing US Army units. But in Beijing, this became an act of disloyalty. Bishop Chen told the audience that Y. Y. Tsu considered wearing that uniform "a glory."

And there was more. After liberation, Bishop Tsu used his KMT passport to travel outside of China, including the trip to Toronto in the summer of 1950 to attend the World Council of Churches meeting. At the convention, the World Council had passed a resolution condemning North Korea's military incursion across the thirty-eighth parallel. But for this audience in Beijing, the emphasis was flipped, with Bishop Chen characterizing the resolution as supporting American aggression and opposing a Stockholm peace accord from 1950. He accused Bishop Tsu, who had penned many articles in the foreign press criticizing the regime's handling of religious matters, of trying to sabotage the Three-Self Movement and acting more American than Chinese. The exiled bishop had studied with American teachers. He socialized with Americans. He kept financial accounts in dollars. He wrote letters in English. He affected an American accent. He traveled more than ten times to America, and his whole family lived there. "With this kind of life," Bishop Chen asked, "how could he help but be pro-American and worship America?"

It was time for self-examination, the senior bishop told the assembled. "We must take the pain and shame and anger of today and transform it into strength," he exhorted. When conference attendees returned home, it was up to them to carry on the work of "convincing, inspiring, educating and remaking all the backward elements within the Episcopal Church."

He closed by saying, "People who love the Church will join the march of the Great Chinese People and shout aloud: 'Long live the Chinese People's Republic! Long live Chairman Mao!'"

SECRET ENEMIES

All of this meant only one thing for Lin Pu-chi. It was time to toe the line or face the consequences.

Confusion, dissension, and internal strife swept over churches as the message from Beijing trickled down to the parish level. Christians were put on notice that there would be denunciation meetings for everyone, denominational churches as well as independent groups such as Watchman Nee's Little Flock. Why was this necessary? For the answer, those who marched to the beat of the Three-Self Movement quoted Chairman Mao: "After enemies who are open, concrete and holding the gun have been overthrown, there are still enemies who are secret, formless and not holding the gun, who will surely struggle with us desperately."

The denunciation meetings and public confessions were part of a process of undoing the past. The history of Christianity was so intertwined with the history of Western imperialism that the Three-Self Movement led Protestants and Catholics to concede that on some level, everyone had been complicit in this ruinous alliance. No one, no matter how respected or prominent, was immune from criticism.

A friend of Bishop Tsu who was the former board chairman of St. John's University described the drama playing out behind the scenes this way: Y. T. Wu, the Protestant leader at the vanguard of the Three-Self Movement, would give a hint to a certain church that so-and-so of its congregation was persona non grata with the government and would have to make a self-confession. Y. T. Wu would pass on the confession to the government's Religious Affairs Bureau. Often, the statement would come back stamped with "not enough." The target then would have to try again, groping in the dark to ascertain what authorities might or might not know about him. People tended to err on the side of too much information, unintentionally playing into the hands of authorities. A former mathematics professor from St. John's had to write four confessions before his testimony was accepted. "We can thus understand better why our bishops made such denouncements of others and themselves at the public accusation meetings," David W. K. Au wrote in his letter to Bishop Tsu. "They really deserve our sympathy more than our bitterness."

Lin Pu-chi's future was uncertain. The religious front that was forming was pulling people like a riptide. Denominational lines were blurring, casting doubt on whether there would be any distinction at all between churches. Lin Pu-chi's work as editor of the *Chinese Churchman* magazine, meanwhile, ceased. His editorial in the June 1951 issue was his last. The piece included the strident rhetoric of the moment, extolling readers to participate in the Three-Self Movement and not to separate political life from religious life. At the same time, the editorial was self-critical in an honest, introspective way. The intrinsic problem of British Anglicans and American Episcopalians, he wrote, lay with their reliance on institutions and traditions. Every service, every prayer followed a rigid form. The clergy had become lazy, delivering messages that were perfunctory, bloodless, uninspiring, all intellect and no emotion. In the editorial, it was as if in using the collective "we," he was actually conceding the failings of the singular "I." The church was weak because its priests were weak. It was like a large wealthy family. And when the family fell, the grand buildings and antiques had no practical value. "But we are not willing to give them up, being afraid of betraying our forefathers," the editorial stated.

A notice on the last page of the issue said the July edition was postponed. The leaders of the Sheng Kung Hui had held a meeting on June 13 to elect five clerics to carry on the work of promoting the "Movement to Resist U.S. Aggression and Aid Korea" as well as the "Three-Self Reform Movement." Lin Pu-chi was among them.

The pressure to conform was mounting, and it didn't matter what Lin Pu-chi might have said or written in the past. The question now was whether he could bend to the political will of the majority, whether he would stand with the masses—or not.

The Church of Our Savior was on a narrow street shaded with sycamore trees in the former French Concession of Shanghai. It held special meaning for the Lin family. In his twenty years in Shanghai, Lin Pu-chi had frequently conducted services at the church, which had moved from Hongkou to the Rue Maresca after being destroyed during fighting in 1937. His daughter, Martha, was married there in 1948 in a ceremony conducted by the American bishop of Shanghai.

After Sunday services on July 29, 1951, more than a thousand people, coming from parishes all over China, returned for an afternoon session on a topic of mandatory study: how the United States had used churches as a form of cultural aggression. One by one, Protestant groups across the city were holding large-scale denunciation meetings, part of the ongoing process of ideological molding. Four other Protestant groups had already staged their mass meetings, and at least a dozen more would follow over the next month.

First to speak was the vestryman of the church, a Shanghai businessman who was actively cooperating with the new regime. Just back from an inspection tour of troops in Korea, he claimed to have personally witnessed Americans using religion as a form of aggression. Army chaplains, he said, were "the claws and teeth" of this cultural assault and were actually spies.

The next speaker was the former dean of the Central Theological Seminary at St. John's University. For more than a century, this man told the crowd, America had manipulated the umbrella group for the church, the Sheng Kung Hui. He criticized himself for thinking religion was above politics and for preventing seminary students from studying political topics.

After him, the bishop from Jiangsu castigated Bishop William Roberts, the Yale-educated American missionary, beloved by many, who taught at St. John's and was a leader of the Sheng Kung Hui for years.

When he finished, it was Lin Pu-chi's turn to speak.

He rose from his seat and walked to the pulpit. He looked down on the faces in the crowd. He saw many friends, clergy as well as people from all over China, fellow believers whom he had met over the past quarter century in his journey from Fuzhou to Shanghai. As a young priest, Lin Pu-chi knew what it felt like to be attacked and punished for his beliefs. In his hometown of Fuzhou, when he was thirty-three years old and a rising star in the church, he was captured and taunted for a day by antiforeign protesters. The mob treated him like a hack for foreigners, no better than a comprador, doing the bidding of British and American clerics. They threw a coarse rope around his neck, pulling him through the streets of Fuzhou and ridiculing him as "a running dog of imperialists."

Now, more than twenty years later, he would have to do the same to his closest friend, Bishop Tsu, using words instead of muscle to bring him down. And of all places, this act of disloyalty would take place in the very parish where both the bishop's father and uncle had been vicars, the latter for almost forty years.

All eyes looked up to Lin Pu-chi as he began to speak.

"I have experienced an intense internal struggle," Lin Pu-chi began. "I stand here today with incomparable compunction, indignation, and grief."

Bishop Tsu had been his teacher at St. John's and his boss at the Sheng Kung Hui offices, he told the congregation. Despite those ties, he explained, "I accuse him with the spirit of placing righteousness above private loyalty and expose his deeds as a lackey and accomplice of American imperialism and degenerate and sinner of our church."

Lin Pu-chi then repeated a litany of transgressions that matched word for word some of the same allegations delivered three months earlier in Beijing in the first denunciation of Bishop Tsu. It was a script, and he was an actor. Bishop Tsu was "ostensibly a Chinese" but in action and thought more American, Lin Pu-chi told the audience. Then, adding a detail that only he would know, he said that the bishop had recounted to him how his grown daughter in California wanted to someday marry an American rather than a Chinese man.

Lin Pu-chi's own sons had homes in Connecticut and Washington, DC, jobs with US hospitals and American lives that they detailed in their monthly letters. Yet here he stood, pressured to castigate Bishop Tsu for perceived offenses that could have been his own. He criticized his mentor, saying, "His whole family is now in America, which proves that he has been completely Americanized."

Bishop Robin Chen had the final word. Y. Y. Tsu was no longer a bishop of any diocese in China. The House of Bishops, too, had severed relations with its counterparts in Hong Kong and Macao and would no longer recognize as members any foreign bishops. They also voted to quit the World Council of Churches. "This is the first accusation meeting in the history of the Chung Hua Sheng Kung Hui," Bishop Chen remarked. "From today, we want not only to develop our Three-Self Movement, but also to cut off all the poisonous influence of America."

Two Sundays later, as parishioners filed into the Church of Our Savior, ushers handed out a sheet with the order of service on one side and church news on the other. One news item was a reminder about a request made in June, urging members to donate funds for planes and guns to oppose America and defend China.

Churchgoers took note, too, that they would be singing a new hymn— the "Christians' Patriotic Hymn."

> Chinese Christians love your country;
> Increase production;
> Do your best to support the front;
> For country, for the Lord's church;
> Quickly donate war weapons to defeat American wolves.

· 13 ·

Missing

Shanghai, 1955

*H*e sat by the living room window, waiting, looking, listening. It had become his end-of-the-month ritual. As soon as he spied the mailman coming down the lane, Lin Pu-chi was out of his chair and reaching for the letters coming through the mail slot on the door. He flipped quickly through the envelopes, hoping to see the thin blue one with a Philadelphia postmark. And there it was.

Paul, his youngest, was now working as a neurosurgeon in that city and married to an American nurse. Lin Pu-chi wrote to him the first week of every month, with Paul replying by the month's end. The patriarch was discreet in what he shared with his son. He had to assume that security agents were monitoring his letters. Paul, too, knew when to be circumspect and hold back on potentially sensitive news. Now was one of those times. Even though the Korean War had ended two years earlier, Paul did not tell his father that he had enlisted as an officer in the US Army medical corps. No one—not the family in Shanghai or agents intercepting the mail—needed to know that he would be shipping out to a hospital in Tacoma, Washington, in the summer of 1955 and living on an army base.

Lin Pu-chi sliced open the envelope and read his daughter-in-law's perfect cursive handwriting. The young couple had married in 1953. It was left to her, not her busy surgeon husband, to keep the family in Shanghai abreast of their lives. Along with the usual patter about home life and family news, she mentioned nonchalantly about sending a birthday gift to Aunt Mary.

He exhaled.

That was their code for the money his son wired to an aunt in Hong Kong. Money transfers had to be handled with subterfuge. Paul could not walk into a bank in Philadelphia and simply send cash to an account in Shanghai. China had severed financial relations with the United States years earlier.

But not so with Hong Kong, which, while still part of the British Empire, remained a Chinese city at heart. The family had to be clever, dance a little two-step so that no one noticed what was going on. Twice a year, in April and October, Paul mailed a check for $500 to Lin Pu-chi's younger sister in Hong Kong. Aunt Mary deposited the money, wrote a check on her account, and then mailed it to Shanghai.

The "birthday gift" had been late this April, leaving Lin Pu-chi to fret. In his last letter, he had addressed his son in Chinese instead of English so that his American daughter-in-law would not understand, sheepishly inquiring: *Do you have any problem with Mother's birthday gift? We hope you will continue to send it, as it is very much needed here.*

It was mortifying to have to admit to his son that the family needed the money to get by. But Lin Pu-chi had no work and contributed nothing to the household income. At a time when he should have been at the prime of his career, he was idle. The only church work he had was substituting at the chapel at St. John's or saying the service in his native Fuzhou dialect for a small congregation in the city. Even then, Lin Pu-chi had to cover the price of his bus fare, receiving no remuneration of any kind from the churches. Once close to the inner circle of leaders in the Anglican and Episcopal Church, he had been shunted aside, replaced by younger clerics more politically in step with the new regime.

This month's letter from Philadelphia included four photos of his son and daughter-in-law with their newborn second child, Daria, who joined her

A studio portrait of Ni Guizhen and Lin Pu-chi from the 1950s. During this difficult period, Ni Guizhen could barely mask her stress and strain. Courtesy of Lin Family Collection.

jiejie, Angela. Lin Pu-chi took the photos and letter to the second floor, where his wife was spending the morning with her sister-in-law Charity, the wife of Watchman Nee. Charity was a frequent visitor, stopping by at least once a week. Martha's two daughters were so accustomed to seeing her that they called her New Granny, or *xin ah-bu* in the local dialect.

Whenever Charity came over, the women retreated to Ni Guizhen's bedroom, closed the door, took out their hymnals, and sang with abandon. Lyrics written by Watchman Nee—some in English, some in Chinese—were favorites. They felt like he was speaking to them through music.

> Oh, let us remember in running our race
> That faith is not feeling, and trust is not trace;
> And when all is seeming as black as the night
> We'll keep on believing and go on with the fight.

"Look, pictures of the baby," Lin Pu-chi interrupted, laying out the snapshots for the women to ogle.

"Who is that one?" Charity asked, pointing to the older child.

"Ah-E," he told her, using his granddaughter's Chinese name, which meant peace and happiness. "Look at her holding that flower, such a mischievous look in her eye! What's in her mind, do you think?"

"And the baby? Her name?" Charity asked.

It was Lin Pu-chi's duty as the patriarch of the family to name all the children in the new generation. American grandchildren received Chinese names; and Chinese grandchildren, English ones.

"Heng," he told Charity. The name meant "perseverance."

"A good name," Ni Guizhen responded.

Perseverance. It was a feeling that weighed heavily on everyone in the room. Mornings like this were a welcome break from their unsettled lives. Both Ni Guizhen and her sister-in-law had serious health issues. Ni Guizhen suffered insomnia so intense that the only way she could sleep was with a nightly sedative plus a tranquilizer. Charity's health was no better. She was losing her eyesight due to diabetes, and her blood pressure sometimes reached precariously high levels.

Stress contributed to the frail health of both women, for neither the sister nor wife of Watchman Nee had heard from him since the police had taken him away three years earlier.

The day Watchman Nee was arrested had been a Thursday, April 10, 1952. Charity had been with him in the office of the China Biological and Chemical Laboratories (CBC). The business was being merged with a state-run company in the northeastern city of Shenyang, but the merger was suspended by government order pending a review of accounts and tax payments.

Without any notice, agents from the Public Security Bureau (PSB) in Shenyang arrived at the CBC compound in Shanghai. They told Watchman Nee that he was needed immediately at the other company. Looking out the window of the office, Charity saw the agents standing on either side of her husband as they led him to a waiting car and drove away.

On a train to Shenyang, officers formally arrested him. Watchman Nee, forty-eight, was charged as part of the "Five-Antis" campaign against illegal activity by the business class. The company was accused of tax evasion and stealing national property. An employee for Watchman Nee's business had informed investigators that CBC inflated the value of a boiler it sold to the state enterprise. The government fined the pharmaceutical business 17,200 million yuan, or the equivalent of $1.5 million.

If the crimes of Watchman Nee had been limited to cheating the government on taxes or contracts, the matter may have ended then and there. But the PSB wasn't finished with him. Agents transferred Watchman Nee back to Shanghai and kept him locked up in a detention center near the South Railway Station.

The only thing the family had been told was to bring some personal items for him—a thermos for hot water and a metal basin for washing—to an address on Huaihai Road in the old French Concession. A relative who dropped off the items inquired about Watchman Nee when she arrived. "Can I ask him to write me a note?"

But she was given a curt "No" and turned away.

For three years, the family had no contact.

A TEACUP ROUND OR SQUARE

Someone like Watchman Nee, with his far-reaching influence, would have been very useful for the Protestant leaders trying to galvanize support for the Three-Self Movement.

The Little Flock had more than seventy thousand members at about eight hundred locations across China. They were doctors and nurses, teachers and students on university campuses, factory workers, professionals, administrators, even bureaucrats with the new government. They lived in urban centers on the coast from Guangzhou up through Xiamen, Fuzhou, Shanghai, Ningbo, Nanjing, Suzhou, and Hangzhou; in northern cities like Beijing and Qingdao; and in river ports like Wuhan and Chongqing in China's interior.

If the Little Flock was expansive before 1949, it became even larger after the communist victory. Many Christian congregations that had been dependent on foreign missions joined the Little Flock, which offered them financial help if they needed it. Some American and British missionaries were so grateful that they handed over their church property to the Little Flock before China kicked them out of the country. The Christian Assembly also welcomed individuals who were outliers in the new socialist state—former members of the Nationalist Party, capitalists, and onetime landlords, drawn by their message of salvation.

With the new religious policy, Watchman Nee played it coyly. He did not immediately reject the Three-Self goals like some leaders of independent Christian groups. But neither did he unambiguously embrace the new order. At best, Watchman Nee strategized that he could carve out neutral ground. After all, his followers were not part of a denominational group like Lin Pu-chi's Anglican Church. Missionaries did not influence them. They were "three-self" even before there was a Three-Self Movement. The Little Flock members were "self-supporting," not relying on overseas funds to run their assembly halls. They were "self-governing," with no hierarchy like that of the Anglican House of Bishops. And they handled their own grassroots expansion, thus being "self-propagating."

But at the same time, Watchman Nee watched what happened to people whose loyalty to the movement was questioned—Christians like Lin Pu-chi. Despite everything his Anglican brother-in-law wrote or said, despite his public efforts to distance himself from foreign missionaries, his allegiance was called into question. Lin Pu-chi was deemed someone whose "love of country" could not be totally trusted by what was now called the Three-Self *Patriotic* Movement. Watchman Nee knew what had happened to his brother-in-law at the Church of Our Savior and the humiliation he faced in denouncing his friend and mentor Bishop Tsu. If someone like that was considered untrustworthy and not patriotic enough, what of him?

A month after the denunciation meeting involving Lin Pu-chi, Watchman Nee tried to more clearly throw his support behind the Three-Self Movement. He gave a series of talks at the Nanyang Road assembly under the heading of "How I have turned over." He admitted being too nonchalant about politics and urged members that it was possible to be good citizens and good Christians. In one address, he told them, "Today, we are the people of the People's Republic of China." The government wasn't asking Christians to give up their faith, Watchman Nee explained. Rather, religion was like a teacup. It could be round or square. The only thing that mattered was that the plate—the socialist state—was the same for everyone. "All of a sudden I realized that the government did not ask you what your cup was; they asked what your plate was."

Such a public pronouncement of loyalty to country was a logical move and an obvious attempt by Watchman Nee to align the Little Flock with current policy. But the problem was that his flock was not willing to follow him. A big meeting at the Nanyang Road assembly to mobilize members behind the Three-Self Movement turned into a chaotic shouting match. People booed a man who stood to read a statement, accusing him of being a government spy. Watchman Nee looked on as the session spun out of control. Government officials did not believe that the outburst at the Nanyang Road assembly was spontaneous and instead suspected that Watchman Nee was plotting antigovernment sentiment from behind closed doors.

Watchman Nee became viewed as someone beyond the control of the government with unchallenged influence over a vast number of people. Communist authorities saw him as someone who potentially could steer not only the religious thoughts of people but their political beliefs as well. He was a threat that had to be contained.

After his arrest in 1952 on tax evasion and fraud, Watchman Nee was the subject of a full-scale investigation into whether he was trying to undermine the revolutionary government. It culminated in August 1955 when PSB agents at the highest level in Beijing quietly began circulating an internal assessment of him—the "Report on the Christian Assembly (Little Flock)." The confidential document, sent to security agents in every province and major city, outlined areas of concern and examples of how the Little Flock was being antagonistic to the government.

It served a key purpose: On its pages was enough ammunition to destroy Watchman Nee and the Little Flock.

SCANDAL

In 1955, the sweltering heat of August carried into September. This was the dreaded "Autumn Tiger," a prolonged stretch of ninety-five-degree temperatures and humidity so heavy it hung on people's shoulders like wet wool coats.

On the third floor of the Lin home, the couple's second son, thirty-year-old Tim, dripped with sweat as he followed his mother's instructions to remove all the furniture from the bedroom. Herself too weak to help, Ni Guizhen was nevertheless well enough to supervise others.

Pick up that chair. Take out that bed. Mop the floor. Whitewash the walls.

There was no time to waste. Tim was getting married, and his bride needed to come home to a fresh, clean room. Lin Pu-chi gave up his study on the third floor to make room for the newlyweds. He moved his typewriter and desk to the attic along with a small cot. With windows on both sides, the bright room caught a breeze in the evening, making it a perfect place to sleep on hot nights.

On October 2, 1955, the family celebrated the marriage of Tim and an outgoing nurse named Emma, the English name for Hu Yimei. More than fifty relatives and friends feasted at a banquet at the old Park Hotel, a twenty-two-story art deco tower on Nanjing Road with the best view of the new People's Square from its Sky Terrace. The daughter of a textile engineer, Emma had met Tim at a party, where they danced and flirted. Not a churchgoer like her future in-laws, Emma knew very little about the family's background. Watchman Nee was not even a name she recognized. No one in the Lin family ever discussed him, not even in the privacy of their home, but particularly not with a newcomer like Emma.

The newlyweds moved into the whitewashed third-floor bedroom the Sunday night of their wedding banquet and by Tuesday morning were back at work—a factory making electric meters for Tim, the hospital for Emma. Emma was heartened at how her new mother-in-law seemed so eager for the company of another woman. She felt happy in her new home.

A month into their marriage, the couple was just coming home from their jobs when a group of men appeared at the front door. They did not wear uniforms, but they carried themselves with unquestioned authority. The plainclothes agents ordered everyone not to move. Emma had no idea what was happening. Startled and frightened, she cowered with the others.

The men climbed the tight stairwell to the second-floor bedroom and immediately started opening drawers, riffling through papers and inspecting photo albums. When they got to the tidy third-floor bedroom with its bare, clean walls and new furniture, they stopped, looked inside, but then moved on, assuming whoever lived there had not been there very long.

In Lin Pu-chi's new study, the men slid open wood panels that led to a storage space under the windows and started pulling everything out. They were like search dogs, sniffing for evidence. "Do you have weapons?" they demanded, thinking the retired priest and his frail wife might be hiding a stash of pistols or knives under the floorboards in order to arm insurgents.

The agents turned up nothing, but the search of House 19 was a warning. The matter of Watchman Nee, too painful and disturbing for anyone in the family to discuss in private, was about to become a national scandal.

On January 29, 1956, after a long evening of fellowship at the Nanyang Road assembly hall that included a symbolic breaking of bread, Little Flock members returned to their homes. Police were lying in wait. At 10:00 p.m., they arrested six leaders of the Christian Assembly and took them into custody. Two were older women, one about seventy who ran a Little Flock bookstore, the other in her sixties and one of the first members of the assembly in Shanghai.

The next day, all the Shanghai members of the Little Flock were summoned to a mass denunciation meeting at the Tian Chan Theater, the one-time opera house in the city center. In a well-scripted meeting that went on for hours, communist cadres inundated the Little Flock audience with evidence of the crimes of Watchman Nee. They called him a counterrevolutionary—*fan geming*. He faced accusations of spying; hostility to the government; fleecing fellow churchgoers; resisting land reform; and plotting against the People's Liberation Army. On top of all of that, he was tarred as morally corrupt, a philanderer who made a mockery of his marriage and paid regular visits to prostitutes.

Four days later, the attack on Watchman Nee moved inside the Nanyang Road assembly hall, officially now a "center of rebellion." Members were ordered to register with the government and write confessions or face the consequences. At the mandatory meeting, Little Flock leaders continued to rail against Watchman Nee before an audience of three thousand people, including followers from the nearby cities of Suzhou and Nanjing.

Everyone was expected to stand and admit his or her own complicity. Ni Guizhen could not escape the pressure to criticize her own actions.

"God opened my eyes," she wailed, "and let me see that it is God who judges the sins at church and also my own mistakes." She said she had allowed herself to be aloof from the world and politics and now regretted her foolishness for not recognizing the will of God in this new era. "In the past, I thought I lived for God and I was faithful and willing to suffer for the Lord. I wanted to be loyal, eager to suffer for the Lord and to be a martyr. Actually, I offended God and offended people."

For Ni Guizhen and her family, even if they wanted to draw the curtains, lock the door, and avoid the stares of neighbors, the newspapers would not let them hide from what was happening. Every day when Lin Pu-chi picked up his copy of the *Liberation Daily*, he read fresh attacks on Watchman Nee and the Little Flock.

On February 1, the newspaper highlighted the charges outlined in the nine-volume, 2,292-page criminal indictment against Watchman Nee. The article was laced with allegations of espionage and intrigue as well as titillating details of Watchman Nee's alleged sexual exploits. Listed among the evidence: a pornographic movie that Watchman Nee allegedly filmed of a Little Flock coworker.

The state accused the preacher with actively passing on sensitive information to Nationalist spies or intermediaries. One tip involved alerting Taiwan about a big military order for seasickness tablets, which Chinese sailors might need for a sea invasion of Taiwan.

Another had Watchman Nee encouraging the enemy to repeat the bombardment of power plants and water stations in Shanghai like they did on February 6, 1950.

The most diabolical plot involved Watchman Nee urging the Nationalist air force to drop snails contaminated with a parasitic disease into lakes used by the Chinese army—and then withholding ingredients to produce an antidote.

As the days passed, headlines grew more and more shrill, with the Communist Party mouthpiece offering daily accounts from Christians who said they were tricked and hurt by Watchman Nee and the Little Flock.

"They Sucked My Blood," screamed one story, quoting a seventy-two-year-old handyman for a Little Flock assembly hall who said he was treated like "a cow or horse" by members before they fired him.

"A Poisoned Christian," read another accusation, this time from a college graduate who said the Little Flock dissuaded him from supporting the "Resist America; Aid Korea" campaign, known in the West as the Korean War.

Under the banner of "A Big Hoax," the *Liberation Daily* condemned the Little Flock for its "Give It Up" campaign that persuaded members to donate money and valuables to the Christian Assembly before communists came to power and took their wealth from them. "What on earth is it?" the paper asked rhetorically. "In fact, this is a trick to cheat money that also involves a major political conspiracy."

By this point, nearly all of the full-time workers and elders of the local churches of the Little Flock throughout China had been arrested. More than a thousand members were rounded up in the cities of Shanghai and Guangzhou and the provinces of Zhejiang and Fujian. Families could not visit the imprisoned and had no word on their conditions or treatment.

If the media blitz was not enough to convince the public of Watchman Nee's guilt, the government staged two exhibits during Chinese New Year to show everyone in Shanghai what it had on him.

Nine days after the Tian Chan denunciation meeting, the national and Shanghai offices of the Three-Self Movement opened "An Exposition of the Criminal Evidence of Watchman Nee." Innocent until proven guilty was not a judicial concept in the people's courts. Instead, the exhibit had one purpose: to present Watchman Nee as a fraud who had duped thousands while hiding under the cloak of a religious man.

All Little Flock members were required to attend, while other Christians—members of denominational churches as well as seminary teachers and students—were also encouraged to take a look.

Tim could not contain his curiosity. He didn't know much about the Little Flock. Growing up, he joined his father for Sunday service at St. Peter's Church instead of going with his mother and sister to Little Flock meetings. As an adult, Tim had let his churchgoing slip and felt no worse for it. His interest in the exhibit was more personal: was the friendly uncle he knew from his youth the same criminal now being pilloried by authorities? He went alone; Emma wanted to stay as far away as possible from the controversy.

At the Allied Health School on Nanjing Road, not far from the Nanyang Road assembly hall, people were divided into small groups of a dozen or so and ushered by an official into a big classroom. The school was empty because of the long holiday for New Year's. All the desks and chairs had been removed to make way for big posters and enlargements of photographs.

The room was silent except for the scratchy sound of a tape recording of two weeping women—the Little Flock leaders Ruth Lee and Peace Wang, who had been arrested only days earlier. The pair admitted that they were counterrevolutionaries.

"If you cooperate, you are free," a cadre was heard assuring the women on the tape recording. "If you refuse, the handcuffs are on the table. You will be taken into prison, where harsher punishments await you. We will deal with you until you deny your faith."

The two exhibits drew 4,700 people over the course of a week. Some women, deeply disillusioned and disappointed, openly sobbed. A few fainted, overwhelmed by the evidence: letters between Watchman Nee and intermediaries for the Nationalist government; confessions that he wrote during four years of captivity; financial documents; and a Little Flock petition, objecting to a government seizure of buildings owned by the group in Guling, the mountaintop retreat outside Fuzhou.

But the one section that caught everyone's attention was the photograph of a naked woman, shot from the head down. This was allegedly the camerawork of Watchman Nee. The evidence included a film projector that he bought in London in 1938, purportedly to view X-rated movies, and ninety-three copies of pornographic books and magazines.

Watchman Nee during a visit to England in 1938. Even as a young man, he was well known in Christian circles outside China. Courtesy of Angus Kinnear family collection.

Tim had to avert his eyes. He hurried out of the exhibit, unconvinced one way or another and mulling over a thought that everyone understood: *If the government says you're wrong, you're wrong.*

VERDICT

It had all come to this: a trial before the People's High Court on June 21, 1956. About one hundred people filled the courtroom, located in the heart of Shanghai near the Bund. All the observers were handpicked and included government officials, church representatives, leaders of the Three-Self Movement, and a dozen members from the Christian Assembly on Nanyang Road.

Absent was anyone from the defendant's family. Charity, who had been at the top of a "wanted" list of Little Flock members, refused to testify against her husband or write a confession. She was detained before the trial.

One of the Little Flock observers was a young medical student, Xu Meili, whose denunciation of Watchman Nee at the Tian Chan Theater was reprinted in the *Liberation Daily*. As bailiffs escorted Watchman Nee into the courtroom, she thought he looked neat, healthy, and calm.

A judge read each charge while a court officer showed Watchman Nee the corresponding evidence, spread out on a table in front of him. He answered questions promptly in a voice that was low. "From the very beginning to the end, all of his answers were 'Yes' without hesitancy," Xu Meili would later observe. "His attitude was submissive, yet without any expression of shame."

After five hours, Watchman Nee rose from his seat for the reading of the sentence. The judge declared him guilty of counterrevolutionary crimes and imposed a fifteen-year sentence to be served at the Tilanqiao Prison, a notorious turn-of-the-century penitentiary built by the British in the city's Hongkou section.

The next time members of the Nanyang Road assembly met for Sunday service, elders of the congregation reported on the trial and proposed the excommunication of Watchman Nee. The assembly endorsed the decision and sent an announcement to Little Flock groups all across the country. It stated, "We represent all brothers and sisters of the Shanghai Christian Assembly to support the sentence of the government heartily!"

In his attic study, Lin Pu-chi began composing his June letter to Paul and Sylvia in Philadelphia.

"It is now a full seven years since Paul and Jim left us, and it is hard to realize how quickly time has elapsed," he wrote. "Aunt Mary sent mother another nice birthday gift, which was gratefully received."

Tim's wife was pregnant but suffering from morning sickness. Lin Pu-chi added that Paul's mother, too, was showing some signs of improving health. Ni Guizhen could now sit up on the sofa for a few hours at a time. "As I told you before," he explained, "her problems began with over-exertion at Tim's wedding time."

Overexertion. Yes, that was one way of putting it. Best to leave out mention of the police search for weapons a month after the wedding.

He dipped his pen into an inkwell. "Then in February, mental strain made her bedridden for a prolonged time."

There was no way to tell Paul about her complete physical collapse in the face of the public shaming and excommunication of her brother, now sequestered in a prison cell. Maybe he could put it in medical terms?

Lin Pu-chi explained to his son that an internal medicine specialist, a friend of Martha's from the hospital, stopped by the house to check on Ni Guizhen. The doctor diagnosed her problem as neurasthenia. The symptoms were fatigue, anxiety, headaches, heart palpitations, and high blood pressure.

The Chinese term for the condition was *shenjin shuairuo*—literally "nerve weakness." A psychiatrist in the West might call it a nervous breakdown.

Lin Pu-chi's letter in English filled one side of the thin sheet of airmail stationery. Now his wife, still bedridden, took the paper and dipped the pen in an inkwell. In the seven years since her sons had left for America, Ni Guizhen had never written directly to them, leaving the task to her husband. Propped up in bed, she began to fill the other side with precise Chinese characters, starting with the term of endearment, *Naung naung die*, "Little brother," the family's pet name for Paul.

"I often miss you and Junmin, especially when I am ill. These years I have really understood how deep the feeling could be when a mother misses her sons who are afar. Although I never wrote to you by myself in the past, my silence tells how my heart misses you."

She explained to Paul that her health had been deteriorating for the past decade. Whenever she became too stressed or "used too much brainpower," she told him her heart seemed to tighten and her body became motionless. In the past three years, her memory and comprehension, even her eyesight, worsened. Lately, she could not tolerate sunlight, and even sitting in a dark room with her eyes shut was uncomfortable.

"You once said, 'Mom, you have always been too stressed.' I know indeed that it is the reason." The culprits, she explained, were "troublesome" household chores. She hoped his wife Sylvia, caring for their two young daughters, did not feel the same life pressures as she did.

She concluded, "I look up to God for His mercy to improve my health."

· 14 ·

Prelude

Shanghai, 1957

*T*he only way to survive Shanghai in the summer was to escape Shanghai in the summer. Lin Pu-chi lived by those words. Though he'd grown up in the furnace of Fuzhou, the older he got, the less tolerance he had for the spirit-draining heat of his adopted city.

In July 1957, after a week of near hundred-degree temperatures, Lin Pu-chi packed his leather suitcase and boarded a river steamer with his wife and granddaughter for a three-day journey on the Yangtze River to the port of Jiujiang, then onward and upward by bus to the mountain retreat of Lushan.

All of the distractions at home receded from his mind as they traveled a tortuous, narrow road, the bus climbing and twisting, rising one thousand feet . . . two thousand feet . . . three thousand feet . . . making tighter turns, more turns, until they arrived at a settlement of stone cottages set in the pines. A cool breeze greeted them, bringing a veil of mist as light as white chiffon wafting across a plaza. Lin Pu-chi breathed steadily, easily, and deeply. He summoned the words of the great poet Li Po: *Let me reach those sublime hills, where peace comes to the quiet heart.*

Lushan was twenty degrees cooler than Shanghai. Since the start of the century, homesick missionaries waited out the summer in the mountains, fleeing not only the mosquitoes and heat in crowded cities but also deadly maladies such as malaria and cholera that arrived in hot months. They built hundreds of villas around one particular peak called Guling, which sounded a lot like "cooling" to their Western ears (a missionary retreat near Fuzhou had a similar name in English but different Chinese characters). They passed the summer gossiping over hands of bridge at clubs, watching their children splash in chlorinated pools, and singing "Rock of Ages" in chapels with stained-glass windows. In the 1930s, Chiang Kai-shek used Lushan as the summer capital of his Nationalist government and moved with his wife to a stone villa, built in 1903 by an English lady who gave the house to the couple as a wedding present. Later, when Chairman Mao took up residence in the same place, he bellowed, "Chiang, here I come," as he passed through the front door.

Home for the next three months for Lin Pu-chi and his wife was a few rented rooms at 132 Pine Tree Road, a stone-block guesthouse with black shutters on wide windows. After all she had been through in the past year—her brother's trial, the splintering of the Little Flock, her health—Ni Guizhen, who was fifty-five, needed time away from Shanghai to recuperate. "Mother can sleep better, feels stronger and can walk more," the sixty-two-year-old Lin Pu-chi wrote to Paul and Sylvia, thanking them for the "birthday gift" that made the trip possible.

Their days were quiet, with time for reading and naps. Lin Pu-chi brought along the classic novel *Hong Lou Meng*, or *Dreams of the Red Chamber*, written 200 years earlier and divided into 4 volumes and 120 chapters. He rationed one chapter a day, spending an hour immersed in the epic tale of love and family. The guesthouse had a cafeteria on the first floor that served simple fare like rice porridge with pickled vegetables for breakfast. The old couple, however, fretted about Julia's thin frame. They feared she wasn't eating well. Lin Pu-chi knew another retired pastor who vacationed in Lushan, and every morning, he hiked with Julia to his friend's cottage, where the friend prepared scrambled eggs for breakfast.

Among the couple's visitors from Shanghai that summer were Watchman Nee's wife and his brother George, a chemist. Charity's health, both physical and mental, was frail. She had been detained for a year for refusing to testify against her husband at his trial and needed the diversion of Lushan as keenly as her sister-in-law did. One day, everyone piled into a hired car and drove from morning until night, seeing one sight after another: overlooks into dark valleys, peaks with names like "Five Old Men," placid lakes, thundering waterfalls, and a quiet Buddhist temple. Ni Guizhen felt so reinvigorated that she stopped taking her sleeping pills and sedatives. Lin Pu-chi promised her they would return every summer if they could.

Nine-year-old Julia enjoyed having her grandparents all to herself. Her grandfather, more relaxed than she had ever seen him, delighted in taking her to explore one of his favorite places: a grotto dedicated to a legendary Daoist figure, Lü Dongbin. He was one of the "Eight Immortals" in the Daoist tradition. Many religious topics intrigued Lin Pu-chi, but from the time he was a student, he was fascinated by the stories of the immortals. The Buddhist path led to nirvana; Christians believed in the resurrection; and Daoism held that man could enter everlasting life. Lü Dongbin was a leader among immortals, or genies. Julia listened intently as her grandfather explained that Lü was a magistrate and scholar from Jiangxi whose sword had supernatural power that he wielded to slay dragons and tigers, ridding the empire of evil.

Lin Pu-chi and his wife alternated between granddaughters on Lushan vacations. Julia accompanied them in 1957, and Terri (shown here) joined the couple in 1958. Courtesy of Lin Family Collection.

"See those characters in the stone? *Shi lu*," Lin Pu-chi asked his granddaughter, leading her to the entrance of the cave. "It means 'way of the genies.'"

The grotto was two stories tall at its mouth and almost fifty feet deep. Ferns draped the rock walls by the entrance. Inside, water trickled down stone, collecting in a pool by an altar. A glass of springwater was thought to have healing power.

As a university student four decades earlier in Shanghai, Lin Pu-chi sought out Daoist priests to question them about the half-human, half-divine immortals. He pored through books on the subject and composed a twenty-page essay in English on the most famous eight genies, which the prestigious *Journal of the Royal Asiatic Society* published in 1918.

"But what are genies?" Julia wanted to know.

"They are happiness," her grandfather explained simply. "They are free from the material world and have drunk the elixir of immortality. They possess wonderful art and perform enviable feats of strength. They drive in chariots of clouds, they mount dragons and storks, they live in palaces of pearl and jade, and they sleep in shady grottoes, like this one."

In the midday sun, Lin Pu-chi unbuttoned his shirt as he and Julia hiked farther up a path. The heat was getting to him. He needed to rest and sat on big rock. He leaned all the way back, closed his eyes, and stretched his arms wide against the smooth, flat surface. Julia looked at him quizzically. Then he began to sing—not hum, but sing with abandon, bellowing an Anglican hymn in English.

Julia was mortified. Other sightseers averted their eyes as they passed him, wondering whether this old man with his shirt undone, lying on a rock and singing with his eyes closed, might be losing his mind.

But this was not a daft man. This was a happy man. He had no job back home, no church flock to tend. His heart was weak, his blood pressure high, and his mood prone to days of deep sadness. But Lushan invigorated him; the mountains lifted his soul.

And just for a moment, resting in the sublime hills, he felt peace come to his quiet heart.

GEESE AND RABBITS

In 1958, Martha moved with her husband and two girls into her parents' house on Lane 170, their *longtang* off Jiaozhou Road. They had been living nearby with her in-laws, but Lin Pu-chi asked his daughter to return home. He was fearful that the government could decide at any moment that he had too much space and assign strangers to move into spare rooms in the house. It was not unfounded paranoia but natural anxiety in the new China.

The communist leaders had just launched a new five-year plan in 1958 called the Great Leap Forward. In the countryside, farm families were consolidated into massive communes, tilling fields as units, sharing their meals in canteens, and collectively raising their babies and toddlers in nurseries. Now Chairman Mao urged peasants to contribute to the industrial development of the country while still feeding its 650 million people. In his mind, China was in a race to catch up with the Soviet Union and the United States. He measured success in steel ingots and expected everyone to chip in, gathering metal household objects and other scrap to melt in makeshift "backyard furnaces." Even the urban families in Lane 170 were called on to do their part. They tore down the wrought-iron fences that used to mark off each front yard and contributed the metal to feed the nation's steelmaking obsession—or to at least meet their quota.

The lunacy of this became clear by 1959. With farmers paying so much attention to collecting scrap metal, they ignored their fields. Local officials lied about their harvests yet still had to make mandatory contributions of grain to the national food coffers. Starving peasants foraged like animals for food, eating bark and boiling weeds. No one called it what it was—an avoidable famine, caused by Mao's irrational zeal to ramp up China's industrial output. And since no one could admit that the emperor wore no clothes, the country euphemistically called this period of universal suffering *Sannian ziran zaihai*, or "three years of natural disasters."

A metropolis like Shanghai was not exempt. People with distended bellies, a telltale sign of malnourishment, could be spotted on the streets. Meat at the dinner table was a rare treat. Food was tightly rationed. Every ten days, each person was allocated an ounce of sugar, an ounce of oil, three ounces of pork, and a nutritional biscuit.

The Lin family ate regular meals of balls of dough made of nothing but flour and water, boiled and then tossed with drops of oil and cabbage leaves in a scalding wok. The dish was bland and chewy but filling. Once in a while, they ate yams or rice porridge, but if the family wanted meat, they had to hunt for it on the black market, offering cash under the table to a farmer for a live rabbit or goose. The smell of the simmering stew made neighbors envious.

For the Lin grandchildren, there was no better entertainment than watching their uncle trying to kill a goose for dinner. Julia and Terri would hang out a second-floor bedroom window and watch Tim chase his quarry in the walled area by the back door near the kitchen. One time, he grabbed a goose by its neck, held it on the ground, and brought down the cleaver like a guillotine— but not forcefully enough to actually sever the animal's head. Blood splattered everywhere as the flailing goose tried to fly away with its head hanging on by a thread. From their perch a safe distance away, the sisters squealed.

The family could afford meat only because of the remittances from the sons in America. But Paul and Jim had no way of knowing that their money was helping; Lin Pu-chi's monthly letters were interrupted from 1960 to 1962, most likely intercepted by public security agents. Famine was embarrassing; what happened in China would stay behind the bamboo curtain.

The world of Lin Pu-chi and his wife was shrinking with each passing year. They no longer left the house for services on Sunday. At the start of the Great Leap Forward, the religious affairs bureau of the government consolidated churches in order to free up property for industrial purposes. The number of churches in Shanghai plummeted from 150 to 20. The Nanyang Road assembly hall ceased to operate and became a factory for making wool scarves. Members of the Little Flock scattered, with some joining official "Three-Self" churches but more following the way of Ni Guizhen. She preferred to pray in the privacy of her home, sharing fellowship with her sister-in-law Charity and one or two trusted friends.

The sisters-in-law shared another routine. Every few months, they took a bus toward the Bund, crossed Suzhou Creek at the old Garden Bridge, and headed into Hongkou District. In a neighborhood that used to include Shanghai's Jewish ghetto, they disembarked in front of a walled complex and passed through a tall, square, black iron gate—the first of two metal doors leading to the "City of the Damned," the turn-of-the-century Tilanqiao Prison.

In 1903, British administrators in Shanghai opened the monstrous jail, the largest in Asia. It could hold as many as ten thousand inmates housed in two thousand cells spread over ten buildings. The execution room had a trapdoor where the corpses of prisoners who were hanged dropped directly into the prison morgue. Armed soldiers in towers kept watch over the complex, which included a jailhouse printing press and sweatshops that cranked out prison-made clothing, toy dolls, and wristwatches.

Charity had to wait five years after her husband's trial before she was allowed to visit him. The first time she saw him, she was permitted to bring some necessities like medicine and soap. A guard inspected her bag before admitting her into a noisy visitors' hall, where a metal mesh screen separated families and prisoners. With more than a hundred people in the hall, prisoners and visitors had to shout to be heard.

When Watchman Nee was escorted into the room, guards made him sit sideways so that they could see his face and hear what he was saying. Charity did not recognize the profile of her husband, his face so gaunt and sunken, his head shorn of hair.

"How are you?" he whispered softly.

How to answer such a simple question? "You see, my hair has all turned gray," was all Charity could muster to fill the gap of many years.

There could be no wailing, no outbursts, no unleashing of emotion. Guards kept their eyes fixed on Watchman Nee. He could not turn his head to look at his wife, who strained to hear him amid the cacophony. His clothes, which were covered with patches, hung on his tall frame, shrunken to about one hundred pounds. Watchman Nee shared a windowless cell with two others. When he spread his arms, he could touch both walls. He had no bed, only a blanket on the floor and a bucket for "night soil." Bedbugs made it hard to sleep. Meals were pushed under an iron door. With his fluency in English, he was assigned a job translating English textbooks and medical journals into Chinese. Instead of toiling in a prison factory, he worked in a bigger room in the prison with a desk and chair.

Charity had gotten only minutes with him that first visit before a gruff guard cut short the session.

"We haven't seen each other for so long," Watchman Nee implored. "Please, can you give us some more time?"

The guard was unmoved. "You just say what you have to say," he barked, as he motioned that it was time to leave.

After that, Charity and one family member were permitted to visit every month for half an hour. Most of her friends had abandoned her after Watchman Nee's imprisonment, fearful of associating with the wife of a political outlaw. All she had was family and Ni Guizhen, her childhood friend and one of her most dependable companions. Sometimes they were allowed to bring Watchman Nee extra food like cooked duck eggs or soy sauce to flavor his bland diet of watery porridge for breakfast and boiled eggplant and rice for dinner. They both wondered how he could stand it.

Inside cell block 3, Watchman Nee confided to his cellmate, an ex-boxer accused of speaking out against Mao's revolution, that he worried about his wife. Her health was so poor. Watchman Nee hoped and prayed that he would be released in time to be with her again. His jailers manipulated feelings like that with all prisoners, including Watchman Nee. During a mass meeting of more than four thousand inmates, Watchman Nee was paraded on stage and told by officials that he could walk out the iron gates of the prison ahead of schedule and reunite with his wife. All he had to do was tell everyone assembled that he was giving up his religion. Two of his former followers—women from the Nanyang Road assembly hall who were imprisoned in 1956—had already done so. Before the crowd, they repeated old accusations against him.

Watchman Nee stood with his eyes closed and head down.

He said nothing.

PITCH PERFECT

Every day, the adults in the Lin household left for work at 7:00 a.m. and did not return until close to 9:00 p.m. It was left to the old couple to watch the three grandchildren. Lin Pu-chi—a onetime pastor, scholar, editor, principal, and church administrator—had mellowed into his new role as babysitter. One of his favorite pastimes was taking Julia to the movies. They preferred the Cathay Cinema on Huaihai Road, next to the Jinjiang Hotel in the former French Concession, not far from their home. In the warm months, Lin Pu-chi liked the coolness of the dark theater, which had a crude air conditioning system consisting of blocks of ice placed under rotary fans—not very efficient, but just enough to cut the heat.

Julia liked romantic films, popular escapist tales served up by China's film industry in the depths of the famine. One of her favorites was China's first musical, the 1961 blockbuster *Liu Sanjie*, or *Third Sister Liu*. The heroine lives in the mountains of Guangxi Province in southern China, collects wood for a living, and spreads revolutionary ideas through folk songs. She falls in love with a fisherman's son but is captured by a local tyrant who wants her as his concubine. Her boyfriend rescues her from the landlord, leaving them to ride off into the sunset, a happily-ever-after ending to a tale of class struggle.

But someone as cerebral as Lin Pu-chi could never be all fun and games. He insisted that his two elder granddaughters learn a new Chinese word each day. He also oversaw Julia's piano practice. From the time she was a young child, Julia displayed uncanny musical ability. Music was always a part of home life, and the piano was a tradition passed down by the women of the family. Ni Guizhen grew up with a piano and taught Martha how to play, and she, in turn, taught Julia. To own a piano was the mark of some degree of wealth and breeding. Most families who had one were Christian, having learned to appreciate the instrument while singing hymns in church. Martha had wanted to pursue music as a career, but Lin Pu-chi vetoed that. She would be a physician like her grandfather, and that was that.

But even he had to concede that Julia was gifted. She possessed the envy of every musician: perfect pitch. From the time Julia was little, her mother could play a chord with both hands and she could identify and play back every note. But like children the world over, she hated to practice. Given the choice of sitting at the piano bench or playing outside in the lane, Julia chose friends over Chopin every time. Sometimes the adults hid her shoes or locked the door to the room so that she would not run off. But often when she practiced, her friends came to her, sitting outside the open window of her house to listen to her play.

Truth be told, Julia was lazy and had a secret that she kept from everyone, even her mother and piano tutor. Her ear was so finely tuned that she could learn a piece just by listening to it. Because it came so easily to her, she never bothered to learn how to read music. The black notes on the page in front of her were a jumbled mystery. Yet she progressed. Martha realized Julia had outgrown the ability of her tutor and asked her sister-in-law, a professional opera singer, if she could recommend a better instructor. She steered Julia to a harpist who taught at the Shanghai Conservatory of Music, the country's preeminent training ground for classical musicians. Miss Hu also was an accomplished pianist. When she went to Miss Hu's home for her lesson, Julia was more intrigued by the giant harp and asked whether she could learn how to play that instrument instead. "You're too tiny," Miss Hu informed her. "The harp will crush you."

Miss Hu taught Julia an important lesson. Julia played music well but used only her hands, not her heart. A professional like Miss Hu infused her music with emotion and seemed to interpret pieces with her entire body. Julia tried to do the same. The first time Terri saw her sister's new, expressive style, she giggled.

Julia was thirteen and ready to start middle school when Miss Hu relayed important news from the Shanghai Conservatory: for the first time in five years, the middle school affiliated with the conservatory would hold open auditions. Before that, only students from good proletarian families were permitted to attend the middle school (the equivalent of a high school in the United States). The children of bourgeois families—the progeny of capitalists or intellectuals—were barred from applying. But the political situation was beginning to ease in the summer of 1962, and the gates of the conservatory would open to everyone, including Julia—if she could play well enough.

The temperature hit ninety-eight degrees the day of Julia's audition at the Shanghai Conservatory's middle school in the former French Concession. Lin Pu-chi had tossed and sweated all through the breezeless night, getting little sleep as he fretted more than his granddaughter about the tryout. Where once he ruled out a career in music for his daughter, now he saw this as his grand-daughter's calling.

"Your sister is very keen that Julia should enter this school," he wrote to his son Paul on the eve of the tryout. "But if she fails, it would be very bad indeed. It means that Julia cannot take music as her life career."

If Julia got into the middle school, all else would fall into place. She could map out each step of her future. From middle school, she would continue to the college-level program and on to a career as a soloist. The director of the conservatory believed that the best teachers produced the best students, and Shanghai in the 1920s had an abundance of stellar musicians from Russia and eastern Europe, many of whom joined the faculty. After 1949, these foreign professors were banished from Shanghai, but their legacy carried on in the quality of their former students on the Chinese faculty.

During audition week, teenage hopefuls lined up on the shaded sidewalk outside the gates of No. 9 Dongping Road. The school was located in the former villa of the Nationalist president Chiang Kai-shek. The generalissimo and his wife were given this house—much like they were given a cottage in Lushan—as a wedding present, this one from the president's millionaire brother-in-law, the former finance minister T. V. Soong. The recital hall used to be the couple's sitting room, where Madame Chiang screened Hollywood films for her family and friends.

Julia was one of two thousand candidates, of whom only fifty would be accepted and of those, only a dozen for the piano program. Other girls visibly shook with nerves as they waited for their turns, but not Julia. She was oblivious to the pressure and viewed the whole thing rather as a lark and a chance to perform.

When her name was called, she breezed through the front doors of a two-story stucco mansion and took her seat at the piano in the recital hall. Her selection reflected her relaxed frame of mind. Instead of a complicated piece by Beethoven or Liszt, she chose a melodic folk song called "Lan Huahua" that highlighted her musicality rather than her dexterity. Adjudicators liked what they heard and cleared her for the next round.

To test her aural ability, Julia was taken into a studio with a teacher who played notes that she had to identify and sing on pitch. Next, the instructor tapped out a rhythm that Julia had to repeat. But the big challenge was learning and performing two new pieces of music. Julia was given one of the études in opus 849 by Czerny and one of the twelve pieces in *The Seasons* by Tchaikovsky. In ten days, she had to perform both before fifty of the top music educators in the city, who would decide whether or not she would be admitted to the school and, eventually, achieve her dream of becoming a professional pianist.

The pressure was on—and she could not read music.

There was no time to waste. As soon as Martha returned from the hospital that night, she and Julia sat side by side at the piano in the family's living room. Martha played the sheet music. Julia listened intently. In her head, she deconstructed the music note by note, chord by chord, and repeated what she heard on the keys of the piano. By the next day, she had committed both pieces to memory, leaving the rest of the week to work on her style.

On the day of her final audition, Julia again felt preternatural calm. The door to the recital hall opened, and she was ushered inside. All the teachers sat in straight rows of wooden chairs. Julia immediately plopped onto a sofa in the front row.

She felt a tap on her shoulder.

"Excuse me, miss," a young professor whispered in her ear. "This is not for you. This is reserved for Mr. Fang."

Mr. Fang just happened to be the chair of the piano department at the main conservatory, with a reputation that outranked everyone in the hall. His opinion could make or break a musician. He had just stepped outside to use the washroom and, luckily for Julia, did not see her faux pas.

Unruffled, Julia composed herself. In the hushed hall, she placed her hands gently on the keys and began. Her Czerny was crisp and tight, her Tchaikovsky full of swelling emotion. Heads in the audience nodded with approval.

Her performance was met with silence. She stood, exited the recital hall, and began the interminable wait for their judgment.

Back-to-back typhoons brought heavy rains bearing down on Shanghai, breaking the heat. On an August morning, a member of the conservatory staff pasted a big sheet of paper on a wall by the front gate. In elegant black brushstrokes were fifty names.

Anxious parents and students elbowed their way to the front to read the names. Some turned around with tears streaming down their faces. Julia turned around with a smile. She would join the school in September, having placed fourth in the piano competition. The fact that she could not read music would be her secret, at least for a while.

V

BAD ELEMENTS

· 15 ·

Lane 170

Shanghai, 1966

*T*he old woman's hands rarely stopped moving. Fingers on metal knitting needles, she guided the yarn, over and around, in and out, one row and another. It soothed her mind and calmed her nerves to settle into her favorite armchair with her knitting. Some older neighbors practiced tai chi to relieve the stress in their lives. Ni Guizhen pulled out her yarn. She could close her eyes, and her fingers would know what to do.

She wondered who would get this black scarf taking shape in her hands. Maybe she'd just give it to her husband, who never left the house in cooler months without his neck covered. Protection against sickness, he always said. In the forty-odd years that they had been married, the man had been sick in bed only twice. *Twice.* Which made his current predicament all the more cruel and frustrating. Since the fall of 1965—seven months ago to be precise—Lin Pu-chi had been confined to bed on the second floor, unable to get up even for a trip to the bathroom. His blood pressure was frighteningly high. When he stood, Lin Pu-chi had to brace his hand on the wall to stop the room from spinning. His legs shook; his chest reflexively tightened. He took daily doses of Chinese herbs, plus medicine that Martha had gotten from the hospital. But nothing seemed to help. Bedridden, he couldn't sit up to write letters to his two sons in America. He couldn't read a novel. He couldn't even scan a newspaper. Often, in the long hours of the day, he ordered everyone out of the room, closed his eyes, and sank into a deep well of despair.

From upstairs, Ni Guizhen heard the clank and clatter of heavy metal. Martha had a special bed sent over from the hospital, and workers were now helping her to put it together. They had a hard time navigating the tight turns in the stairwell of the three-story house.

Ni Guizhen placed her knitting in her lap and reached for her Bible on the end table. She opened it and gently picked up a faded pink rose petal

Ni Guizhen was constantly knitting. When her adult son Paul went off to the United States, she knitted him a sweater with a big "P" (for Paul) on the front. Courtesy of Lin Family Collection.

pressed between the pages. Her daughter-in-law in Philadelphia had tucked the petal into the fold of her last letter. With her mind's eye, Ni Guizhen saw the circular rose garden by the stone house, heard her American grandchildren playing in the yard. She knew them only by photographs, which she kept under glass on top of her bedroom dresser. She had fashioned a collage of images: two granddaughters in pink tutus at a ballet recital; school pictures; a family portrait on Christmas morning.

"Mother," Martha called. "Come upstairs."

Ni Guizhen slowly climbed the winding steps to the second-floor bedroom. She was relieved to see Lin Pu-chi propped up by pillows in his new bed. He gave her a wan smile.

"The bed can be cranked up and down," explained Martha, showing her how. "This way at least he can sit up and do things. For now, only let him sit up maybe four times a day. To eat, or maybe to use the toilet."

Martha gathered her things to leave. "I have to hurry back to the hospital," she said. "Good luck."

Lin Pu-chi immediately asked for his fountain pen and a sheet of airmail stationery. He hadn't written to Paul in Philadelphia since last fall.

"Rest," Ni Guizhen chided.

"I've been resting for seven months," he replied. Lin Pu-chi placed the paper on a book to use as a makeshift desk for writing in bed. He jotted the date of June 9, 1966, in the upper right corner and picked up where he had left off seven months ago.

"Maybe in another two months," he wrote with shaky penmanship, "I hope to be able to stand up and walk. My trouble is that my heart and nerves got old and feeble after 72 years."

By August, Lin Pu-chi began to mend. But just as his health was improving, his nerves were starting to fray. He read with increasing alarm reports in the newspaper about a new revolution. On May 16, Mao released a notice that enemies of the communist cause had infiltrated the party with the intent of bringing back capitalism. On June 1, an editorial in the *People's Daily* heralded the start of a "Cultural Revolution," a political campaign to "sweep away all cow-demons and snake-spirits." Reading those words made Lin Pu-chi shudder. It brought him back to 1927, when he was paraded through the streets of Fuzhou as a "running dog." The imagery in the *People's Daily* article came straight from Chinese mythology, but in the hands of propagandists, the demons and spirits meant "class enemies" who were masquerading as loyal members of the Communist Party.

Fear began to seep into the Lin household like a vapor. Political campaigns were nothing new. But this one seemed broader, more sinister. The whole country was exhorted to wipe out "black categories" of people—landlords, rich peasants, counterrevolutionaries, capitalists, and intellectuals. Behind the screen of power in Beijing, communist titans were locked in a high-stakes power struggle. Mao was out to destroy his rivals by using force inside and outside the Chinese Communist Party. The seventy-two-year-old leader may have been worshipped like a political deity, but he acted like a paranoid old man who was threatened by adversaries such as the president, Liu Shaoqi, and the party's general secretary, Deng Xiaoping. Mao was manipulating the passions of rebellious youth to shake up the party apparatus from top to bottom. Students from universities and high schools and even youngsters from middle school were urged to attack authority figures. Mao's "Red Guards" were exhorted to strike down old customs in "struggle sessions" against teachers or officials.

Mao's wife, Jiang Qing, who directed what happened in arts and culture, endorsed rough tactics, telling students: "If good people beat bad people, it serves them right." And if good people beat good people? Well, she rationalized, misunderstandings happen. Through the looking glass of the Cultural Revolution, she said: "Without beatings, you do not get acquainted."

On August 18, Mao greeted almost a million Red Guards in Tiananmen Square who passionately waved his little red book of sayings. With the chairman's blessing, a multitude of students set out from the capital to root out enemies. Mao let them travel wherever they wanted for free on a crusade to eliminate the "Four Olds"—old customs, habits, culture, and thought.

For students and their red allies in factories and mills, "capitalist road-ers" were treasured quarry. And in the hunt for targets, all roads led to that one-time epicenter of wealth and decadence, that Western carbuncle on the socialist body politic—Shanghai.

BAD ELEMENTS

The summer of 1966 was hot even by Shanghai's muggy standards. By Au-gust, Red Guards were making their presence known on the streets. Banging drums and gongs and shouting slogans, they marched in columns to the local Communist Party headquarters. They waved the national flag and carried red banners with the battle cry to "Destroy the Four Olds!"

Inside the Lin household, fourteen-year-old Terri anxiously asked her father, "Will they come here?"

Again and again, he assured her, "Don't worry."

The families who lived in the twenty-four identical homes on Lane 170 off Jiaozhou Road had a reputation for being wealthier than most and better educated. Neighbors in the *longtang* included a pediatrician, ophthalmologist, and obstetrician, as well as teachers and professors, nurses, and chemists. Before 1949, one couple owned a sewing machine factory employing dozens; another homeowner practiced law in Shanghai's international court system. Most families had Bibles in their bookcases, and several had been active members of the Christian assembly of Watchman Nee, who at one point had lived in a lane on the opposite side of Jiaozhou Road.

The tan brick terraced homes with European-style gables, while spacious by Chinese standards, were really just one room on top of another, connected to the spine of a circular staircase. Three generations of Lins lived in House 19. The grandparents occupied the second-floor bedroom, while Tim, his wife, Emma, and their two children had the big room on the third floor. Martha and her two daughters slept under the eaves in the attic. Her husband had a cot in a tiny room between floors that was once the room for the *ayi*, the family housekeeper from the countryside.

At her middle school, Terri had plunged with enthusiasm into the first phase of the Cultural Revolution. Long sheets of white paper, pots of black ink, and big brushes appeared in her classroom. Students were encouraged to make "big character posters"—*dazibao*—criticizing teachers, even principals. Most were only obnoxious rants: "Teacher Wang, why do you pressure your students so much?"

If someone came up with a good line, others would copy it, substituting another teacher's name. Posters went up everywhere. Walking home from school, Terri lingered for hours, reading all the missives plastered on walls between her middle school and Lane 170. She had no clue why so-and-so was being singled out as bad. But it didn't matter. All of her classmates were writing posters, and she joined in.

The campaign quickly turned ugly. Pumped up on the rhetoric of class war, packs of Red Guards left their schools and factories and fanned out into Shanghai neighborhoods like jackals sniffing for meat. On August 22, a secret directive from Beijing had gone out to police departments across the country, forbidding officers to interfere with the actions of Red Guards, however violent.

Rebel students and workers ordered tailors, beauty salons, barbers, boutiques, and coffee shops to close their doors and reform their ways by catering to workers, peasants, and soldiers. On billboards and street signs advertising silk clothing or perfumes, students scrawled, "For whom are such articles made, for the proletariat or for capitalists?" Along the Bund, workers removed the iconic brass lions standing guard outside the front entrance of the Hongkong and Shanghai Bank while others chiseled away emblems and crests on granite facades, trying to wipe away all vestiges of Shanghai's aristocratic past. Students proposed new names for buildings, such as the People's War Hotel for the Peace Hotel, and the Anti-Imperialism Building for the old Customs House.

With crimson armbands on their upper arms, teenage rebels thought nothing of randomly singling out strangers on the sidewalk to taunt. The mere sight of a man in fashionable trousers or a woman with a stylish haircut—evidence of decadent ways—was enough for a verbal thrashing.

"We are Red Guards!" attackers would shout, as if that alone were enough.

The family in House 10 felt the jackal's bite first.

On a sticky day in late August, a mob of students charged into Lane 170, looking for a music teacher named Ho who lived with her husband and three children. The intruders were middle school students, boys in shorts and girls with blunt-cropped hair, none older than fifteen. Neighbors peeked from behind pulled curtains as they dragged the petite teacher from her living room. The students rampaged through the house, tearing pictures off walls, taking away a baby grand piano, and scooping up armfuls of books and record albums, all the while chanting, "Down with old culture!"

On a two-by-three-foot piece of blackboard, Red Guards scrawled Teacher Ho's name with a big red X through it and hung the sign around her neck with wire. Her crime: she was a stern and exacting teacher, which made her unpopular. The attack was less about revolution than revenge. Like schoolyard bullies, students ordered her to stand on a little table by her front door while making her husband and children submissively bow beside her with their heads down.

One of her accusers, wielding an electric razor, grabbed the teacher by her hair, shaved one side of her head, and left the other tangled and unruly. They called this a yin-yang head, the branding for a "bad element," popularized by Red Guards in Beijing and now copied in Shanghai. The teens commanded the teacher's twenty-year-old son to make sure that whenever she left the house, she carried at least twenty pounds in a dunce cap on her head.

"How am I supposed to do that?" he responded to this irrational demand.

"Put bricks in it. Her head must hang low!"

At her school, Red Guards made Teacher Ho watch as they burned her books and sheet music in a revolutionary pyre. When the fire subsided, they ordered her to take off her shoes and walk across the hot ashes. Onlookers jeered as the teacher with her shaved head limped home. From his third-floor room, her son could hear his mother's approach from blocks away before he saw her. He waited by the front door to quickly pull her inside and push away abusers who tried to follow her into her home.

House 7 came next.

Red Guards sounded their arrival in the lane with drums and gongs. With a swipe of paste from a paintbrush, they plastered a *dazibao* on the front door of the house of a family named Ge. The lineage of these neighbors made them targets. The grandfather had been a wealthy lawyer with a British wife. In the eyes of Red Guards, the taint of decadent Western influence coursed through the veins of his four adult children. They stripped the house, only six doors from the Lins.

The next evening, the Lin family sat at a round table on the first floor, eating dinner in silence. They quickly finished the meal and cleared the table. The women rinsed bowls and chopsticks in the sink. The old people got ready for bed.

From outside, a chanting crowd turned the corner off Jiaozhou Road and started heading down the lane.

Thump, thump, thump!

Burly men banged their fists and heaved their shoulders into the front door, smashing it open and yelling, "Down with the bourgeoisie!"

These were not scrawny middle-school students but laborers from Tim's factory, the Shanghai Meter Works. Tim worked in an office with engineers and designers. But these were men from the factory floor, strong men who welded steel and assembled electric meters for the power department.

As the adults and children hurried down the steps into the living room, the leader of the group ordered them not to move. "In the corner, there," he barked. "Just stay where you are."

One of them dragged Tim by the arm, pulling him outside and pushing him down on his knees.

"Head down," the man barked.

Circling him, his coworkers barked into his face, "Down with Lin Tingmin! Down with Lin Tingmin!"

With practiced precision, the intruders ran up the stairwell, going from room to room in search of evidence of a comfortable life and the "four olds" of culture and thought.

In the attic, they hauled away a keepsake pigskin trunk, handmade in Fuzhou for Ni Guizhen's trousseau. They slid open wooden doors to a crawl space under the windows and upended boxes. They pried up floorboards, looking for stashes of money, gold bars, or silver dollars, as well as anything

Before their lives were upended, Lin Pu-chi and Ni Guizhen enjoyed getting away to the seashore or mountains. Here, they visited Dalian in northeastern Liaoning Province in 1964. Courtesy of Lin Family Collection.

incriminating that would link the family to condemned ways—stocks and bonds, bank certificates, deeds, or even something as innocuous as scroll paintings, damnable evidence of old culture.

In the room Tim shared with his wife, Emma, and two young children, his coworkers rifled through drawers, grabbing jewelry: pearl earrings, jade bracelets, and wristwatches. They ran their rough fingers over silk scarves in a drawer, pulled wool coats from a closet, and gathered leather shoes into a box. They took heavy cotton quilts and blankets; thick wool sweaters knitted by Ni Guizhen; a radio and record player—anything and everything they could carry in their arms.

Lin Pu-chi, still too weak to walk downstairs, pressed close to his wife on the edge of his hospital bed, not daring to move when men barged into their second-floor room. An intruder spied Ni Guizhen's photo collage on top of the dresser. With a swipe of his hand and a smirk on his face, he pushed away the glass, sending it crashing to the wooden floor. The man ripped up all the snapshots: seaside vacation pictures, Paul's family at Christmas, baby pictures. Next, he took scissors and shredded a brocade bedspread.

"You cannot enjoy this kind of life," screamed this vigilante for Chairman Mao.

Only when the intruders had grabbed all that they could carry did they leave the house.

Silently and slowly, the family began to clean up the mess. Tim walked past his parents' room and saw his mother furiously ripping something into pieces. She was destroying bank certificates purchased with money that the couple had received from their sons in the United States. There must have been hundreds of dollars in CDs, all made out anonymously by the bank.

"What are you doing?" Tim asked her with alarm.

"I don't want them to see this," she answered without looking up.

He ripped the certificates out of her hands and hurried into the bathroom. He shredded them into tiny pieces and flushed everything down the toilet.

"They could find the paper. This way everything will be destroyed and gone."

No sooner had the family started restoring order to the house than a new crew arrived. Two big trucks rumbled down the narrow lane. A dozen men from the office of Martha's husband, John, jumped out of the truck beds.

Up went an accusation poster on the door, charging John with "exploiting the labor class." His late father had been a successful entrepreneur who manufactured and exported embroidery—fine bed linens and tablecloths, delicate handkerchiefs and ladies' blouses. The family invested its profits in real estate and, before 1949, had owned enough property, including forty rental houses, to cover six city blocks. After their assets were seized by the state, John was assigned to work for the government office that managed the very houses his family used to own.

Running from floor to floor, the men from the Housing Bureau didn't bother with small items like books or clothing. They went straight for furniture—bookcases, tables, armchairs, and wooden stools.

"You own too much," one sneered.

The intruders ordered Julia and the other children to sit on the bed with their grandparents on the second floor. Julia couldn't see what was happening downstairs but feared for her piano, a J. Strauss & Son upright model. To Red Guards, a piano marked a family as exploitative capitalists. Only a rich man could afford such an instrument. But Julia had spent her childhood practicing on this piano, its sound like a comforting, familiar voice. In the bench, she kept her favorite sheet music—Rachmaninoff's Concerto no. 2 and Chopin's Piano Concerto no. 1, plus twenty-four Chopin études.

Not the piano, Julia silently pleaded. She tried to will the men rummaging through the house to bypass the tall upright in the corner. *Please, please not the piano.*

Downstairs, a worker rolled a dolly into the living room. The intruders pushed the piano away from the wall, tipped it back, and wheeled it out the door. They scooped up all of Julia's books and sheet music as well as her Deutsche Grammophon LPs, gifts from her aunt in Hong Kong, and tossed everything into the truck bed.

The driver turned on the ignition, set the truck in reverse, and pulled out of the lane. They had stripped the house, leaving only the bedframes.

Two raids by two groups, all in the span of a few hours in one night—and it wasn't over.

Around midnight, without noise or theatrics, men in military-style green uniforms entered the house without knocking. The earlier groups were amateurs. These were professionals. They didn't say who they were or why they were there. They didn't shout slogans or paste posters on the front door. Everyone recognized these men as agents from the local office of the Public Security Bureau (PSB). The eyes and ears of the party, they kept meticulous files on "class enemies," including a thick dossier on Ni Guizhen, the sixty-four-year-old sister of Watchman Nee.

The PSB agents knew that this late hour was best for interrogations—the targets weakened by back-to-back raids and relentless verbal and physical torment.

Officers took the adults one at a time into John's small bedroom between the second and third floors. Waiting on the other side of the stairwell in the grandparents' room, the others strained to make out the muffled voices coming from behind the closed door.

"Has your wife committed crimes against socialism?"

"Is your husband a bad element?"

"Your sons in America, have they told you to do things to harm the security of our country?"

The answer was always no, but this was how "struggle" played out in families. Wives were goaded to turn on husbands, brothers on sisters, children on parents.

"Ni Guizhen," an agent gruffly summoned. "Get the old woman."

The men of the family helped her to her feet, her legs unsteady from exhaustion. The officers in the room sat her on a wooden chair. They took the shade off a lamp and shined the light in her face. They had many questions for the loyal older sister of Watchman Nee. The preacher had been jailed since 1952 on trumped-up charges of crimes against the state. Until his imprisonment, she had been an active member of his Christian assembly and was a close friend of his wife, Charity. The interrogators wanted to know what had happened to her brother's circle of followers and pressed Ni Guizhen on her religious activities.

"When did she pray?"

"Where did she pray?"

"Who joined her?"

They said they knew about the flow of money from Hong Kong and bombarded her with questions about it.

"Where was she getting it?"

"What did she do with it?"

A group of Christians in Hong Kong, known inside the family simply as "the observatory group" for the location of their meeting place in Kowloon, regularly sent funds to Shanghai. The family knew that Ni Guizhen sometimes helped to channel money to destitute friends, including Charity.

Ni Guizhen softly mumbled an answer, which only seemed to inflame her interrogators.

Another mumbled reply, then, *thwack*!

"We know you're not telling us everything!"

A whimper. Then another backhanded slap across the face.

The others, on the opposite side of the door, flinched at the sound.

The officers demanded to know what she did with the money.

"Where's the bank book?"

Ni Guizhen confessed that she didn't have it. Her son had destroyed it.

When the door opened before dawn, Ni Guizhen stood in the doorway, held up by the officers, exhausted and limp, her hair tousled, looking at her husband and children with confused, fearful eyes.

Lin Pu-chi wrote no letter to his son in Philadelphia that August. When he finally reached out to him in September, he switched from his flawless English to terse Chinese. With straightforward words, he sent a disguised warning, knowing that the PSB agents would steam open his letter after he posted it.

"Do not send your December birthday gift," he wrote in Chinese without explanation. "I have told your brother and Aunt Mary the same. Our lifestyle is quite satisfactory. All are well. Please do not worry about us."

HOUSE 19

During the Red Terror that exploded that August and extended through September, some 150,000 households in Shanghai were ransacked. The bounty of valuables confiscated by Red Guard units and rebel workers included gold bars, gold and silver jewelry, 3.3 million in US dollars, 370 million yuan in cash and bonds, and 2.4 million yuan in silver dollars.

That autumn, pedestrians along the Bund became accustomed to the sight of bloated bodies floating facedown in the murky Huangpu River. In September alone, 704 people in Shanghai committed suicide, while another 354 others were killed in Cultural Revolution violence.

The Cultural Revolution splintered families. One by one, the adults in House 19 were sent away. Martha was reassigned to a rural commune on an island at the mouth of the Yangtze River, more than twelve miles by ferry from Shanghai. She saw her daughters only when she could travel home on her days off. Emma, a nurse, also was sent to the countryside, to a tiny dispensary in Pudong on the other side of the Huangpu River, three hours away. She had to entrust her children to their grandparents, who had a hard enough time just taking care of themselves. It was left to eleven-year-old Kaikai to go to the market in the morning to buy vegetables and meat to cook for his seven-year-old sister, Lin Yu.

Tim was not around to help. When he reported to work after the August raids, rebel workers at his factory detained him. His coworkers shaved his head and forced him to sleep on the concrete factory floor. Communist cadres in charge of his "work unit," or *danwei*, as state-run enterprises were called, questioned him around the clock.

"What's that in your ear?" an inquisitor demanded.

"My hearing aid," Tim told him, explaining how a childhood illness had damaged his hearing. The uneducated men had never seen such a device.

"Are you sure it's not for spying for America?!" they accused.

His interrogators knew about the money coming from the United States. They had gotten a tip. Ni Guizhen had made the mistake of confiding to someone at her church about destroying the bank CDs, purchased with money from her sons—and that person had informed the Red Guards.

"You're lying!" a guard accused Tim with a smack across his head.

For weeks, rebel workers held Tim captive at his factory, refusing to let go of their suspicion that he was an agent for Washington.

John also went to work one day and did not come home. His coworkers detained him indefinitely, giving Martha no reason and only instructing her to bring him a bedroll and food. They kept him locked in a windowless basement bunker that had been built as an air-raid shelter in the 1930s. The Cultural Revolution empowered "good workers" to act as prosecutor, judge, jury, and captor in dealing with class enemies. John had two black marks against him: he was the scion of a capitalist family and a devout Christian who was intensely loyal to Watchman Nee. To squeeze confessions from him, his tormentors strung up his arms by his thumbs, leaving his feet on the ground.

Only the old people and grandchildren remained in House 19. All of the children dreaded going to school. Word traveled fast through the neighborhood about the ransacking of the house and the family's branding as "bad elements." Kaikai got punched in the face in a classroom brawl. Terri and Julia faced constant taunts from Red Guards, who reminded them, "If the father is a hero, the son is a hero. If the father is a scoundrel, the son is a scoundrel."

Terri had to report once a week to the Red Guard unit at her middle school and reveal to them everything that happened in her home. After Tim

During the Cultural Revolution, girls wore pigtails. Like all Chinese, Julia (left) and Terri sported Mao buttons. Courtesy of Lin Family Collection.

came home following six weeks of detention, workers from his factory asked her to record his movements. Desperate to curry favor with the Red Guards, she agreed. In the upper right drawer of a desk in the living room, she kept a notebook and jotted down who came and went in the house. She noted the hours when Tim left the house and returned, who visited her grandmother, and how long they stayed.

"You need to help us," the Red Guards told her. "Make a clear demarcation from your family. Stand on the side of the proletariat."

Despite her efforts to please, Terri remained a pariah, shunned by her classmates and now resented within the family. She felt that even neighbors in the lane avoided making eye contact with her. Every day she was force-fed the notion that all those around her, from her grandmother to her father and uncle, were nothing more than capitalist roaders, counterrevolutionary sympathizers, and "running dogs" of American enemies.

The Red Guards even had a song for people like her:

> I am a cow devil and snake spirit.
> I am the enemy of the people.
> I have committed a crime.
> I deserve the punishment of death.
> People should smash me into pieces.

Eventually, schools stopped teaching and became nothing more than headquarters for the Red Guards. Terri stayed home, retreating to her attic bedroom, cursing the turn in her life, her family, and her fate. At the start of the year, she had friends and thoroughly enjoyed school. Just last spring, at a track meet for the whole school, her classmates cheered her as she finished third in the four-hundred-meter race. She ran so hard and so strongly that she fainted at the finish line.

Now she lived in constant dread of another attack. She couldn't sleep through the night. Every loud noise, squeak, or bang made her wake with a start, panicked that Red Guards were knocking down the front door and terrified of reliving that night in August when all the trouble began.

Alone all day in her room, she studied her chemistry and physics textbooks. When she finished that, she read the only novel still left in the house, the 1,300-page, two-volume *Dream of the Red Chamber*. It was one of her grandfather's favorite books, which he managed to hide from attackers during the many raids. The first chapter of the love story opened with a couplet that seemed to be speaking to her:

> Truth becomes fiction when the fiction's true;
> Real becomes not-real where the unreal's real.

Terri needed to keep her hands and mind busy. Tedium was her enemy. She wanted her friends back. She wanted to break from her family and, as Red Guards constantly prodded her, to cross that "line of demarcation" to stand with them. She felt emotional whiplash. She hated her family, she loved her family, she hated her family.

In the fall of 1966, Red Guards from Beijing and other cities, traveling freely with Mao's blessing, continued to wander the streets of Shanghai, making mischief. Strangers to the city, they looked for homes with big-character posters on front doors, which served as inadvertent signposts for bourgeois targets. When some of them came down Lane 170, looking in windows, Terri opened the door and invited them to stay in the house.

"We have too much space," she told them.

They settled into the living room and, to the horror of the other family members, roamed the upper floors, ate the family's food, and ordered them around as if they were household staff. They demanded that the family pay each of them five yuan a month for living expenses.

Four months later, the Red Guards left. After they did, the family never regained the use of their living room. Once it had been decided that they had too much space, housing authorities assigned another family—good workers with proletarian credentials that burned red—to take over the spacious living room as their own dwelling. From then on, the Lin family had to use a back door to enter their home of more than twenty-five years.

NEIGHBORS

Schools had Red Guards to carry out the revolution. Factories had rebel workers. And the *longtang* of Shanghai had old housewives to man the front lines of class warfare. They ran "neighborhood committees," a fixture of residential life since the founding of the socialist state and responsible for making sure the message of Mao reached all the people, including retirees or housewives who stayed at home and didn't have work units to guide their political education. The cadres were tasked with indoctrinating old people with new thoughts. At meetings, everyone recited sayings from the little red book of Mao quotations and sang hymns of praise to the chairman:

> The East is red; the sun rises.
> China has got Mao Zedong.
> He seeks happiness for people
> And he is the people's savior.

Most of the cadres were older women who made it their business to know everyone else's. With armbands to identify them, they sat in little booths at the entrance of lanes, keeping track for police and the PSB of everything going on.

In Lane 170, a tiny, middle-aged woman named Jinping, who had a fierce personality, was assigned to make sure all of the older residents reported to their committee—in particular, the sister of Watchman Nee. Jinping worked as a housekeeper for two single sisters who lived on the third floor of House 22. She took her job very seriously. In the early months of the Cultural Revolution, neighbors had to attend three sessions a day at the committee room in Lane 120 on the other side of Jiaozhou Road. If Jinping didn't see Ni Guizhen and her husband heading across the street, she pounded on the door, demanding to know why they were late.

Inside the committee hall, Ni Guizhen knew all the faces around her. In quieter days, if they had passed each other in the lane, she would have greeted neighbors by name and asked about grandchildren or chatted about the weather. She recognized many as fellow Christians who used to worship alongside her at her brother's assembly hall. But any friendship that once bound her to these people was now replaced with public scorn. For some, it was real; for others, it was a disguise they wore to survive.

In this neighborhood chapel to Mao, the old people forced Ni Guizhen to kneel before them like a sinner. She couldn't stand up until she "confessed" her misguided ways. She told them what they demanded to hear:

"I come from a bad family."

"My son-in-law is a capitalist roader."

"My brother is a counterrevolutionary."

"My sons are running dogs in America."

Ni Guizhen was crumbling under the strain. One morning, she felt too weak to get out of bed. Tim helped his mother to sit up, but there was no way she could walk. He couldn't get her to the meeting. He panicked at the thought of what Jinping would do if his mother didn't show up.

Ever the tinkerer, Tim found four caster wheels from furniture and attached them to a square piece of wood to fashion a makeshift wheelchair. Helping his mother down the stairs, he placed her in a wicker chair atop the wooden platform and wheeled her down the lane to again face her accusers.

"Rebellion is justified!" the cadres chanted as a greeting.

Every morning, the first thing everyone in the lane heard over a public address system was *East Is Red*, the anthem of the Red Guards, declaring Chairman Mao the savior of the People's Republic. The last thing they heard before they went to sleep was *Internationale* with its prophecy, "We want to be the masters of the new world. This is the final battle."

That battle continued to play out in House 19. Red Guard units and PSB officers made frequent unannounced visits and always went straight for the easiest target, Ni Guizhen. During one raid, the Red Guards ordered Julia and Terri with their younger cousin Kaikai into a bedroom while berating their grandmother in her second-floor bedroom.

Like their grandparents and parents, the cousins had to write endless confessions, admitting to classmates that they came from a bad family. It was all they heard, drummed into their heads, all day, every day. They were bad. They were scoundrels. They must break from the past. Confused and no longer able to discern truth from lies, they felt the inevitable pull to cross over to the other side.

They agreed to take action, knocked on the door of their grandmother's room, and entered. Red Guards, who surrounded her bed, looked up. Julia, the oldest of her generation and the more reserved of the two sisters, spoke in a low but direct voice for all of them. With Terri and Kaikai beside her, she told the old woman, "We will not follow you. We are not on your side."

The betrayal hit the old woman hard. She implored with a weak, shaky voice, "What have I done?"

They avoided her gaze. As they turned to leave, Julia could not hold back her tears.

Terri, however, could not leave the matter alone. More forceful than her older sister, she was unable to tamp down her deepening resentment and anger. Her "blood was boiling," as the lyric from the *Internationale* went. "Fight for the truth! The old world shall be utterly routed."

The next time they were alone in the house, Terri confronted her grandmother. She lashed out at the old woman, blaming her for everything bad in her life.

"I hate being born into this family!" Terri screamed. "You have done so many wrong things!"

This time, Ni Guizhen did not submit. She shot back with equal intensity. "Why are you reporting on us to the Red Guards? Why are you taking notes on all of us?"

"The church is bad," Terri countered. "And Watchman Nee, he is the cause of all of our troubles!"

She stormed out of the old woman's room and ran up to the attic.

The argument had been a short but ferocious squall, which Terri immediately regretted the next day. She knew she had to apologize.

As she softly stepped into her grandmother's bedroom, she saw her grandfather gently talking to his wife. Ni Guizhen sat on the edge of the bed. Her face seemed slack. She held her left hand in her lap. Lin Pu-chi whispered to Terri that her grandmother seemed to have suffered a small stroke during the night.

Ni Guizhen could no longer move her hand.

· 16 ·

Yellow Music

Shanghai, 1968

*E*ach day for Julia started like every other. From Jiaozhou Road, she rode her Flying Pigeon bicycle two miles to her school in the old French Concession. She passed under the stone archway of 9 Dongping Road and parked her bike next to hundreds of identical black bikes.

The campus of the middle school for the Shanghai Conservatory of Music was a mix of aging villas and slapdash utilitarian brick buildings. In the days before the Cultural Revolution, music seemed to rise from every corner of the school. On hot mornings, students would throw open the windows of small practice rooms. Pianists practiced regimented scales, their fingers flying back and forth over black and white keys. Sopranos reached for high notes in arias, competing with the equally ambitious efforts of those playing violins, flutes, cellos, and bassoons. Each note from every voice or instrument could be traced back to a teenage virtuoso who yearned to be the country's next great soloist. Julia was one of them. When she entered the school at thirteen, she took private lessons twice a week in a second-floor studio in one of the villas. She learned pieces by Czerny, Bach, Mozart, and Beethoven as well as mandatory "red" music, such as "The Sky of the Liberated Region," which contained the lyric "The mercy of the Communist Party is endless!"

But as the years went by, Julia played less Bach and Beethoven and more revolutionary music. Finally, in the spring of 1966, Chairman Mao allowed his wife, Jiang Qing, and her cohorts to launch their campaign to wipe out anything perceived as bourgeois in the arts and culture. This left little room for Julia and her classmates to enjoy something as indulgent as learning Western classical music. Instead, they watched radical students torment teachers at cruel "struggle sessions." The principal of the high school, a refined pianist who always wore a prim Western dress, had to take turns slapping the face of another piano instructor in front of the entire student body—a popular form

215

of punishment meted out by Red Guards throughout China. But that was nothing compared with what older students at the college-level conservatory were doing. Red Guards confined a renowned violin professor in a dark closet under the stairs for nine months before assigning him to the job of cleaning and maintaining 122 toilets in classrooms and dormitories.

By the start of 1968, the campus on Dongping Road was silent.

Julia at eighteen went through the motions of school. Teachers did not teach. Students did not practice. No one performed recitals. They were all too busy "participating in revolution." The only thing young musicians heard eight hours a day was the constant monotone of revolutionary rhetoric.

Conservatory students from "good families," whose parents were factory workers, poor peasants, or, even better, the offspring of high-ranking Communist cadres, ruled the school. They formed the nexus of a Red Guard unit; others were divided into a caste system based on their proletarian purity. Julia was grouped with other untouchables. In her assigned study group, she was placed with three other girls from "bad families." They gathered daily in a practice room to work on assignments. One day it could be dissecting an editorial from the *People's Daily*. Another day it might be prepping for "self-criticism" sessions, mandatory public confessions that were a treacherous exercise in acting. Before all your peers, you had to admit your failings while criticizing others, knowing that what you said could bring even more trouble to someone else.

Only once did Julia witness a student, a piano prodigy two years younger named Xu Feiping, refuse to voice a self-criticism. Xu Feiping was the son of a Christian pastor who grew up playing hymns on the island of Gulangyu in Fujian Province, which was famous for producing some of the best musicians in China. He played Chopin's difficult Etude no. 2 so furiously and with such command that his older classmates listened with envy. When it was time for his self-criticism, Xu Feiping stood in silent defiance, unwilling to attack mentors who had nurtured his talent. His supporters watched with unspoken awe while his tormentors used his stubbornness to harass him even further.

Among the three fellow castoffs in Julia's study group, one pianist had a father who was an English professor at the Shanghai Foreign Language Institute. Another was a child of capitalists. And the third was the daughter of an electrical engineer who had earned his graduate degree from the University of California in Los Angeles. That would have been a source of family pride in the old days but now branded him as an intellectual, one of the black categories. He was kicked out of his family's house and moved with his wife and children to a much smaller apartment.

Julia, of course, had them all trumped: her father was a capitalist; her great-uncle was an imprisoned Christian, accused of being a counterrevolutionary; her grandfather was a minister educated in America; and her uncles, doctors who had fled in 1949, were now American citizens. The other girls thought nothing of Julia's tainted lineage. The pariahs stuck together. And for that she was grateful. During their study sessions in the practice room, the four of them would close the door, shut the windows, and freely chatter, setting aside, if only for a moment, all talk of revolution and struggle.

By the end of the school day, Julia could not wait to escape and race home on her bike. But the house on Jiaozhou Road offered little in the way of solace or privacy. If the practice room felt like a cell, her home was a birdcage. Neighbors kept a watchful eye on the three generations living inside House 19. On more than one occasion, Julia caught a neighbor—an older man with no job—just standing by the door, peering inside and listening. The family had to assume that whatever he heard and saw—or thought he heard and saw—would get back to the neighborhood committee.

Ni Guizhen no longer had to make daily confessions before her neighbors as she had in the first months of the Cultural Revolution. But young Red Guards still made surprise visits to the house to verbally attack and humiliate the old woman. Curiously, none of her young tormentors ever seemed to turn their attention to her husband, Lin Pu-chi, the retired Anglican priest. They seemed more inflamed by Ni Guizhen's bloodline as the sister of Watchman Nee, an imprisoned enemy of the state, than her husband's past life as a leader in the Protestant Church.

The constant stress was taking a toll on Ni Guizhen's health. She had heart disease, a cholesterol level that was precariously high, and unrelenting insomnia. Worst of all, her mind was slipping. Terri, who spent her days in the house, could sense it. Unlike Julia, she did not have to go to school and stayed in her bedroom, reading or just brooding. Terri came up with mental exercises to battle boredom. She took apart a radio and put it back together, and when she was done with her radio, she did the same with her bicycle.

Alone under the eaves in the attic, Terri sometimes could hear her grandmother talking to herself in her room. Even more alarming was when she heard the old woman laughing at no one in particular. Other days, Ni Guizhen would lie in bed, silent and still, her quilted cotton jacket buttoned tight, a black knit cap on her head. She was lonely and missed her closest friend, the wife of Watchman Nee, Charity. Before, the sisters-in-law used to gather in Ni Guizhen's room to pray or sing hymns from the palm-size Little Flock hymnal. But since the start of the Cultural Revolution, Charity was under house arrest and faced constant surveillance by public security officials. Once, Ni Guizhen sent Julia to Charity's house to check on her aunt, but officers stopped her, grabbing the handlebars of her bike and demanding to know why she had come.

With the other adults gone all day, Lin Pu-chi was left to care for his wife, a role reversal for the two of them. Just two years before, he was the one who had been bedridden for months. Now it was his turn to tend to his ailing wife. He propped her up in bed three times a day so that she could eat or read her Bible. He made her a thin porridge of rice and water and fretted over her weight loss—almost twenty pounds in the past year. At night, he gave her two pills to help her sleep and knew that if she clutched her chest when she woke in the morning, he had to quickly give her nitroglycerin, kept in a medicine bottle on the nightstand.

YELLOW MUSIC

Though Julia no longer had a piano to play at home or school, she was not about to let her skills slip. She had worked too long and hard to backslide now. She asked her grandmother to teach her how to knit, thinking this at least would be a good way to build dexterity in her fingers. Making a sweater was not the same as mastering the F minor scale, but what alternative did she have? In her attic room, Julia also set out to replace her sheet music, which had been destroyed by Red Guards when they ransacked the home in the summer of 1966. With borrowed music from classmates, she painstakingly copied each note of twenty-four études by Chopin.

But if she was going to hold onto her piano skills, she needed a piano. Some families had escaped the notice of Red Guards and still had theirs. Julia asked around and found friends willing to let her practice in their homes. One was her mother's supervisor, another obstetrician from the hospital. The doctor's old upright was woefully out of tune, but Julia could not be choosy. She went to the woman's home as often as she could, conscious not to wear out her welcome. Adding to her circuit of pianos, Julia asked her piano teacher from the conservatory whether she could practice some afternoons at her home. The woman, who had a son and daughter who also were music students and understood her predicament, allowed Julia to come by every so often.

But Julia's favorite place to play was at the house of Third Uncle—San Shu, the younger brother of her father. He lived in the Sun family's home, a spacious villa on Yuyuan Road that his father had purchased in 1946 with ten gold bars, profits from the family's embroidery business, China Handwork.

Third Uncle, an accountant at a shipyard, was a self-taught violinist, and his wife was a professional singer for the Shanghai Lyric Opera House. He delighted in bringing together family and friends with people from her circle of musicians. Before Red Guards ransacked his home at the start of the Cultural Revolution, the couple owned an enviable library of music: the latest recordings of compositions by Verdi, Puccini, and Paganini, performed by such greats as Maria Callas and Renata Tebaldi. His living room became a popular salon where amateurs could mingle with professionals and enjoy an evening of music.

Apart from Third Uncle's home, Julia's options for musical entertainment were limited. The only productions that Madame Mao deemed acceptable were eight "model" works: five revolutionary operas, two ballets, and one symphony. Julia had nowhere to go to hear a classic Italian opera like the tragic tale of lost love in *Madama Butterfly*. But she could see the *Raid on the White Tiger Regiment*, about a Chinese battle against US-backed troops in Korea, as many times as she wanted.

Despite all the constraints on music, Third Uncle thought it was all right to continue his soirees. The gatherings, he reasoned, were only for the enjoyment of his family and friends. He also felt that the atmosphere in Shanghai had eased ever so slightly. Everyone was still careful to toe the revolutionary line, but there was not the same anarchy in the streets as during the first months of the Cultural Revolution.

Julia went as often as she could to Third Uncle's parties, sometimes not waiting for an invitation. If there were risks, she, too, ignored them. She was

Julia was able to play back a piece after listening to someone else play it. As this photograph shows, she eventually learned how to read music, but not until after she entered the middle school affiliated with the Shanghai Conservatory of Music. Courtesy of Lin Family Collection.

a naïve teenager who yearned to hear the music of Mozart and Chopin, even as Madame Mao tried just as hard to control the artistic offerings for Julia and eight hundred million other Chinese.

Once, a famous violinist from Hong Kong visited Third Uncle and asked Julia to accompany him on the family's Moutri upright piano. When the visitor began playing Mendelssohn, Julia's heart swelled just hearing a master perform the Violin Concerto in E Minor, op. 64.

At one point, the violinist leaned over and whispered, "The chords on your left hand should be cleaner."

Julia was thrilled. She wasn't embarrassed by the correction. She craved instruction of any kind, even if it was only one brief comment.

Before Chinese New Year in 1968, the Year of the Monkey, Third Uncle sent a message to the Lin home, inviting his brother's family to his house on Sunday night, January 21.

Julia was the first one out the door, cycling the twenty minutes to Third Uncle's house at the end of a quiet lane. She hurried up the steps to his rooms on the second floor. Third Uncle used to share the villa with another brother. But at the start of the Cultural Revolution, Red Guards decided that the two families enjoyed too much space, an unacceptable extravagance in crowded Shanghai. The local housing bureau moved a couple named Wang into rooms on the first floor. The newcomers, laborers with good proletarian credentials, did not get along with their more cultured neighbors and openly bickered over trivial matters like the noise and music coming from upstairs.

Close to twenty people crammed into chairs and onto stools in Third Uncle's living room. His brother-in-law and several of his friends, including the sons of prominent Communist cadres, were among the guests. Julia ignored the snacks and tea set out by her aunt and sat down immediately at the piano bench. She plunged into Mozart before moving on to Liszt. The mood was relaxed and happy; music flowed freely. Third Uncle picked up his violin while his wife, Ailin, entertained guests with some of her favorite arias.

Hours passed and the party showed no signs of ending. From outside, his wife thought she heard shouting. She stood up to peek out a window. She heard heavy footsteps landing on steps and harsh voices growing louder and louder.

Before she knew what was happening, strangers burst open the front door of the apartment. Guests froze. Julia's hands stopped. Fight or flight was not a choice, only fright, terrifying, heart-pounding fright. She knew what came next. Everyone knew what came next.

"What are you doing?!" accused a Red Guard, storming into the living room. "Are you playing banned music?"

The neighbor downstairs had tipped off the Red Guards from the opera house. Ailin looked at the six faces before her and recognized them as dancers and singers who, on any other night, would have shared the stage with her. The young men chastised Third Uncle's guests for playing "yellow music"—*huangse yinyue*, the phrase Red Guards used to dismiss any music they considered promiscuous and sleazy. Striptease music with long trombone pulls and thumping drums was yellow music. In their judgment, so was a Mozart sonata. They searched every person, took down names, and ordered each guest to report the next morning to the Red Guards in their work units. As they left, the intruders made sure to grab all of Third Uncle's new albums from Hong Kong.

When the door shut, the guests silently got up to leave, weighed down with dread as they filed down the stairs, past the door of the Wang family and into the cold night.

Red Guards at the conservatory were waiting for Julia.

She kept her head down, trying hard not to make eye contact with anyone as she passed through the archway and walked her bike into a parking spot. But on the second-floor balcony of one of the villas, the Red Guards spied her and began hurling insults.

"You dog!" they taunted. "Look at the dog!"

They didn't call out her name but just kept screaming, "You daughter of a dog!"

Before, Julia was only one of many unfortunate students with bad family backgrounds. But after the previous night, she was notorious. Accounts about what happened at Third Uncle's house spread quickly from one student to another. Six girls with red armbands, validating their pedigree as Red Guards, ordered Julia into a classroom. Two years before, she would have counted them among her friends. One was a piano student like her. But now their faces were twisted with hatred and anger. All of them came from the reddest of red families, and they were fired up for punishment.

Julia didn't know it, but another group of Red Guards from the conservatory had gone to her home and dragged her father, John, to the school. John had only recently been released from detention at the housing bureau, where he had endured months of physical and mental abuse in a windowless basement bunker. The Red Guards placed him in a classroom next door to the one where Julia was held. Not a strong man to begin with and cowed from months of deprivation during his own detention, John was not about to antagonize his young interrogators.

"Stand on the stool!" a Red Guard commanded.

John stood on a stool.

"Bend over!"

He bent at the waist, wobbling and struggling to keep his balance.

"Did you play yellow music?"

"No," John softly answered.

"I can't hear you!"

"No."

A Red Guard kicked the stool out from under him. With nothing to break his fall, John landed hard on the cement floor.

"Stand up!" a teen shouted. "On the stool."

John slowly crawled to his feet and climbed back onto the stool.

Again, the same question and the same denial.

With his leg, the student again knocked the stool out from under John.

Sprawled on the floor, the older man clutched his injured back.

Next door, Julia sat at a desk, her eyes downcast as the girls continued to berate her.

"Why were you playing yellow music? Answer us. Why were you playing yellow music?"

Julia could absorb a lot. She was not one to argue or fight. She avoided conflict. But this constant accusation about playing yellow music was ludicrous. These girls knew the difference between Mozart and dance hall jazz. But the Cultural Revolution had turned otherwise sane classmates into sadistic bullies. Closing in on Julia, they were determined to make her feel like nothing but a lowlife pornographer, the trash of society.

The more they pushed, the more steeled Julia became. Finally, she snapped, challenging them instead of giving them what they wanted to hear. Her urge to fight eclipsed her fright.

"It was not yellow music!" Julia firmly shouted. "It was classical music, Mozart! Why are you saying this?"

Shocked by her insolence, one of the girls—a fellow pianist—grabbed a Ping-Pong paddle that was lying nearby and yanked Julia's right hand onto the desktop. She looked like a snarling dog, baring its teeth right before it lunges and bites. The girl raised her arm high above her head and came down with ferocious force on Julia's knuckles. She raised her arm again, wielding the paddle as if she were chopping chicken with a cleaver.

Each blow made Julia wince, but she fought back her tears. She would not give this classmate the satisfaction of seeing her cry.

At home, Julia raced up the stairs, running past her grandparents' room and heading straight for the attic. She burst in on Terri, who looked up from her book with shock.

"Julia, what happened, why are you crying?"

Her older sister cradled her right hand. "I don't know if I'll be able to play again," she whimpered.

Her fingers, black and blue with bruises, looked like they'd been pumped up with air. The sisters sat in silence.

Martha returned late that night and determined that nothing was broken. Julia cried in her arms. She felt responsible for the mess and was convinced that her reckless desire to play music at Third Uncle's house now had made matters even worse for the family.

"I'm sorry," she confided to her mother. "It's just that I love music too much."

Julia's father, however, did not come home. Red Guards returned him to his work unit, where he again was locked in a basement bunker.

Two days after her beating, Julia had to return to school. Her body tensed when she walked through the archway into the conservatory campus. Red Guards immediately spied her and taunted from a balcony, "Dog! Dog! Dog!"

She lowered her head and parked her bike.

SENT-DOWN YOUTH

Sometimes, Julia could not help but ask her mother, "Why didn't you leave for the United States with your brothers?"

"Why, Julia," Martha would answer with a smile, "if I had left, you wouldn't be here."

Julia was left to read about the world that might have been in letters that still arrived every month from Philadelphia and Norfolk, Virginia. The uncles in America described uncomplicated, comfortable lives. They took family vacations to places like Martha's Vineyard and Puerto Rico. Their children learned how to ski and how to golf, how to ride horses and how to dance. They listened to the Beatles and watched *The Magical World of Disney* and *The Ed Sullivan Show* on television on Sunday nights. The families celebrated baptisms, first communions, birthdays, and graduations. The uncles bought new cars, enjoyed promotions at their hospitals, and invested in second homes. Paul bought a farm with an eighteenth-century stone house and barn on eighty-six acres. Jim owned a house on a lake and a motorboat. They were landlords, intellectuals, capitalists, and Christians—and no one in America seemed to mind.

Julia and Terri read notes that their cousins who were closest in age to them sometimes included in the letters from Philadelphia. Angela told them about coming in twelfth out of ninety-two students in a citywide spelling bee. Daria described going to a school fair with a Ferris wheel at her Catholic private school.

It was harder for the Shanghai cousins to reply with any news from inside their home. Julia could never truthfully share with her cousins what was happening at her high school. After all, what would she say?

Dear Angela and Daria,
Today at school we attended a mass meeting at a big theater. Two Red Guards dragged the head of the conservatory, a very famous composer named He Luting, onto the stage. They made him bow his head and wear a dunce cap. It was broadcast on live television, so everyone in the country could hear us shout at him, "Knock down the anti-communist He Luting!"
Your cousin,
Julia

The Philadelphia cousins wrote about getting honors on their last report cards. Terri, meanwhile, hadn't been to formal classes at her middle school since the start of the Cultural Revolution in 1966. She was a captive in her own home, passing the days by reading and rereading the few books that Red Guards hadn't confiscated in earlier attacks on the family home.

But that was about to change.

On December 22, 1968, the *People's Daily*, the most influential newspaper in the country, ran an editorial with a pronouncement from Chairman Mao, who said: "The intellectual youth must go to the country, and will be educated from living in rural poverty."

Even Mao could not ignore the fact that the Cultural Revolution was spinning out of control. He needed to do something with the Red Guards to move them out of cities and on to other things. When Mao spoke, people listened. With the mere utterance of those words in the *People's Daily*, he launched a mass migration of millions of teenagers and young adults, who left their homes in cities to live and work among peasants in the countryside.

Julia and the other musicians from her class at the conservatory were assigned to a reeducation camp for intellectuals in the farming district of Fengxian, just south of Shanghai. But Terri and her former classmates from middle school would be sent farther away. They could choose between relocating to the impoverished South or frigid North.

The thought of living among peasants so far from home terrified some classmates. But the idea thrilled Terri, who picked the place farthest from Jiaozhou Road.

At last, Terri had a way to escape her attic.

· 17 ·

Barefoot Doctor

Jilin Province, 1969

*T*erri scanned the faces in the schoolyard, hoping to see her mother's tiny frame breaking through the crowd at any moment. Her sister Julia had come to see her off at the Xinzha Middle School, but Martha had to work the overnight shift at the hospital and was running late.

Hundreds of students lingered over good-byes with their parents. Girls wept in the arms of their mothers, while boys tried hard not to show emotion. A dozen military trucks idled on the basketball courts, waiting to shuttle students to a transport ship to take them to the northern port of Dalian.

Julia did not try to hold back her tears. It was damp and chilly on this March morning in Shanghai, but where Terri was going, the weather was still frostbite cold. Just the thought of it made Julia fret for her younger sister.

"Don't worry," Terri reassured. "I'll be okay."

There would be no crying for Terri. She could have gone to a commune in Anhui Province, about two hundred miles to the west of Shanghai, but instead chose a more remote option, relocating with other classmates to Jilin Province in the icy heart of northeastern China.

The idea of starting anew and living among strangers exhilarated Terri. She was only sixteen and for the first time in years felt in control of her life. Shanghai represented her past and all that was wrong with her family. But in a new place among new people, she believed she had a shot at defining a different future.

Terri had a plan. Her whole life, she had expected to grow up to be a doctor just like her mother. Of the sisters, Julia was always "the musical one," while Terri was "the scientific one." At school, she excelled in classes like biology and chemistry. In her attic bedroom, she read an anatomy textbook with as much concentration and enjoyment as her novels. With her move to the countryside, Terri was determined to rewrite the script of her life. She

225

made up her mind that she would become a rural medical worker, a "barefoot doctor," a *chijiao yisheng*.

She first heard the term in an editorial in the *People's Daily* on September 15, 1968, which advocated for barefoot doctors to bring basic health care to more people. Mao attacked the health-care profession, with its many Western-trained experts, for skewing services to urban residents while ignoring the needs of peasants. The vast majority of people had nothing. To change that, Mao wanted to train a new class of rural medics who would be "half farmers, half doctors." They would receive a few months of training and then return to village clinics to bring basic health care to peasants.

Terri found the idea exhilarating. She wanted to become this new model worker, who could stand shoeless in a field one moment and then wield a syringe in a clinic the next.

Many students shared the same ambition. To accommodate them, a clinic in Shanghai held a four-week crash course before the students were dispatched to the countryside. Terri learned the basics of first aid, such as how to suture a cut, how to treat a kitchen burn, and how to care for a cold.

Her obstetrician mother also had arranged for her to get further training in delivering babies. For two weeks, Terri was allowed to shadow a team of doctors, nurses, and midwives at Xinhua Hospital, observing them in the labor room as they handled as many as ten deliveries at a time. They showed Terri how to coach a mother through her first contractions to the final push. Only once did Terri flinch; she nearly fainted the first time she saw a doctor use a scalpel to make an incision to prevent tearing during childbirth.

An eager and focused student, Terri felt pressured to learn as much as she could, as fast as she could. Sleep would have to wait. For two weeks, she didn't go home and allowed herself only a few hours a day to nap at the hospital.

Martha arrived at the Xinzha schoolyard just in time to say good-bye. She came alone. Her husband was still being detained by Red Guards, who had locked him up after the piano episode at Third Uncle's house a year earlier.

After a busy night in the delivery room, Martha looked exhausted yet calm. She knew that this move, however difficult it would be for everyone, was the best thing for her daughter.

Workers strained to lift Terri's two big leather trunks onto a flatbed truck. It was heavier than others. In between wool scarves and socks, Martha had tucked stainless steel medical instruments, including clamps, a scalpel, and scissors, as well as acupuncture needles, alcohol, and several doses of penicillin. Some mothers sent their children off with stashes of dried fruit or nuts, hidden like surprise gifts in the folds of their luggage. Martha tucked into Terri's trunks her textbook on obstetrics and gynecology, plus another manual on common medical ailments and basic procedures.

The students, pressing shoulder to shoulder, held onto the side of the truck. Terri locked her eyes on her mother's reassuring face. She had no idea when she would see her parents again.

Daughter and mother exchanged small waves as the truck lurched into gear and pulled away.

The young passengers trudged up the gangplank of a commercial ship like cattle through a chute. They descended into a dark cargo hold improvised to handle passengers. Terri took a place among rows of blankets laid side by side on the steel floor. Everyone clambered to the top deck to watch the Shanghai skyline fade away as the ship sailed down the Huangpu River.

For most of the city teenagers, this was their first time on a seafaring vessel. The rocking motion of the ship on the open ocean lulled Terri into a deep sleep. Some of the girls around her were not as lucky. Seasick, they had a hard time holding down their dinners.

After three days at sea in the dark, cold, and increasingly smelly cargo hold, all the passengers were anxious to disembark in the port of Dalian. Their legs were still wobbly from ocean travel when they were immediately transported to waiting trains. So many students packed into the railcars that Terri had to stand most of the time. Students took shifts sitting on hard seats or the floor. Some unfortunate travelers could find spare space only in the toilet compartment.

The teenagers looked at the wintry landscape racing past their windows with silent disbelief. It was much worse than Terri had imagined. She and her classmates came from a city with granite skyscrapers, streetlights, and lush parks. All they saw now were flat, brown fields. Occasionally, swirls of yellow dust would spin like tops in the sky.

Dry, cold winds from Siberia constantly raked across this part of China, the ancient homeland of the Manchu people, the last imperial rulers, whose Qing dynasty ended in 1911. Outsiders called the northeastern region Manchuria—a name not used by the Manchu themselves—and coveted its bountiful farmland as well as its rich deposits of oil, coal, and iron ore. Czarist Russia pushed into Manchuria, establishing a naval base on the coast in the late nineteenth century, while Japan made a grab for the whole region. In 1932, Japanese invaders installed the last emperor, Puyi, as the puppet ruler of the Nippon state of Manchukuo in Jilin's capital of Changchun. In Mao's China, there was no more Manchukuo or Manchuria, only Dongbei, its proper Mandarin name, meaning "East-north."

After a day and night on the train, the students arrived at a rail station on the outskirts of Changchun, the vital industrial center of Dongbei. In 1958, the city's First Automobile Works manufactured China's first domestic passenger car, the Red Flag or Hongqi. The luxury sedan, with its black-lacquer finish and grinning steel grill, was reserved for special passengers like high-ranking communist cadres or visiting dignitaries. The pride of socialist China, the Red Flag could trace its lineage to capitalist Detroit: its engine was modeled after a Cadillac, and its chassis looked like that of a 1955 Chrysler.

Terri put on the mustard yellow quilted jacket that each of the students had been given when they left Shanghai. Herded onto trucks for another leg of the journey, the Shanghai transplants got their first taste of Dongbei's notorious weather. Unforgiving winds slapped their faces, making it hard to breathe. On the back of the flatbed truck, they pressed closer together for warmth.

"I picked this place because I thought I'd be in the wilderness among wolves and tigers," joked one city boy named Liyu as the truck rumbled over dirt roads.

But there were no forests, no mountains, nothing, in fact, surprising or random about the landscape. Barren fields unfolded like bolts of brown corduroy. Rows of tall poplars, planted as a defense against wind erosion, stood ramrod straight along the roadside. Streets were empty except for the occasional truck hauling mounds of muddy beets to sugar mills.

Pulling into the town of Yihe, the mood of the teens sank even lower. Men with wooden carts pulled by mules were waiting for them. The Shanghai students were a thousand miles from home, and their journey still wasn't over. They had even farther to travel into the cold night.

A single oil lamp illuminated the thatched-roof home of a peasant. Old men and women, packed into a room, ogled their young guests.

Terri and five other girls sat awkwardly and stiffly on the edge of an eight-by-eight-foot brick platform called a *kang*. It was so high that their legs didn't touch the ground. The room had no furniture, an unfamiliar concept for the modern Shanghai girls. In this part of rural China, life revolved around the *kang*, which was warmed from inside by a fire. The girls were told that this was where they would eat, sleep, and lounge.

No one spoke as each side sized up the other. Farmers wearing hats with earflaps lined with dog fur envied the hard leather shoes of the city girls and silently wondered how long soles like that would last in the fields. The Shanghai teens, staring at the leathery skin of old farmwives, had the urge to reach out with their smooth fingertips to see what it felt like.

"You children must eat," urged an older man named Gao, ladling soup from a big wok into six bowls. He was a widower with a grown son. He told the girls that he was assigned to look after the twelve "educated youth" from Shanghai, dubbed *zhishi qingnian*, who would be staying in the village.

Terri (kneeling in the center of the second row) photographed with other Shanghai students who were sent to a village in the frigid Northeast to "learn from peasants." She worked as a "barefoot doctor" and delivered her first baby at the age of sixteen. Courtesy of Lin Family Collection.

Their new home was less of a town than a cluster of houses near a bend in the dirt road. Gao explained that he and his neighbors—150 people spread among 25 families—were part of a household collective, and he was the top cadre.

"If you have problems, you come to me," he instructed.

The girls wrapped their numb fingers around the warm soup bowls, slurping steaming broth and devouring thin slices of potato. No one took off her quilted jacket or wool hat. Even though they sat indoors, they could still see their breath.

More than five days after leaving Shanghai, the sent-down youth were finally at their destination. The reality of it terrified them. Mao's abstract command to "learn from peasants" had now come into sharp focus: a drafty house with no furniture, no electricity, no running water. From now on, a hot shower would be a luxury they enjoyed once a year if they were willing to travel to a public bathhouse ten miles away. Families read by oil lamps and used cornstalks to fuel fires for cooking or heating *kangs*. Wood was far too precious to waste.

Sleeping that first night under a heavy quilt, side by side with the other girls, Terri could hear them crying themselves to sleep. Shanghai with its streetcars and bustle was now something relegated to their nighttime dreams.

Terri ignored them. Instead, her mind raced. All she could think about was getting started.

BIRTH

Gao rapped his knuckles on the window of the house.

"Get up, get up," he shouted.

The sky was just starting to lighten, though it was well after seven. Dawn came late in the Far North.

Gao introduced the teens to a middle-aged woman who was missing a few teeth and wore a dark blue scarf around her head. Everyone called her Auntie, or Da Niang, and she was going to give the students their first life lesson: how to cook Jilin style.

Pouring a few precious drops of oil into a wok, she fanned the fire under the black cauldron. She measured out cornmeal, added some flour and hot water, and poured the mixture into small pancakes in the wok. This was *da bingzi*. Forget rice. At this time of year, it was all anyone ate. There were no greens, no pork, no chicken. The only winter vegetable was last year's garlic preserved in salt. Meat was a luxury enjoyed only once a year. Families killed a fattened hog for their New Year's celebration and literally ate until they got sick. With the holiday just passed, it would be another eleven months before the students would see pork in their bowls.

Next on the agenda was a lesson outside. The city students bundled up with mittens, hats, scarves, and coats and followed Gao into the fields. He handed everyone a small hoe.

"Watch me," the old cadre explained.

Bending over, he dug up the stump of a corn stalk from the hard ground and gave the roots a few swipes with the hand hoe to knock off dirt. He filled in the hole, patted it smooth, and moved on to the next.

Terri tried to imitate Gao. She followed each step. Her big mittens made it too hard to hold the stalk and hoe, so she took them off for a better grip. But the next time she came down with the hand tool, she swiped her finger with the blade.

Blood dripped down her hand. She winced from the pain and squeezed the deep gash to make it stop bleeding. Mortified, she looked around, hoping no one noticed that on her first day, she was her first patient.

Terri didn't waste any time telling Gao or anyone else who would listen about her plan to become a barefoot doctor. Her collective was part of the bigger town of Yihe, located a short distance away. She traveled to the clinic there to volunteer her services. Expecting a warm welcome, she got the opposite. The clinic workers were unwilling to add any of the "sent-down" youth from Shanghai to the staff. These were prime jobs, which kept them indoors and not laboring in the fields during winter months. Many of the women were the wives of commune leaders. They closed ranks.

Undeterred, Terri looked for pregnant women on her own.

She found one living not far from her house. Emboldened by the moxie of youth, she went right up to the woman and asked whether she could help her with her pregnancy.

"I've trained at a top hospital in Shanghai," Terri told her neighbor, trying hard to impress her. "I know what to do. I brought equipment with me, too, the best you can use for a delivery."

The pregnant mother seemed receptive to letting this young stranger help her. Even a teenager with only a little practical experience was better than no help at all. In the countryside, death was part of the birth experience. It wasn't unusual for a mother to lose one infant, often more, to infection or complications.

But when the time came, the pregnant woman opted to call an elderly neighbor to help her instead of sending for Terri. The old woman approached the birth of a child as she would the birth of a calf. She severed the umbilical cord by cinching it off with a piece of sorghum rope and then using a shard of glass to cut it. Nothing was sterilized.

Horrified by such methods, Terri knew enough to realize that this could cause an infection like tetanus.

Which was exactly what happened.

The newborn girl lived for two days. The family buried her tiny corpse in a shallow grave in a nearby field. Soon after, Terri saw wild dogs dig up the body and rip it apart with their fangs.

Terri resolved to establish herself as someone who could be trusted to help with childbirth, even though, at sixteen, she was still a child herself.

Another woman in the village was due to have her fourth child in June and agreed to let Terri help. As soon as this mother went into labor, Terri hurried to her house. She brought her scissors and clamps and a metal box for sterilizing the instruments in boiling water. Martha had also given her strips of white wool fabric to use as bandages.

The thirty-year-old woman lay on her *kang* with her knees up. Taking a deep breath, Terri tried to remember everything she had learned at her mother's hospital.

The delivery progressed frighteningly fast. No sooner had the baby's crown appeared than Terri was guiding the slippery child into the sunlight. She quickly clamped the umbilical cord.

"A boy!" she shouted to the woman.

But there was no response.

The mother had passed out.

"Wake up!" shouted Terri, putting the wailing newborn down and gently patting the woman's cheeks.

The mother was breathing but still unresponsive.

What to do, what to do?

Reflexively, Terri reached for her acupuncture kit. Somewhere in the recesses of her mind, she had filed away the fact that applying needles simultaneously on the very tips of fingers and toes was so painful it could rouse a person from unconsciousness.

Terri inserted the thickest needles she had, fearful about losing this first patient.

Stay calm, she told herself. *This will work.*

As she pushed the needles in deep and twisted, the woman stirred. Her eyes opened. Terri exhaled.

She gave the mother a bowl of water with sugar and began cleaning the bloody blankets on the *kang*. Afraid the woman might pass out again, Terri sat next to her for hours to make sure she would be all right. She held the swaddled baby boy in her arms. The child slept peacefully.

Back home, on her *kang*, Terri wrote a letter to her mother. She recounted every detail of her first delivery and how she used acupuncture to revive the mother. She closed by saying that for the first time in years, she felt truly happy.

Word spread fast. *This girl from Shanghai knew what she was doing.*

Women from other villages started seeking her out. Sometimes at night, a horse-drawn cart would pull up to the house and a stranger would get out and ask for the girl who delivered babies. Terri would hesitate. Was this safe, taking off to some unknown place with a man she had never met before? But she never refused. And the morning after, she would return to her house just as her friends were getting up. She was expected to grab her hoe and join them in the fields. No one was excused from farmwork.

The workers at the commune clinic, who had originally spurned Terri, eventually asked her to join them. Two days a week, she walked from village to village, handling everything and anything: infected cuts, fevers, boils, blisters, toothaches, stomach pains, babies with diarrhea, and wives with burns. She knew when to prescribe penicillin to a sick child and when to give an analgesic to a farmer with a sore back. Her life acquired a structure and meaning. People depended on her. She had a purpose.

The more babies she delivered, the more her reputation grew. But even with her growing confidence, Terri knew the limits of her abilities. Early on, she had a patient with narrow hips and a very petite frame. With some women, you could just look at them and know they were built to bear children. This one was not one of them. Terri strongly advised the family that it would be safer for the woman to deliver her baby at the commune hospital. A doctor might have to perform a cesarean section.

The husband had to go out of town for several weeks, leaving only his mother to help his wife. As the due date drew near, Terri went to check on the woman at her home. Opening the front door, she immediately gagged from a pungent, heavy odor.

"What happened?" Terri asked the mother-in-law, who was slumped, exhausted in a chair.

Not replying, the old woman pulled Terri by the hand into the next room. It looked like the aftermath of a desperate struggle, with blood smeared all over the *kang*. Terri gasped.

The mother-in-law had ignored her advice to send the woman to the hospital. When the pregnant mother started having trouble during labor, the old woman panicked and sent someone on horseback to fetch a doctor. But it was too late. No one at the commune hospital was available to help. The woman bled to death after delivering a son.

Her body, now stiff and cold, was trussed with rope on the floor, awaiting cremation. On a *kang* in another room, a baby boy slept. He was the couple's firstborn.

The family tried to keep him healthy, feeding him goat's milk, but the child died two months later.

By summer, villagers had built the sent-down youth their own house. It was a simple one-story, mud-wall dwelling, big enough for six boys and six girls. The boys slept on a *kang* in a room on one side of the building and the girls on a *kang* on the other. In the center of the house was a kitchen with two stationary woks: one for cooking and one for boiling water. Heat from fires under the woks was channeled via pipes into the space under each *kang*.

All of Terri's roommates were from her Shanghai middle school, but she hadn't known any of them beforehand. She was as much of a blank slate to them as they were to her. For that, she was relieved. No one knew whether her father was a factory worker or a former business owner, and no one asked. Her value was measured in tangible ways. How much corn could she harvest? How many babies could she deliver? How many sick people could she treat? Terri ceased being that scared, lonely girl in the attic of her Shanghai house. No longer did she just imagine a different life. Now she was living one.

Her first year passed quickly, the days following the rhythm of the seasons. After the autumn harvest of corn, soybean, and sorghum, the girls stayed inside for the worst of the winter weather. With temperatures plunging below zero, they ventured out only to do farmwork for a few hours a day. The rest of the time was devoted to mandatory political study and sleep, luxurious sleep. They rested indulgently like hibernating bears. Otherwise, they sat on their warm *kang* and read Mao's quotations as well as the works of Engels, Marx, and Lenin.

When the days grew longer and warmer, the daily pace quickened. Everyone was under pressure to meet grain quotas set by the commune. Fields of corn had to be planted and harvested by hand. Most of Terri's housemates had lived pampered lives in the city. Now their palms were callused and their backs sore from endless days of fieldwork, tending to crops without the benefit of tractors. If the students fell behind in their output, the whole collective fell behind. The households under the watch of Comrade Gao got paid only if they harvested at least twenty tons of grain a season. The city teens were twelve more mouths to feed and seen by the collective as more of a burden than a benefit.

By summer, the sent-down youth took to the fields as soon as the sun came up and didn't leave until after eight at night. Exhausted, they would take their dinner outside to eat and sit cross-legged on the ground. Their bowls in their laps, they watched the orange sun slip behind the green waves of corn.

At times like that, Terri thought to herself, *Yes, this life is good.*

At the start of harvest season in the fall of 1971, Terri felt worn out like never before. She tried to will herself through her grueling schedule and ignored her symptoms. But one night, aching and shaking with chills, she took her temperature and found that she had spiked a fever of 104 degrees. For ten days, she curled up on her *kang*, unable to move and suffering sharp pains in her stomach. Her urine turned dark yellow. The whites of her eyes looked the same color as beer.

Terri knew enough by now to diagnose her symptoms: she had an inflamed liver. Most likely, she had contracted the virus that causes hepatitis A, which was easily spread through contaminated food or water. She probably caught the disease from a patient and now risked spreading it to everyone in her house as well as her village. She could not gamble on causing an outbreak, not with so many crops to harvest and quotas to meet. But she would need months to recuperate. With winter approaching, she felt she had only one choice.

In a letter home, Terri alerted Martha that she was coming home. As a present for her family, she bought a live chicken from a neighbor, placed it in a burlap bag with corn kernels, and boarded a southbound train for Shanghai.

· 18 ·

Passages

Shanghai, 1971

$\mathcal{T}$his was what it meant to come from a "bad" family. At any given moment, someone could be taken away without warning or explanation and with no redress for the target or any of the people around him. At one point during the Cultural Revolution, all the men of the household were gone. Martha's husband, John, had it worst. He was removed from the house twice, the second time for half a year. The tormentors from his work unit frequently strung him up by his thumbs. When a cellmate made a noose, using cloth scraps twisted into a rope, and hanged himself from a hook in the ceiling, John thought of doing the same. Only his faith stopped him.

Lin Pu-chi, though not physically harmed like his son-in-law, faced pressure to "confess" to imaginary crimes.

Once, he was summoned to a "study group" with more than one hundred other former Christian workers. It was held in an old Protestant church near the Bund, where Sichuan Road crossed Suzhou Creek. When he didn't return home, the family had no idea what had happened to him. Several weeks passed, then two months, until one day, Martha got a call with a curt command: "Come get your father."

She arrived at the gate of the church and found him waiting with his belongings in a bag. The sight of her walking toward him alarmed and startled the old, bearded man.

"What are you doing here?"

"I've come to take you home."

"Take me home?" he repeated. Relief erased the fear from his face. "I thought I was going to prison."

The "Study Group for Christian Leaders" in the Huangpu District had determined that Lin Pu-chi was an American spy. After all, it was undeniable that he received regular mail from the United States, not to mention money.

Although the decision did not lead to jail, it did result in self-inflicted punishment. Lin Pu-chi stopped writing to his sons in America. He told his son Jim in a letter, "I'm too old. I'm tired of writing. I don't want to write anymore."

PRODIGAL DAUGHTER

Since returning to Shanghai, Terri ended up most afternoons with her grandparents. The old couple—Lin Pu-chi was seventy-six, his wife sixty-nine—rarely left their room. They slept in two small beds, aligned perpendicularly against the walls. The space was sparsely furnished with a tall, mirrored armoire and a folding table where they ate their meals. A glass door with a transom window led to a porch overlooking an alley running the length of the lane. Part of the porch was enclosed. This was where Lin Pu-chi liked to sit and write. Otherwise, he stayed in his bed. His blood pressure remained frightfully high, and he could not walk without the help of a cane.

Lin Pu-chi surrounded by his Shanghai grandchildren in 1971. Behind him are Terri (top left) and her older sister, Julia; next to him are Lin Yu (bottom left) and her older brother, Kaikai. Courtesy of Lin Family Collection.

Terri's relationship with her grandparents was much better than it had been five years earlier. At the start of the Cultural Revolution, she had been a strident, impressionable teenager of fourteen who saw the world in black and white, good and bad, revolutionary and reactionary. When Red Guards commanded her to break from her past and distance herself from her family, she obeyed them. She said and did whatever was necessary to survive. But now, in the fall of 1971, she was nineteen and less certain about whom or what to believe. The people closest to her had endured unspeakable cruelty, all in the name of revolution, a revolution that made less sense with each passing year. Her grandmother had been forced to her knees to confess her "sins" to accusers. Her father had been locked up for more than half a year. Her pianist sister was beaten and almost had her hands broken, and for what? Playing Mozart?

Terri had returned to a house, not a family. Martha came home only on weekends. She worked at a rural clinic on an island in the Yangtze River estuary, a few hours away. Julia was permitted to travel back to Shanghai once a month, if that. She had been sent with her conservatory class to a "reeducation camp" in a farm district on the outskirts of the city. The musicians split their time between working in the fields and studying Mao. It was a socialist solution for exorcising intellectuals—such as piano and violin virtuosos— of indulgent ways. The classmates, with their delicate fingers and soft palms, toiled next to peasants in rice paddies, bent over, barefoot, arms sunk up to their elbows in brown muck. They lived in fear of contracting the parasitic "snail fever," or schistosomiasis. The thought of becoming a host for flatworms a half-inch in length repulsed and terrified the musicians.

At home, Terri again had the company of her father, but he moved from room to room like a faint breeze. Quiet to begin with, he seemed even more withdrawn after the housing bureau released him from detention. They had punished him for the sins of his father, an entrepreneur who built a family fortune from creating beautiful embroidery. After his release, John returned to work in the housing bureau, but as a repairman fixing roofs instead of as an office clerk keeping the books.

In her grandparents' room, Terri liked to sit at the foot of Lin Pu-chi's bed while he rested on his back with his eyes closed and talked to her like a teacher addressing students. He filled the hours of the day discussing his favorite novels and history books. His knowledge ran deep. He had loved learning from the time he was a schoolboy in Fuzhou, reading the dictionary for pleasure, through his years as a graduate student in philosophy in Philadelphia and decades later as a teacher and principal in Shanghai. With his big, powerful voice, he could hold forth just as easily about the first emperor of China as the first president of the United States.

"Tell me why there was a civil war in America," Terri once asked, launching Lin Pu-chi into a detailed discourse on President Abraham Lincoln and slavery.

Lin Pu-chi delved into the teachings of great Chinese philosophers like Confucius and his disciple Mencius as well as Western ones like Aristotle and Plato, whom he had studied at the University of Pennsylvania. He never spoke openly about his Christian beliefs. That was still too risky a topic, even in the privacy of his home. But they talked about wanting a life with meaning and purpose.

"You should learn English," Lin Pu-chi told his granddaughter at one point. His own command of the language remained flawless.

"Why bother?" Terri answered. "There's no use for English in China."

"America is a beautiful country," he replied wistfully. "And strong."

Terri shuddered. To utter such thoughts aloud, even in the privacy of your own home, was to court trouble. He had been accused of being a US spy. Indeed, America was Meiguo, "beautiful country." But the bamboo curtain, in place since 1949, kept Chinese families separated from their American relatives.

"You should go to America to study."

Terri did not reply.

BESSIE

On a cold December morning in 1971, Ni Guizhen was making such a racket in her bedroom that everyone in the house wondered what was going on. She opened dresser drawers and closed them. She took out all of her gray cotton tunics and black pants and folded them into piles on the floor. If you didn't know better, you would think she was packing for a very long trip.

"Bessie," whispered Lin Pu-chi, using the pet name for his wife, the diminutive of her Christian name, Elizabeth. He called her this only when it was just the two of them. Gently, he asked, "Bessie, why are you doing this?"

She didn't reply, but Lin Pu-chi could hear her mumbling a phrase over and over. "*Naung naung die, naung naung die.*" She had reverted to the Fuzhou dialect of her youth as she repeated, "Little brother, little brother." This was the term of endearment the family used when referring to the youngest son, Paul, who had immigrated to the United States more than two decades ago.

Lin Pu-chi let her be. Her mind was not the same. Red Guards no longer ambushed her with surprise visits to the house. But she bore emotional scars from the beatings and interrogations, the betrayal of Christian friends, and the public vilification of her favorite brother, the still imprisoned Watchman Nee.

The Little Flock had scattered. When Ni Guizhen prayed, she did so alone. Most days, she stayed in bed, her mind unsettled as she mumbled over and over, "I've done nothing wrong."

There was another reason, too, for the added stress in her life. A month before, Ni Guizhen was devastated by news of the death of her friend Charity, the wife of Watchman Nee. Her sister-in-law had been standing on a stool when she fell, most likely from a stroke. Three days later, on November 7, 1971, she died. Ni Guizhen had been closer to Charity than to any of her own sisters. The two had known each other as young women in Fuzhou and reconnected when the Lin family moved to the old International Settlement. Charity and Ni Guizhen saw each other often at meetings of the Christian assembly.

During the Cultural Revolution, Charity was singled out. With a husband in prison and herself branded an opponent of the communist regime, she was kept under constant surveillance and relegated to the job of street sweeper. The college graduate was getting a socialist lesson in humility: no one was too good for the lowest job. Her black hair turned gray, prompting neighbors to mockingly call her "White Hair." During one violent interrogation, Red Guards whipped her with a belt buckle. They took particular delight in finding the most humiliating forms of punishment. Once, Charity and two other Christian women were forced to put shoes on their hands, bend at the waist and spread their arms like an airplane. It had no purpose other than to demonstrate the power of her accusers over their victims. "Do you still believe in Jesus?" a Red Guard demanded. Charity unequivocally answered yes, enraging them so much they hurled shoes at her.

Ni Guizhen's clothes were still scattered all over her room on December 14. Lin Pu-chi got up first, put on his slippers, and shuffled with his bamboo cane to the bathroom next to their bedroom.

When he returned, he noticed that his wife had not moved. She was still in the same position. He shook her shoulders, gently at first, then with increasing vigor.

Lin Pu-chi yelled for his daughter-in-law Emma, a nurse who had just returned home after working the overnight shift at the hospital.

"*Hurry*," the old man called.

His shouts woke up the household. Everyone ran down the stairs into the bedroom. Emma knelt by the bed of Ni Guizhen, trying to rouse her. She never stirred.

In the late morning, Terri helped her aunt bathe the old woman's lifeless body and dress her in simple black clothes. They placed a black knit cap on her head. Emma bought a new pair of cotton shoes for her feet. Workers from a funeral home took her body away.

Even in death, Ni Guizhen did not escape punishment. At the crematory, the family was forbidden to have a proper memorial. In 1969, she had been officially labeled a counterrevolutionary like her brother, with public security and military authorities handing down "Decision No. 1213," an indelible black mark on her reputation.

The mortician refused to fix her face with makeup or dress her in better clothes. The family could send no flowers or banners of tribute to the funeral home, which would not present her body in a proper viewing room. Instead, her corpse was placed on a steel gurney and wheeled into a dimly lit hallway. The relatives would have a few minutes, no more, before she was cremated.

Julia and Martha, who both returned from the countryside, joined their immediate family members to pay their respects. Other friends stayed away, knowing the risk of showing support for a "bad element."

The family felt reproachful eyes everywhere. There could be no crying, no dramatic displays of grief, no prayers, no words. They had to remain blank slates. By now, they knew the unspoken rules of the game and what was expected of them. To show too much remorse would be interpreted as having sympathy for a counterrevolutionary and could be used against them at the next interrogation or struggle session.

Standing at the head of the gurney, Lin Pu-chi leaned over his wife's body. They had just celebrated their fiftieth wedding anniversary that March. Lin Pu-chi used to think she was such a stubborn woman. In the early years of their marriage, they fought bitterly over her decision to join Watchman Nee's Christian assembly instead of staying by his side and playing the role of a pastor's wife at his church. She paid for her allegiance to her brother. Yet after all the abuse and intimidation, she remained fiercely loyal to him. She was, as Lin Pu-chi came to see her in the twilight of their lives, a woman of uncompromising faith.

Lin Pu-chi stroked her head. His voice trembled as he murmured his English nickname for her, the one only he spoke, so that no eavesdropper would understand.

"Bessie," he whispered. "My Bessie."

The bad news came in threes.

In late May 1972, on a rutted road in the mountains of Anhui Province, a labor-camp worker drove a tractor over White Cloud Mountain, pulling a cart with a sick prisoner. The inmate, wearing a threadbare, torn jacket over his bony shoulders, barely stirred. By the time the tractor arrived at a labor camp clinic, the prisoner was dead.

Before he was taken away to the clinic, Watchman Nee wrote a letter to the sister of his late wife. His prison sentence ended on April 12, 1972, and he needed somewhere to live. Prison officials told him that he could not return to Shanghai or Beijing, where he might reconnect with followers, and was allowed to reside only in a small village or town. Watchman Nee knew it would be a burden for any of his relatives to take him in. A nephew on Charity's side of the family finally agreed to assume responsibility for him. But before this could happen, Watchman Nee had complained of chest pain and a racing heartbeat. Guards sent him to the clinic for medical attention.

Watchman Nee was sixty-eight when he died, six months after the passing of his wife, five months after his sister. When relatives came to get his ashes at the labor camp, a guard gave them a piece of paper that had been tucked beneath his pillow. With a weak hand, he had written in Chinese characters: "I shall die for believing in Christ."

AMERICA, MEIGUO

Terri purchased a ticket for a midnight train to Changchun. Nearly a year earlier, she had arrived in Shanghai to recuperate from her illness. Her last blood test in the fall of 1972 was good, leaving her with no reason to stay any longer in the terraced house in Shanghai. It was time to return to the farmhouse on the edge of a cornfield.

A few hours before her departure, Terri tiptoed down the stairs, past her grandfather's door, thinking he would already be asleep and she would slip out the back door. But Lin Pu-chi heard her and called her inside. He had something to tell her. He explained how for months he had mulled the idea of going to the United States to visit his sons.

Lin Pu-chi was emboldened to do so after reading about the improving relations between the two nations. On February 21, 1972, an extraordinary meeting took place in Beijing: Chairman Mao hosted President Richard Nixon at his residence. No American president had visited China since the founding of the communist state in 1949. But Nixon astutely understood how a thaw in relations with China could change the balance of power with the vexing Soviet Union. Mao, too, was a master manipulator. He knew that better relations with Washington would leave Moscow as the odd man out. The *Liberation Daily* newspaper, the Communist Party mouthpiece, devoted its entire front page to articles and a photograph documenting the visit. At a banquet, the newspaper dutifully reported that the flags of both countries hung side by side as a band played *America the Beautiful* as well as *Sailing the Seas Depends on the Helmsman*.

"I want to go to America," Lin Pu-chi told his granddaughter. "I've applied for an exit permit at the police station."

This was precisely what the family did not want to hear. Tim had pleaded with his father not to submit an application, begged him not to go down this road. Lin Pu-chi risked drawing needless attention to everyone by openly expressing his desire to travel to the United States. He had been accused of being a US spy. To now ask for permission to travel to Philadelphia to see his son was suicidal, Tim warned.

True, the recent turn in diplomatic events was positive. But what if the political situation did an about-face, as it often did? What if "America the Beautiful" reverted to "America the Ugly"? What then? Lin Pu-chi's trip request would be in his dossier with security officials and could be used in the future as ammunition against him.

But Lin Pu-chi ignored the warning. He explained to Terri: "I want you to come with me. I would go first, then after six months, you could follow me. You could study English in the States. It's not difficult to learn."

With his wife gone, the old man's desire to see his American sons grew even stronger. Perhaps it was a premonition. He suffered from heart disease. How many years did he have left?

He wanted to see his sons.

"You have such potential," Lin Pu-chi told Terri. "You like to read. You would be a very good student."

"*Ah gong*," Terri replied in Shanghai dialect. "Grandfather, I have to go."

Pulling away, she noticed his eyes welling up. By the time she was out his bedroom door, she heard uncontrollable sobbing.

· 19 ·

Father, Hello!

Shanghai, 1972

*I*n socialist China, you did not go looking for a job; a job found you.

After more than a year at the reeducation camp, Julia was permitted to move back to the house on Jiaozhou Road in early 1972. She was twenty-two and finally assigned to her first job. Cadres in charge of securing work for musicians placed Julia as a piano accompanist for singers at the Shanghai Light Opera House. It wasn't her dream job; she yearned to perform and not just to play in the shadow of others. But her assignment got her out of the rice paddy and into the rehearsal hall.

Before the Cultural Revolution, the lyric opera company staged full Western operas like Verdi's *Aida*. But those days were over. Madame Mao had commandeered the nation's artistic direction, and theatrical troupes everywhere were restricted to performing productions based on eight revolutionary plots, transformed into operas and ballets. Eight plays for eight hundred million people, as everyone privately snickered. But in the early 1970s, her seesaw policies tipped again, this time in favor of musicians. They were permitted to play Chopin or Mozart but only to hone their skills in order to create more and better revolutionary music. Mastering the piano and violin was a means to an end, not an end in and of itself.

At the reeducation camp, Julia and her classmates had nine pianos at their disposal. The old uprights were lined up against the walls of a cafeteria. So great was their pent-up desire to play that the pianists rarely gave the keyboards a rest. With no walls to separate them, they let forth a constant cacophony of sound that made village neighbors rue the day they arrived.

Julia went to work at the opera house as it was trying to replenish its ranks of singers and dancers after years of cutbacks and restrictions. Teachers from the troupe needed fresh talent and traveled from town to town, auditioning hopefuls. Julia played pieces for young singers. The girls rubbed their cheeks with blush and pulled their hair into pigtails with bright pink bows. Even proletarian performers needed good looks to go with their good voices.

Julia was happy to be working and playing music again. But there was something missing from her life: her old J. Strauss & Son upright piano.

Other musicians told Julia that the government was letting families reclaim pianos that were seized during earlier raids. In August 1966, an estimated 150,000 homes in Shanghai were ransacked by marauding packs of Red Guard rebels, who carried away gold, cash, jewels, clothing, artwork, books, furniture—anything that represented the "four olds" of customs, habits, culture, and thought. The Red Guards destroyed some confiscated possessions, dumping the rest in warehouses or storage rooms to collect dust for years.

Out of curiosity, Julia traveled to the Cultural Assembly Hall in the former French Concession, where the government was storing pillaged upright pianos. (The grand pianos were at another site on the Bund.) Julia knew this theater. When she was little, Martha took her there to see visiting ballet companies from the Soviet Union. But *Swan Lake* was a distant memory. *The Red Detachment of Women* or *The White-Haired Girl* were the only ballets performed on the stages of China.

From the lobby, Julia entered a vast, dark, musty space with row upon row of uprights, looking like tombstones in a piano graveyard. Each piano represented a family, a story, and the shared terror of watching Red Guards destroying homes and hauling away anything that suggested a bourgeois lifestyle. Julia walked among the pianos, occasionally touching a dusty key. Years of neglect had damaged the instruments. Worms had eaten through the wool on hammers. Ivory keys were missing. Julia spied a Strauss—*her Strauss.* Her heart fluttered as if she had bumped into a long-ago friend. But immediately she could see that the piano was badly damaged. The wooden top was warped and split in two. Julia learned that there had been a fire in the hall and many of the pianos, including hers, had been ruined by water.

Julia was crestfallen. She could not retrieve her old piano, and a replacement was prohibitively expensive. Martha pledged to find a way to raise the money. She had recently returned to her hospital job; the price of a piano equaled about four months of her salary, or four hundred yuan. Martha scrimped on meals, skipping meat at every dinner and adding more cheap cabbage. Every spare yuan was put into the piano fund. It took months before Martha and Julia had saved enough to travel to another piano graveyard, this one in the Hongkou District, more than an hour away by bus. Inside a former church, Julia scanned the used pianos for sale, all of which had been plundered from homes. She tested the quality by playing scales and settled on a Mozart model with a full sound and good tone. Martha counted out her yuan to seal the purchase as one family's loss became her family's gain.

Every day after work, Julia practiced until late in the night. Like so many of her generation, she was propelled by a sense of urgency, of having to make up for lost years of training. The Cultural Revolution, with all of its trauma and illogical policies, had stunted her growth as a musician. Julia put pieces of soft cloth between the hammers and strings of her Mozart upright to soften the sound so that she could play without disturbing her neighbors.

Among her ardent fans was her grandfather, who delighted in hearing music, however muted, filling the house again.

DIPLOMATIC THAW

To no one's surprise, the neighborhood police, who controlled issuing all travel permits, had denied Lin Pu-chi's request to visit the United States. But the old man still had hope. Relations between China and the United States

In 1972, Lin Pu-chi, a widower, traveled to Beijing with his daughter, Martha (right) and an unidentified relative. Courtesy of Lin Family Collection.

continued to improve, with Nixon's top national security adviser, Henry Kissinger, returning to Beijing in early 1973 to meet Mao and continue negotiations for better diplomatic ties. The headline in the *People's Daily* on February 18 read: "The two had a frank and extensive talk in an unrestrained atmosphere."

Lin Pu-chi's sons in the States learned that the improvement in US-China relations meant they could now place direct telephone calls to Shanghai, ending years of limited communication for the family. Lin Pu-chi immediately set up a date for Paul to call and passed on the number for a public phone at a corner store near the house on Jiaozhou Road. As the day approached in the spring of 1973, Lin Pu-chi rehearsed pronouncing the names of his grandchildren, some of which—like Damien and Stefanie—were strange to his ear. It had been years since he carried on a conversation in English. On the appointed evening in Shanghai—morning in Philadelphia—a clerk from the shop came running to the house, yelling up the stairwell, "*Waiguo dianhua!* Foreign phone call!"

With his cane, Lin Pu-chi waddled down the block. Neighbors stared as he reached the store and grabbed the receiver from the clerk. "*Wei?*" he asked, immediately switching to English. "Hello? Paul? Paul?"

"Father, hello!"

Lin Pu-chi's throat tightened as he pictured his son at his home in Philadelphia, surrounded by his wife, five daughters, and one son. He knew them only from photographs and the monthly letters, faithfully written by his daughter-in-law to keep him connected to their lives.

The phone connection was poor. It took a second before something Lin Pu-chi said in Shanghai was heard in Philadelphia, causing each to step on the other's sentences. Lin Pu-chi tried to think of some tidbit to say to each person as Paul passed the phone from one person to another.

"Xuehua," he greeted his daughter-in-law Sylvia, using the Chinese name he gave her twenty years ago when she married his son. It meant "Snowflake." "How I love your letters."

"Damien, you're the horseback rider?"

"Jennifer, how is your dancing?"

It had been twenty-four years since Lin Pu-chi had said good-bye to his sons on the tarmac of the airport in Hong Kong. The call lasted just ten minutes. Still, Lin Pu-chi hung up feeling ebullient. When Martha got home from the hospital, he told her, "Paul speaks very good English. He sounds just like an American." For now, all he had was a phone call. But he hoped that maybe soon, there could be a visit.

"Don't practice too much," Lin Pu-chi kindly cautioned Julia as he made his way down the stairwell.

It was Wednesday, May 9, 1973.

After the death of his wife, Lin Pu-chi relocated to a smaller bedroom where the maid used to sleep, making room for Martha and her husband to move into the bigger second-floor bedroom, where Julia's piano was also moved.

Practicing that morning, Julia could see out of the corner of her eye that her grandfather was holding a fishbowl in his arms as he gingerly maneuvered the stairs. His goldfish had died, and he was heading to the bathroom to flush it down the toilet. He left the door open.

Julia continued practicing a difficult Chopin étude. Minutes passed, ten, maybe more. She paused. It occurred to her that her grandfather should have climbed back up the stairs by now. He was so quiet. She walked over to the bathroom to check on him. The door was ajar.

He had been sitting on the closed toilet seat, emptying water into the sink, when he collapsed. His body slumped to the side, his head dropped into the sink. Julia could see that his face had turned dark yellow.

A thousand miles away, a village cadre came running through the cornfields, waving a piece of paper for Terri. There were no telephones in her village.

At his funeral, a portrait of Lin Pu-chi from 1967 was flanked by wreaths, one sent by his sons, Paul and Jim, in the United States. Courtesy of Lin Family Collection.

The only way her family could reach her was via a telegram. The message from Shanghai was brief: *Come home. Grandfather died. Mother.*

This time, the family was permitted to hold a proper memorial. Lin Pu-chi did not have the same problem of "guilt by association" as his late wife. He was dressed in his best Mao suit, with a black wool cap on his head. His sons in America paid for big wreaths of paper flowers, each one with long white ribbons bearing their names and those of their wives in Chinese characters. Friends sent baskets of silk lilies and carnations. In one wreath, the family placed an enlargement of a portrait of Lin Pu-chi that he had taken on his birthday in 1967. It showed his thick salt-and-pepper hair parted and slicked to the side; his beard, wispy and white, was neatly trimmed on the tip of his chin. Looking straight into the camera lens, he had given the photographer just the hint of a crooked smile.

The funeral director hung a banner in a viewing room with big characters that read, "In Memory of Dear Father Lin Pu-chi." Everyone in the family wore black armbands and stood around his body for a final photograph. Terri stood at his head, her eyes downcast.

· 20 ·

Lost

Jilin Province, 1973

$\mathcal{E}$very time Terri traveled to Shanghai, it became that much harder for her to return to the countryside.

The simple life in faraway Jilin Province, such a welcome change when she first arrived, now was a constant reminder of all that she left behind in the city. It wasn't just missing the material comforts—the occasional pork dish for dinner, sleeping on a mattress, toilets and bathtubs. Instead, her discontent came from a deeper place. It was late 1973 and she was twenty-one, living in a village far from everyone who meant anything to her. She had reinvented herself as a barefoot doctor, but she felt like she was wandering in a dense forest with no signposts.

Terri was not the only one who was restless. Millions of young people who had been sent down to the countryside now longed to be sent back home. Some of her housemates began to find escape routes. One friend was able to finagle a transfer to a tractor factory in the nearby city of Chang-chun. He came from a family of workers with an unblemished proletarian background. They used their *guanxi*, or the personal ties that greased all relationships in China, to find him a good production job. Another Shanghai transplant—the son of a doctor—got placed in a medical school. Terri could barely contain her resentment toward him. This friend had shown no interest in medicine. *She* was the one who became a barefoot doctor. *She* was the one who read medical textbooks by the light of a kerosene lamp. But his family had better *guanxi* than hers, and the survival of the fittest in socialist China was all about connections. Universities began to reopen in 1970, but admission was not based on standardized examinations or intellectual merit. Instead, students were recruited from communes, factories, and military units. These "worker-peasant-soldier students"—or *gong-nong-bing xueyuan*—needed the support of the cadres from their work units as well as "recommendations from the masses." Terri's background dogged her even now. She came from a bad family; there was no way any medical school or university would award a precious slot to someone like her.

Terri felt impatient whenever a housemate left, and she began losing interest in her work as a barefoot doctor. She had delivered almost forty babies in her years in the village. But instead of gaining confidence, she started to lose her nerve. Peasant women were so lacking in proper nutrition and prenatal care that they often faced complicated deliveries. Terri had more than one close call with mothers who almost died on her watch. It made her tentative and cautious.

One by one, the Shanghai youth, now adults in their twenties, moved out of the house that the villagers had built for them. By the end of 1975, Terri slept alone on her *kang*. She could not imagine spending her entire life in the far reaches of Jilin Province and wrote to her neighborhood committee in Shanghai, requesting permission to return. This was not a decision that she could make alone; local cadres back home had to approve her move. The reason she presented: she was not physically fit for farmwork. In addition to her bout with hepatitis, she had a slight curvature of the spine, confirmed by X-rays taken by a specialist in Shanghai. Even before receiving a reply from the committee, she pulled out her two leather trunks and packed all of her clothes and medical instruments.

The autumn winds began blowing down from Siberia. She put on her quilted jacket, the one she had been given as a teenager when she left Shanghai seven years ago. Outside, a villager waited to drive her in a horse-drawn cart to the main village, the first leg of her journey home.

WORK

Terri always liked taking things apart and putting them back together. Radios. Clocks. Bicycles. When she was younger, it had kept her busy, her mind as well as her hands. It made her think. At the start of the Cultural Revolution in 1966, with no classes at school to attend, she could spend days pondering the workings of the gears of her bike. That same curiosity extended to the wiring and mechanics of the human body. It was what intrigued her about medicine.

But never did she imagine that at this stage of her life she would be reduced to sitting at a big round table with others her age and assembling cheap toys by hand. The job consisted of taking parts from piles—mounds of springs, screws, and plastic forms—and making wind-up toys that looked like chickens or airplanes or cars and would end up in the hands of Shanghai children. It was mind-numbing work that paid her seventy fen a day, equal to pocketing a quarter and a dime in the United States. Terri barely earned enough to eat.

The cadres in charge of households in her neighborhood had a problem on their hands. There were many jobless returnees exactly like Terri. Only the state could provide them with employment because only the state—or some smaller units, such as cities or districts—had the capital and property to create jobs. There were no private companies; entrepreneurs were aliens who existed only in capitalistic societies. Needing to find work for all the returning youth, the neighborhood committee for Terri's lane started the toy-making workshop. About forty laborers—mostly men and women in their twenties plus some housewives from the neighborhood—toiled in a Maoist version of Santa's workshop.

Terri stayed at the toy-making job for several months before transferring to another worksite run by her local district, this one an equipment factory in the textile industry. She learned how to use milling machinery to shape cones that would hold thread or yarn for weaving into bolts of cotton or wool.

Terri's shift started at 2:00 p.m. and ended at 11:00 p.m. Her factory was only ten minutes away by bicycle, but she liked to take a longer path home, going out of her way to swing past the hospital where she had trained years before, learning the basic skills of a barefoot doctor. In the midnight darkness, Terri often would pause outside the hospital gates and watch people coming and going. It was so easy for her to imagine herself among them, striding up the stairs and into the maternity ward, making rounds and using her stethoscope to listen for a fetal heartbeat, coaxing a first-time mother through a hard delivery and smiling at the sound of a wailing, healthy newborn.

Instead, Terri milled cones for knitting machines, day in and day out. Same design, same specifications, day in, day out. This was her life.

Mei banfa, she convinced herself. There was no other way.

A decade had passed since Terri painted big-character posters as a middle-school student, extolling an end to old ways and customs. When Mao told her to go off and live among peasants, she willingly followed his command. All of that upheaval and sacrifice led to a dead-end job in a knitting factory. Veteran workers treated the "sent-down" youth like interlopers and did not try to hide their contempt for them. Terri and her peers, meanwhile, talked incessantly about giving up their spots on the factory floor for seats in a university classroom. It was a conversation that millions all over the country were having.

Change was afoot. Everyone could feel it. The year started with the death of Premier Zhou Enlai on January 8. The outpouring of grief for him was genuine and overwhelming. It started as a trickle on March 19 with students from a Beijing middle school laying a wreath at the Monument to the People's Heroes in Tiananmen Square. In days, it grew into a torrent of humanity—millions and millions of mourners jamming the square, carrying the premier's photograph and burying the base of the ten-story obelisk under a mountain of funeral wreaths. Most people viewed Zhou as the sane counterweight to the fanatical Gang of Four, and they flocked to Tiananmen Square not just to mourn him but also to telegraph to leaders their widespread discontent with the extreme tactics of the Cultural Revolution. Tucked amid the paper-flower wreaths were messages of protest, scrawled anonymously.

Then, on September 9, an era ended. The Xinhua News Agency sent out a news bulletin alerting the country that Chairman Mao had passed away at ten minutes after midnight. In the days to follow, every workplace and school was required to show its respect for the departed father of socialist China. At the theater where Julia worked, actors and musicians indulged in much wailing and overt mourning, with one performer trying to outdo the other. But Julia hung back, unable to shed a single tear for the man she held responsible for causing her family so much pain.

The nation got its first glimpse of who would fill the power vacuum with the passing of Mao in an editorial in the *People's Daily* on October 18. The losers: Madame Mao and her three henchmen. All were arrested, ending the decade-long nightmare of the Cultural Revolution. The man who rose to power was the four-foot-eleven-inch Deng Xiaoping, a pragmatic, reform-minded leader who seemed to have nine political lives. At the start of the Cultural Revolution, he had been denounced as the "number two capitalist roader" and exiled to a remote factory to toil as a laborer for three years. Mao brought him back into the fold in 1973, only to depose him again. Opponents accused Deng of instigating the Tiananmen Incident after Zhou's death. But with the Gang of Four behind bars, allies of Deng elevated him to the status of "paramount leader" with control of the Communist Party and country.

Deng repudiated the Cultural Revolution and, soon after regaining power in July 1977, turned his attention to restoring order in higher education. One of his first acts was reinstating a national college entrance examination, or *gaokao*. No longer would "worker-peasant-soldier students" have priority over others. Intellect would decide who entered college and who didn't.

Martha often told Terri, "If you want to go to the university, I will support you. You don't have to worry about anything. I have bought a lot of books and will help to get you ready for the *gaokao*."

"You would be a very good doctor," Martha said. But while Martha was pushing Terri to try, someone new in Terri's life was pulling her back.

His name was Sui. He was an actor with Julia's theatrical troupe. Handsome, with a square face and thick hair parted in the center, he projected a strong personality whether onstage or in a room. He smiled easily and loved to talk. Originally, Sui sought the attention of Julia, but she showed little interest in him. Instead, Julia preferred a quiet, bookish teacher named Victor, who was introduced to her by her aunt. Spurned by one sister, Sui turned his sights to the other. Terri had never before enjoyed the attention of a man. Five years her senior, Sui told her things that she enjoyed hearing. "You're so much smarter than people your age," he told her. "Your future will be good."

Terri welcomed his company. His flirtation was a diversion from the tedium of her life. They rode bikes together and sometimes met up with his friends, talking and drinking *baijiu*, a potent liquor, late into the night. Alone with him, Terri succumbed to his advances more willingly than was prudent for a single woman. He was forceful, and she was not able to resist him.

When the topic of the national examination came up, Sui discouraged Terri from trying. "You shouldn't waste your time," he kept telling her. Even though he gave the impression of someone who was also well read, it was an act. He could hold forth on *Das Kapital*, even though he had read only a few pages of Marx's treatise. He was, after all, a performer.

Sui wanted Terri to marry him and forget about sitting for the examination. Terri was torn. She listened instead to her mother and tried to break up with him, but he would have none of it. He threatened her. If she refused him, he would tell everyone about her intimate relationship with him. Terri knew the risk. Her reputation would be ruined by whispers, leaving no prospect for marriage to anyone.

In late 1977, more than five million people sat for the national examination. Some were only teenagers trying to make the next logical step in their education. Others were adults in their twenties and thirties, members of China's "lost generation" who were struggling to recast their lives before it was too late.

Terri was not among them. On December 24, 1977, she begrudgingly went with Sui to the Civil Affairs Bureau to register for a marriage license. They bickered all the way. In the end, Terri felt she had no choice but to acquiesce.

That night, her parents hosted a somber dinner to mark the occasion.

REPLACEMENT

Almost a year later, on the morning of December 16, 1978, everyone in the Lin household on Lane 170 listened intently to a radio bulletin being broadcast over the neighborhood loudspeaker. The Xinhua News Service had put out an urgent news flash: China and the United States were renewing diplomatic relations. The announcer read: "Starting from January 1, 1979, the Chinese and American sides will acknowledge each other and establish diplomatic relations."

In a large brick house in suburban Philadelphia, decorated for the Christmas holiday, a physician listened to a live television address from the Oval

Office of the White House. President Jimmy Carter read from a statement in his hands: "The normalization of relations between the United States and China has no other purpose than this: the advancement of peace. It is in this spirit, at this season of peace, that I take special pride in sharing this good news with you tonight."

Paul Lin's mind began racing. If relations between the two countries were reverting to normal, that meant he could get a visa and return to Shanghai to see his family. Up until then, travel to China was limited and complicated. But the renewal of diplomatic relations, with the reopening of embassies in the two countries, would make it easier for "overseas Chinese" in the United States to return and visit their Chinese families.

The Year of the Goat in 1979 got off to an auspicious start. Madame Mao was behind bars and Deng Xiaoping packed for a trip to Washington, DC, in late January to cement the deal at the White House. Deng was making history at home, too, by setting China's economy in a new direction. As he saw it, central planners would follow the demands of the marketplace instead of trying to plan out every detail of production. Deng best summarized his approach to a socialist economy with Chinese characteristics with his quote: "It doesn't matter whether a cat is white or black, it is a good cat as long as it catches mice."

Terri felt as if she were watching a train pulling away without her. She was entering her third year at the factory, trapped in a loveless marriage and still living at home. Her husband spent most nights with his own family. When the second national examination came around in 1978, Terri again missed it. The reason this time: she was pregnant.

Bitter and full of regret, she stopped discussing college. Her mother pitied her and began to consider the only other option available for Terri to move on with her life. It was called the *dingti* system, a replacement plan enabling an older worker to give up a spot for an adult child. The planned economy was not producing enough jobs to meet the demand for work. Martha would have to retire in order for Terri to take her place. She was fifty-seven and a highly experienced obstetrician and gynecologist as well as a professor, who had been trained at the medical school of St. John's University, one of the top programs in the country. Officials at her hospital approved her job swap with Terri, but it would not be a one-for-one exchange allowing her daughter to step into a job of equal merit and responsibility.

Martha broke the news. "We can do this, but you will have to be the lowest person at the hospital," she explained.

A job was a job was a job, so it made perfect sense in the socialist scheme of things for an esteemed physician to be replaced by a "service girl," akin to a hospital orderly.

Terri nevertheless took the job in early 1979 in the hope that maybe she could work her way up through the ranks, if not as a doctor, then in some other fashion. Already in the last trimester of her pregnancy, she waddled to the bus stop at 6:30 a.m. and traveled for almost an hour to the hospital. Handed a mop and bucket, she cleaned floors. Her workplace was far from egalitarian. No job was lower than hers. She delivered trays of food to patients, cleared tables, washed dirty bowls, and filled thermoses with hot water. For patients who couldn't get in and out of bed, Terri emptied and cleaned their bedpans. Her belly was so big that simply bending over to empty her bucket was an effort. At her new job, she earned a little more than she had at the factory, about thirty yuan a month.

Not long after starting at the hospital, Terri came home one night to find her mother and uncle excitedly discussing an airmail letter that had arrived that day. The postmark was Philadelphia. Martha smiled as she shared the news.

Their youngest brother, Paul, wanted to bring some of his children to visit them in June.

HOMECOMING

Terri gave birth to a girl on April 20, 1979. Two months later, Paul and his daughters arrived from Philadelphia. No one knew what to expect. Throughout the 1950s and 1960s, Lin Pu-chi had written to Paul and his wife, Sylvia, nearly every month. But after he died, communication between the two households became sporadic. For the younger generation, all that they knew was that Lin Pu-chi's youngest son was now a wealthy man with an Italian wife and six children, three of whom would be traveling with him.

Paul was twenty-two when he left home in May 1949—almost thirty years ago to the day. He had spent more years in America than in China. His siblings viewed the reunion with excitement and apprehension. What would he be like? More foreign than Chinese? Surely living abroad for so many years had changed him. They hoped Paul could still speak to them in the Shanghai dialect. If not, Julia's husband, Victor, an English teacher, would serve as translator. For all the questions they had for Paul, they expected him to ask them just as many, and that would be a challenge. They had to decide how much to reveal to him about the devastating era—for the country and his family—that had just ended. Martha and Tim did not dare tell him the truth, at least not the whole truth. They felt a need for circumspection and reticence, fearing that this new period of openness could be fleeting, that there might well be a return to the repression of the Cultural Revolution.

The first thing they all noticed was how different Paul looked compared with every other man in the household. On his first full day in Shanghai—June 18, 1979—he came out of his room wearing a pair of lightweight pale blue trousers and a starched button-down white Oxford-cloth shirt, both from Brooks Brothers if anyone had asked. Chinese men had a choice of black or gray for pants. Paul's face was full and his hair worn in a crew cut. The family silently studied his daughters, too. One of them wore tight-fitting blue jeans, and another wore running shoes in fluorescent orange and yellow, another oddity in monochromatic China.

As they stepped outside for a morning walk, Paul seemed tired and subdued. He had stayed up late talking to Uncle George, the younger brother of their mother. Unlike Paul's siblings, George had decided there was much that needed to be said about the past, and he didn't hold back. Paul could not process everything he had just learned. His siblings could sense it but said nothing.

The extended family strolled down a small street where sidewalk vendors were selling breakfast food. Paul perked up when he spied a man placing long strips of dough in a wok of hot oil. "*Youtiao!*" Paul enthused to his daughters. "I used to buy these on my way to school." He bought a bundle of the greasy, Chinese-style crullers and passed them out. As the English-speaking foreigner in the sky-blue pants went from one vendor to the next, buying fried pancakes with green onions, hunks of rice cake, and bottles of cold soy milk, people stopped and stared, unaccustomed to Americans in their midst. Martha and Tim hung back a few steps, relieved to see their youngest sibling enjoying himself.

After the walking breakfast, followed by another sit-down breakfast at the house, Paul had business to tend to. First things first: he needed to register at the local station of the Public Security Bureau. Though relations between the United States and China had improved, allowing for family reunions like theirs, the authorities still insisted on knowing the comings and goings of all foreigners.

"What is the purpose of your visit?" an officer questioned Paul, inspecting his passport and looking for the visa.

"To see my family," Paul replied in rusty Chinese.

"How long will you be here?"

"Two weeks," Paul informed them.

"Where will you go?"

"Nanjing, Suzhou, Hangzhou, and Beijing."

The first full day was jammed with sightseeing, starting with a stroll along the fabled Bund and then a visit to a Buddhist temple; the Children's Palace for a puppet show; and a stop at the vast People's Park, built on the grounds of the former Shanghai Racecourse. Topping off the day was a feast at the

Xin Ya Restaurant on Nanjing Road. At a big round table, Uncle George sat next to Paul and toasted him with warm beer. Guests ate their way through a procession of dishes: cold meats, mushrooms, shrimp with peas, eggs, squab, squid, melon soup, chicken, fish, duck, noodles, another soup, and dessert of sticky rice filled with black-bean paste and floating in almond milk.

Satiated, exhausted, and happy, everyone slept soundly that night.

When Terri and Julia were young girls growing up in the 1950s, in the aftermath of the "Resist America, Aid Korea" conflict (known to Americans as the Korean War), they learned songs with lyrics such as "Defeat the vicious wolves of American imperialism."

For most of their lives, the United States was China's enemy, so having American uncles was a problem for the family. After all, their grandfather, Lin Pu-chi, had been falsely accused of being part of a US spy ring. Everyone knew that his letters to and from his sons were monitored by authorities. Paul assumed as much, which was why he never told his father that in the wake of the Korean War, he had enlisted in the medical corps of the US Army. The American military needed to replenish its stateside ranks of doctors, and in 1955, Paul, who had become a US citizen, signed up for two years. His father and siblings would never know this. If public security officers in Shanghai had known that letters going to Paul Lin were actually forwarded to Captain Paul Lin at the Madigan Army Hospital in Tacoma, Washington, it could have made a difficult situation catastrophic.

But since the death of Mao and rise of Deng Xiaoping, China had made a sharp pivot. Yesterday's enemies were today's new friends. At House 19 in Lane 170, the family wanted all their neighbors to see their Philadelphia relatives, these so-called American wolves. There had been times during the Cultural Revolution when some of these same people used the family's American ties as a reason to condemn them. But now, having relatives from the United States was more a point of pride than a source of shame.

From the time he walked into the house, Paul was the focus of attention. He seemed to be enjoying the reunion, but every now and then he became quiet, withdrawn, pulled by an undertow into dark thoughts about the past few years. Paul had been eager to visit Shanghai and step back into the past, to sleep in his old home, to spend time with his sister and brother, to meet their children and spouses, and to say hello to old friends. But the trip also gave him a chance to say good-bye to two people who were no longer there—his father and mother.

A soot-belching steam engine pulled into the station in Suzhou, a smaller city west of Shanghai known for its elegant villas, walled gardens, canals, and beautiful women. Paul and his daughters, plus Martha and Tim, arrived in the late morning. The air was hot and dry, a break from steamy Shanghai. If foreigners were a rare sight in Shanghai, they were alien creatures in smaller Suzhou. China had been sealed off from Western travelers for so long that the only impression most people had of foreigners was what they saw on television. Even that exposure was limited since most families did not own TV sets. After a stop at the Suzhou Friendship Store, a foreigners-only souvenir and antiques shop, Paul and his daughters drew a crowd of gawkers that was so large it spilled from the sidewalk into the street, stopping traffic.

The group wasted no time heading to its destination. Climbing into two big black taxicabs, they took a road out of town that cut through rice paddies and fields planted with rows of beans, tomatoes, and cabbages. The drivers stopped at a small bridge over a canal. They could go no farther. Everyone got out and crossed the bridge to a cluster of one-story brick houses that were part of the Huangshan production team. Martha and Tim led the way. Children peered from doorways, spied the foreigners, and darted back inside. A petite, gray-haired farmer with a wooden rake over her shoulder smiled when she saw the entourage of visitors but ran away screaming after one of Paul's daughters snapped a photograph of her.

"She thinks your camera will steal her soul," explained Victor, who was traveling with the group and helping with translation.

They followed a path up a hill overgrown with weeds. On either side were rows of gravestones, packed one next to another. As Paul climbed higher under low pines, he reached down to pick flowers among the weeds. His daughters followed his lead, snapping off stems to form sprays of tiny white flowers, purple clover, and small yellow blossoms.

Turning off the trail, they stopped at a two-foot gray stone marker. All the weeds around it had been cleared, and the big chiseled characters on the tombstone were freshly painted in red and black. This was the grave of Ni Guizhen and Lin Pu-chi. On the right side were the dates of their birth and death; on the opposite side were the names of their children.

Paul paused before the gravestone, his three daughters standing behind him. He knelt and put the bouquet of wildflowers on the rectangular cement base. He bowed his head, showing no emotion. Any bitterness or anguish he had felt about what Uncle George had told him only days earlier remained hidden.

Then slowly, he began to recite a prayer in English, his daughters quickly joining him: "Our Father, who art in heaven . . ."

Helpless to undo the past, he moved on.

"May they rest in peace," Paul murmured softly before turning and heading down the hillside.

VI

REVIVAL

· 21 ·

Faith

Fuzhou, 2015

I settled into my first-class window seat on a bullet train from Shanghai to Fuzhou, which, according to the timetable, would cover 346 miles in exactly 5 hours and 1 minute. The electronic scroll above the door to our compartment ticked off our accelerating speed in kilometers per hour.

280 . . . 281 . . . 282 . . .

I used the calculator on my cell phone to do the conversion; we were close to hitting our cruising speed of 185 miles per hour. The light was dimming in the hill country of northwestern Fujian, where groves of bamboo stood like giant feather dusters. The mountains were getting tighter, the tunnels more frequent. At one point, I counted five in quick succession, the sound in the car alternating from a vibrating hum to a loud whoosh as the train shot from one tunnel to the next.

It was close to midnight when I checked into my hotel on the north shore of the Min River. I had come to Fuzhou to retrace the steps of my grandfather Lin Pu-chi and his brother-in-law Watchman Nee. Both men began their religious journeys in Fuzhou before moving to Shanghai, where their worlds intersected and sometimes collided. Lin Pu-chi worked within the denominational church, while Watchman Nee distanced himself from foreign missions and cultivated a popular independent religious movement. When they died in the early 1970s—Lin Pu-chi at home in Shanghai, Watchman Nee in a labor camp in Anhui—each had reason to despair. Religion of any sort had no place in this society, this new China. Protestant churches were shut down during the Cultural Revolution, while followers of Watchman Nee, branded a notorious counterrevolutionary, dared not utter his name.

I remember when China announced in 1979 that it would reopen churches. We were visiting our relatives at the time and had just spent the day visiting a temple with a five-story gold Buddha sitting in lotus position. Victor, my cousin's husband, who spoke fluent English, told us that he had heard the news on the radio. He predicted that it would have little effect on people. Maybe some old people would return to churches, Victor explained, but his generation had little interest in religion because of their indoctrination during the Cultural Revolution. In a journal entry for June 22, 1979, I wrote: "After what happened to my grandparents, it's a wonder that anyone in the family has any religious beliefs left at all."

We were both monumentally wrong. Article 36 of the Chinese constitution, adopted in 1982, granted "freedom of religious belief," and the reopening of churches sparked a revival with so much momentum that China could soon have the largest population of Christians in the world. Fenggang Yang, a sociologist at Purdue University who arrived at that estimate by extrapolating from current trends in China, thinks that could happen by 2025.

Chairman Mao extolled the masses to "serve the people." His successor, Deng Xiaoping, encouraged a generation to get rich, and they did it with gusto. But without Mao or Deng to glorify, many Chinese have felt a spiritual hollowness that they increasingly fill with religion of all kinds, not just Christianity.

And how many Christians are there in China?

It is a simple question that is impossible to answer. China's churches are all over the place, literally and figuratively. The government requires churches, temples, and mosques to register with the State Administration for Religious Affairs, which oversees China's five recognized religions: Protestantism, Catholicism, Buddhism, Daoism, and Islam. There are no denominational distinctions among Protestants, no Anglican versus Presbyterian churches; since the 1950s, everyone must be part of the Three-Self Patriotic Movement (TSPM) and its sister organization, the China Christian Council, which operates seminaries and prints Bibles.

It would seem like a straightforward exercise to tally the population of Christians in China by adding up all the people belonging to churches under the auspices of the TSPM and its Catholic counterpart. But that's where things get complicated. A majority of Christians choose to practice their religion outside the sphere of the government. They operate off the grid in "house churches." These informal gatherings can take place in apartments, auditoriums, offices, or even outdoors and attract anywhere from a handful of people to thousands. Some of these groups worship in a way that would be similar to the Catholic Mass or a Protestant service. Others operate on the fringe and bear the imprimatur of charismatic individuals with idiosyncratic beliefs. What all share, however, is an aversion to government oversight.

The official population of Protestants and Catholics in China is twenty-nine million, according to the "Blue Book of Religions" report published in 2010 by the state-supported Chinese Academy of Social Sciences. But the real number may be more than double that figure. The Pew Research Center in Washington, DC, estimates that China's Christian population is closer to sixty-seven million, or 5 percent of the country's population. Researchers examined public opinion surveys, church membership reports, and Chinese government statistics. In a 2011 report on global Christianity, Pew estimates that Chinese Catholics number about nine million and Protestants an additional fifty-eight million, of whom about thirty-five million are "independents" with unregistered churches.

By comparison, eighty-eight million people belong to the Chinese Communist Party.

When I arrived in Fuzhou in the summer of 2015, I had the city of Wenzhou on my mind, and this made me anxious. If you drew a straight line north from Fuzhou along the coast of the East China Sea, it would be 160 miles to Wenzhou. Both cities have vibrant Christian communities; the number of Protestants and Catholics in Wenzhou is so large that the city is called the "Jerusalem of the East." But in 2014, tension increased between the provincial government of Zhejiang, where Wenzhou is located, and its churches, even ones registered with the government. Provincial authorities had launched a campaign to remove large crosses from churches. The official reason: they were "illegal structures" that violated zoning rules. The unofficial reason, according to religious and political observers of China, was unease among local Communist Party leaders with the strong public profile of churches in cities such as Wenzhou.

The cross campaign made headlines around the world when the provincial government demolished the five-million-dollar Sanjiang Church in April 2014. The church loomed large by the side of a highway in a new economic zone. Members refused to remove their giant cross on a 180-foot spire. They signed petitions and protested. Authorities responded by razing the entire building, claiming it occupied five times more space than authorized.

From then on, the news in Wenzhou only got worse. Five months later, viewers of CNN saw a late-night clash, captured by amateur video and security cameras, between riot police swinging truncheons at members of a different church, who had barricaded themselves in a failed attempt to stop the removal of the cross on their church. In an eighteen-month span, provincial authorities had demolished or removed crosses from more than a thousand churches in Zhejiang, of which many were officially registered congregations. Social media lit up with images of protests. Christians made crosses from wood and painted them red or wore T-shirts with crosses. Catholic priests, led by the bishop of the Wenzhou Diocese, openly criticized the cross removals as "an evil act."

The overriding question: Where was this coming from? Was it just the action of an overzealous provincial party boss who didn't like seeing so many red crosses rising from rooftops in a new economic zone? Or was it coming from higher up? Earlier in the year, President Xi Jinping had urged religious groups of all stripes to pledge their loyalty to the state and had warned against foreign influence. If this was the start of a campaign to rein in churches, the people most at risk were Christians operating on the edge of the system. In Fuzhou, this group included many of the people I hoped to soon meet.

ANCESTORS

My daughter, Cory, joined me for the first leg of my trip to Fuzhou. She had not been back to China since we lived in Beijing from 1996 to 1999, when she was a little girl and I was covering Asia as a correspondent for the *Philadelphia Inquirer* and Knight-Ridder Newspapers. Now she was twenty-two, and we were seeing Fuzhou with an elderly cousin. His father was my grandfather's younger brother, whose eagerness to marry forced Lin Pu-chi to cut short his studies in Philadelphia in 1920. In Chinese tradition, we started our tour with a pilgrimage to the gravesite of the patriarch, Dr. Lin Dao'an, my great-grandfather whom missionaries had trained as a doctor. The day was oppressively hot, alternating between showers and full-on sun. At Gao Gai Mountain on the edge of town, we followed a meandering stone path under pines. When we could climb no farther, we looked into the thicket of weeds for the grave and carefully began sidestepping down a steep, muddy embankment.

The stone sarcophagus of Dr. Lin stood amid knee-high wild grass. It was shaped like a cross and had pitched sides inscribed with red characters. The writing recorded when he was born and when he died and mentioned his three sons, including Lin Pu-chi, but none of his three daughters. Next to the sarcophagus was a small headstone with three names: these were Lin children who never made it to adulthood. We said a prayer and placed bouquets of burgundy, yellow, and white chrysanthemums at the base of Dr. Lin's grave.

I was apprehensive about our next stop, Christ Church Cathedral, where in 1927 the Anglican Church appointed a thirty-three-year-old Lin Pu-chi as the congregation's first dean in charge. A year earlier, I had heard from contacts in Fuzhou that the city intended to tear down the old church to make way for development. We parked in the lot of the old YMCA on the waterfront, which had been converted into a nightlife complex with restaurants and bars. Cory and I followed our cousin down a lane, past shoddy brick homes and cinderblock apartments. I was relieved to spy the church's distinctive twin towers above the rooftops. The cathedral had survived the wrecking ball, but I could hear the crunch of metal on brick and the beep of construction vehicles moving in reverse. As it happened, everything but the church was being demolished. The metal arm of a crane took big bites out of buildings, while front loaders removed bricks and concrete and leveled the ground.

The pastor in charge of Cangxia Christ Church, renamed after the neighborhood, grew up in a Christian family. I had met Pastor Sun four years earlier on my first visit to the church. He told me then that during the dark days of the Cultural Revolution, his family did not keep a Bible in their home. Instead, his father wrote down passages of scripture, which everyone read and shared. The pastor had worked at the cathedral since it reopened as a registered church in 1985. Over tea in his office, he explained to me the congregation's recent good fortune. The demolition was stopped on a technicality: the building had historic status as part of the city's cultural heritage and was protected by law. Fuzhou, like many other cities in China, had belatedly recognized the value of its architectural legacy and was preserving some historic structures, even building ersatz "old" neighborhoods.

My daughter and I climbed three flights of stairs and stepped outside to the rooftop between the towers. In the middle of this platform stood a three-foot-tall red cross, outlined with neon. In the distance, I could make out another church with a big cross, a Catholic congregation, I was told. As

The author, left, standing atop Cangxia Christ Church in Fuzhou in 2015 with her daughter, Cory. Courtesy of Kaikai Lin.

I surveyed the neighborhood, what struck me was the utter absence of any effort by this old church's Anglican founders to have it blend in with its Chinese surroundings. When the cornerstone was laid with much fanfare in 1924, a powerful nationalistic current was lifting the Chinese people. Rather than respond to that emerging spirit, missionaries designed a church in their own image. It looked British, not the least bit Chinese.

Every Tuesday, Thursday, and Sunday, Pastor Sun and two others conducted services for about one thousand members. Inside the cathedral, I could make out the bones of its Anglican past. The chancel in the front of the church, where the choir sat, had four rows of high-back, dark wooden benches that faced each other. Under a sign listing the hymns for service was a grand piano. I had hoped to see the eagle lectern donated by the Lin family in 1927, but it had been removed or destroyed long ago. The only furnishing from the original building was a hexagonal stone baptismal font. Everything else—slatted pews, pulpit, lectern, and altar—were replacements.

During the Cultural Revolution, the church was converted into a factory to make medicine. I will never forget what the pastor said to me the first time we met in 2011. I had asked whether the bad old days could ever return, when churches closed and Christians went underground.

"Impossible," he said at the time with a wave of his hand. "There are too many believers."

Another cousin, this one from the Ni side of the family, flew up from Hong Kong to join me for the next leg of my journey. His father and my grandmother had been siblings. I had asked him about the legacy of Watchman Nee: What had become of his Little Flock? For the answer, we were off to see a ninety-eight-year-old man.

In Fujian, some followers of Watchman Nee decided to join churches with the Three-Self Movement. But many more preferred to worship at house churches. My cousin and I drove an hour south to Fuqing County. Along the highway, I saw one twenty-story apartment block after another, a dreary landscape of runaway development that had metastasized all over China. We pulled off the main road and headed down a narrow road. Immediately, something caught my eye: a bright red sign with two vertical lines of characters, pasted on the side of a gray cement wall. It was a reference to Ephesians 1:15: *Faith in the Lord Jesus, Love unto all the saints.*

This was a village of Christians. We entered a five-story building and took the elevator up. The entire year-old building was a house church, including a meeting hall on one floor, a canteen on another, and apartments. As we entered a conference room, a young man was finishing a study session and left to turn the space over to us. Photographs covered all the walls—group shots showing a very old man known as Brother Lin (no relation) posing with visitors from all over the world.

Like me, they wanted to meet this man who had spent twenty-four of the past sixty years in prison for his religious beliefs. Brother Lin was convicted four times for everything from being part of Watchman Nee's "counterrevolutionary" inner circle (1956) to writing reactionary hymns (1963); criticizing the Three-Self Movement (1983); and disturbing social order (1999).

Brother Lin toddled into the room but seemed spry and sharp. His plain white cotton shirt hung loosely on his small frame. Sitting in an old-style wooden Chinese chair, his feet just brushed the ground. He wore a hearing aid but had no trouble following the conversation or understanding why I was there. The mention of my grandmother's name reminded him of the only time he had met her. Brother Lin had just been released in 1957 from a year in prison after his first conviction. Watchman Nee was behind bars, but his coworkers from the Little Flock gathered in Shanghai for a meeting to plan for the future. Brother Lin, undeterred by his recent prison stay, came up from Fuqing for the two-week meeting. One Sunday, he gave a sermon at the Nanyang Road assembly hall and afterward shared lunch with my grandmother, Ni Guizhen, and her friend Charity, Watchman Nee's wife.

"We chatted a lot," he told me. "She inquired about my family, how many children I had, were they boys or girls." Brother Lin, then forty, was a teacher who struggled to support his family. The day after their lunch, Ni Guizhen sent him four sets of clothing for each of his young children. More than fifty years later, he remembered this act of kindness. "This left a deep impression on me," he told me through my cousin.

Brother Lin had something he wanted to show me. It was a pair of old frayed baggy pants and a shapeless padded cotton jacket. Both looked like a crazy quilt of threadbare patches in indigo blue, black, gray, and white, all held together with crude, thick stitches. I had read in his memoir about these tattered clothes. This was what he wore when he was released from a labor reeducation camp in 1973; he wrote that he could not bear to throw the clothes away. He proudly showed me the pants and coat that he had worn for ten years and seventy-five days.

In the past, just meeting a foreigner like me could have gotten him in trouble—and did. In 1983, after he received an overseas Chinese Christian, Brother Lin was arrested. One of the charges against him was that he had played a role in reprinting a banned book by the late Witness Lee, a close coworker of Watchman Nee, who left China in 1949 for Taiwan and later California. Authorities accused Witness Lee of being behind the "Shouters Sect," a Christian group with a call-and-response style of worship that the Public Security Ministry labeled a cult.

Students in China's official seminaries are banned from reading Watchman Nee's books to this day. He still bears the "counterrevolutionary" label. But online, anyone can get access to all of his works—from his opus *The Spiritual Man* to compilations of sermons, essays, and testimonies. Interest in Watchman Nee, who died in 1972, remains strong both in and out of China. A Chinese professor and expert in religious history, Wang Aiming, described Watchman Nee to me as "a spiritual giant" among Chinese Christians. Part of what made him different from his contemporaries—other famous independent preachers like John Sung and Wang Mingdao—was his global appeal. Nee had traveled extensively in Asia, Europe, and the United States during the 1930s and published books and periodicals in Chinese and English, extending his reach far beyond Shanghai.

Brother Lin told me that every Sunday about one hundred people gathered at this building. Sometimes they invited Christians from other places—only the previous Saturday more than five hundred visitors from another town had joined them in fellowship. Overseas Christians came and went frequently. Brother Lin recounted a German visitor telling him, "Watchman Nee not only belongs to China, but he belongs to Germany as well." Members of the Fuqing local church had traveled abroad, attending Christian gatherings in the United States, Japan, and Europe. "Even I had a chance to visit Taiwan," the old man enthused. "Imagine a guy like me who had once been sentenced to twenty years, and now I have that freedom. Things have really changed for the better."

How was this happening? How could a group that, in the government's eyes, bore the stigma of a cult operate so openly?

After my years of living in China, I knew that nothing in China was black and white, only shades of gray. Indeed, it was possible for the situation in Fujian to be the antithesis of neighboring Zhejiang. It all came down to local leaders, and Brother Lin explained to me that the situation began to change in Fujian in 2003. He and others in the local church in Fuqing realized that unless they were able to remove the label of being a cult with an aberrant theology, they would always face problems. "If we wanted to fix the issue of cults once and for good, we must let people know the truth, in the right way," he explained. "I appealed to the government a first time, a second time, telling them about our faith, our activities, our political stance, our contribution to society. The walls between us gradually fell down." Communication was in writing at first but was followed with face-to-face meetings between church members and provincial authorities.

The last big crackdown was in 1996, when more than sixty Christians in Fujian were arrested and sent to labor camps or forced to undergo reeducation. Brother Lin told me that before his group established "mutual trust" with the government, eighteen Christians were jailed, including two of the men sitting beside him. But in the past eight years, no one had been arrested.

We had been talking for more than an hour. Brother Lin was tired. In parting, I asked him and the others whether they feared that the situation could abruptly change and they could be arrested. Their answer for me: "China is a vast country. We can't say for sure about the whole China, but in Fujian Province, the communication has been going well."

REPUTATIONS

After Mao died in 1976, Chinese society began the slow process of recovering from the trauma of the Cultural Revolution. One aspect of healing was allowing people who were wrongly accused of crimes against the country to restore their reputations. A formal process—called *pingfan*, or political rehabilitation—was put into place, through which victims or their families could request an official clearing of the record.

My family has a document dated August 23, 1986, and titled in big red characters "Shanghai Public Security Bureau Decision." It stated that Ni Guizhen in 1969 was labeled a counterrevolutionary by the Shanghai Public Security office, the court, and a military committee. Her alleged crimes were using "religion to conduct counterrevolutionary activities." Specifically, she had been accused of participating in "secret networks and gatherings" to spread reactionary opinions, accepting funds from Hong Kong churches to support counterrevolutionaries, and "maliciously defaming Chairman Mao." The PSB had reexamined her case on August 21, 1979, and ruled that the earlier crimes were true. But since she was dead by then, the counterrevolutionary label could be removed. It was only a half victory. Seven years later, the family petitioned the government to take another look at her case. This time, the PSB ruled that the earlier criminal allegations were "not proper." In writing, they decided to "give Ni Guizhen redress." My grandmother was no longer an enemy of the people.

In another document, dated August 27, 1984, the Shanghai Religious Affairs Bureau reexamined the case against Lin Pu-chi, who died in 1973. In August 1971, my grandfather was accused of being part of an American spy ring. "The decision is now negated upon the approval by higher-level leaders," the decision read. From 1969 to 1972, a Shanghai "study group" targeted Christians. This was a form of political persecution, the statement said. "For that reason, any untrue statement made by the study group should be overturned."

Portrait of Lin Pu-chi and Ni Guizhen from 1948. Their records were purged of charges made during the Cultural Revolution. Courtesy of Lin Family Collection.

And what of the reputation of Watchman Nee? I asked that question in 1999 for a magazine piece about Christianity in China that I wrote for the *Inquirer*. It came up in an interview with three Protestant leaders in Shanghai who spoke on behalf of the official Three-Self Movement. I prefaced my question with the observation that China took great pride in the fact that churches were free of foreign or denominational influences and had been reshaped, like the economy, with Chinese characteristics. Didn't Watchman Nee advance precisely that form of self-supporting religious movement? Wasn't he an independent, uniquely Chinese Christian voice?

My query prompted a sharp response from one of the elderly pastors. She repeated for me in flawless English the crimes of Watchman Nee, as if it were 1956 and we were sitting in the Tian Chan Theater, witnessing his denunciation session. She said that he had committed adultery, was a capitalist, and sent damaging intelligence to spies for Taiwan and the exiled Nationalist Party. Added another pastor: "We don't talk a lot about Mr. Nee himself."

But by 2015, I found that opinions were beginning to soften. Privately, Chinese theologians and scholars suggested to me that the time had come to reconsider the reputation of Watchman Nee. Many universities in China had centers of Christian study with scholars and graduate students who were inquiring into Watchman Nee's ministry, teachings, and historic impact. At the grassroots, meanwhile, the influence of Watchman Nee on the current generation of Christians remained strong. A mainland scholar estimated for me that about fifteen million Chinese Christians would identify Watchman Nee as the strongest influence in their faith life.

Even with the restrictions that still exist under the atheistic rule of the Communist Party, the Christian revival in China is expected to continue unabated. Fenggang Yang, the Purdue sociologist, projected that if current trends progressed at even a modest growth rate, China could have as many as 225 million Christians by 2025. Compare that to the United States: the Pew Research Center estimated that in 2010, about 247 million Americans identified as Christian, but the trend was on a downward slope.

On a summer Sunday in 2015, two dozen people filled a sparsely furnished ground-floor apartment in the Nantai neighborhood of Fuzhou. It was close to 9:00 a.m., and almost all the little plastic stools in the living room were taken. In the center of the room was a small folding table with a glass of grape juice and a plate of wafers set on a white tablecloth. Everyone held black hymnals on their laps and sang with vigor. I was told I could follow along in English on my smartphone by going to www.hymnal.net and searching for number 214, "According to Thy Gracious Word." Alas, I had no Wi-Fi connection.

In between the third and fourth hymns of the morning, stragglers walked into the room. A young father held his toddler in his arms and gripped her tiny green backpack in his hand. They took seats on a stool in the back. The girl chattered while holding the ear of a fluffy stuffed toy rabbit.

In my Catholic church back home in Philadelphia, congregants were seen but only heard when reciting the liturgy. But in this living room, everyone who wanted to participate did participate. People took turns in a kind of call and response, making short, spontaneous comments in Chinese that were answered in English with "Amen."

> We are all family. Amen!
> It doesn't matter what our surnames are, we have the same Father. Amen!
> We are all priests. Amen!
> We must spread the gospel, spread the truth. Amen!
> Whoever we meet, we should speak to them. Amen!
> Thank God I can get together with all of you this morning. Amen!

I looked around. Men sat on one side of the room, women on the other, many of whom wore small black lace caps. The head coverings reminded me of the round white veils we wore at Mass in my childhood. Some women pressed their eyes shut. It was an older crowd, but there was a smattering of couples with children. Everyone seemed engaged and connected, and it was at that moment that I thought of my grandmother.

In chronicling my family's history, I had plotted what had happened to them starting at the very beginning, all the way back to the fisherman from Fujian who was the first member of my father's branch of the family to convert to Christianity. But I had a harder time understanding every "why" in their journey. One of the questions that I continued to wrestle with was why my grandmother upset the harmony in her marriage by walking away from her husband's church to join the Little Flock of her brother. I had my theories, but it wasn't until just then, in the informal setting of this house church, that I understood. I felt it. It was the intimacy of shared fellowship, the yearning for connection in a turbulent world. I pictured her sitting on a wooden stool in the terrace house on Hardoon Road in Shanghai, listening to her younger brother put into language she could understand the mystery of man's spirit and soul.

The assembled turned their attention to a middle-aged member who delivered the main message of the day from Acts 20, verses 17 through 38. The apostle Paul was saying good-bye to the elders in Ephesus after three years with them. He was headed to Jerusalem and almost certain imprisonment. Paul warned them of the dangers they faced and expressed his sadness in parting. "Have we done that?" the speaker asked the group. "Labored for the Lord like Paul?"

After he finished, people passed around the plate with the wafer pieces and dipped spoons into the cup of juice, the symbolic body and blood of Christ. There was another round of spontaneous call and response and more singing. The clock on the wall read 10:05 a.m. when the service ended and everyone got up to leave. Women stacked the blue plastic stools. The father lifted his toddler and picked up her green backpack. One man told me that he would attend another service that evening, a much larger and younger gathering of about a hundred people.

Next Sunday, they would return.

Epilogue

$\mathcal{O}$n a late August afternoon, I stood at my desk in my Pennsylvania farmhouse talking via a video link to my Aunt Martha, who sat at her computer in an old brick house in Sydney, Australia. We were continuing a conversation that began three decades earlier. I spoke to Martha every few months, picking up threads of the family story. On this day, I asked her about returning to church after the death of Mao and the end of the Cultural Revolution.

I knew that Martha, who at the time was ninety, was a steadfast Christian. I wanted to know: when she heard the news in 1979 that the doors of churches would reopen, did she immediately return?

"No," she replied. Martha was by nature taciturn, but her succinct answer still caught me off guard. She went on to explain that it wasn't until she moved from Shanghai to Australia that she resumed an active and open practice of her faith. Every Monday, she joined a group of followers of Watchman Nee in Sydney. I pressed her on why she had waited a decade.

"Fear," she replied.

Martha continued. She and her husband, John, who had been tormented by Red Guards and held in captivity for almost a year, did not trust the authorities enough to expose themselves with such a public return to church. Instead of joining an approved congregation or reconnecting with an unofficial house church in Shanghai, they kept their spiritual life confined to the privacy of their home.

The trauma that the family experienced, beginning well before the Cultural Revolution, explained why one by one, everyone in the house on Jiaozhou Road left China. They were pushed by harsh treatment as much as pulled by new opportunities.

Julia was first to go. In May 1980, she and her husband, Victor, relocated to Chicago, where he studied business at Roosevelt University. Their son, then four, stayed behind in Shanghai with Martha and did not join them until just before his eleventh birthday in 1987. Julia studied piano at the American Conservatory of Music in Chicago, followed by postgraduate work at Indiana University. As a teenager, Julia had lost critical years of training during the ten-year Cultural Revolution, which derailed her dream of a solo career. In Chicago, she built a successful business as a tutor who was popular among Chinese immigrant parents and also worked as the music director of a large Protestant church, performing and recording Christian music on the side. She told me that once, when she was at a piano competition with some of her students, she recognized another piano teacher, a woman from Shanghai who had been in her conservatory class. This woman was one of the classmates who smashed her hand with a Ping-Pong paddle as punishment for playing classical music during the Cultural Revolution. I was shocked by the story. If it were me, I would have created a scene and loudly faced my nemesis. But Julia, a gentle and forgiving soul, did not dwell on the episode. She was startled to see a ghost from her past but did not confront her. She moved on.

Our cousin Kaikai, Tim and Emma's oldest, was next to leave. In Shanghai, Kaikai made and repaired rattan furniture for a state-run store that sold household items and kitchenware. He had a special skill, however, that would serve him well in the future: He enjoyed sewing and was good at it. After the Cultural Revolution, young people put away their Mao suits and craved contemporary styles. Kaikai made his friends copies of fashionable clothes that he found in Hong Kong magazines, outfits like a Levi's-inspired jean jacket paired with flared trousers. In 1981, when he was twenty-five, he bought a ticket for Los Angeles and landed in the States with fifty dollars in his wallet. After bouncing from job to job, including hotel handyman and rattan repairman, he parlayed his sewing skills into a clothing business. At first, he took on contract work for other manufacturers but then started to design and make his own line—KK 88, a women's sportswear label with pieces selling for $100 to $300 at boutiques and department stores like Nordstrom. By age fifty, Kaikai was financially secure enough to live the American dream: he retired early and spent his days traveling the world with his wife. On his Chinese-language blog, he shares photos of everything from emperor penguins on the beach in the Falkland Islands to castles in the Rhine Valley. When last I looked, he had more than nine million views.

After Kaikai settled in Los Angeles, his parents, Tim and Emma, left Shanghai for California, and were followed by their daughter, Lin Yu, and her husband, who opened a clinic for Chinese medicine in San Jose. Lin Yu shared her brother's entrepreneurial zeal and became a distributor of a Japanese-made massage chair. She and her husband bought a vast home in the hills outside the city. Tim and Emma lived nearby.

In 1987, Martha moved to Australia, where her husband had relatives. Their daughter Terri and granddaughter Jean joined them. Terri, the barefoot doctor whose education was interrupted by the Cultural Revolution, divorced her husband in the early 1980s. When she got to Australia, she earned a degree in accounting at the age of forty-two and worked for several years in Sydney. But in the 1990s, she realized that China offered her better career choices. China was evolving from the sick patient of Asia into a forceful economic superpower, and foreign companies needed people like Terri who could navigate both China and the Western business world.

When I was posted in Beijing in the 1990s for the *Inquirer*, Terri worked for a foreign joint venture that made auto parts in Changchun, China's Motor City in the northeastern part of the country. She lived in a luxury hotel whose doormen wore mink fur hats. In a twist of fate, her apartment was an hour's drive from the old mud-walled house where she spent seven years as a "sent-down" youth living with peasants during the Cultural Revolution. Terri's career took her all over Asia. She lived for several years at a time in China, Japan, Taiwan, and South Korea before returning to China in 2008 to handle finances for an American multinational that had a factory in the southern city

In 1999, while working for a joint venture, Terri Sun visited the village in northeastern China where she lived for seven years as a "barefoot doctor." Here, she is greeted by a villager who remembers her. Courtesy of Jennifer Lin.

of Shenzhen. A few years later, Terri decided to slow down and returned to Australia to start her own business as a China consultant.

The last ones in the family to leave China were my grandparents Ni Guizhen and Lin Pu-chi.

My grandmother died in 1971 and my grandfather in 1973. Their cremated remains were buried at the nearest cemetery, sixty miles west of Shanghai in Suzhou. But in August 2002, my Uncle Tim dug up their graves, placed their bones in plastic bags, and wrapped everything in red cloth. He had his reasons. Their gravesite suffered from neglect and was overgrown with bushes and weeds. Tim was getting old and would be making fewer and fewer trips to China. With no family left in Shanghai, there would be no one visiting their graves to maintain the site.

I was visiting Los Angeles in 2004 when Kaikai took me to see our grandparents' new burial site at Forest Lawn Cemetery in the city of Glendale. The pastor and his wife were interred at the Cemetery of the Stars, joining in eternity the likes of Walt Disney, W. C. Fields, Nat "King" Cole, George Burns, and Gracie Allen. Their urns were stored in a marble niche in the Columbarium of Courage, just past a bronze plaque in memory of baseball Hall of Famer Casey Stengel and a giant mosaic of the signing of the Declaration of Independence.

In life, Lin Pu-chi never visited Los Angeles; Ni Guizhen never set foot in the United States. But in death, they rest in a meticulously manicured memorial park near the interchange of the Glendale Freeway and Interstate 5.

The last time I was inside the old Lin home in Shanghai, Terri joined me. It was a few months before the 2008 Beijing Olympics, and I was doing a story about her for the *Inquirer*. I wrote in the newspaper that the real story of China's progress was told not through the billion-dollar stadiums in Beijing but through the lives of people like Terri. In her lifetime, she went from being a hospital janitor to earning more money than I could ever imagine as an executive for a multinational business. Like so many of her generation, she was impatient to make up for lost time.

At the back entrance of House 19, we knocked at the door, and one of the tenants, who recognized Terri and knew the Lin family, invited us inside for a look. Two families now occupied the house. We climbed the narrow staircase to the top floor. The place smelled of mildew, just as it had during my first visit. No one lived in the attic, and the woman fumbled for a key on her chain to open the door.

The dusty alcove below the slanting eaves was where Terri used to sleep with her mother and older sister. Some of the family's furniture, relics from the past, remained. Off to one side stood an old dressing table with a smoky mirror. In a corner were two antique leather trunks, which our grandmother had taken with her from Fuzhou, decades ago.

"This still looks the same," Terri commented, her eyes darting around the room.

I could tell she was uncomfortable, anxious. Memories resided here, bad ones. She bent to show me a sliding wood panel, painted aqua and smudged with decades of dirt and dust. It led to a crawl space. She explained that when mobs ransacked the house—Red Guards from schools and factories, public security squads, you name it, there were so many over the years—they would throw open the panels and search for anything incriminating. I took pictures and we left.

I heard my grandfather's voice only once—during the phone call in 1973 when I was fourteen. I said little more than hello. But there were many times when I felt like he was talking directly to me through his writing. Just days before I had to send the final draft of this manuscript to the publisher, a graduate student in Hong Kong, who was familiar with my research, sent me an article dated February 3, 1932, that Lin Pu-chi had written for the Chinese-language *Faith Newspaper*, or *Xinyi Bao*. My grandfather told readers that the study of China's church history was "indispensable" because "every society and every nation must use the past as a mirror." But he lamented the paucity of books on the Chinese church, adding that materials that could be used to compile a history were scattered and incomplete. Missionaries did a good job of chronicling their experiences. But the task of sorting out China's church history, he noted, would be difficult, requiring "sufficient time to devote to searching for materials and editing them."

It has taken me just shy of four decades to reach this point in the telling of my family's story. The one who showed me the way was Lin Pu-chi. A prolific writer with a restless mind, he left a paper trail for me to follow, starting from when he was a teenager until his final years. I found a piece he wrote as a student at Trinity College for an English essay contest. I read articles from his days as a college editor at St. John's University; his sermons as a priest at St. Peter's Church; dozens of essays in Chinese and English in church periodicals; even short stories about love and marriage that he penned as a young university man. And always, I went back to his letters, my guideposts into the past. It was odd how I found clues about him where earlier I had seen none. One was a photograph he sent us, a portrait of him wearing the white tunic and black tippet or scarf of an Anglican priest. With his owlish wire-frame glasses and coal black hair parted to the side, he looks straight into the lens of the camera. He wrote "Christmas 1956" in black ink at the bottom. His birthday fell on December 25, and most years he marked the occasion by posing for a birthday photograph. Only now did I see the picture for what it was. The faint smile,

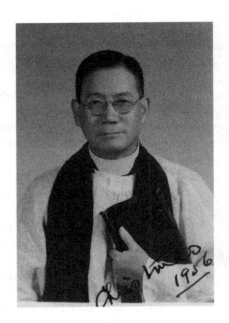

Almost every year, Lin Pu-chi had his photograph taken on his birthday on Christmas Day. This one from 1956 reveals a quiet defiance. When it was taken, he had been shunted aside from his duties within the church. Courtesy of Lin Family Collection.

the unflinching gaze: this was the face of quiet defiance. It was taken in a year that began with the public vilification of his brother-in-law Watchman Nee—the denunciation meeting at the Shanghai opera house, the newspaper articles attacking the Little Flock, the arrest of coworkers, the unbearable pressure on his wife to condemn her brother—and ended with his own loss of position in his church. Not viewed as revolutionary enough, he was shunted aside from any position of influence or responsibility in the reconstituted church under communism. He stood outside the inner circle and preached only when he was asked to fill in for others. But in that Shanghai photographer's studio, he posed for the camera, Bible held high in his left hand, in full Anglican dress, uncowed.

I want to ask my grandfather a question: why did he never tell his children about being seized by an anti-Christian mob in his hometown of Fuzhou in 1927? I only learned about the incident in a book on Fuzhou Protestants by Ryan Dunch, a professor at the University of Alberta and expert on Christianity in China. After researching the matter and finding multiple references in articles from the era, diplomatic dispatches, and missionary letters, all applauding how the young pastor comported himself under unimaginable pressure, I viewed the episode as a proud moment for Lin Pu-chi as well as a cautionary example of the dangers faced by Chinese Christians in their contact with foreigners. But with his own family, he chose not to make it part of his narrative. He did, however, tell his mentor about it. In his memoir, published in 1935, the Reverend William S. Pakenham-Walsh wrote about his twenty years in

China and quoted from a long letter my grandfather had sent him, reminiscing about the early days of Trinity College in Fuzhou but also describing the attack. The older missionary described the mob violence in his memoir. Lin Pu-chi's children never read this book or even knew of its existence until I told them about it. If not for happenstance, any memory of the episode within the family would have disappeared when Lin Pu-chi died in 1973.

I have a question for my grandmother, too. Like my father, when he heard about her suffering for the first time in 1979, I felt the same urge to go back in time to protect her from harm. If she were here today, I would ask her why she didn't capitulate when neighbors forced her to kneel and renounce her brother Watchman Nee. Or when interrogators took her behind closed doors and roughed her up. As I listened to one person after another recount the abuse against her, I wanted to whisper in her ear and say, *It's okay. Spare yourself. Lie if you must. In your heart, you will know it's not true.* But she didn't; she wouldn't. She held firm. Her devotion to her brother and her religious beliefs was unwavering.

But it was in these lingering questions that I found my answers. When Mao Zedong stood on the rostrum of the Forbidden City on October 1, 1949, to proclaim the creation of the People's Republic of China, there was reason to think this was the death of religion. The Chinese Communist Party was composed of avowed atheists, and Christianity was seen as a foreign religion that would wither away.

When churches reopened in 1979, again the skeptics said nothing would come of it. Even before liberation, the number of Chinese people who were Protestant or Catholic was very small, no more than 1 percent of the population. The roots of Christianity were shallow. The religion had not been *Sinified*.

And this was where the skeptics were wrong. In very different ways, Lin Pu-chi and Watchman Nee built a religious foundation that would prove to be sturdy enough to support the religious revival in China today. But equally as important was the conviction of believers like my grandparents. It cannot be measured by surveys. It cannot be calculated. It must be witnessed. After all that they had been through, after the physical abuse and mental torment, after the accusations, humiliation, and betrayal, Lin Pu-chi and Ni Guizhen never let go of their beliefs.

To the end, the family in Shanghai remained faithful.

September 2016
Doylestown, Pennsylvania

Acknowledgments

$\mathcal{M}$y father, Paul M. Lin, M.D., called this project my "obsession," and he was right. It began with my first stories about China—a two-part series written in 1979 while I was a summer intern for the *Bucks County Courier Times*—and ends with the publication of this book.

None of this would have been possible without the cooperation of my family in Shanghai, who endured my endless questioning and graciously provided answers to everything, even if it meant revisiting traumatic episodes from the past. I am thankful to my aunt Martha Sun and her daughters—Terri Sun and Julia Tsien—for their patience and generosity. They sat for multiple lengthy interviews over the course of many years and also located old photographs, translated materials, pointed me to other sources, and responded to hundreds of e-mail queries. My cousin Terri and I had our first long interview in 1986. We sat and talked every night for a week in her living room in Shanghai, beginning a conversation that basically has never ended. She joined me on many reporting expeditions in China: to the Lin ancestral hall in Fujian, to the gravesite of Watchman Nee in Suzhou, to the village where she lived as a barefoot doctor, and to the old house in Shanghai.

Her sister, Julia, also opened up her world to me and in 2007 allowed my son, Karl, to make a documentary about her life as a pianist during the Cultural Revolution. Julia's husband, Victor, our translator during the family's 1979 visit, continued to help me with translation over the years. At key points in my reporting, my cousins who are the children of Uncle Tim and Aunt Emma came to my aid. In 2004, Kaikai took me to our grandparents' new burial site in Los Angeles and in 2015 traveled with my daughter, Cory, and me to Fuzhou to see family landmarks. His sister, Lin Yu, supplied photographs and critical documents and arranged Skype interviews with her parents in San Jose. On my grandmother's side of the family, Sam Nee of Hong Kong gave me as much time as I needed to help me understand Watchman Nee. He also showed me places in Fuzhou from our shared past.

The deeper I got into my research, the more interested and engaged my father became. He enjoyed our interviews and thrilled every time I found a new photograph of his father or discovered some long-ago article, like the love story that Lin Pu-chi wrote in 1919 as a seminary student. When my father retired, he took all of the handwritten letters from Lin Pu-chi—which my mother, Sylvia Lin, had the foresight to save—and transcribed them on the computer, making it easier for me to study and deconstruct them later on. Meanwhile, his brother, Jim, who lived in Tampa, contributed his keen memory and uncanny eye for details. After one interview, he sent me a follow-up note, describing the bedraggled European refugee who came to the house to beg for food in the 1930s. A writer of narrative nonfiction craves images like that. A long-ago neighbor of the Lin family, Boling Dong, whose house was in the same lane in Shanghai, also provided me with vivid details from the 1960s.

The one person who has witnessed my obsession almost from the start is my husband, Bill Stieg. I know you're supposed to save the best for last, but I could not continue without acknowledging right here and now his role in this book. Bill is a graceful writer and thoughtful editor, who gave me honest criticism, constructive ideas, and endless encouragement. He literally read every word of every draft of every chapter—and changed more than a few, always to make the narrative stronger. He encouraged me to follow the story wherever it took me, whether it was back to China for more reporting or jetting off to London or Austin, Texas, to comb through archives. Through more than thirty years of marriage, he has made life seem like an endless adventure, full of possibility, and for that, I am eternally grateful. It is no exaggeration to say that this book would not have come to fruition without Bill working beside me.

I have been fortunate through this odyssey to have friends and family in my corner. My sisters—Angela, Daria, Damien, and Stefanie—shared my curiosity about the family history. They carefully read my drafts and cheered me on. My children, Cory and Karl, were good listeners and knew that when Mom was in her "zone," writing in the attic, they should tiptoe lightly. They were troupers, too, at ages three and five, when I announced to them that we were "moving to China!" Later in life, they accompanied me on separate reporting trips to China to research my book.

My *lao pengyou*, old friends from my days as a Beijing correspondent, offered critiques and indulged me by listening to me yammer on about this project for years and years. Thank you to Rod Mickleburgh and Lucie McNeill; Richard Tomlinson and Tess Poole; Mary Kay Magistad; Renee Schoof and Bob Erskine; and Vivian Polishuk. My former news assistant in the China bureau of the *Philadelphia Inquirer* and Knight-Ridder Newspapers, the incomparable Guo Hui, worked with me as I dug into the past. Her daughter, the equally talented Wei Xinyi, joined me on expeditions to the Shanghai municipal archives. Meanwhile, in Germany, my research assistant for the book, Mei Chen, provided prompt translation of documents, chapters, and articles and checked my manuscript for historical accuracy. The reporting for many sections depended on her contributions. Another translator and longtime friend who aided me was Chen Yourong, who was also my first Chinese-language tutor, a job that required enormous patience. Meanwhile, in Australia, Colin Hall provided new material on the life of Watchman Nee.

Because I wanted to write this book as a narrative, I relied on diaries, letters, and articles that I found in archives to bring the places and people to life. Henry Hong took me on a walking tour of Shanghai to show me some of the sites from my family history, including the Wing On neighborhood and Third Uncle's house. Archivists, meanwhile, fed my obsession and were as thrilled as I was with every little discovery. Gratitude goes to Ivana Frlan and her team at the Cadbury Research Library's special collections at the University of Birmingham in England; Martha Smalley and Joan Duffy at the Yale Divinity School Library; Sarah Dana of the Archives of the Episcopal Church in Austin, Texas; Kaiyi Chen and Nancy Miller at the University of Pennsylvania; and the library staffs of the Episcopal Divinity School, Drew University, and Princeton Theological Seminary.

Over the years, numerous scholars gave freely of their time to help me understand the history of Christianity in China. Joseph T. H. Lee of Pace University and his wife, Christie C. S. Chow, led private tutorials to guide me through the teachings and legacy of Watchman Nee. Daniel H. Bays, who wrote *A New History of Christianity in China*, answered questions, read my manuscript, and offered encouragement. Robert André LaFleur of Beloit College shared his boundless insight into Chinese history, Buddhism, and Confucianism. In Hong Kong, Philip L. Wickeri, an adviser on historical studies for the Anglican archbishop, opened up his archives, sharing books and documents as well as making important suggestions. On two occasions, he invited me to present papers on my research at academic conferences in Hong Kong, allowing me to connect with Chinese scholars who also provided direction and information on archival sources. To those many Chinese experts, thank you for your interest and guidance at critical stages of my reporting.

Along the way, I have met many kindred spirits, including fellow researchers working on family histories or interested in China's Christian history. While wandering online, I stumbled upon the work of George Niu of Fuzhou, who had an English-language blog on the rich missionary history of his hometown. George located for me a rare photograph of my grandfather from 1920. He also introduced me to Chen Zhaofen, an expert on the history of the hospital where my great-grandfather worked as a surgeon.

I got to know many helpful "mish kids," the children of missionaries, including Peyton and Mary Craighill, and Helen Roberts and her daughter, Katherine Granfield. Luckily for me, Frances Slater, a retired geography professor in London, spent years researching the life of her relative, Archdeacon John R. Wolfe, a Fuzhou missionary for more than a half century. She published much of her research, including primary sources, in several books. Her efforts saved me multiple trips to archives. Also sharing materials with me was the daughter of Angus Kinnear, the biographer of Watchman Nee who authored *Against the Tide*. In London, Fiona Putley allowed me to look through her father's files and photographs, two of which appear in this book.

As a reporter for more than thirty years, I could count on my former colleagues at the *Inquirer* for their expert opinions. Avery Rome applied her sharp pencil to the first draft of my manuscript, while Sue Warner, Jeff Gammage, Emilie Lounsberry, and Andy Cassel provided thoughtful feedback on an ongoing basis. At critical junctures in the reporting of this book, editors Bill Marimow and Stan Wischnowski gave me time away from work to move the project forward.

I also owe appreciation to the many inquisitive friends whose unwavering curiosity in my topic bolstered my confidence when I needed it most, people like Jane Pepper, Linda Harris, Bob Fu, Robert Strauss, Joshua Bergey, Kathy Hacker, Miriam Hill, Monica Yant Kinney, Maria Panaritis, David Beverage, Wayne Baumgaertel, and the Dance Moms of Doylestown.

Finally, I want to thank Jessica Papin, my agent with Dystel and Goderich Literary Management, who believed in this project from the very beginning, and the editors of Rowman & Littlefield, who have taken my obsession and put it between two hard covers.

Notes

PROLOGUE

The scene at the Tian Chan Theater was based on *Liberation Daily* newspaper, February 1–10, 1956; Lily M. Hsu, *My Unforgettable Memories: Watchman Nee & Shanghai Local Church* (Longwood, FL: Xulon Press, 2013), 113–51; Angus Kinnear, *Against the Tide: The Unforgettable Story Behind Watchman Nee*, rev. ed. (Eastbourne, UK: Kingsway, 2005), 264–79; and Basil Sun, *A Higher Ground: Testimony of a Tortuous Life Journey* (Sydney: Aukeli, 2001), 49–53.

CHAPTER 1: COOK

To re-create the world of Chinese converts and missionaries in Fujian in the mid-1800s, I relied on *Church Missionary Society Annual Proceedings, 1862–1917; CMS Annual Letters of the Rev. John Wolfe, 1862–1910*, published in 2007 by John Fitzgerald and Frances Slater in a print-on-demand publication, *JRW: CMS Annual Letters*, at http://www.lulu.com/johnfitzgerald; *For Christ in Fuh-kien* (London: Church Missionary Society, 1904); Daniel H. Bays, *A New History of Christianity in China* (Malden, MA: Wiley-Blackwell, 2012); Ellsworth C. Carlson, *The Foochow Missionaries 1847–1880* (Cambridge, MA: Harvard University Press, 1974); Ryan Dunch, *Fuzhou Protestants and the Making of Modern China 1857–1927* (New Haven, CT: Yale University Press, 2001); Eugene Stock, *The Story of the Fuh-kien Mission* (London: Seeley, Jackson & Halliday, 1890); and John Wolfe, "The Fukien Mission," *Church Missionary Gleaner*, October 1894.

14   *His arrival as a passenger*: Donald MacInnis, *China Chronicles from a Lost Time: The Min River Journals* (Norwalk, CT: Eastbridge, 2009), 200–202.

14   *It didn't help*: MacInnis, *China Chronicles*, 200.

15   *Missionaries seized the moment*: Carlson, *Foochow Missionaries*, 64–66.

15   *"I preach and preach"*: Carlson, *Foochow Missionaries*, 65.

16   *When Wolfe arrived*: In his annual letters to the CMS office in London, the archdeacon recounted his travels and work in the region around the village of Erdu, which at the time was known as Nitu.

16   *In Ningde*: Stock, *Fuh-kien Mission*, 158–59.

17   *giving up their worship of idols*: Stock, *Fuh-kien Mission*, 162.

17   *Lin Yongbiao was an old man*: Genealogical records at the Lin Ancestral Hall in Erdu, Fujian Province, recorded the time and date of the birth of Lin Yongbiao; his son Lin Dao'an; and his grandson (my grandfather) Lin Pu-chi. The *jiapu* also contains some biographical details, such as when individuals died, burial sites, and information on heirs.

18   *foreigners were out to poison*: Rev. John E. Mahood to CMS board, Sept. 8, 1871; Carlson, *Foochow Missionaries*, 128–32.

19   *road to Fuzhou*: Many early missionaries wrote vivid descriptions of Fuzhou and Fujian province, cited in Stock, *Fuh-kien Mission*; Stephen Livingstone Baldwin, *Frank Leslie's Popular Monthly*, Dec. 1884, http://foochow-mission.blogspot.com/2014/09/foo-chow.html; Lloyd Llewellyn, "Fuh-chow, the Banyan City," *Church Missionary Gleaner*, June 1, 1899; MacInnis, *China Chronicles*.

21   *temples on Black Stone Hill*: John Fitzgerald and Frances Slater, *Wu Shih Shan Affair*, in a print-on-demand publication at http://www.lulu.com/johnfitzgerald, reprinted: Trial transcripts and court filings that appeared in the *Hong Kong Daily Press* from April through August 1879; 1878 article on the conflict that appeared in the publication *Fair-Play, Hong Kong*; Carlson's paper, "The Wu-shih-shan Incident of 1878," in *Festschrift for Frederick B. Artz* (Durham, NC: Duke University Press, 1964).

22   *Stewart was in charge of the project*: The Reverend Robert Stewart, letters to the CMS board, September 6 and 14, 1878, from the Australian National University online database for *The Flower Mountain Murders*, compiled by Ian Welch, part II, 185–92, https://digitalcollections.anu.edu.au/handle/1885/7273.

CHAPTER 2: DOCTOR

After the death of my great-grandmother, Zhan Aimei, the magazine for the Fujian Diocese of the Anglican Church ran a brief obituary, *CHSKH Fukien Diocese Monthly* 10, no. 4 (April 15, 1943): 12–14. I used that to retrace her life.

She met her future husband in Funing (known today as Xiapu). The most detailed description of missionary life in that walled city was found in Elsie Marshall, *For His Sake: A Record of the Life Consecrated to God and Devoted to China* (Oxford: Religious Tract Society, 1896). Marshall, one of the eleven missionaries and children killed in Gutian in 1895, studied Chinese in 1893 in Funing.

To further re-create the world of my great-grandparents, I reviewed the annual letters to the London-based Church Missionary Society from twenty-nine missionaries and one Chinese cleric stationed in the Fujian cities where they lived, including Mary Isabella Bennett, Funing, 1902; Maria Dechal Boileau, Funing, 1890–1894; Janet Clarke, Funing, 1894–1895; Jemima Clarke, Funing, 1894–1904; Rosamond Clemson, Funing, 1896–1899; Hugh Mortimer Eyton-Jones, Funing, 1891–1896; Augusta Frederica Forge, Hinghua, 1899–1902; Florence Annie Forge, Hinghua, 1903; Emma Sophie Goldie, Funing, 1888–1891; Anna Louisa Greer, Funing, 1899–1900; Gertrude Maude Harmar, Funing, 1899–1901; John Hind, Funing, 1903–1904; Marcus Mackenzie, Funing, 1898–1902; John Martin, Funing, 1886–1890; Isabella Mears, Funing, 1891–1893; William Pope Mears, 1891–1893; Sydney James Nightingale, Hinghua and Sieng-iu, 1899–1904; W. S. Pakenham-Walsh, Fuh-kien, 1901–1904; Kathleen Power, Funing, 1892; John Riggs, Funing, 1889; Leonard Star, Funing, 1898–1899; Charles Shaw, Hinghua, 1894–1901; Thomas de Clare Studdert, Funing, 1898–1903; Mary Synge, Funing, 1899–1902; Samuel Synge, Funing, 1897–1903; Birdwood Van Someren Taylor, Funing and Hinghua, 1890–1903; Christiana Van Someren Taylor, Funing and Hinghua, 1893; Edith Marian Thomas, Funing, 1897–1900; Ting Chung-seng, Sieng-iu, 1903; and W. S. Walsh, Funing, 1898.

On the work of Fujian missionaries from Dublin University, I also consulted: R. M. Gwynn, E. M. Norton, and R. W. Simpson, *"T.C.D." in China: A History of the Dublin University Fukien Mission, 1885–1935* (Dublin: Church of Ireland, 1936); Project Canterbury, *A History of the Dublin University Fuh-kien Mission, 1887–1911* (Dublin: Hodges, Figgis, 1911).

27   *The stone bridge*: Robert Nield, *The China Coast: Trade and the First Treaty Ports* (Hong Kong: Joint Publishing (H.K.), 2010), 149–73.

28   *The cook enrolled his son*: Multiple interviews with his granddaughter Martha Sun, 1980 to present.

28   *He selected the cook's son*: Y. Y. Huang, *Streams of Living Water* (Singapore: Diocese of Singapore, 1972) 101–3. Also see Chinese People's Political Consultative Conference, Culture and History Committee, *Xiapu Cultural and Historical Materials*, "A Promoter of Western Medicine in Xiapu: Mr. Taylor," no. 8, 104–6.

28   *To reach Funing*: Church Missionary Review, *The Dublin University Mission in China*, vol. 59 (July 1906).

29   *The deacon immediately dismissed*: Taylor defended his medical missionary work in "Twenty Years' Experience in the Training and Employment of Medical Students," *China Medical Journal*, Shanghai, Oct. 1901. Taylor and his wife, Christiana, regularly reported on their work in CMS publications, including *Medical Missionary Quarterly*, 1892–1895, and *Mercy & Truth*, 1896–1899.

30   *"We were thought to be spies"*: Taylor recounts this in *Medical Missionary Quarterly* in 1892, which reprinted his "Paper #2."

30   *a military officer asked him for help*: Eugene Stock, *The Story of the Fuh-kien Mission of the Church Missionary Society* (London: Seeley, Jackson & Halliday, 1890), 307–9. The treatment of addicts was discussed in Donald MacInnis, *China Chronicles from a Lost Time: The Min River Journals* (Norwalk, CT: Eastbridge, 2009), and Kathleen L. Lodwick, *Crusaders against Opium: Protestant Missionaries in China 1874–1917* (Lexington: University Press of Kentucky, 2009).

31   *two out of three patients were addicts*: Taylor made multiple references to the prevalence of opium addicts among his patients in annual letters. It was also referenced in Gwynn et al., *"T.C.D." in China*, 31.

31   *Another British cleric in Funing*: Rev. Hugh M. Eyton-Jones, annual letter to CMS, December 6, 1895.

35   *Elsie tried not to laugh*: Marshall, *For His Sake*, 54.

35   *the nearly blind woman*: Rev. Dr. S. Synge, annual letter to CMS, December 17, 1901.

35   *felt like a barn*: Marshall, *For His Sake*, 45.

37   *the world opened up inside the classroom*: Descriptions of students were gleaned from the annual letters of teachers, including Rosamond Clemson, Janet Clarke, and Edith Thomas.

38   *celebrated with a banquet*: Marshall, *For His Sake*, 61–62.

38   *A young English lady*: Marshall, *For His Sake*, 39–41.

CHAPTER 3: FIRSTBORN

39   *On a Monday morning*: W. S. Pakenham-Walsh, *Twenty Years in China* (Cambridge: W. Heffer & Sons, 1935), 40–51. Also see W. S. Pakenham-Walsh, "The Reform Movement in China" (London: Operative Jewish Converts' Institution, 1911), in which he describes the mood in the country from 1900 to 1910.

41 *the Anglican mission was "half asleep"*: W. S. Pakenham-Walsh, annual letter to CMS, January 13, 1908.

41 *"you will never get ten boys"*: Pakenham-Walsh, *Twenty Years in China*, 45–47.

42 *voluntary incarceration*: R. S. Maclay, *Life among the Chinese* (New York: Carlton & Porter, 1861), 145–46. Additionally, Ralph Gold of the YMCA photographed the vacant examination center in Fuzhou.

45 *Autumn winds brought rumors*: Many missionaries described the battle between Qing and revolutionary forces. Among them are the American physician H. N. Kinnear, who provided a detailed account in his annual report for the Foochow Missionary Hospital for the year ending January 31, 1912. Rev. Pakenham-Walsh also published an unsigned diary of the week of fighting in the English-language newspaper, the *Foochow Daily Echo*. While the account ran without his name, the newspaper clip was sent to the CMS office in London, and both Pakenham-Walsh and a colleague told the home office that he had penned the unsigned newspaper account.

47 *lop off the braids*: Missionaries in Fuzhou described the rush of men to cut off queues in 1911, including Edith Couche in the unpublished manuscript *The Garden of the Lord: The history of the C.E.Z.M.S. Work in China* (no date).

50 *On the third Sunday in February*: Eleanor Harrison, a missionary with the Church of England Zenana Missionary Society, described the ceremony for the consecration of the Trinity College chapel in an undated letter from 1913. She made particular note of seeing the son of Dr. Lin, adding that he was bound for the ministry.

CHAPTER 4: LIGHT AND TRUTH

The main sources for this chapter were Mary Lamberton, *St. John's University, 1879–1951* (New York: United Board for Christian Colleges in China, 1955); Andrew Y. Y. Tsu, *Friend of Fishermen* (Ambler, PA: Trinity Press, n.d.); F. L. Hawks Pott, *A Short History of Shanghai* (Shanghai: Kelly & Walsh, 1928); issues of *St. John's Echo*, 1915–1917; and catalogues for St. John's University, 1915–1920.

53 *Inside Alumni Hall*: "St. John's University: Closing Exercises," *North China Herald*, February 8, 1913, 379–80.

54 *In September 1915*: W. S. Pakenham-Walsh, *Twenty Years in China* (Cambridge: W. Heffer & Sons, 1935), 114.

55   *By 1915, the foreign population*: Samuel Couling, *Encyclopedia Sinica* (London: Amen Corner, E.C., 1917), 508.

59   *He was a senior theology student*: Lin Yutang reflected on his years at St. John's University in *From Pagan to Christian* (Cleveland and New York: World, 1959), 35.

60   *Only three students competed*: The winning speech of Lin Yutang and a description of the oratory contest were published in the *St. John's Echo* in January 1916.

62   *the fifth anniversary*: November 1916 issue of the *St. John's Echo* and the *North China Herald*, October 14, 1916, 84–85.

64   *Watching the students waving from the deck*: Lin Pu-chi, "The Departure of Chinese Students for America," *St. John's Echo*, September 1916, 22–23.

CHAPTER 5: A MODERN MAN

For capturing the world of Chinese students abroad, I relied on coverage in *Chinese Students' Monthly (CSM)*, December 1918–June 1920.

67   *Heavy smoke poured*: A description of ship life on the SS *Nanking* came from three sources: Stacey Bieler, *"Patriots" or "Traitors": A History of American-Educated Chinese Students* (Armonk, NY: Sharpe, 2004); Xu Zhimo, "To My Family and Friends upon My Departure for the U.S. on August 14, 7th Year of the Republic," in *The Complete Works of Xu Zhimo*, ed. Jiang Fucong and Liang Shiqiu (Taipei: Zhuanji Wenxue Chubanshe, 1969), 6:99–102; and Ezra Caryl and Grace Brownell letters, September and October 1918 (William L. Clements Library, University of Michigan).

67   *veritable ship of scholars*: Cross-reference of the ship manifest and *Who's Who of the Chinese Students in America* (Berkeley, CA: Lederer, Street & Zeus, 1921).

69   *he began to write a story*: Lin Pu-chi, "The Comedy of Ignorance," *Chinese Students' Monthly*, June 1919, 488–94.

70   *Lin Pu-chi caught the Pacific Limited*: All information in this chapter on train lines and timetables was provided by the National Railway Historical Society.

71   *In late August a deadly influenza virus*: *Encyclopedia of Greater Philadelphia*, s.v. "Influenza ('Spanish Flu' Pandemic, 1918–19," by Thomas Wirth, http://philadelphiaencyclopedia.org/archive/influenza-spanish-flu-pandemic-1918-19/; 1918 Influenza Epidemic Records, http://www.phmc.pa.gov/Archives/Research-Online/Pages/1918-Influenza-Epidemic; *Philadelphia Evening Public Ledger*, September 18–November 11, 1918.

72   *Lin Pu-chi officially became a student*: Records of the Divinity School of the Protestant Episcopal Church in Philadelphia, held at the Episcopal Divinity School in Cambridge, MA.

73   *At the Friday night gathering*: Issues of *Chinese Students' Monthly* magazine, 1918–1920, provided information on activities at the University of Pennsylvania as well as the national alliance.

74   *It was a precarious time*: Lin Pu-chi expressed his views on the political situation in China in "A Dissertation on Modern Changes," *St. John's Echo*, October 1916, 19–23, and in his short story, "The Comedy of Ignorance."

76   *Troy was a small enough city*: Coverage of the conference was included in *Chinese Students' Monthly*, November 1919. Daily reporting on the event was also provided by the *Troy Times*, September 6–15, 1919.

CHAPTER 6: SECOND DAUGHTER

Interviews: Martha Sun, Paul, James, and Tim Lin.

81   *Even with her door shut*: Lin Heping acknowledged the possibility of missing the wedding of her daughter Ni Guizhen in her testimonial, *An Object of Grace and Love*, written in 1943 and translated by Hilda Holms with additional revisions by Martha Sun.

82   *Lin Heping was not born into a high station*: Lin Heping, *An Object of Grace and Love*.

82   *Lin Heping left for Shanghai*: Information on the McTyeire School was found in the following: *McTyeirian Yearbook*, 1917; McTyeire High School catalogue, 1917; Women's Foreign Missionary Society, *Annual Report*, 1920, 259–62; and Heidi A. Ross, "'Cradle of Female Talent': The McTyeire Home and School for Girls, 1892–1937," in *Christianity in China: From the Eighteenth Century to the Present*, ed. Daniel H. Bays (Stanford, CA: Stanford University Press, 1996), 209–27.

82   *no girls with bound feet*: Julia Bonafield's letter on the practice of foot binding appeared in the *Chinese Recorder*, vol. 25 (Shanghai: Presbyterian Mission Press, 1894), 497.

82   *The physician Xu Jinhong*: Ryan Dunch, *Fuzhou Protestants and the Making of Modern China, 1857–1927* (New Haven, CT: Yale University Press, 2001), 45–46.

85   *The visitor's name was Yu Cidu*: Silas Wu, *Dora Yu and Christian Revival in 20th Century China* (Boston: Pishon River, 2002), 171–80.

86   *The ranks of Chinese Protestants*: Daniel Bays, *A New History of Christianity in China* (Malden, MA: Wiley-Blackwell, 2012), 94.

87   *The experience left the seventeen-year-old tormented*: Angus Kinnear, *Against the Tide: The Unforgettable Story Behind Watchman Nee*, rev. ed. (Eastbourne, England: Kingsway, 2005), 47–55.

CHAPTER 7: RUNNING DOG

To understand the anti-Christian and antiforeign movement in Fuzhou and China, I consulted Jonathan Tien-en Chao, "The Chinese Indigenous Church Movement, 1919–1927: A Protestant Response to the Anti-Christian Movements in Modern China" (PhD diss., University of Pennsylvania, 1986); Ryan Dunch, *Fuzhou Protestants and the Making of Modern China 1857–1927* (New Haven, CT: Yale University Press, 2001); Xi Lian, *Redeemed by Fire: The Rise of Popular Christianity in Modern China* (New Haven, CT: Yale University Press, 2010); and "The Anti-Christian Movement" (pamphlet, Young Men's and Young Women's Christian Associations of China, Shanghai, 1925).

91   *The procession was about to begin*: A. W. R. Norton, "Impressions of the Laying of the Foundation Stone of the Cathedral," *Fukien Diocesan Magazine*, 1924, 7–9.

92   *Even among Chinese Christians*: Angus Kinnear, *Against the Tide: The Unforgettable Story Behind Watchman Nee*, rev. ed. (Eastbourne, England: Kingsway, 2005), 110–23.

94   *His barbed opinions*: "The Chinese Christian Answers the Missionaries' Questions," *Chinese Recorder*, January 1927, 23–27.

94   *Another time, he challenged*: Lin Pu-chi, letter to the editor, *Chinese Recorder*, June 1924, 407–9.

94   *In Fuzhou, as many as ten thousand*: US Consul Ernest Price, report, September 13, 1925.

95   *On August 30, 1925*: Lin Pu-chi, letter to Rev. W. P. W. Williams, August 30, 1925; W. P. W. Williams, letters to CMS, September 4 and November 26, 1925.

96   *The Northern Expedition, as it was known, faced little resistance*: Accounts of the situation in Fuzhou were taken from US Consul Ernest Price, "Political Conditions, Fukien Province, China, January 1926" (annual report, 1926); *Foochow Messenger*, January 1927, 16–21; *Missionary Herald* (Boston), March 1927, 100–105; and Bishop John Hind, letters to CMS, January 7 and 11, 1927.

98   *What they saw*: A reconstruction of the orphanage attack was based on: US Consul Ernest Price, letter to Americans in Fuzhou, Jan. 15, 1927; report to legation, January/February 1927; "Foochow Mob Outrages," *North China Daily News*, January 26, 1927; Alice and Neil Lewis, letter, September 5, 1927; Bishop Hind, letter to CMS, January 18 and 21, 1927; John Gowdy, letter to Eric North, Fukien Christian University, Board of Trustees, January 21, 1927; "What Happened at Foochow," *Chinese Recorder*, April 1927, 288–90; and Foochow Consul G. S. Moss, letter to Sir Austen Chamberlain, political report for March quarter, 1927.

98   *It was a conical stone structure*: W. S. Pakenham-Walsh, in *Twenty Years in China* (Cambridge: W. Heffer & Sons, 1935), describes a baby tower in Fuzhou, infanticide, and the Roman Catholic orphanage, 95–97. Also see W. Somerset Maugham, *On a Chinese Screen* (London: Heinemann, 1922), 166–70.

99   *The following Sunday*: In a letter dated January 17, 1927, and reprinted in the *Missionary Herald* in April 1927, Betty Cushman described the attack and her guests, Lin Pu-chi and his wife. A description of events that day was also reported by the US Consul Ernest B. Price in his report for January/February 1927.

102   *Its American president*: John Gowdy, letters to Trustees of Fukien Christian University, December 23 and 29, 1926.

102   *At the start of 1927*: Roderick Scott, "A Great Minority Victory—Overturnings in China," *Christian Education*, Nov. 1927, 136–44; Fukien Christian University, "News Sheet for Alumni and Friends," Dec. 1, 1927.

103   *Lin Pu-chi still enjoyed*: In a letter to his mentor W. S. Pakenham-Walsh, Lin Pu-chi recounted the episode, his reaction, and praying to St. Stephen. Pakenham-Walsh described the attack in his memoir, *Twenty Years in China*, 118–25. Lin Pu-chi also was quoted in the *Church Missionary Outlook*, November 1928, describing his internal thoughts: "I just prayed for myself that I might be brave, and for them that their eyes might be opened."

    To re-create the scene, I relied on other accounts of the incident, including John Goly, letter to FCU trustees, March 30, 1927; Bishop John Hind, annual letter to CMS, 1927–1928; Ida Belle Lewis Main, unpublished memoir; *Chinese Recorder*, May–June 1927, 390; British Consul, Foochow, April 6, 1927; *Church Missionary Outlook*, Rev. E. M. Norton, "Making Men: The Work of a Christian School in China," November 1928, 225–27; and Reuters, "Communist Fury at Foochow," *North China Daily News*, March 28, 1927.

CHAPTER 8: ALMA MATER

Interviews: Martha Sun, James Lin.

For the history of Trinity College Fuzhou, I consulted R. M. Gwynn, E. M. Norton, and B. W. Simpson, *"T.C.D." in China: A History of the Dublin University Fukien Mission 1885–1935* (Dublin: Church of Ireland, 1936); Y. Y. Huang, *While Drinking Water Remember Its Source: A History of Trinity College, Foochow and Anglican High School* (Singapore: Singapore Malaya, 1971); and W. S. Pakenham-Walsh, *Twenty Years in China* (Cambridge: W. Heffer & Sons, 1935).

107 *The clock on the dormitory wall*: Hind described the fire, the presumption of foul play, and the impact on the mission in a January 4, 1928, letter to Joseph G. Barclay, general secretary of East Asia for the Church Missionary Society in London.

108 *Bishop Hind suspected*: Bishop Hind's diocesan bulletins, November 21 and December 6, 1927; Rev. E. M. Norton, "The Present Situation in the Christian Schools of Foochow," *Fukien Diocesan Magazine,* January 1928, 9–12.

108 *But internally, the school struggled*: Bishop Hind, letter to CMS general secretary Barclay, May 9, 1927.

109 *Before the fall term started*: Bishop Hind's letter to members of the diocese, November 28, 1927.

109 *After the meeting*: The date of the delivery of the registration letter was mentioned in Gwynn et al., *"T.C.D" in China,* 64.

110 *Every day at 11:30 a.m.*: *Report of the Chung Hua Sheng Kung Hui Fukien Church Day Schools,* 1928, 8–9.

111 *He respectfully declined*: Rev. E. M. Norton refers to "canonical obedience" in *Church Missionary Society Annual Report 1929–30, Fukien Mission,* 371–72.

112 *Not everyone in the Trinity community*: Norton, *Annual Report,* 372; Gwynn et al., *"T.C.D" in China,* 64–65.

113 *One by one, teachers in the Middle School*: Norton, *Annual Report,* 372.

113 *One night in May*: Additional descriptions of this episode were found in Rev. W. P. W. Williams, "Standing Committee Meeting, Fukien Diocesan Synod, Review of the Year July 1928–1929"; and Fujian CPPCC Cultural and Historical Records Committee, ed., *A Selection of Cultural and Historical Records,* Vol. 5, *Christianity and Catholicism* (Fuzhou: Fujian People's Publishing House, 2003).

115 *They acted decisively*: Lin Pu-chi, letter to Joseph G. Barclay, Church Missionary Society, London, April 25, 1930. Includes "Report of Trinity College for the First Half of 1929."

115 *"Things went on without a hitch"*: "Report of Trinity College for the Second Half of 1929."

116 *In his article for the missionary magazine*: Lin Pu-chi, "Four Cardinal Principles for the Development of the Chinese Church," *Chinese Recorder*, June 1924, 353–60, and July 1924, 445–50. (Note: His name is misspelled as Liu Pu-chi.)

116 *in his first three terms*: Lin Pu-chi, letter to Joseph G. Barclay, Church Missionary Society, November 13, 1930.

116 *In the spring of 1930*: Lin Pu-chi, letter to Joseph G. Barclay, November 13, 1930.

118 *Lin Pu-chi told the bishop that he would seek new work*: Bishop Hind, letter to Joseph G. Barclay, Church Missionary Society, January 2, 1931.

CHAPTER 9: WATCHMAN NEE

Interviews: Martha Sun, James, Tim, and Paul Lin.

121 *The rector rushed from room to room*: St. Peter's Monthly, March–October, 1932.

122 *At 11:10 p.m.*: North China Daily News, January 29, 1932. Also see Stella Dong, *Shanghai: The Rise and Fall of a Decadent City* (New York: HarperCollins, 2000), 213–17.

122 *When he arrived on March 5*: St. Peter's Monthly, March 1932. Also see American Church Mission, *District of Shanghai Newsletter*, March 1932, 3–12.

124 *like few other churches in China*: Lin Pu-chi, "A History of St. Peter's Parish," in *20th Anniversary Volume St. Peter's Church*, September 1933, 3–12. Also see Philip L. Wickeri, *Reconstructing Christianity in China: K. H. Ting and the Chinese Church* (Maryknoll, NY: Orbis), 24–25.

124 *The previous rector*: Duan Qi, "Christianity and Chinese Nationalism: St. Peter's Church in Shanghai during the War against Japan" (paper presented at a conference sponsored by the Hong Kong Sheng Kung Hui, Hong Kong, June 7–9, 2012).

124 *Lin Pu-chi's indignation*: Description of Haskell Road in Larry Fein, "Shanghai Roots: A City of 'Gones' 49 Years Later," *Chicago Tribune*, November 9, 1986.

125 *It was October 9*: Lin Pu-chi, "National Day in the National Disaster," *St. Peter's Monthly*, October 1932, 1–2. Also see Duan, "Christianity and Chinese Nationalism."

126 *The Lin family had joined*: All About Shanghai and Environs (Shanghai: University Press, 1934–1935), 33–34.

126   *The Public School for Chinese Boys was*: Shanghai Municipal Council, *Report and Budget*, years 1931, 1933, 1935, 1937, 1938, 1939, 1940.

128   *Watchman Nee once complained*: Watchman Nee, letter to Norman Baker of the China Inland Mission, September 19, 1938 (private collection of Angus Kinnear).

128   *In 1933, Watchman Nee*: Angus Kinnear, *Against the Tide: The Unforgettable Story Behind Watchman Nee*, rev. ed. (Eastbourne, England: Kingsway, 2005), 146–52.

129   *Watchman Nee once regaled the family*: Kinnear, *Against the Tide*, 162–67.

129   *the population of Shanghai*: American Church Mission, *District of Shanghai Newsletter*, January 7, 1934, 2–3.

131   *Outsiders called their group*: Kinnear, *Against the Tide*, 140–41.

132   *On Sunday morning*: Kinnear, *Against the Tide*, 200–201.

133   *The Bible, he told them*: Watchman Nee, *Normal Christian Faith* (Anaheim, CA: Living Stream Ministry, 1994), 27–28.

134   *This was more than a family squabble*: *Report of the Ninth Meeting of the General Synod of the Chung Hua Sheng Kung Hui*, April 17–25, 1937, 31.

135   *The US Navy*: "Rising Storm—The Imperial Japanese Navy and China 1931–1941," Imperial Japanese Navy Page, accessed March 24, 2016, http://www.combinedfleet.com/Chefoo.

CHAPTER 10: ISLAND OF SHANGHAI

137   *As her teenage sons looked on*: James Lin, letter to Paul Lin, April 8, 2011.

137   *helping the refugees who had flooded Shanghai*: Lin Pu-chi, "Christmas This Year," *Chinese Churchman* 30, no. 20 (1937).

138   *To the rest of China*: Christian Henriot, "Shanghai and the Experience of War: The Fate of Refugees," *European Journal of East Asian Studies* 5, no. 2 (2006): 220–21.

138   *Any Chinese resident*: Stella Dong, *Shanghai: The Rise and Fall of a Decadent City* (New York: HarperCollins, 2000), 257.

138   *During the three-month Battle*: Frederic Wakeman Jr., *The Shanghai Badlands: Wartime Terrorism and Urban Crime, 1937–1941* (New York: Cambridge University Press, 2002), 6.

139   *Before dawn*: Shanghai Municipal Council, *Report for the Year 1941 and Budget for the Year 1942* (Shanghai: North-China Daily News & Herald, 1941), 49.

139   *It galled students*: Mary Lamberton, *St. John's University, 1879–1951* (New York: United Board for Christian Colleges in China, 1955), 184.

140   *The American physician*: Helen McCracken Fulcher, *Mission to Shanghai: The Life of Medical Service of Dr. Josiah C. McCracken* (New London, NH: Tiffin, 1995), 197.

141   *The summons that foreigners*: Donald Roberts, "Our Pootong Camp Experience," Archives of the Episcopal Church, December 10, 1943.

142   *This presented a crisis for Lin Pu-chi*: The circumstances of Lin Pu-chi's employment at the China Biological and Chemical Laboratories from 1944 through 1945 were included in a statement by him on April 12, 1969.

142   *Ni Guizhen had a younger brother*: Interviews with Martha Sun, James Lin, and Paul Lin.

142   *When Watchman Nee became involved*: Angus Kinnear, *Against the Tide: The Unforgettable Story Behind Watchman Nee*, rev. ed. (Eastbourne, England: Kingsway, 2005), 211–21.

144   *"I envy you"*: Kinnear, *Against the Tide*, 214.

145   *In one of his first articles*: Lin Pu-chi, "Pleading for Church Preachers," *Chinese Churchman* 35, no. 5 (1946): 3–4.

146   *St. John's medical school had a sterling reputation*: Kaiyi Chen, *Seeds from the West: St. John's Medical School, Shanghai, 1880–1952* (Chicago: Imprint, 2001), 57–75.

147   *By 1947*: Events are based on Kinnear, *Against the Tide*, 220–36; James Chen, *Meet Brother Nee* (Kowloon, Hong Kong: Christian, 1976), 56–68; and Witness Lee, *Watchman Nee: A Seer of the Divine Revelation in the Present* Age (Anaheim, CA: Living Stream Ministry, 1997), 316–21.

148   *He compared his foray*: Chen, *Meet Brother Nee*, 64.

148   *a large property*: Lee, *Watchman Nee*, 318.

149   *"Brother," Watchman Nee explained*: Lee, *Watchman Nee*, 320.

CHAPTER 11: BUND TO BOARDWALK

Interviews: Paul and James Lin.

A description of the scene at St. John's University on the eve of the Communist victory was gleaned from the letters of Frances and Donald Roberts, who both worked at the university, to their children in the United States, which are held at the Yale Divinity School missionary archives. The letters were written in 1949 and dated May 15 and 20; June 2, 4, 6, and 10; and July 17 and 18.

CHAPTER 12: AMERICAN WOLVES

Interviews: Martha Sun, Paul and James Lin.

165   *On the eve of the Communist victory*: Lin Pu-chi, "A Christian's Proper Attitude to the Current Situation," *Chinese Churchman* 38, no. 1 (1949): 1–3.

166   *But the bishop felt bound by duty*: Y. Y. Tsu, *Friend of Fishermen* (Ambler, PA: Trinity, 1953), 156.

166   *Lin Pu-chi made his thoughts known*: See Wallace C. Merwin and Francis P. Jones in *Documents of the Three Self Movement: Source Materials for the Study of the Protestant Church in Communist China* (New York: National Council of the Churches of Christ in the USA, 1963). Also see both Daniel Bays, *A New History of Christianity in China* (Oxford: Wiley-Blackwell, 2012) and Philip Wickeri, *Seeking the Common Ground: Protestant Christianity, the Three-Self Movement, and China's United Front* (Eugene, OR: Wipf and Stock, 1988), who discuss the importance of the "Message from Chinese Christians to Mission Boards Abroad."

168   *At the Sheng Kung Hui national office*: Tsu, *Friend of Fishermen*, 149.

168   *he had made the wrong decision*: Tsu, *Friend of Fishermen*, 157–60.

168   *Premier Zhou had warned*: Taken from "Notes on Report of Conference with Premier Zhou Enlai regarding the Christian Church in China," July 27, 1950, Bishop Y. Y. Tsu, China historical correspondence, Archives of the Episcopal Church, Austin, Texas.

169   *Zhou summoned*: "Delegates in the Whole Body of Christian Conference Accuses Agents of Imperialistic Crimes. Severely Blames Frank Price and Others of Being Tools of Imperialistic Aggression. Unanimously Begs the People's Government to Give Severe Punishment," *Ta Kung Pao*, Hong Kong, April 24, 1951. Taken from New China Agency report from Beijing, April 22.

170   *It fell upon his colleague*: Statement of Bishop Chen, "I Accuse Y. Y. Tsu, Running Dog of American Imperialism," included in personal papers of Y. Y. Tsu, Archives of the Episcopal Church, Austin, Texas.

171   *Confusion, dissension, and internal strife*: Excerpt from David W. K. Au, letter to Y. Y. Tsu, October 18, 1951.

171   *process of undoing the past*: Chen Chonggui, "Why Do We Denounce?" *Tian Feng Weekly* 11, no. 22, June 9, 1951, 1–3. Also see Wu Yaozang, "A Summary of the Christian Three Self Reforming Movement in the Past Eight Months," *Chinese Churchman* 40, no. 6 (June 15, 1951): 4–6.

172 *His editorial in the June 1951 issue*: Lin Pu-chi, "Talking Earnestly with the Clergymen of Our Church in the Three Self Movement," *Chinese Churchman* 40, no. 6 (June 15, 1951): 8–10.

172 *The Church of Our Savior*: Lin Pu-chi, "Accusing the American Lackey and Church Degenerate Zhu Youyu," *Tianfeng*, 1951, 9. Also, the Hong Kong–based *Ta Kung Pao* ran an account of the denunciation session on August 5, 1951, under the headline, "Announcement of the Shanghai Episcopal Church Leaves the World Council of Churches Forever." A translation was included in the personal papers of Bishop Y. Y. Tsu.

CHAPTER 13: MISSING

Interviews: Emma and Tim Lin, Martha Sun, Basil Sun.

Lin Pu-chi described scenes in the family home in his monthly letters to his son in Philadelphia, Paul M. Lin.

The following sources provided information on the arrest, denunciation, indictment, and trial of Watchman Nee.

Books

Lily Hsu with Dana Roberts, *My Unforgettable Memories: Watchman Nee & Shanghai Local Church* (Longwood, FL: Xulon Press, 2013).

Angus Kinnear, *Against the Tide: The Unforgettable Story Behind Watchman Nee*, rev. ed. (Eastbourne, England: Kingsway, 2005).

Xi Lian, *Redeemed by Fire* (New Haven, CT: Yale University Press, 2010).

Newman Sze, *The Martyrdom of Watchman Nee* (Culver City, CA: Testimony, 1997).

Silas H. Wu, *Shell Breaking and Soaring: The Imprisonment and Transformation of Watchman Nee* (Boston: Pishon River, 2004).

Articles

Joseph Tse-hei Lee, "Watchman Nee and the Little Flock Movement in Maoist China," *Church History: Studies in Christianity in China* 74, no. 1 (March 2005): 68–96.

Jialin Liang, "Investigation into Ni Tuosheng's Guilt," *Jian Dao Magazine*, no. 17, January 2002.

Fuk-tsang Ying, "Watchman Nee and the Three-Self Reforming Movement," in *Anti-Imperialism, Patriotism and the Spiritual Man: A Study on Watchman Nee and the "Little Flock"* (Hong Kong: Christian Study Centre on Chinese Religion and Culture, 2005), 31–98.

178   *The Little Flock had more than seventy thousand members*: Estimates vary. According to Lee, in 1955, the government put the numbers at 80,000 members at 870 locations

179   *He gave a series of talks*: The series of talks—titled "How Did I Turn Around?"—were reprinted in Lily Hsu's memoir, *My Unforgettable Memories*, 304–35.

180   *in August 1955 when PSB agents*: The secret document was a primary source for Joseph Lee in "Watchman Nee and the Little Flock Movement in Maoist China."

182   *"God opened my eyes"*: Hsu quotes Ni Guizhen in her memoir, 118.

182   *On February 1*: Coverage in *Liberation Daily*, February 1, 2, 3, 4, and 8, 1956.

183   *Nine days after the Tian Chan denunciation*: Hsu, *My Unforgettable Memories*, 122–30. In addition, the exhibition was described by relatives of Watchman Nee, including Tim Lin, Basil Sun, and Xu Fengxian.

185   *One of the Little Flock observers*: Hsu, *My Unforgettable Memories*, 135–37.

CHAPTER 14: PRELUDE

Interviews: Julia Tsien, Martha Sun.

188   *one of the "Eight Immortals"*: The immortals were described by Lin Pu-chi in an article published in 1918 and written under his Christian name with a regional spelling of his last name. Peter C. Ling, "The Eight Immortals of the Taoist Religion," *Journal of the North-China Branch of the Royal Asiatic Society* (1918): 53–75.

192   *When Watchman Nee was escorted into the room*: The sister-in-law of Watchman Nee, Xu Fengxian, described the meeting in an interview in Shanghai on June 17, 2003, that was shared with the author. Conditions inside the jail were also described by Angus Kinnear, *Against the Tide: The Unforgettable Story Behind Watchman Nee*, rev. ed. (Eastbourne, England: Kingsway, 2005), 284–90.

193   *All she had was family and Ni Guizhen*: Silas H. Wu, *Shell Breaking and Soaring: The Imprisonment and Transformation of Watchman Nee* (Boston: Pishon River, 2004), 73–81.

193   *Inside cell block 3*: Wu, *Shell Breaking and Soaring*, 69–72.

CHAPTER 15: LANE 170

202   *The summer of 1966*: To re-create the attacks on families in Lane 170, I interviewed Martha Sun and her daughters, Terri Sun and Julia Tsien; Tim Lin, his wife, Emma, and children, Kaikai Lin and Lin Yu; Sun Guoguang, the brother-in-law of Martha Sun; and Boling Dong, a resident of Lane 170.

203   *The campaign quickly turned ugly*: Song Yongyi, "Chronology of Mass Killings during the Chinese Cultural Revolution (1966–1976)," *Online Encyclopedia of Mass Violence*, published online August 25, 2011, http://www.massviolence.org/Chronology-of-Mass-Killings-during-the-Chinese-Cultural. Also see Guo Jian, Yongyi Song, and Yuan Zhou, *The A to Z of the Chinese Cultural Revolution* (Lanham, MD: Scarecrow, 2009).

203   *With crimson armbands*: Description of street scenes in Shanghai were found in *Far Eastern Economic Review*, September 8, 1966, 443–45.

209   *During the Red Terror*: Statistics were collected by Elizabeth J. Perry and Li Xun, *Proletarian Power: Shanghai in the Cultural Revolution* (Boulder, CO: Westview, 1997).

211   *The Red Guards even had a song*: Lyrics to all songs mentioned in this chapter were taken from Lu Xing, *Rhetoric of the Chinese Cultural Revolution: The Impact on Chinese Thought, Culture and Communications* (Columbia: University of South Carolina Press, 2004).

CHAPTER 16: YELLOW MUSIC

Interviews: Julia Tsien and Basil Sun.

215   *the middle school for the Shanghai Conservatory*: For an understanding of classical music in China, I relied on Sheila Melvin and Cai Jindong, *Rhapsody in Red: How Western Classical Music Became Chinese* (New York: Algora, 2004).

CHAPTER 17: BAREFOOT DOCTOR

Interviews: Terri Sun, Martha Sun, and Julia Tsien.

CHAPTER 18: PASSAGES

Interviews: Terri Sun, Martha Sun, Julia Tsien, and Emma Lin.

239   *Charity was singled out*: Angus Kinnear, *Against the Tide: The Unforgettable Story Behind Watchman Nee*, rev. ed. (Eastbourne, England: Kingsway, 2005), 281–84.

240   *on a rutted road*: Kinnear, *Against the Tide*, 295–98.

CHAPTER 21: FAITH

262   *We were both monumentally wrong*: Fenggang Yang, "When Will China Become the World's Largest Christian Country?" *Slate*, sponsored by the John Templeton Foundation, December 2, 2014.

262   *The official population of Protestants and Catholics*: I consulted the Pew Research Center's Forum on Religion and Public Life report on "Global Christianity," December 2011; and a Council on Foreign Relations background paper on "Religion in China," June 10, 2015.

263   *The cross campaign made headlines*: Ian Johnson, "Church-State Clash in China Coalesces around a Toppled Spire," *New York Times*, May 29, 2014; Tom Phillips, "China's Christians Protest 'Evil' Communist Campaign to Tear Down Crosses," *Guardian*, July 27, 2015; Ishaan Tharoor, "Why China Is Removing Crosses from Hundreds of Churches," *Washington Post*, May 14, 2015; and "Render unto Caesar," *Economist*, July 25, 2015.

267   *Brother Lin was convicted four times*: Brother Lin documented his life in his unsigned testimonial, *God's Grace Is Great* (Taipei City: Taiwan Gospel Bookroom, February 2004).

Bibliography

BOOKS

Aikman, David. *Jesus in Beijing: How Christianity Is Transforming China and Changing the Global Balance of Power*. Washington, DC: Regnery, 2003.

Ballard, J. G. *Miracles of Life*. London: Fourth Estate, 2008.

Banks, Robert, and Linda Banks. *View from the Faraway Pagoda*. Victoria, Australia: Acorn, 2013.

Bays, Daniel H. *A New History of Christianity in China*. Oxford: Wiley–Blackwell, 2012.

———, ed. *Christianity in China: From the Eighteenth Century to the Present*. Stanford, CA: Stanford University Press, 1996.

Bays, Daniel H., and Ellen Widmer, eds. *China's Christian Colleges: Cross-Cultural Connections, 1900–1950*. Stanford, CA: Stanford University Press, 2009.

Bieler, Stacey. *"Patriots" or "Traitors": A History of American-Educated Chinese Students*. Armonk, NY: Sharpe, 2004.

Blair, Margaret. *Gudao, Lone Islet: The War Years in Shanghai*. Victoria, BC: Trafford, 2008.

Carlson, Ellsworth C. *The Foochow Missionaries, 1847–1880*. Cambridge, MA: Harvard University Press, 1974.

Chen, James. *Meet Brother Nee*. Kowloon, Hong Kong: Christian, 1976.

Chen, Kaiyi. *Seeds from the West: St. John's Medical School, Shanghai, 1880–1952*. Chicago: Imprint, 2001.

Chinese Students' Alliance in the United States of America. *Who's Who of the Chinese Students in America*. Berkeley, CA: Lederer, Street & Zeus, 1921.

Church Missionary Society. *For Christ in Fuh-kien: The Story of the Fuh-kien Mission of the Church Missionary Society*. London: Church Missionary Society, 1904.

Couche, Edith. *The Garden of the Lord, being The History of the C.E.Z.M.S. Work in China*. Records of the Church of England Zenana Missionary Society, Cadbury Research Library Special Collections, University of Birmingham, CEZ/G/EA 2/1V.

Craighill, Marion G. *The Craighills of China*. Ambler, PA: Trinity, 1972.

Dong, Stella. *Shanghai: The Rise and Fall of a Decadent City*. New York: HarperCollins, 2000.

Dunch, Ryan. *Fuzhou Protestants and the Making of a Modern China 1857–1927*. New Haven, CT: Yale University Press, 2001.

Fitzgerald, John, and Frances Slater. *1895 Hwa-Sang Massacre* (self-published compilation of news accounts and missionary records). Raleigh, NC: Lulu, 2007.

———. *Wu Shih Shan Affair* (self-published compilation of trial transcript and newspaper accounts of the trial). Raleigh, NC: Lulu, 2009.

Fulcher, Helen McCracken. *Mission to Shanghai: The Life of Medical Service of Dr. Josiah C. McCracken*. New London, NH: Tiffin Press, 1995.

God's Grace Is Great. Taipei City: Taiwan Gospel Bookroom, 2004.

Gray, G. F. S., and Martha Lund Smalley. *Anglicans in China: A History of the Zhonghua Shenggong Hui*. New Haven, CT: Episcopal China Mission History Project, 1996.

Griggs, Katharine Mary. "The Wonder of the Road, or Bandit & Barbed Wire" (unpublished memoir of 1920–1950 missionary work in Fujian).

Guo, Jian, Yongyi Song, and Yuan Zhou. *The A to Z of the Chinese Cultural Revolution*. Lanham, MD: Scarecrow, 2009.

Gwynn, R. M., E. M. Norton, and B. W. Simpson. *"T.C.D." in China: A History of the Dublin University Fukien Mission 1885–1935*. Dublin: Church of Ireland, 1936.

Hamrin, Carol, ed. *Salt and Light*. 3 vols. Eugene, OR: Pickwick, 2009–2011.

Harrison, Henrietta. *The Missionary's Curse and Other Tales from a Chinese Catholic Village*. Berkeley: University of California Press, 1913.

Hewitt, Gordon. *The Problems of Success: A History of the Church Missionary Society, 1910–1942*. Vol. 2. London: SCM Press, 1971.

Hind, John. *Fukien Memories*. Belfast: James A. Nelson, 1951.

Hook, Marion. *Save Some: C.E.Z.M.S. Work in Fuh-kien*. London: Church of England Zenana Missionary Society, 1900.

Hsu, Lily M. *My Unforgettable Memories: Watchman Nee & Shanghai Local Church*. With Dana Roberts. Maitland, FL: Xulon, 2013.

Huang, Y. Y. *While Drinking Water Remember Its Source: A History of Trinity College, Foochow and Anglican High School*. Singapore: Singapore Malaya Printing and Publishing, 1971.

Huntington, Virginia E. *Along the Great River*. New York: National Council of the Protestant Episcopal Church, 1950.

Johnston, Tess, and Deke Erh. *Hallowed Halls: Protestant Colleges in Old China*. Hong Kong: Old China Hand, 1998.

Kindoff, Jason, and Carol Lee Hamrin, eds. *God and Caesar in China: Policy Implications of Church-State Tensions*. Washington, DC: Brookings, 2004.

Kinnear, Angus. *Against the Tide: The Unforgettable Story Behind Watchman Nee*. Eastbourne, England: Kingsway, 1974.

Lambert, Tony. *China's Christian Millions: The Costly Revival*. London: Monarch, 1999.

Lamberton, Mary. *St. John's University, 1879–1951*. New York: United Board for Christian Colleges in China, 1955.

Lee, Witness. *Watchman Nee: A Seer of the Divine Revelation in the Present Age.* Anaheim, CA: Living Stream Ministry, 1997.

Lewis, Ida Bell. *The Education of Girls in China.* New York: Teachers College, 1919.

Lian, Xi. *Redeemed by Fire: The Rise of Popular Christianity in Modern China.* New Haven, CT: Yale University Press, 2010.

Lin Heping. "An Object of Grace and Love" (unpublished testimony, 1943).

Lin Pu-chi. *History of St. Peter's Parish: XX Anniversary Volume.* Shanghai: St. Peter's Church, 1933.

Lin Yutang. *From Pagan to Christian.* Cleveland: World, 1959.

———. *My Country and My People.* London: Heinemann, 1936.

Lodwick, Kathleen L. *Crusaders against Opium: Protestant Missionaries in China 1874–1917.* Lexington: University Press of Kentucky, 1996.

Lu Xing. *Rhetoric of the Chinese Cultural Revolution: The Impact on Chinese Thought, Culture and Communication.* Columbia: University of South Carolina Press, 2004.

Macfarquhar, Roderick, and Michael Schoenhals. *Mao's Last Revolution.* Cambridge, MA: Belknap, 2006.

MacInnis, Donald. *China Chronicles from a Lost Time: The Min River Journals.* Norwalk, CT: Eastbridge, 2009.

———. *Religious Policy and Practice in Communist China: A Documentary History.* London: Hodder and Stoughton, 1972.

Maclay, R. S. *Life among the Chinese.* New York: Carlton & Porter, 1861.

Mariani, Paul. *Church Militant: Bishop Kung and Catholic Resistance in Communist Shanghai.* Cambridge, MA: Harvard University Press, 2011.

Marshall, Elsie. *For His Sake: A Record of the Life Consecrated to God and Devoted to China.* Oxford: Religious Tract Society, 1896.

Maugham, W. Somerset. *On a Chinese Screen.* London: Mandarin, 1997.

Melvin, Sheila, and Jindong Cai. *Rhapsody in Red: How Western Classical Music Became Chinese.* New York: Algora, 2004.

Merwin, Wallace C., and Francis P. Jones. *Documents of the Three Self Movement: Source Materials for the Study of the Protestant Church in Communist China.* New York: National Council of the Churches of Christ in the USA, 1963.

Nee, Watchman. *Concerning Our Missions.* Shanghai: Gospel Book Room, 1939.

———. *Normal Christian Faith.* Anaheim, CA: Living Stream Ministry, 1993.

———. *The Spiritual Man.* Vol. 1. New York: Christian Fellowship, 1968.

Nield, Robert. *The China Coast: Trade and the First Treaty Ports.* Hong Kong: Joint Publishing (HK), 2010.

Pakenham-Walsh, William S. *Some Typical Christians of South China.* London: Marshall Brothers, 1905.

———. *Twenty Years in China.* Cambridge: W. Heffer & Sons, 1935.

Palmer, David A., Glenn Shive, and Philip Wickeri, eds. *Chinese Religious Life.* New York: Oxford University Press, 2011.

Perry, Elizabeth, and Li Xun. *Proletarian Power: Shanghai in the Cultural Revolution.* Boulder, CO: Westview, 1997.

Pott, F. L. Hawks. *A Short History of Shanghai.* Shanghai: Kelly & Walsh, 1928.

Project Canterbury. *A History of the Dublin University Fuh-kien Mission, 1887–1911.* Dublin: Hodges, Figgis, 1911.

Richmond, Annette B. *The American Episcopal Church in China.* New York: Domestic and Foreign Missionary Society of the Protestant Episcopal Church in the United States of America, 1907.

Spence, Jonathan. *The Search for Modern China.* New York: Norton, 1990.

Standard Guide Book. *All About Shanghai and Environs.* Shanghai: University Press, 1934–1935.

Stead Sisters. *Stone-Paper-Scissors: Shanghai 1921–1945.* Deddington, Oxon: Panos, 1991.

Stock, Eugene. *The History of the Church Missionary Society: Its Environment, Its Men and Its Work.* London: Church Missionary Society, 1899.

———. *The Story of the Fuh-kien Mission of the Church Missionary Society.* London: Seeley, Jackson & Halliday, 1890.

Stursberg, Peter. *No Foreign Bones in China: Memoirs of Imperialism and Its Ending.* Edmonton: University of Alberta Press, 2002.

Sun, Basil. *A Higher Ground: Testimony of a Tortuous Life Journey.* Sydney: Aukeli, 2001.

Swedberg, Claire. *In Enemy Hands.* Mechanicsburg, PA: Stackpole, 1997.

Sze, Newman. *The Martyrdom of Watchman Nee.* Culver City, CA: Testimony, 1997.

Tsu, Andrew Y. Y. *Friend of Fishermen.* Ambler, PA: Trinity, n.d.

Turner, H.F. *Ring Out the Old, Ring In the New: New Ideas in Old China.* London: Church of England Zenana Missionary Society, 1908.

Wakeman, Frederic, Jr. *The Shanghai Badlands: Wartime Terrorism and Urban Crime, 1937–1941.* New York: Cambridge University Press, 1996.

Waley, Arthur. *The Opium War through Chinese Eyes.* Stanford, CA: Stanford University Press, 1958.

Wickeri, Philip L., ed. *Christian Encounters with Chinese Culture: Essays on Anglican and Episcopal History in China.* Hong Kong: Hong Kong University Press, 2015.

———. *Reconstructing Christianity in China: K. H. Ting and the Chinese Church.* Maryknoll, NY: Orbis, 2009.

———. *Seeking the Common Ground: Protestant Christianity, the Three-Self Movement, and China's United Front.* Eugene, OR: Wipf and Stock, 1988.

Williams, Peter John. *Philadelphia: The World War I Years.* Charleston, SC: Arcadia, 2013.

Wu, Dongsheng John. *Understanding Watchman Nee: Spirituality, Knowledge, and Formation.* Eugene, OR: Wipf and Stock, 2012.

Wu, Silas H. *Dora Yu and Christian Revival in 20th Century China.* Boston: Pishon River, 2002.

———. *Shell Breaking and Soaring: The Imprisonment and Transformation of Watchman Nee.* Boston: Pishon River, 2004.

Ye, Weili. *Seeking Modernity in China's Name: Chinese Students in the United States 1900–1927.* Stanford, CA: Stanford University Press, 2001.

Ying, Fuk-tsang. *Anti-Imperialism, Patriotism and the Spiritual Man: A Study on Watchman Nee and the "Little Flock."* Hong Kong: Christian Study Centre on Chinese Religion and Culture, 2005.

Yu, Joshua. *The Cross & Suffering*. Alhambra, CA: Chinese Christian Testimony Ministry, 2005.

MAGAZINES, ARTICLES, DISSERTATIONS

Chao, Jonathan Tien-en. "The Chinese Indigenous Church Movement, 1919–1927: A Protestant Response to the Anti-Christian Movements in Modern China." PhD diss., University of Pennsylvania, 1986.

Chinese Students' Alliance in the United States of America. *Chinese Students' Monthly (CSM)*. December 1918–June 1920.

Clemson, Rachel. "A Lady Missionary in China." *Wide World Magazine*, October 1900.

Conlin, W. "Fukien Then and Now." *Church Missionary Society*. No date.

Cushman, Betty. "The Story of the Foochow Looting." *Missionary Herald*, April 1927, 130–32.

Duan Qi. "Christianity and Chinese Nationalism: St. Peter's Church in Shanghai during the War against Japan." Paper presented at a conference sponsored by the Hong Kong Sheng Kung Hui, Hong Kong, June 7–9, 2012.

Fujian CPPCC Cultural and Historical Records Committee, ed. *A Selection of Cultural and Historical Records*. Vol. 5, *Christianity and Catholicism*. Fuzhou: Fujian People's Publishing House, 2003.

Henriot, Christian. "Shanghai and the Experience of War: The Fate of Refugees." *European Journal of East Asian Studies* 5, no. 2 (2006): 215–45.

Lee, Joseph Tse-Hei. "Watchman Nee and the Little Flock Movement in Maoist China." *Church History: Studies in Christianity in China* 74, no. 1 (March 2005): 68–96.

Liang, Jialin. "Investigation into Ni Tuosheng's Guilt." *Jian Dao Magazine*, January 2002.

Liu, Qianguang. "A Brief Biography of Mrs. Lin Dao'an." *CHSKH Fukien Diocese Monthly* 10, no. 4 (April 15, 1943): 12–14.

Lloyd, Llewellyn. "Fuh-chow, the Banyan City." *Church Missionary Gleaner*, June 1, 1899.

———. "Has China Changed?" *Church Missionary Gleaner*, January 1916.

Norton, A. W. R. "Impressions of the Laying of the Foundation Stone of the Cathedral," *Fukien Diocesan Magazine*, 1924, 7–9.

———. "Making Men: The Work of a Christian School in China." *Church Missionary Outlook*, November 1928, 225–27.

Scott, Roderick. "A Great Minority Victory—Overturnings in China." *Christian Education*, November 1927, 136–44.

Taylor, Birdwood van Someren. "Twenty Years' Experience in the Training and Employment of Medical Students." *China Medical Journal*, October 1901.

Taylor, Christiana. "The Stewart Memorial Hospital, Hing-hwa." *Mercy & Truth*, October 1898, 234–37.

Wolfe, John Richard. "The Fukien Mission." *Church Missionary Gleaner*, October 1894.

———. "Pressing Missionary Problems in Fuh-kien." *Church Missionary Review* 60 (June 1909).

———. "Some Events in the Fukien Mission, 1861–1911." *Church Missionary Gleaner*, January 1912.

Xu Yihua. "St. John's University, Shanghai as an Evangelizing Agency." *Studies in World Christianity* 12, no. 1 (2006): 23–49.

Xu Zhimo. "To My Family and Friends upon My Departure for the U.S. on August 14, 7th Year of the Republic." In *The Complete Works of Xu Zhimo*, edited by Jiang Fucong and Liang Shiqiu. Taipei: Zhuanji Wenxue Chubanshe (1969), 6:99–102.

Yang Fenggang. "When Will China Become the World's Largest Christian Country?" *Slate*, December 2, 2014.

SELECTED WORKS BY LIN PU-CHI (EARLIEST TO LATEST)

"The Departure of Chinese Students for America." *St. John's Echo*, September 1916, 22–23.

"A Dissertation on Modern Changes." *St. John's Echo*, October 1916, 19–23.

"The Tragedy of the Jade Ring." *St. John's Echo*, February 1917, 13–21.

"An Estimate of Yuan Shih-kai." *St. John's Echo*, October 1917, 10–20.

★"The Eight Immortals of the Taoist Religion." *Journal of the North-China Branch of the Royal Asiatic Society for the Year 1918* 49:53–75.

"The Comedy of Ignorance." *Chinese Students' Monthly*, June 1919, 488–94.

★★"Four Cardinal Principles for the Development of the Chinese Church." *Chinese Recorder*, June 1924, 353–60.

"The Church and the Ninth of May." *Chinese Recorder*, June 1924, 407–9.

★★"Four Cardinal Principles for the Development of the Chinese Church, cont." *Chinese Recorder*, July 1924, 445–50.

"The Christian Church and the Rising National Spirit in China." *Church Missionary Review*, March 1926, 38–49.

"An Ancient Creed and Modern Faith." *Chinese Recorder*, April 1926, 253–60.

"A Brief History of the Churches in Fujian." *Chinese Churchman* 19, no. 19 (1926): 11–15.

"An Explanation of the Virgin Birth." *Chinese Churchman* 19, no. 23 (1926): 13–17.

"The Chinese Christian Answers the Missionaries' Questions." *Chinese Recorder*, January 1927, 23–27.

"The Mission of Christian Education." *Chinese Churchman* 10, no. 19 (1929).

"National Day in the National Disaster." *St. Peter's Monthly*, October 1932, 1–2.

★ Published under the name Peter C. Ling, which combines his Christian name, Peter, with the spelling of Lin used in Fuzhou.

★★ Lin Pu-chi's name was misspelled as Liu Pu-chi.

"Explanation on Revising the Book of Common Prayer." *Chinese Churchman* 27, no. 19 (1934): 3–5.

"Education Is Life." *Magazine of Public Schools for Chinese Children* no. 6 (1935): 25.

"Christianity and Revolution." *Chinese Churchman* 29, no. 19 (1936): 11–14.

"National Calamity and the Trial of Confidence." *Chinese Churchman* 30, no. 16 (1937): 7–9.

"Christmas This Year." *Chinese Churchman* 30, no. 20 (1937): 4–5.

"Christian Reflections in Extraordinary Circumstances." *Chinese Churchman* 31, no. 6 (1938): 1–5.

"Pleading for Church Preachers." *Chinese Churchman* 35, no. 5 (1946): 3–4.

"A Christian's Proper Attitude to the Current Situation." *Chinese Churchman* 38, no. 1 (1949): 1–3.

Index